Compliments of **Wheaton College**

Since 1860
For Christ and
His Kingdom

WHEATON, ILLINOIS 60187

Gods best to you and your efforts for His Praise

from Walter

WHEATON COLLEGE

A Heritage Remembered 1860-1984

Paul M. Bechtel

Harold Shaw Publishers
Wheaton, Illinois

*To the students, faculty, alumni,
and other friends of Wheaton College with gratitude,
and to Mary with thankfulness.*

Cover photo: Ken DeJong

Photos within text include the work of Walter Danylak, Carlos Vergara, and Jim Whitmer.

Printed in the United States of America

ISBN 0-87788-347-5

Library of Congress Cataloging in Publication Data
Bechtel, Paul M.
  Wheaton College: a heritage remembered, 1860-1984.

  Includes bibliographical references and index.
  1. Wheaton College (Ill.)—History. I. Title.
LD6041.W562B43   1984   378.773'24   84-10710
ISBN 0-87788-347-5

First printing, September 1984

CONTENTS

FOREWORD

Institutions, like people, are the product of their heritage. Although tempered by the complexities of contemporary environment, their roots determine their character and shape their destiny.

Even so, an institution can drift from its founding distinctives unless the thread of original purpose remains unbroken. This, then, is the unique nature of a history such as this. It reveals the extent of fidelity to founding principles, while chronicling growth and maturity within these original ideals.

In the providence of God, the history of Wheaton College, written by Paul M. Bechtel, is testimony to our continuing commitment to a liberal arts education that is distinctively Christian. That commitment integrates faith, learning, and living, espousing a world view within biblical truth. As Wheaton's sixth president, recently inaugurated, I am privileged to inherit a legacy carefully preserved by my predecessors who averaged nearly 25 years each in office, revealing their remarkable dedication to a common task. Their singular goal to keep Wheaton true to founding convictions, while adapting through the years to changing times, is a God-given heritage.

This history is appropriately presented during the 125th anniversary of Wheaton College. I commend it to you for new insights into the character of Wheaton, for an enlightening account of its many moments in time, and for renewed understanding of its tradition, purpose, and destiny under God.

J. Richard Chase, President
September 1984

PREFACE

The history of a college has many of the elements of a drama: absorbing characters, diverse scenes, intense crises centering in fundamental issues, moments of inspiration and transformation. Small midwestern colleges, originating largely in the nineteenth century, before the emergence of state universities, exhibit all those qualities. Heroic effort and sacrifice brought them into being; their founders' confidence in the future of a free society strengthened them; an earnest quest for knowledge characterized them.

These pioneer institutions played a crucial role in the cultural and social advancement of the midwestern states east of the Mississippi—Ohio, Indiana, Illinois. Nearly all of the colleges were Christian, creating a fusion of faith and culture that gave moral direction to the era. Many of the frontier colleges were founded by eastern revivalists who were graduates of Yale, Princeton, or Dartmouth. Hoping to transform a spiritual wilderness into a Christian society, these men made a frontal attack on the ignorance and secularism of the rapidly expanding upper Mississippi Valley.

In 1800 there were 25 colleges in the young United States, all in the East; by 1860 there were approximately 175, many of them established in small towns west of the Alleghenies. They aspired to train clergymen, evangelists, and enlightened civic leaders, equal to the demands of a new age filled with promise. The tides of nationalism and local pride were running strong, the latter often realizing its finest expression in the founding of a college. Without parallel in European education, these Christian colleges developed as a uniquely American phenomenon.

Founded in 1853, Illinois Institute, which became Wheaton College in 1860, was among those early prairie institutions, established by the pioneers who first came to these broad lands of tall grass, sweeping winds, and uninterrupted sky.

As these words are being written, Wheaton College is preparing to celebrate its 125th anniversary, beginning in September 1984 and continuing through the academic year. If they are vitally alive, neither people nor institutions fear aging. Rather, such milestones are times of celebration and rejoicing. For Wheaton this special year is an occasion for thanksgiving for God's providence in preserving the College as a liberal arts institution dedicated to knowing and doing the will of the One who is the source of all knowledge and wisdom.

There are several ways of writing a college history. I have chosen to tell the story of Wheaton College as a chronicle of events occurring during the administrations of five presidents, and the beginning of the sixth. The book is primarily about the people who made up the campus community—their commitments, behavior, personalities, and accomplishments. Some attention has been given to the philosophical, theological, political, and educational trends that have influenced the life and practices of the College. Where there have been meritorious achievements, I have tried to let them speak for themselves. Where there has been conflict, I have attempted to give an objective account of the events, noting the occasional internal strains and opposing ideas that are inevitable in the growth of an institution.

Sifting through the voluminous, carefully kept college archives, reading hundreds of pages of old records, letters, campus publications, and Board of Trustees minutes was a rewarding experience, enlightening, often inspiring, sometimes amusing. I early realized that there was far more material than could be used, making it necessary to deal only representatively with many events, groups, and individuals in order to tell the story in a prescribed number of pages. Readers who have been among the makers of history at Wheaton, or who have simply observed the flow of events for a long time, will understand that need for selectivity. For readers unacquainted with the College, I trust this work will be a helpful introduction to its history and achievements.

I am grateful to many friends and colleagues for sharing with me their experiences as students and faculty members, their insights, and their encouragement. The Advancement Office of Wheaton College initiated the project and supported it from the beginning. As chairman of the committee giving oversight to the work, Richard Gerig was continuously helpful. Other members of the committee were Peter Veltman, Edward Coray, Paul Snezek and Leland Ryken. For any textual error that may have escaped the eagle eyes of perceptive counselors, I take full responsibility.

I am immensely appreciative of those who have read the manuscript in its entirety or in part, and who kept me from stumbling at many points:

Miriam Fackler, Ruth and Edward Cording, Mark Noll, David Roberts, Wil Norton, and Lawrence Bechtel. Arthur Holmes, Gerald Hawthorne, Clyde Kilby, Hudson Armerding, and others made valuable suggestions. Staff workers in many campus offices were unfailingly gracious in their search for requested material. This research undertaking could not have proceeded far without the continuous and enthusiastic assistance of archivists Bill Favata and Roger Phillips. I wish also to acknowledge my indebtedness to the late Steven Barabas, professor of Bible, discerning scholar, wise counselor, warm-hearted friend. Donna Van Conant and Lucy Unger were faithful and skilled typists.

To my wife Mary, for ready encouragement and helpful insights, I am deeply grateful.

Wheaton, Illinois
January, 1984

PRESIDENT JONATHAN BLANCHARD, 1860-1882

CHAPTER 1

Jonathan Blanchard
and the Founding
of Wheaton College

I WAS BORN, SAID PRESIDENT JONATHAN BLANCHARD TO THE
listeners gathered around him, "on the Green Mountains, in the town of
Rockingham, Vermont, January 19, 1811." The occasion was the eightieth
birthday celebration of the first President of Wheaton College, January 19,
1891. Trustees of the College, faculty, and students had been invited to hear
their venerable leader read a brief sketch of his life. Simple, straightforward,
without rhetorical adornment, the account moved through adventurous
years as he rose from New England farm boy to elder statesman among the
nation's educators and reformers.

Had the occasion allowed him time to comment on his forebears, he
might have told of five generations of Blanchards in Massachusetts and Vermont who were part of his heritage. His father, also Jonathan Blanchard,
had moved from Billerica, Massachusetts, to Vermont to establish himself as
a farmer. Like others who pushed into the new state from central and western Massachusetts, he was driven by the land hunger that has shaped human history from the beginning. In Rutland he met and married Mary
Lovell, and together they became the parents of fifteen children, the younger Jonathan being the eleventh.

In the fall of 1826, at the age of fifteen, Jonathan took the stage to Chester, about ten miles north of Rockingham, to begin his preparatory school-

ing in Chester Academy. With only his own meager savings to rely on and his parents' good wishes, he knew he would need help to pay his expenses. How providential it was, therefore, that he was invited to live in the house of the preceptor of the school, the Reverend Uzziah Cicero Burnap, and to perform routine chores in return for his board and lodging. The most important consequence of Jonathan's living in the Burnap home was his meeting with Asa Burnap, who had come to Chester to visit his brother Uzziah. During evening walks Asa led the young student into some hard thinking about his life and his soul's need. Though the older Blanchards were not professing Christians, they had taught their children to revere the Bible as the Word of God and to live upright lives. Under Asa Burnap's leading, Jonathan saw the need to confess his sinful nature and to accept Christ as Savior and as Deliverer from the old nature.[1]

In August 1828, after two years at Chester Academy, Jonathan said goodbye to his family, climbed aboard a stagecoach, and began the eighty-mile journey to college. He traveled northward through the beautiful Green Mountains to Uzziah Burnap's old school, Middlebury College, founded in 1800 with seven students. Chester Academy had prepared him well. Admission to the College required the student to be versed in Latin and Greek grammar, to parse Virgil, Cicero's Orations, and the New Testament. In addition, he was to understand the structure of Greek and Latin poetry, to be familiar with ancient and modern history, and show a sufficient knowledge of arithmetic, fractions, and decimals. The catalog of Middlebury College showed a four-year curriculum laden with classical literature, several levels of mathematics, chemistry and geology, rhetoric, history, natural theology, and evidences of Christianity. Jonathan's interest in verse continued throughout his life.

In July 1829, young Blanchard joined the Congregational Church in Middlebury. That act was perhaps the beginning of his serious reflection on the course of his life. The church was also the place of worship for Samuel Bent, whose daughter Mary was later to become Jonathan's bride. Though more than half of his classmates at Middlebury later chose to study law, Jonathan chose a different route. Charles Albert Blanchard states in his autobiography that his father, as a student, often went to preach or help in small rural churches. On one of those occasions, Charles records that his father walked back to the College through a mountain path. Pausing at a spur, he saw "a rocky, narrow, forbidding valley" and to its left "there opened a wide and beautiful plain, green with grass and beautiful with trees." Looking slowly from right to left, the young man seemed to see symbolically set before him two ways of life. A career in law would lead through the pleasant valley to power, affluence, and the possible acclaim of multitudes; the Christian ministry would lead through the rocky valley. Recalling the experience for his son years afterward, Jonathan's words reflected a moment of decision: "On that mountain I stood and deliberately chose the narrow, harder path."[2] His graduation from Middlebury College in a class of twenty-seven in 1832 marked the first major step toward the fulfillment of that vow.

Anti-Slavery Crusader

In the fall of 1834, Blanchard entered Andover Theological Seminary, already a distinguished institution, with enrollees from Harvard, Princeton, Yale, Dartmouth, Bowdoin, Williams, and Amherst. There Jonathan, as a second-year student, met Theodore Weld, an anti-slavery crusader who had, unknown to the administration, come to the seminary to recruit young men as anti-slavery lecturers in the eastern states. To the astonishment and disapproval of Andover's President Woods, Jonathan, along with other students, cast in his lot with Weld's cause and announced his intention of leaving the seminary. In the fall of 1836 the Anti-Slavery Society held a conference in New York. There seventy appointees of the society, Jonathan Blanchard among them, were commissioned as lecturers; and in the tradition of the early church, they went forth to declare a holy cause, the total abolition of slavery.

Jonathan's assignment took him to Pennsylvania. As he journeyed, his mind may have drifted back to a time when a Unitarian minister asked him: "Mr. Blanchard, what society would you bring mankind into? What is a perfect state of society?" In recalling that incident for his friends at his eightieth birthday gathering, he declared that the minister's question had thrilled him. He added, "I have since thought and written more on that one theme than any other."[3] Surely in Blanchard's engagement in the anti-slavery cause his young life was committed to one of the much needed reforms antecedent, as he believed, to the emergence of a perfect society, for where slavery and ignorance prevail, the ideal society is not possible.

"I lectured amid mobs in Pennsylvania, where I made the acquaintance of Gov. Ritter, Thaddeus Stevens, and a young girl of seventeen, who became afterward the dear companion of my life."[4] Thus, in brief, Blanchard summed up his experience in Pennsylvania. In those hazardous days the youthful reformer was being seasoned and shaped into a fearless campaigner, ready to challenge awesome adversaries. Jonathan had been sent to Harrisburg as a replacement for another anti-slavery lecturer who had been driven away by his opponents.[5] Like an ancient prophet he traversed the land, denouncing the monstrous evil of slavery, an offense to God and humanity. But he realized his need for additional training, and in 1837 traveled down the Ohio River by steamer to Cincinnati to enter Lane Seminary.

While lodging at a boarding house in Harrisburg, Jonathan met Mary Avery Bent, the young principal of the girls' high school, who could trace her ancestry back through generations to Mary Allen Adams, niece of Samuel Adams. The two young people were attracted to each other almost at once. However, letters from friends cautioned Mary about too close an alliance with an abolitionist.[6]

Having earlier decided to spend a year in the South, Mary did not allow the budding romance to divert her. After a year in Montgomery, Alabama, however, she returned to the North, and she and Jonathan were married at her home in Middlebury on September 17, 1838. She was nineteen; he was twenty-seven. They could not have dreamed they would spend more than fifty years together. Over the years, the Wheaton years particularly, Mary, one of a family of ten children, was to be the great center of strength and encouragement Jonathan needed. Often depressed by one reverse or another and by his own unstable health, he found in Mary a steady, confident, generally unperturbable companion.

Little detail has survived of their wedding and their wedding trip to Saratoga Springs, New York, or of their journey via the Erie Canal to Niagara Falls and then down the Ohio River to Cincinnati, a thriving city of 30,000, where Jonathan had been graduated from Lane Seminary in the spring.

When the newlywed Blanchards arrived in Cincinnati, Jonathan had already been installed as pastor of the Sixth Presbyterian Church. Most of its members were abolitionists and had chosen their new minister for that reason. He did not feel, it seems, that he had compromised his earlier Congregationalism by accepting a New School Presbyterian pulpit.[7] He was ordained in the church, with Dr. Lyman Beecher preaching the sermon and Dr. Calvin Stowe, husband of Harriet Beecher Stowe, offering the ordination prayer.

On the question of abolition, Cincinnati was a divided city; but Jonathan had no fear of antagonizing special interests nor was he intimidated by elements seeking to silence the abolitionist forces. Prior to his coming, an unruly crowd had dumped into the Ohio River the press on which James Birney had been printing The Philanthropist. When Birney turned over his paper to a young physician acquaintance, it was published without further peril.[8] That paper, under its new editor, often carried notices of Blanchard's activities. It noted on January 1, 1839: "Rev. J. Blanchard will deliver a discourse on the sinfulness of American slavery and its remedy, next Wednesday evening at half past six o'clock, in the church on Sixth Street." Still later it announced a meeting of the Cincinnati Anti-Slavery society in the Sixth Church, at which Mr. Blanchard was to speak.[9] Through his strong stand against slavery and his public opposition to the licensing of additional taverns, Jonathan was coming to be known throughout the city.

The young minister's conviction that slavery is sin furnishes a key to understanding Blanchard's intense investment of his energies and skills in the abolitionist cause. The progress of his career from the Middlebury days to his final years in Wheaton as abolitionist, anti-Mason, and temperance advocate—to name only major causes—might lead to the conclusion that here was a man motivated principally by great social reforms. But an examination of his notebook and diary makes clear that these were necessary applications of one central driving motive: love for God and service for others in God's name. To the privacy of his diary he confessed on January 26, 1844: "It is my purpose, through free and intimate mercy, to devote the remnant of strength, both of soul and body which sin has left, only to the service of my blessed Jesus."[10] Like the great classical devotional writers, he chided himself often for want of humility. "So above all things deceitful is my heart," he wrote, "and inordinately in love with praise, that I can detect in it a desire to beautify this writing so that, when I am dead it may cause admiration in those who may chance to read it." In a time of lethargy he acknowledged "that my heart lies at a dead calm."[11] As a youth of twenty-one he had written, "And may I have grace, more and more, daily, to feel weaned from the world and consecrated to Him—and more ardent in my desire to see the world brought under the blessed influence of the Gospel of Christ. Amen."[12]

In the summer of 1844, Hiram Kellogg, president of Knox College in Illinois, whom Jonathan met at the World Anti-Slavery Convention in London, wrote to Blanchard suggesting that he become an agent in the East for Knox College, then severely pressed financially. Jonathan did not accept the invitation, but at the urging of Kellogg and some of the community leaders he did travel to Galesburg the following April to get acquainted with the Knox situation. Already the trustees of the College had asked Kellogg to resign, which he agreed to do in May. He recommended Jonathan as his successor.[13] In June Blanchard was unanimously chosen by the Board.

The eight-year sojourn in Cincinnati was ending. Jonathan presented his resignation, with regret, to accept the Knox College opportunity. In Cincinnati four children had been born to the family. The arrival of the first of these is noted in the diary, July 24, 1839, with gratitude and a new sense of dependence on God: "This day at eleven o'clock God gave to us a healthy son; and with him a new set of emotions, fears and hopes. May God keep me and give me faith to plead the covenant which he has mercifully made to believing parents, that he will be a God to their children."[14] The child was named Jonathan Edwards, after the great New England preacher and theologian, surely with some expectation that the bearer of an honored name would himself be the agent of mighty works for the Lord. A diary entry on October 25, 1840, however, reads: "The city has been shaken by a powerful revival. Our church has received more than 100 members; our little Edwards is gone home before us."[15] Of the two boys and two girls born in Cincinnati, only Mary Avery and Catherine Lucretia survived infancy.

After a two-week delay the Blanchards' long and arduous journey to Galesburg was begun on Monday, November 24, 1845. The steamer should have reached St. Louis before Sunday, but by Wednesday, the first snowfall of the year slowed progress, and the next day brought extreme cold. By Saturday the ship was still more than a hundred miles from St. Louis.[16] With strong convictions that Sunday travel was sinful, and despite the fact that the weather was severe, that one of the children was ill, and that they would have to disembark in Missouri, a slave state, Mary and Jonathan asked to be put ashore at Cape Girardeau. For three weeks they waited for the weather to break. Then, using what Jonathan later estimated was about a fifth of their savings,[17] they purchased a wagon and two horses to make the 350-mile trip to Galesburg—long days of wagon travel over a narrow road in the December cold which is hard for modern readers to imagine. Grateful for an occasional hospitable homestead along the way, Jonathan and Mary followed the Illinois River to Peoria, crossed a fifty-mile stretch of prairie, and arrived in Galesburg early in January. To honor their convictions about Sunday travel had taxed their energies severely, but they had done so ungrudgingly.

Knox College Years

When the Blanchards arrived in Galesburg, they put up at once at a small hotel then operated by ex-president Kellogg of Knox College. A student band and a delegation of townspeople arrived in the evening to welcome the newcomers. Ernest Elmo Calkins says of Jonathan that "he arrived in the town, tall, commanding, strikingly handsome, faultlessly dressed in silk hat and frock coat, a dynamic reformer."[18] He was thirty-five, filled with energy, and stirred by dreams of large usefulness for the little prairie college he had been called to serve. Soon he had purchased a small tract of land and built a house near the College, where he lived unpretentiously with his growing family. There, each morning, he milked his two cows and cared for his hogs before leaving for school.[19] Minutes of the Board of Trustees indicate that within six months Jonathan had worked out a comprehensive plan to assure Knox College's stability and growth: the purchase of forty acres of land; authorization of the erection of a main building; provision of money for library books; and the raising of $20,000 for the establishment of professorships.[20]

The Knox years cannot be chronicled in detail here, but certain highlights were essential to the development of the future president of Wheaton College. Jonathan wrote that he found Knox College "$5,000 in debt and running behind five dollars a day."[21] He submitted to the college treasury $6,000 given for his personal support by J. P. Williston, who like other eastern benefactors was attracted to Knox by its strong anti-slavery stand. For his Wheaton College listeners at his eightieth birthday party, the aged Blanchard recalled that he "wrote the College diploma, procured the college seal, a library, graduated thirteen classes and left Knox College free from debt, and worth $400,000."[22]

In his inaugural address at Knox in June 1846, titled "The Kingdom of Christ: and the Duty of American Colleges Respecting It," President Blanchard set forth a favorite theme: "A sound and thorough education is of priceless value. Yet an education without moral and religious excellence, an enlightened intellect with a corrupt heart, is but a cold gas-light over a sepulcher, revealing, but not warming the dead."[23] Head and heart must be joined in a God-centered union. As president of the College, living in a small community of 130 families, Jonathan did not forsake the common touch. Nonetheless, local citizens thought him a little pretentious when he appeared at his first commencement in full academic regalia.

After eleven years at the helm of Knox College, Jonathan Blanchard resigned in 1857 amid controversy and acrimonious exchanges between himself and some members of the Board of Trustees. He was also strongly at odds with George W. Gale, long-time member of the faculty, founder of Knox College, and pioneer settler of the town that bore his name. Although in the beginning Gale had appeared enthusiastic about the new leader of Knox College, calling him a "man of God and an uncompromising enemy of slavery . . . a man who acts on the dictates of conscience whatever difficulties may lie in his path,"[24] he had steadily grown jealous, it seems, of the president's capabilities and emerging popularity. "My offense is simply that I am here and popular"[25] Jonathan wrote to Solomon P. Chase, an old friend who was at that time United States senator from Ohio. Furthermore, through the 1850s Gale became more conservative politically and far less aggressive on the anti-slavery issue than Blanchard. Actually Jonathan had offered to resign earlier, three years after his arrival in Galesburg, when tensions had arisen between himself and Gale—then aging and dyspeptic—and several members of the Board. But a majority of the Board members, confident in their president, had no desire to accept his resignation.

Later President Blanchard's resignation was urged in a resolution to the Board of Trustees proposed by Orville H. Browning, never a friend to Jonathan. After an all-day session the Board accepted the resolution by a vote of eleven to ten and requested the resignation of both Blanchard and Gale. When word of the trustee action quickly spread among the students, all of the seniors except one, a relative of Gale, announced they would not attend commencement. Other students declared they would not return to Knox in the fall. *The Students Farewell*, published in the summer of 1857, condemned Gale's followers and charged Gale himself with "deception," "forgery," and "misrepresentation."[26] A number of townspeople and friends, including Dr. Edward Beecher, brother of Henry Ward Beecher, urged reinstatement of the president. The best that came out of those efforts was a compromise, that Jonathan should resume his position on the faculty for one year. "When I resigned the presidency at Knox College," Blanchard later wrote, "the Board employed me at an advanced salary, to teach another year, and graduate the next class, which I did."[27]

On October 15, 1859, Geraldine Cecilia, the last of the twelve Blanchard children, was born in Galesburg. Mary Blanchard, an extraordinary woman in spite of sometimes fragile health, cared for the children and presided over a busy household, where visitors were frequent. Often, when her husband was away on trips to the East in search of funds, she responded to his college correspondence. In November 1848, she had given birth to Charles Albert, the most notable of the children. Jonathan wrote shortly after to Thaddeus Stevens of this son, "about whom I care more than I supposed I should."[28]

In April 1859 Jonathan was appointed pastor of the First Congregational Church of Galesburg, to serve for one year, though he had been invited to numerous pastorates and received no less than six invitations to college presidencies elsewhere.[29] His distresses at Knox and subsequent resignation did not prevent Beloit College, Congregational in background, from inviting him to be the speaker at its June commencement.

Among the academic proposals Jonathan received was one inviting him to become president of Illinois Institute at Wheaton, founded by the Wesleyans. The Institute was essentially a preparatory school, offering additionally a few freshman and sophomore college courses. "As to Wheaton," Mary wrote in April 1859 to her husband, then on one of his frequent trips to Chicago, "I have some thoughts which I will open to you when I see you." Mary Blanchard was understandably reluctant—as was his friend and counselor J. P. Williston—to have him accept the offer from Illinois Institute, the poorest and weakest of the institutions that had offered Blanchard their presidencies.[30] In Galesburg, Mary and Jonathan had a comfortable home and a substantial amount of land. In spite of Mary's reservations, however, Jonathan determined to move to Wheaton, and early in the fall began to wind up his affairs in Galesburg.

Board minutes of Illinois Institute for November 23, 1859, note that the meeting "was opened by prayer by the Rev. J. Blanchard." At the same meeting seven new members, all Illinois Congregationalists, were added to the Board of Trustees, several of them appointed at Jonathan's suggestion. These included Owen Lovejoy, the brother of the martyred abolitionist Elijah P. Lovejoy, who was later to introduce the bill to outlaw slavery in the United States. Seated also were the Reverend Flavel Bascom, of Dover, Illinois, and Moses Pettengill, a reformer and successful businessman from Peoria. Clearly the Wesleyans had lost control of the Institute. Before he had officially taken over the presidency, Blanchard was beginning to lay the foundations of the college he envisioned.

The First Years of Wheaton College

Why did Jonathan Blanchard come to Illinois Institute, the floundering little prairie college? He answered the question himself as he spoke to his family and college friends on that wintry birthday night in January 1891.

Why did I come to Wheaton?...I answer: 1. Because Wheaton is near Chicago, the Gate City between the Atlantic and Pacific, between Western Europe and Eastern Asia. 2. Because the Wesleyans had given up their Institute on condition that their testimony against the lodge be maintained. 3. But the chief reason was, I believed the Lord had need of Wheaton College, to aid in preparing the way for His coming.[31]

Jonathan moved to Wheaton to preside over the destinies of Illinois Institute, which had been dedicated to anti-slavery principles by the small Wesleyan denomination in conference at Batavia, Illinois, in 1851.

The Wesleyans, having resolved to found an educational institution, acted with dispatch. They drew up a subscription list dated at Longtown, Illinois—by which name the Wheaton area was then known—and placed the names of Warren and Jesse Wheaton and Erastus Gary at the head, inviting each to contribute $300. Those efforts soon brought gifts of nearly $2,100.[32] The site chosen for the Institute was a rise of ground adjoining the Wheatons' own extensive properties. Without anyone's urging, the Wheatons bought the forty acres, and donated it to the Board of Trustees. Filled with gratitude and a deep sense of God's guidance, a small group of Wesleyans made their way through the prairie grass to the new site, there to dedicate in prayer the institution they envisioned.

Illinois Institute began its first full year in 1854, in a building made of limestone from nearby Batavia. During the year 140 students were enrolled; the following year the number rose to 270, including more than a hundred public school students who used part of the lower floor. By the next year the Institute's assets were nearly $30,000, and the school began to operate under the presidency of Lucius C. Matlack, a strong anti-slavery leader and one of the founders of the Wesleyan Church.

Competent though he was, Matlack was unable to establish the Institute on a solid financial basis; the nationwide financial crisis of 1857 imperiled all philanthropic enterprises. Soon the school was running behind on its obligations: loans, salaries, daily upkeep. At its meeting on July 5, 1858, the trustees examined several methods of undergirding the Institute; but if the plans should fail, it was suggested as a last resort that the trustees announce the immediate suspension of the Institute, and also propose a plan for selling out and paying off the debts of the little school.

In July of the following year President Matlack resigned, declaring, "I have no salary—no revenue whatever and am in debt with a heavy expense upon me constantly." He withdrew his resignation when the trustees resolved to make "a vigorous effort to secure the $100 required by President Matlack as a condition of his acceptance of the temporary presidency the ensuing term."[33] By contemporary standards the sums of money by which the destiny of the struggling institution hung in the balance were small. Certainly those who managed the affairs of Illinois Institute believed that the preserving hand of God was at work to save the prairie school from perishing.

On December 29, 1859, the trustees authorized publication of a "communication" in The Congregational Herald. The statement, headed "The Wheaton College," noted that in May a proposal made to the Congregational Association meeting at Bloomington to take over and endow Illinois Institute had been declined. Instead, the statement went on, "friends in Wheaton and DuPage County have made the most praiseworthy efforts to enlarge and place it upon a permanent foundation." These friends had given cash, loans, and lands "rated at the present low prices, above twenty thousand dollars." The trustees were pleased to announce that "Rev. J. Blanchard, late President of Knox College, has been appointed to the presidency and will enter upon his duties at the opening of the term January, 1860."[34]

Jonathan's arrival in Wheaton was unheralded. He arrived alone, having urged Mary and the children to delay their coming until early spring. When he stepped down from the train that had brought him from Galesburg in January 1860, a panoramic flow of images from the past may have coursed through his mind: his boyhood among the hills of Vermont; the maturing years at Middlebury and Andover; the making of an anti-slavery crusader in Pennsylvania; his rising star as a national figure among abolitionists during his pastorate in Cincinnati; and, finally, the era of testing and achievement at Knox College. As he stood at the railway station and gazed toward the two-story limestone building on the hill, he must have anticipated the problems of assuming the leadership of a nearly bankrupt institution. But Illinois Institute stood for principles dear to his heart: abolition, temperance, anti-secret societies. He was forty-nine and, although never physically robust, he was prepared to expend his energies without restraint in his new assignment.

In its communication to *The Congregational Herald*, the trustees commended the college at Wheaton in terms much like those that have been used ever since. The institution was, they said, "within an hour's ride of Chicago." Further, "the site of the college is healthy and delightful; and families in the city who wish to have their children away from its noise and temptations, and yet within an hour of home, will find in Wheaton instruction for both sexes in the various branches of academic and collegiate education." In carefully chosen words the document declared the intention of the trustees "that the instruction and influence of the Institution shall bear decidedly against all forms of error and sin. The testimony of God's word against slaveholding, secret societies, and their spurious worship; against intemperance, human inventions in church government, and whatever else shall clearly appear to contravene the Kingdom and coming of our Lord Jesus Christ, are to be kept good."[35] The commitment to reform by Wheaton College and its president was clear.

The transition of the name from Illinois Institute to Wheaton College came about through President Blanchard's skillful negotiations with Warren L. Wheaton, who in the 1830s had come with his brother Jesse from Pomfret, Connecticut, to the community that was to bear his name. First Blanchard persuaded him to make the College a gift of fifty acres of choice land, a parcel lying south of the Northwestern Railway tracks extending south to what is now Illinois Street and east to President Street. Then, in a letter to Warren Wheaton, dated December 5, 1859, Jonathan proposed that the institution be hereafter known as Wheaton College. "This," he said, "will at least save your heirs the expense of a good monument."

The transaction would be advantageous to Wheaton, since his adjoining lands would certainly increase in value. Further, Jonathan would himself build a house worth at least $3,000 in a ten-acre plot east of Wheaton's holdings, thus assuring him that all of the land would be in the town. Finally, Jonathan and other associates would provide Wheaton and his family $6,000 compensation if within five years there were not at least $25,000

Warren L. Wheaton

worth of buildings under college control.[36] Warren Wheaton agreed to the proposal, though he later said he wished the quality of his life to be his monument rather than an institution or a set of buildings. On January 9, 1860, the trustees unanimously agreed to adopt the name of Wheaton College.

On July 3, 1860, to allay any fear of job insecurity, the Board agreed "that the present faculty be employed as the future faculty of the institution." The names of the first faculty members of Wheaton College are listed in the college catalog for the academic year 1860-61. They represent, symbolically, all the dedicated instructors and distinguished scholars who have followed them at Wheaton in spending their lives in Christian higher education.

Heading the list was Jonathan Blanchard, who, in the tradition of the scholar-president of a bygone era, was listed as professor of intellectual and moral history. Oscar F. Lumry, A.M., son of Rufus Lumry, a trustee and early pastor of the Wesleyan Methodist Church, was professor of Greek and Latin. The professor of mathematics and natural philosophy was George H. Collier, A.M. German and French were taught by Paul Shuman, a friend of the Honorable Francis A. Hoffman, Lieutenant Governor of Illinois, and a trustee of the College. Alfred Hadley Hiatt, M.D., taught hygiene and physiology, practiced medicine, and operated a drugstore, which still does business in Wheaton under the Hiatt name. Music was taught by Freeborn Garrettson Baker. George Fredric Barker, Ph.B., was designated professor of chemistry and geology. He may or may not have had any say in formulating the single sentence paragraph about his department in the catalog under appointees: "The Institution has expended over sixteen hundred dollars in philosophical and chemical apparatus, which is of the best quality."

Barker had been graduated from Yale and taught both there and at Harvard for a year before his arrival at Wheaton. Later he taught physics for many years at the University of Pennsylvania. A man of great distinction in his field, he served in 1879 as president of the American Association for the Advancement of Science.[37] The Reverend William Beardsley is listed as tutor in the preparatory department, and Mrs. A. Whittier served as principal of the Ladies Department. These eight men and one woman first breathed intellectual life into the institution so recently named Wheaton College. Many of the early instructors were ministers with seminary training, but few college teachers in those years had the rigorous graduate level preparation now regarded as essential for college teaching.

Early Curriculum

This faculty presided over a curriculum uniform for all students, largely classical in nature, and very much like the pattern set by eastern colleges. There was nothing of the variety of course options so essential to modern higher education. However, the fixed curriculum had at least the advantage of giving students a continuity of experience, a common intellectual foundation on which to base values and moral norms. Confronted with the academic rigors facing the 1860 Wheaton students, modern prospective Wheatonites might have hesitated a good while before casting in their lot with the college on the hill.

For admission to the freshman class, early Wheaton students were required to pass examinations in geography, English grammar, American history, ancient and modern history, natural history, physiology, arithmetic and algebra, Latin grammar, Caesar and Virgil, Xenophon's *Anabasis*, rhetoric, and astronomy—a formidable battery of intellectual hazards clearly reflecting the classical character of the students' preparation. But the actual admissions procedure may have been less awesome than it seems, if Charles Blanchard's experience was typical. In his *Autobiography*, describing his admissions examination, he noted: "It was about the close of the war. We were more interested in that subject at the time than in any other. We met in what was called 'the large recitation room.' The faculty of the day, mostly men, was present, my father presiding. A few questions were asked each of us in Latin, Greek, Algebra and English. We answered as we might, I think none so poorly as I did, but we were admitted to standing in the Freshman class."[38]

Having already had two years of Latin and Greek in preparatory school, students were ready for the demands of translating Cicero, Livy, Horace, and Tacitus in Latin, and Xenophon, Thucydides, and the Pauline Epistles in Greek during the freshman and sophomore years. In mathematics, algebra, geometry, trigonometry, analytics, and calculus were routinely expected of everyone. Crowded into the junior year were mechanics and hydrostatics, chemistry and mineralogy, pneumatics, optics, electricity, astronomy, geology, physiology, and the option of French or German for one year. (These were descriptive lecture courses, without full laboratory requirements.) The senior year offered psychology, political economy, a study of the United States Constitution, philosophy of the plan of salvation, evidences of Christianity, history, elements of biblical criticism, and intellectual and moral history. Teaching the intellectual and moral history was part of President Blanchard's busy day.

The Wheaton program of studies was the essence of a liberal arts education in 1860. Noticeably missing from the required curriculum were art, music, and English literature; but art and music were available to those who chose them as non-credit supplements to their program, for which they paid a special fee. An organized program of athletics lay well in the future.

The first catalog listed the names of all students and their home towns under columns headed "Gentlemen" and "Ladies." Most of the students were from northern Illinois, though S. Q. Dewey had journeyed all the way from Richmond, Massachusetts. Home towns such as Blackberry, Sugar Grove, and Blood's Point, all in Illinois, are named. M. J. Sheridan was from Yellow Head and Q. Smith from Ox Bow. The catalog notes that there were three juniors, five sophomores, and thirteen freshmen. The Preparatory School enrolled twenty-seven, and the Ladies' Course seventeen; the Academy—

equivalent to the modern high school—had 143 students. In all, 208 students were under the supervision of Wheaton College. The Academy continued to operate on the grounds and under the authority of the College until the end of World War II. From the beginning, Wheaton education was coeducational, a system in which Jonathan Blanchard strongly believed, as he had previously made clear at Knox College. He had been inspired by the example of Oberlin College in admitting four women students in 1837, making it the first coeducational institution of higher education. Educational rights for women was one of the causes of the time, like prison reform and the emancipation of slaves.

Under the heading "Government, etc." is the clear statement that the "faculty will exercise a parental and moral oversight of the character and conduct of students."[39] This concept of *in loco parentis* evoked no challenge from any quarter a century ago, but in the late 1960s was largely nullified by the courts. All officers of the College had the power to suspend disorderly students until the next faculty meeting, at which the offenders were required to appear, hear the charges against them, and listen to the judgment pronounced. Students were required to be present at all college exercises, and to treat "their officers with respect and their fellow students with decorum."[40] Church attendance was required; and students were not to leave town, be out at night, leave their rooms during study time, or be absent from examinations without permission. Rigid as that code of restraints and obligations was, the system continued largely unmodified into the early decades of the present century.

Following the general statement of government, there is a precise bill of particulars: things "positively disallowed: offensive or indecent conduct, the propagation of infidel principles, profaning the Sabbath, the use of liquors or tobacco, careless use of fire [when student rooms were equipped with coal stoves for winter heating], or entering the marriage relation while a member of the college." Taboo also was "playing billiards and like games," probably because they were regarded as time wasters, and because unsavory connotations were associated with the billiard parlor of the time.

Added to the 1868-69 catalog was a new prohibition: "throwing water, fire or filth from the windows." The statement concludes with a word of caution on "the deportment of the sexes toward each other." Any evidence of either foolish or improper conduct would result in separation from the institution "if admonition fails to correct it."[41] In summary, everything would be forbidden that hindered, and everything required that would enhance the purpose of the College: "to encourage the improvement of mind, morals, and heart." The list of prohibitions continued unaltered from 1869 to 1894, when the statement of conduct disappeared entirely from the catalog. In 1907 a statement of prohibitions reappeared, limited to alcohol, tobacco, and secret societies. Though it had never been countenanced on campus, dancing was included among the prohibitions for the first time in 1914.

In imposing limitations on student conduct Blanchard was not acting capriciously. Any activity that weakened mind and body, he earnestly believed, would inhibit the emergence of that perfect society which, he was persuaded, was realizable. The perfected society would usher in the Kingdom. In this unfolding of the divine plans for human society, Wheaton College was to have a crucial role.

The library of the College contained some 600 volumes, which also included the libraries of the two literary societies. All were said to be works "valuable for reference or general reading." Tuition was $24.00 a year in the College, $21.00 in the Ladies' Course. Instruction in instrumental music was $12.00 a term while vocal music cost only $1.00. Contingency expenses were $1.00. Board for ladies, together with a room containing a stove and bedstead, could be had for $1.70 a week, with the cost for men a bit higher. A sixteen-week fall term, beginning early in September, was followed by winter and spring terms of twelve weeks each. No mention is made of a Christmas recess, since Jonathan never believed in or celebrated Christmas as a Christian festival, either at the College or in his home. During his first Knox years classes had been held even on December 25. At Wheaton the fall term ended on December 24 and classes resumed on January 8. Commencement was set for July 2.

Finally, in the sixteen-page catalog there was the sort of confident assurance found in most college catalogs: "considering the nature of the population, the general interest taken in the college, etc., it is believed that better instruction, at less cost, cannot be obtained in the United States."

First Commencement

Bound into the final catalog of The Illinois Institute, 1859-60, is a copy of the program of the first Wheaton College commencement, held on July 4, 1860, at Jewell's Grove. There was no room in the College large enough to hold the graduates, their friends and relatives, and the townspeople who wished to attend the ceremonies.[42] At 8:30 in the morning the men graduates assembled at the College chapel and proceeded to the Methodist Episcopal Church, where they were to meet the ladies and any townspeople who wished to join the procession to Jewell's Grove. Led by the county sheriff, and enlivened by the Naperville Brass Band, the company reached their destination, some two miles northwest of the College, ready for the exercises at ten o'clock.

Each of the graduates delivered an original oration followed by music. George H. Beecher, of Galesburg, son of Rev. Edward Beecher, spoke on "The Theory of Popular Amusements," followed by A. M. Chadwick of Wheaton, whose discourse was titled "A True Estimate of England." Two students engaged in a discussion, Charles E. Marsh of Galesburg for the affirmative and J. P. Stoddard of Lafayette for the negative, on the subject, "The Permanence of the Federal Government." Other subjects treated were "The Mission of the Teacher," "The Sublimity of Achievement," and "The Course of Study in American Colleges." Yet to come was the address by the Rev. L. C. Matlack, who had served as President of Illinois Institute in its last years, and the conferring of degrees, together with remarks by President Blanchard. (Three of the graduates, including George Beecher, nephew of Harriet Beecher Stowe, had followed Jonathan from Knox to Wheaton.)

In the life summary which Jonathan Blanchard presented to his well-wishers on his eightieth birthday, he said little about the onset and consequences of the Civil War, though he hinted strangely that the conflict had been incited through a Masonic conspiracy: "in 1832 Freemasonry had fallen in the North, gone South and organized the war." Evidently he did not see in the firing on Fort Sumter on April 12, 1861 some foreshadowing of an end to the iniquitous system of human bondage in America. But throughout the war he occasionally wrote words of support for the Union cause, and it is known that he once considered joining the army. The College, however, did send sixty-seven men into the war, all of whom served in the Union Army, some dying for the cause. Others returned to Wheaton after peace came. One of the returnees was Walter Hart, a graduate of the class of 1870 along with Charles Albert Blanchard. He and George Hand, another student, entered the Army together. "Both of these were captured by the rebels on the same day and shut up in the same military prison," Charles Blanchard noted in his autobiography. Hand was a large man, "strong and stalwart," but "he wilted like a leaf and in about a month died." Hart was "smaller, physically inferior, apparently, but lived out months of imprisonment."[43]

In 1861, as the war intensified, commencement exercises were omitted. It was probably with the clear understanding that the war could have closed the College that Jonathan wrote in the 1861-62 catalog: "Hitherto God hath helped us. We live, while other institutions have gone down by the war drainage and the times; and we have increased our Faculty by the addition of a Professor of Natural Science, while other Colleges are diminishing their teaching force."

In February 1861, the General Assembly of the state of Illinois and Governor Richard Yates had granted the College its charter, stating that there was hereby "created and established, at Wheaton, in the county of DuPage, in this state, a college for the instruction of youth in the various branches of literature, the useful arts and the learned and foreign languages. The said institution shall be called by the name of Wheaton College." The three-page document names the trustees and describes their corporate powers, notes the authority of the president and faculty to prescribe the curriculum, and confirms the right to grant degrees. Included also is a statement acknowledging the right of the trustees to attach to the College "an academical or preparatory department, a female department and a common school department." About the last of these three supplementary divisions the charter is specific: "And when such common school department shall be in operation, agreeably to the common school laws of this state, the trustees shall be entitled to draw their proportion of the township, school, college and seminary funds for such scholars as may attend."[44]

For President Blanchard this was a significant statement; it acknowledged the need for and support of common schools. He had always given strong encouragement to the public educational system; such schools were essential to a free and responsible society. When at a gathering in Galesburg in 1858, a local citizen suggested that a planned public high school might draw off students from Knox Academy, a substantial part of the College, Jonathan had risen to his feet and declared: "If Knox Academy stands in the way of public schools for Galesburg, perish the Academy."[45]

Student Life

Some notion of what student life was like at Wheaton College in the 1860s can be derived from statements in the catalogs of that decade. Since the institution was organized principally as a learning center, study hours, including class periods, were prescribed and carefully monitored. At 6 a.m. the tower bell awakened students, who began their rigorous day with breakfast at 7.[46] Classes commenced at 8 and ran until 11:30 in the morning; afternoon requirements were from 1 to 4 p.m., and evening study hours from 7:30 to 9:30. Daily chapel services were given to "highly interesting and instructive Lectures by the President" and the reading of student essays twice a week "under the personal supervision of the President." One of the student editors writing in Voice of Our Young Folks, an eight-page monthly campus paper that lasted for one year, 1868-69, describes a part of the student day. "Eight o'clock! let us take our way to the college chapel. The seats are filled with students, for all must 'go up to worship' at this daily 'Shiloh' of ours. We enter a long, low room, somewhat humble in appearance now, but soon to give place to one of fairer proportions. A hymn in which all may join, a lecture and a prayer by the president, an essay, perhaps by a senior, and then we separate to our study-rooms or classes."[47]

From the beginning, the weekly prayer meeting was attended by most of the students. They were "a source of great good, for scarcely a term passes without quite a number of conversions; and during the year many who came here irreligious, return to their friends rejoicing in Christ."[48] A student writer noted: "Tuesday evening! It is the time for the students' prayer meeting. We gather in the lecture room and one of our number reads a chapter from the Bible, and opens the services of the evening. The room is full and we feel the spirit of God is there. Some of our fellow students who hitherto have 'lacked one thing' are here inquiring for the 'King's Highway.' Oh! Sacred spot. Oh! holy hour."[49]

Much of the student social life centered in the literary societies. When Jonathan Blanchard arrived at Wheaton, there was a single literary society, Beltionian, which had a membership of both men and women. Debates, declamations, original essays, and poetry filled the evenings, frequently continuing well beyond allowed limits of time. In the fall of 1861 a faculty committee was asked to consider separating the ladies from the Beltionians into a society of their own. Consequently in the spring the "ladies belonging to the Society considered it expedient to withdraw their active support"[50] and form the new Aelioian Society, which was to meet on Friday afternoons. Fannie Townley, writing in a light vein several years later in the resurrected *Voice of Our Young Folks*, said of this division: "Whether it was good that man should be alone in this matter, and that Eve should keep this garden of literature without the aid of Adam, judge ye!"[51] Another waggish student spoke of Aelioians as "a training school for the coming millennium of 'Women's rights.' " Beltionians he tagged as the "gas works of the institution."[52]

Student housing was available for extraordinarily modest costs. "Unfurnished rooms outside the College, can be had for from twenty to fifty cents per week," the 1870 catalog announced. For those rooming off campus, mostly men, "table board" cost $2.50 a week. Many of the men lived in the faculty homes that ringed the campus. Rooms in the Ladies' Hall were furnished with "stove, bedstead, mattress, table, chairs, lamp, washstand and crockery for the same." Young women were reminded that "as at Mt. Holyoke, Rockford and other like institutions," they would, "in addition to the care of their rooms, work one hour each day in the household." Board, tuition, fuel, and lights for those living in Ladies' Hall were offered at a package rate of $150 a year.

Students wishing instruction in "painting in oil colors" could have five lessons a week for $60 a year. Vocal music, at a rate of $1 a term, was offered by "Prof. Baker, a distinguished teacher," while instrumental music was $39 a year. Instruction was also given "on the piano and melodeon." A modest effort to keep the student body healthy is suggested in the statement that "the system of physical culture, as taught by Dr. Dio Lewis, is continued with excellent results."

To meet a contemporary need, add students, and open a new source of revenue, a commercial department was instituted as part of the college program in 1863. The catalog noted the justification that "many of the Literary Institutions of the West are pressed with applicants of both sexes for instruction in various branches of commercial education."[53] Students were offered instruction in bookkeeping and penmanship, lectures in commercial law, phonography (shorthand), and telegraphy, for which "a separate room is furnished with Registers and Sounders, representing several telegraph offices."[54] Of the telegraphy course it was said that "this is a rare opportunity for ladies, who are now fast being employed as telegraph operators at good salaries." In 1866 there were 146 enrolled in this department, and Charles A. Blanchard, then only eighteen and a freshman in the College, was listed as teacher of penmanship. For disabled Civil War veterans a one-fifth reduction in tuition was offered.[55]

The College was responding to a call for vocational training at a time when the rapidly expanding Midwest was appealing for large numbers of people prepared in business skills. But that was not a full swing toward vocationalism. The liberal arts concentration was still to be the center of Wheaton's academic vision.

CHAPTER 2

The Administration
of Jonathan Blanchard

J ONATHAN BLANCHARD DROVE HIMSELF UNSPARINGLY. HE
traveled, lectured, organized and promoted agencies for social justice, and
labored in the cause of Christian higher education. Never a physically robust man, he suffered from chronic dyspepsia and periods of weakness. In
the hope that his health might be improved, the trustees granted him a six-
month leave of absence in the spring of 1864, enabling him to fulfill a long-
held desire to see territory west of the Mississippi. With sixteen-year-old
Charles at his side, he set out by covered wagon across Illinois, and pressed
on beyond the great river. Since many wagon trains were moving in the
same direction, it was easy for father and son to link up with one of them.

Having passed through Nebraska, Colorado, Wyoming, Montana, and
Idaho, they came finally to Salt Lake City, where the Mormons were building their city and rearing the great temple on the square. When Jonathan returned, he found that the college department had enrolled one senior, one
junior, one sophomore, and seven freshmen. By 1870 there were 247 students at Wheaton College, but of those only 51 were in the college program:
22 men and 29 women.

Restored to health after his trip to the West, Jonathan Blanchard began
energetic efforts to establish a financial base for the College that would insure stability for the present and encourage growth in the future. His first

appeal, a request for $5,000, presented in person at a meeting of the Society for Promoting Collegiate and Theological Education, in Marietta, Ohio, was refused.[1] Quite dejected, he realized that he had made the journey to Ohio in vain. But shortly thereafter he did secure $8,000 from friends in the East, including J. P. Williston, the inventor of indelible ink, and Ichabod Washburn, the country's leading wire manufacturer. Evidences of a developing financial strength were noted at the annual meeting of the Board of Trustees in June 1866, in which the "President read a statement setting forth the prosperous state of the college for the past year."[2]

Blanchard noted also "7000 dollars raised on his endowment" and "1560 dollars raised" on the endowment of Professor Webster. To aid him in his quest for funds, John Calvin Webster had traveled to the East carrying a copy of a letter to Blanchard endorsing the work at Wheaton from Blanchard's friend and fellow abolitionist, Chief Justice of the Supreme Court Solomon P. Chase, great grandfather of Wheaton's sixth president, J. Richard Chase. At this time it was not uncommon for some professors to seek funds from private individuals, paid to the College, to create an endowment fund from which their salary, or part of it, was paid.

One significant element of President Blanchard's leadership was his concern for the education of blacks. He had heard with gratitude at the Board meeting in June 1864 a circular read from the Lovejoy Monument Association, proposing the endowment of "Lovejoy Scholarships for the education of colored persons in such of our literary and professional institutions as will receive the recipients of these funds to equal privileges and on the same terms with the white students." Jonathan guided the trustees in the preparation of an enthusiastic response: "Resolved that this board approve the proposed plans of perpetuating the name of that Christian patriot Owen Lovejoy and that we proceed to the endowment of a scholarship of $1,000 upon the condition required by the monument association and to be called the Lovejoy scholarships."[3] Though no great number of black students came to Wheaton College in the early years, several black men, assisted by Lovejoy scholarships, did register after the Civil War. All of these lived in President Blanchard's residence, where they received every courtesy. Not only blacks, "but students of other races soon came to Wheaton, and practically all made their residence with the president, thus giving a cosmopolitan atmosphere to the home."[4] Jonathan had a tender heart for the slaves, for ex-slaves, and for all who had helped those in bondage in their struggle for freedom.

During the Blanchard's administrations a grave located on the northeast corner of the lawn of Williston Hall was annually decorated in the spring as part of a chapel service conducted by the junior class. Here James Burr, an anti-slavery worker who had been engaged in helping slaves escape to freedom from Missouri to Illinois, was buried. Before his death at age 45 in 1859 in Princeton, Illinois, he had asked to be buried in Wheaton, perhaps because of the Wesleyans' strong stand against slavery. A five-foot tall stone marking the site of the grave was familiar to generations of Wheaton students. In 1928 the Board of Trustees authorized the moving of the body and gravestone to a cemetery near Wheaton. A small white ground-level stone, a few feet north of the dining hall, now marks the place where the grave had been.

Main Building Enlarged

The college catalogs from 1868 to 1870 carried an engraving of the proposed new building planned by the trustees in 1866. In part, the inscription beneath the picture read: "The front is to be 235 feet in length facing south. The wings to contain laboratories, a cabinet, gymnasium, dormitories and a domestic hall. The center building is to contain a chapel for religious exercises and rooms for Lectures and Recitations. We want FIFTY THOUSAND DOLLARS for this building in addition to funds already provided." A similar announcement and appeal was carried on the letterhead of the College.

Erected in 1853 at the cost of approximately $2,000, the original main building was a plain structure, forty-five by seventy-five feet. The initial step in rebuilding was to raise the roof of this structure thirteen feet, thus creating a four-story rather than three-story building. Elevating the roof produced a two-story room on the third floor extending the length of the building, which was long used for chapel services. In 1868 the trustees authorized the building of a west wing that would be twice the area of the old building, for which addition the cornerstone was laid on September 1, 1868.

Chairman for this historic moment in the life of the young College was Professor O. F. Lumry, who listed for his hearers a number of items sealed into the cornerstone: catalogs of Wheaton College and Chicago Theological Seminary, a record of the Beltionian Literary Society, and copies of *The Northern Illinoisian, The Advance, The Congregationalist, The Christian Banner,* and *The Voice of Our Young Folks.* Professor J. C. Webster, in the address of the day, commented on the hilltop location of the building: "It will give this building a beautiful appearance, and, if its fine architectural proportions be realized, will render it the admiration of the millions of travelers who will pass and repass it on this great central thoroughfare to Omaha and the Pacific." What Professor Webster failed to foresee was the row of houses at the bottom of the hill, the college service center—where the Billy Graham Center now stands—, the athletic field stadium, and the stately trees, all tending to obscure the view of the campus for the railroad traveler. But he was clear in his conception of the College, not as a showpiece but as a center for learning: "I take it to be the grand purpose of this college, not merely to bring out, strengthen, and refine, but to sanctify the powers of the mind—to subsidize all human learning to the precepts and instructions of the Great Teacher."[5]

When Charles Blanchard was graduated in 1870, he was relieved at not having to march to Jewell's Grove for the commencement ceremonies. The new west wing, makeshift and unfinished though it was, provided the setting for the year-end exercises. Charles's *Autobiography* offers some details of the occasion: "Our class graduated in the west part of what is now the central building. It was not completed at the time and rough boards were laid down for flooring on which a temporary platform was erected . . . .Most of our class received some little gift of some sort; and I remember that my dear mother sent me a little bunch of flowers." Since that day he had seen "mountains of flowers," he recalled, but he did not think they "represented so much earnest and true affection as that little bouquet I received that day." Young Blanchard's commencement oration was "The Natural Immortality of Man," a theme that like most such orations, did not work out to anyone's particular benefit. At the time, Charles questioned its truth. Later he said: "Now that I am older, I still question it. God alone has immortality as a natural possession."[6]

On the night of Sunday, October 8, 1871, a spectacular sight appeared which no Wheatonite of that day would ever forget. A great red glow, awesome and frightening, filled the eastern night sky. Excitement spread among the students at the news: a great fire was raging in Chicago. Whipped by a strong wind, the flames were leaping from wooden building to wooden building, engulfing both business and residential areas. One student noted in his diary: "Monday, October 9, Fire raging in Chicago all day. . . . The people of Chicago call for food and clothing."[7] For several days Jonathan Blanchard, aided by students and faculty, drove wagonloads of food, collected in Wheaton, to the stricken city. Through twenty-seven hours the fire raged, destroying some seventeen thousand buildings and claiming 250 lives.

Work on the west wing of the Main Building went slowly, partly because funds were low, and partly because economic sluggishness just about dried up gifts to the College. Nevertheless, on October 5, 1872, the last stone of the octagonal tower was set, the American flag was raised, and the announcement of the head mason, Mr. Austin, that the work was finished was welcomed with a cheer by those who had come to witness the event. The "old bell rang out, as well as its cracked and feeble utterance would permit, the joy of the great occasion."[8] As a demonstration of gratitude and affection, friends and students presented President Blanchard with a new set of office furnishings, including "carpet, furniture, and paintings." Professor Lumry, who had been connected with the College longest, made the presentation speech, to which President Blanchard responded with thanks "for this agreeable surprise." The day was happily concluded when "the faculty and their wives and members of the Ladies Advisory Board with their husbands adjourned to the new and beautiful dining hall and took tea with the steward and matron, Mr. and Mrs. Bissell and their family of about fifty students."[9]

Before Christmas in 1872 a new 1,000-pound copper and tin tower bell, cast in Troy, New York, at a cost of $500, was chiming the hours for church

Blanchard Hall in 1871. Then known only as the Main Building.

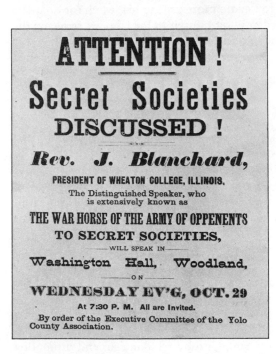

A public announcement of one of President Blanchard's many anti-secret society meetings.

services, classes, mealtime, athletic victories, and notable events. Engraved on the bell were the college name and the date, as well as the college motto in Latin, *Christo Et Regno Ejus* ("For Christ And His Kingdom"). John L. Stratton, class of 1876, who sponsored the project and raised the money among his fellow students to purchase the bell, later wrote: "The trade winds passing the Tower have kissed the bell and circled the globe with its message. Missionaries across the seas have heard it in their dreams." Now a recording of the tower bell begins each morning chapel. Over the years countless students have climbed the long wooden stairway to the Tower to ring the bell; three sets of seven rings announce an engagement, seven sets of three a wedding.

Other improvements came with the new building, as the 1873-74 catalog announced. "Fuel is taken to each floor by an elevator, sparing the young ladies that onerous task." "Neither study, pains, nor expense have been spared to make these buildings perfect in their adaptation to the health, purity and progress of young ladies and gentlemen in a mixed institution." The dining hall had been enlarged to "seat comfortably two hundred boarders." Regrettably, expenses for the new building had exceeded by $5,000 the estimated cost of $50,000. To meet the indebtedness, therefore, the trustees authorized the borrowing of $10,000, secured by the campus and buildings. Operating needs, together with obligations for the new west wing, left the College at the end of 1873 with a debt of $20,000. Relieved of his teaching duties by the trustees in 1870 to devote more time to his search for financial assistance, President Blanchard now set himself to the labor of reducing the college debt. His task was made no easier by the death the preceeding year of J. P. Williston, one of the College's most consistent and generous benefactors.[10]

Secret Societies

When the Civil War ended, the cause in which Jonathan Blanchard had labored so ardently for nearly thirty years came to a conclusion: the abolition of human slavery in the United States. In the early days of his anti-slavery lecturing Blanchard could not have foreseen, nor would he have chosen, the means by which his dream of freedom for Negroes was fulfilled. Still, the fact that the Fourteenth Amendment had brought an end to slavery was deeply gratifying.

But what now? To a man within whose heart the zeal for social reformation burned strongly, and who still clung to the vision of a perfect society there had to be other worthy causes. If American culture was to advance toward perfection, some of the grosser evils that blighted the land had to be purged. As a Christian it was his duty to expose and chastise evil: "He must speak, write, vote, support public men and measures, and sustain public papers on the sole principle of honoring God by rebuking sin and promoting holiness on the earth."[11]

And so Jonathan gave his energy to a new cause. He felt that secret societies were both un-Christian and undemocratic—un-Christian in that society members gave sworn allegiance to a ritual of their own devising, undemocratic in that some were excluded by their race or religion. Masonry was a "conspiracy against God and the human race."[12] The inferences were clear for Blanchard: "That Freemasonry must be destroyed if the country is to be saved; that fellowshipping Freemasonry is destroying the church; that voting for adhering Masons is voting for men who in practice deny the first principles of republican government . . . we must unite to withhold our fellowship and votes from known adherents of the lodge, if we will be consistent Christians or consistent Americans."[13]

Modern readers, now little interested in secret societies, may wonder what all the stir was about. But in the years both before and after the Civil War, the anti-secret society struggle was an issue in national politics and in various church councils, resulting in innumerable rallies in churches, town halls, and public auditoriums. Anti-lodge activity is significant in the history of Wheaton College because Jonathan Blanchard was so active in it and because through him the cause became institutionalized. Everywhere he went in his wide anti-lodge speaking activity, he was introduced as the President of Wheaton College. His frequent allusions to the subject must have been tiresome to some of his friends. Even Charles did not mind confessing in his *Autobiography* that, as a young man of nineteen, he "wearied of its continual mention," and asked one day at dinner, "Father, can we not speak about something in this house beside Freemasonry? I am extremely weary of the whole subject."[14] Nevertheless, Charles was himself later to lecture widely on it.

Jonathan Blanchard was the first president of the National Christian Association, founded in Aurora, Illinois, in the fall of 1867, by a gathering of eighty-seven ministers, laymen, and ex-Masons. A major arm of the Association's campaign against secretism was the *Christian Cynosure*, a four-page newspaper, the first issue of which appeared in Chicago on July 23, 1868. The paper continued to be published regularly until recent years. Earlier it often carried news about Wheaton College—indeed, many details of the college history during the Jonathan Blanchard era are found nowhere else.

The first issue of the paper appeared under the title, *Christian Banner— Opposed to Secret Societies*. It was not to be financed by the sale of stock, but was to be issued "upon the faith and intelligent piety of the friends of light and truth against secrecy and error."[15] One of those friends was Philo Carpenter, who came to Chicago from Massachusetts in 1832 by canoe, canal, and lakes, bought a 160-acre tract of land near what was to become the "Loop" of the central city, and by astute management of the land and other business involvements became a wealthy man. Exercising wise stewardship over his resources, Carpenter supported many philanthropic and reform causes, among them anti-slavery and anti-secret society efforts. When he died in 1886, Jonathan wrote a commendatory obituary notice, in which he revealed that Carpenter once said to him: "When we get along with this slave business we must give our attention to the lodge, and we must have a paper to represent us." Blanchard further observed that Carpenter had paid for the first issue of the paper, gave the building in which it was printed at 221 West Madison, and remained a generous supporter for many years.[16] The building and its presses were destroyed in the great Chicago fire.

Though the central function of the *Cynosure* was to carry on an unrelenting campaign against the lodge, it steadily enlarged its interests and in time became a widely read sixteen-page journal. The public meetings of D. L. Moody were frequently reported in commendatory terms, though Blanchard was distressed that Moody tolerated lodge men on the platform with him. On one occasion Blanchard wrote to the *Cynosure* of hearing Moody at Northfield, Massachusetts: "A whole day and evening was spent studying Christ's second coming and not a word to warn young men against joining a giant system which lies directly across his path and prevents his coming to men."[17] Later, he was praising one of Moody's sermons and acknowledging that he had sometimes censured him. But now "I understand him better than ever I have."[18]

The *Cynosure* had its well-wishers, like the reader who wrote, "Thank God for the *Cynosure*. It stands next to my Bible for light and truth."[19] It also had its enemies, among them, Jonathan thought, postal workers who destroyed some of the copies before their delivery to subscribers. To Charles G. Finney he wrote: "The Masons are haunting and hounding me to death."[20] One irate citizen wrote to Blanchard declaring that "your fanatical paper and your lectures shall only add damnation to you. If possible we will crush you." It would please him, the writer added, to see Blanchard suffer the fate of William Morgan, a Mason and resident of Batavia, New York, who in 1826 was murdered by other Masons, so it was claimed, for revealing Masonic secrets.[21] The incident aroused a national wave of indignation and national feeling. Many Masons resigned from the order; some lodges disbanded. Several anti-Masonic newspapers appeared, giving hope to some that secret societies would perish.

The Morgan affair, which had occurred when Jonathan was a boy of fifteen, had had much to do with fixing his resolve to oppose lodgery. The decline of secret societies before the Civil War did not continue into the post-war era, however; after 1865 they began to evidence new strength. In a brief history of the College published in the *Wheaton College Record* in 1910 to mark the fiftieth anniversary of the institution, Charles Blanchard wrote, speaking of the resistance to secret orders: "It was a blow on behalf of the home, in behalf of wives and children, worse than widowed and orphaned because of lodge influence upon husbands and fathers. It was a blow for the Church of Jesus Christ, robbed of its young men."[22]

A prohibition against membership in secret societies had been written into the first catalog of Wheaton College, the legality of which was tested in the courts of Illinois in 1865. Fifteen students, with the encouragement of local lodge members, joined the Masons; one went to the daring length of posting notices of meetings on the college bulletin board. Confronted with the threat of dismissal for defiance of college rules, all but two of the men withdrew from the order. The two who refused to resign were suspended. Wishing to test the legality of the College's action, the Wheaton lodge in 1865 presented their case to the Illinois Circuit Court, which ruled in favor of the College. Undaunted, the Masons appealed to the Supreme Court of Illinois, which confirmed the ruling of the lower court, declaring that the College was "in the place of parent," and was entitled legally to establish and enforce reasonable rules of behavior.

In Time of Stress, a Steady Vision

When the class of 1870 was graduated from Wheaton College, it included among its seven members three young men who had become intimate friends: Charles Albert Blanchard, Herman Augustus Fischer, and Henry Lyman Kellogg. Fischer and Kellogg had lived at the Blanchard home and shared the family meals. Herman Fischer, one of ten children of German-born parents, entered Wheaton on the basis of a letter he had received from the president of the College addressed to "Mr. Herman Fischer who expects to attend Wheaton College, Addison, Illinois." After his graduation, Fischer was appointed principal of the preparatory department; two years later he became professor of mathematics in the College. At the Blanchard home his affection had settled on Julia Waters, one of Jonathan's daughters whom he saw daily. Three years after his graduation Herman and Julia were married, and shortly afterward set out for a year in Leipzig and Heidelberg. Eventually their family numbered twelve children, ten of whom were graduated from Wheaton College; five of the seven sons were graduates of Harvard Law School. Herman Fischer, Sr. was to serve the College for fifty years. Of him Charles Albert Blanchard wrote: "He is one of the best all-round teachers I have ever known, doing successful work in mathematics and German, which were his choice, but also being equipped for instruction in Latin, Greek and other studies."[23] For many years he was also the efficient treasurer of the College, aiding regularly, when he was not teaching, in the unending task of searching for funds.

While Charles was engaged in anti-Masonic work in the East, he met Margaret Ellen Milligan to whom he was married in October 1873 in the Eighth Street Reformed Presbyterian Church of Pittsburgh by A. M. Milligan, father of the bride and pastor of the church. The couple's five children were Jonathan, who died in infancy, Mary Belle, Julia, Rachel, and Clara. There was also an adopted son, Paul, who married, lived in Chicago, and was killed in an automobile accident there. Julia Blanchard served the College in various roles for many years, in particular as the first full-time librarian from 1912 to 1948.

Liberalism and Evolution

When Herman Fischer set out for Germany and advanced study there—American universities were not yet offering graduate programs—he faced some hazard. Increasingly, after the Civil War, American scholars were being drawn to the German universities in admiration of their professionalism and intensity of research. The emphasis was on the quest for new knowledge rather than on conservation of the classical heritage. The American professor was the transmitter of the wisdom of the ages; the German professor was the researcher, the investigator. In American higher education of the times the influence of German scholarship is clear, since "it is estimated that between nine and ten thousand Americans studied in Germany from 1815 to 1914."[24] American institutions did not become replicas of German universities; but the German influence was transmitted through Americans who returned to American colleges and universities with a new professional concept of scholarly teaching.

The first generation of such students were attuned to humanistic and aesthetic values. But the second generation of American scholars in the German universities during the latter half of the nineteenth century were less humanistically inclined. They became absorbed in professional German scholarship, with its intensive devotion to analytical research in quest of new knowledge.[25] They also absorbed the rationale and methods of theological higher criticism, which they appropriated and applied to their academic pursuits. Not all Americans studying abroad succumbed to these characteristics of German university scholarship—certainly Herman Fischer did not—but the broad tendency among students was to accept the assumptions of German rationalism and its challenge to the supernatural elements of biblical Christianity. The higher criticism, transmitted into American scholarship, was a central element in the rise of theological liberalism. Through its influence there followed a loss of the evangelical convictions to which many Christian educational institutions had earlier been committed.

Jonathan Blanchard was not unmindful of the perils implicit in this new stream of thought. Writing in the *Congregational News* in January 1892, when some of the consequences of German scholarship were clearly discernible, he said: "German universities have done more to make the Bible contemptible than have all other causes since Luther rescued it from the convent of Erfurt."[26] But since the president himself taught the crucial courses which rationalism and liberalism might affect—Mental and Moral Philosophy, Christian Evidences, Philosophy of the Plan of Salvation—he could commend the ideas acceptable to historically evangelical theology. These senior courses were small enough to meet in the president's office, where the intimate relationship of instructor and learner generated confidence in Blanchard's wisdom. Under those circumstances doctrinal infidelity was unlikely to arise. That Jonathan felt assured he could grant a measure of freedom to his students without serious consequences is evident from the statement in the 1877-78 catalog description of the courses in Mental and Moral Philosophy: "Free discussion is encouraged in all these studies, and students are not expected to adopt without question the views of either textbook or teacher, but to think for themselves."[27]

The debates over Darwinian evolution which began in America in 1860, the year following the appearance of *The Origin of Species*, seemed in the earliest days to have provoked no agitation on the Wheaton campus. First among Americans to champion the theory was Asa Gray, a distinguished Harvard botanist, a Christian, who believed that natural selection did not impair the idea that nature is the consequence of a preordained design. Henry Ward Beecher held a similar view, while Phillips Brooks rejected the thesis. If the assumptions of evolution were true, then the fixed certainties of the old classical curriculum would be subject to doubt.[28] President Blanchard was not unaware of the implications of Darwinism nor of the consequences of evolutionary teaching on Christian education. At the 1871 commencement he invited the Reverend S. B. Goodenow to speak on "Creation, a Supernatural Work," an exposition that was expanded into a series of articles in the *Christian Cynosure*, beginning on September 28, 1871. Speaking editorially of the series, Jonathan said: "Under this examination the poor 'theory' is reduced to an absurdity with the convincing clearness of a geometrical demonstration." He called the evolutionary hypothesis the "sickly product of a trifling intellect."[29]

Not until 1927 was there a doctrinal statement in the College catalog dealing with origins. During the early years, the daily chapel service, the required Sunday church attendance, and Tuesday prayer meeting, together with the Christian classroom instruction, seemed adequate to maintain on the campus a spiritual tone of commitment to Christ. With a dedicated Board of Trustees, a president and faculty unwaveringly devoted to historic Christianity, and a student body trustful of their mentors' spiritual integrity, Wheaton College did not falter theologically, nor succumb to the liberal unorthodoxy that captured many other educational institutions.

It was probably propitious that early attempts to have the Congregationalists assume a large portion of the financial needs of the College failed. It forced the College to be largely independent, freeing it from such denominational dependence as led other colleges into theological liberalism. It was not swept into liberalism by the changing vision of a parent body. Crucial, too, in preserving the conservative-reformist posture of the College were the instructors drawn to Wheaton by Blanchard and the trustees. Many of them were reformers from the anti-slavery days, or recent alumni of the College who shared the president's views.[30]

One of these former abolitionists was James Barr Walker, who took over the president's teaching responsibilities in intellectual and moral philosophy in 1870, thus freeing Blanchard for administrative work and fund raising. Charles Blanchard acknowledged that he was much influenced by this man, who was his instructor in moral philosophy. Walker was the author of *The Philosophy of the Plan of Salvation*, a widely known text that had been translated into five languages. He also frequently wrote for the *Cynosure*. In 1876 he became the National Christian Association's candidate for president under the banner of the American Party, which ran candidates in four campaigns, beginning in 1872. In accord with the values of Blanchard and the spirit of Wheaton College, the American Party platform called for prohibition, the banning of lodges, Sabbatarian legislation, and an amendment to the Constitution proclaiming the United States a Christian nation.[31] From 1871 to 1880 Walker was pastor of College Church, a Congregational affiliate. Since the church was supported for the most part by the faculty, students, and community, its services were held in the college chapel.

Another faculty member, professor of commercial law, was Novak E. Gary, son of Eldridge Gary, the first settler of Wheaton, and brother of Judge Elbert M. Gary, later chairman of the board of United States Steel. Art was given significant emphasis through the teaching of Sarah H. Nuting, who had come from western Vermont in 1871, and remained until the turn of the century.[32] Science was taught through Jonathan Blanchard's era by recent graduates of Wheaton with limited training, but whose complete dedication to the ideals of the College was evidenced in part by the readiness of the faculty to accept meager, and sometimes delayed, salaries. In 1881 the trustees acknowledged that instructors had received only half of their promised salaries for the year and had to supplement their income by Sunday preaching or various business efforts.[33]

Although Wheaton was later to write into its doctrinal statement a commitment to premillennialism, President Blanchard had no rigidly fixed theological position on the millennium to which faculty and students were expected to subscribe. After printing D. L. Moody's sermons on Christ's premillennial return, he said editorially in the *Cynosure*: "For ourselves, we believe in the premillennial and postmillennial coming of Christ, both; that his coming will take the world by surprise; that it will be attended by terrible judgments; that the day is near and hasteth greatly; and that the Scriptures that describe it are given for use; and we like Mr. Moody on the subject because he seems to have no definite theory drawn out in detail but wishes to impress his hearers with the fact of its near approach."[34]

Campus Scene

Amid all his busyness Jonathan was able to shift many of the routine administrative duties to the care of Charles Albert Blanchard, who at the June 1877 meeting of the trustees had been named "to continue indefinitely as assistant to the president." Charles Albert spoke of his father as "a man of oak and iron . . . stormy and tempestuous when the winds are raving."[37] The *Christian Press* of Cincinnati had said of him: "President Blanchard . . . probably has more warm friends and more determined enemies than any minister of the gospel in the West! This arises from his peculiar natural temperament which leads him to attack whatever appears to him sinful with the whole strength of his nature . . . with all his faults he is a noble Christian man, and would scorn to do a mean thing or refuse a reparation when betrayed into doing a wrong thing. He may have great faults, but he also has great virtues."[38]

Through all the tense episodes he endured, Jonathan had been encouraged by the unfailing support of Mary. In Cincinnati, Galesburg, and Wheaton she had been a faithful and enthusiastic partner in her husband's enterprises. Possessed of extraordinary patience, energy, and devotion to the Lord's will in her life and the life of her family, she was a woman of sturdy pioneer quality. The day before Jonathan Blanchard died, he said to his daughter Julia, Mrs. Herman A. Fischer, "Make mother's memory not only 'blessed' but a blessing." The result of that appeal was the publication of *Blessed Memories: Life of Mary Avery Blanchard*. When Mary came to Wheaton, Julia records, she found a "struggling institution dedicated to reform, poor and deeply in debt." When she promptly gathered about her "a band of willing-hearted, willing-handed workers, chapel and dormitories were washed, white-washed, papered or painted, as the case required."[39] One neighbor said: "I think we would have died when we first came to Wheaton if it had not been for Mrs. Blanchard." She explained that when a niece had been taken ill with smallpox, no one would come near the house except Mary, who came every day. "Her work for the college and her motherly interest in the students was unceasing,"[40] Julia noted.

Revivals from time to time at College Church and within the college community were strongly encouraged by Jonathan Blanchard, who usually reported them in the *Cynosure*. In 1880 a campus revival, supported by evangelistic meetings, was given the following notation:

> The revival of Wheaton College continues. After five weeks nearly all the students professed the new birth, and quite a number not connected with the institution. In order to reach more of the latter class, the meetings this week are held in the Wesleyan Church.[41]

Those kinds of Christian experience, together with the daily chapel service, did much to create an environment uniquely conducive to personal devotion, Christian service, and scholarship at Wheaton. Virtues desirable for the Christian were without pretention honestly cultivated.

Literary societies continued to be the center of student social life, as they were at most colleges of the time. By now there were three societies at Wheaton—for men, the Beltionian and Excelsior; and for women, the Aelioian. According to Professor Edwin Hollatz, "the first known intercollegiate contact [in speech events] occurred when Beltionian Literary Society accepted a challenge from the Natural Science Society of North-Western College in nearby Naperville for a literary contest."[42] The two schools competed in declamation, oratory, and debate on November 20, 1878. Beltionian was declared the winner in oratory; their opponents won the declamation; and the debate, "Resolved: That Religious Freedom should be tolerated in the United States," was declared a tie. In reporting the event, the *Wheaton College Record* said: "The contest cannot fail in stimulating the members of both societies to more earnest society work especially in debating." The following year Wheaton hosted the event, which drew a crowd of 600 listeners in the college chapel.

Two months earlier the *Wheaton College Record,* a six-page monthly paper sponsored by the Literary Union, had made its appearance. J. D. Nutting's offer to publish ten issues, 250 copies each issue, for $160.00 was gladly accepted. In preparing copy and editorials, the "Belts" seem to have taken the largest responsibility. Thomas E. Kennedy, the editor, was a Belt, who later became the son-in-law of Jonathan Blanchard. On campus it was often jocularly said that "the Belts had the brains, while the Celts had the money."[43] Whether for want of brains or money, the paper published only six issues. What is now known as the *Wheaton College Record* made its appearance as the official college paper in 1890, under the editorship of President Charles Blanchard, who in editorials, news of College Church, and accounts of his travels, pled for various reform causes, and invited student and alumni contributions.

Although the catalog description of appropriate student conduct was explicit, not everyone submitted to the letter of the law. Darien A. Straw, a student in the seventies, who was to be associated with Wheaton for fifty-eight years, in the course of an interview in 1947 recollected that

> We had problems with boys and girls [in the seventies] who didn't obey the rules, more in proportion than now. But the College didn't waste time with them. It was straighten up or go.[44]

Organized student activity, apart from the "lits" was to await a later day in Wheaton history. "We did not have many athletic contests in those days," Straw noted. "Generally finding acceptance on other college campuses, sports at Wheaton was nothing more than boys and girls at play—never organized, never systematized."[45]

During the latter half of the nineteenth century college students everywhere were themselves largely responsible for developing an extracurriculum, operating side by side with the curriculum. Through the variety of organizations and machinery—later known as student activities—young men and women learned many supplementary skills and insights that never were a part of formal education, although sometimes students lost sight of the curriculum in their eager pursuit of extracurricular activities.

Except for the continuing burden of financial needs, the College moved through the remaining years of Jonathan Blanchard's presidency with relative calm and few changes. The college department remained small, rarely exceeding fifty students. In Jonathan's last year there were only twenty-nine, but the supplementary divisions kept the enrollment consistently at 200 or above. The Conservatory of Music had twice as many students as the College had; art was also popular.

In 1880, conscious of advancing years and waning strength, President Blanchard submitted his resignation to the Board of Trustees, who were unready to accept it. The preceding August he had suffered a physical breakdown which called for rest and a change of scene. Accordingly, he and Mary decided to visit their youngest daughter Sonora Carolina and her husband

Thomas E. Kennedy in San Jose, California, a journey that took them through areas Jonathan and Charles had visited years earlier. When he returned—he was now seventy and encouraged by the fact that the College was out of debt—Jonathan once again pressed the trustees to accept his resignation. In June 1882, the request was honored, and the Board designated "that his future relation to the college be that of President and Professor Emeritus." A special resolution expressed thanksgiving that he "for twenty-two years conducted the affairs of this institution with great sacrificial fidelity and success." The resolution further declared that "the endowment of the professorship of Mental and Moral Philosophy was given in large part to him personally, but was by him transferred to the Treasury of the College." In consequence the Board voted to set aside from the income of that professorship $500 to be paid to him semi-annually.[46]

Although Jonathan Blanchard's active days as a college teacher and administrator were now over, his reforming efforts were not. Wheatonites look back to him as the first of an exceptional line of skillful teachers who loved their fields of learning and their students. As an administrator Jonathan Blanchard was a paradox: a perfectionist, idealist, hardheaded go-getter. He saw the difference between what is and what ought to be and could be. From near demise he raised Illinois Institute to a new, soundly organized college with steadily enlarging promise. He exercised every effort to get and hold a good faculty at Wheaton College. Resisting strains of thought alien to biblical Christianity, he kept the institution unalterably committed to historic Christian orthodoxy. He was colorful, resolute, sometimes irascible in administrative style. Confident that he was laboring in righteous causes, he remained relentless in his efforts to see that they bore fruit.

PRESIDENT CHARLES A. BLANCHARD, 1882-1925

CHAPTER 3

Charles Albert Blanchard:
The Vision Continues

WHEN IN SEPTEMBER 1882 CHARLES ALBERT BLANCHARD came to the presidency of Wheaton College, as everyone expected he would, he was thirty-three years of age. Born in Galesburg on November 8, 1848, he was the fifth of the twelve Blanchard children. At Mary Blanchard's death in 1890, Charles was the only one of her five sons surviving. In his *Autobiography* he observed that he was born in a year of revolutions. Long slumbering European nations, where freedom had been denied for centuries, were beginning to demand reform. Among the progressives who allied themselves with nationalism was the Duke of Sardinia, Charles Albert, whom Mary, "greatly interested in the struggle for Italian freedom," much admired. It was she, Charles wrote, "who was chiefly interested in naming me after this Sardinian duke who was struggling for the nationalizing of his people."[1] Charles Albert Blanchard cherished his name and its significance for his life. He had been "named for one of the soldiers in the army of freedom" and "it has seemed to me that it would be unspeakably base not to have a share myself in the war."

During Charles Albert's boyhood the Blanchard home, spacious and hospitable, was a place of ceaseless activity. Besides their own growing family, Jonathan and Mary, both children of large families, often accommodated their own brothers and sisters for varying periods of time. Charles had before him a pattern of family concord that certainly influenced his own life. "I have never heard of any family strifes in either of my parents' homes," [2] he wrote. Nor any in his own, he might have added.

Christian nurture began early in the family circle, where every Sunday evening for more than twenty years, Mary gathered the children around her. The little ones "sang their hymns, recited Bible verses, psalms and chapters...while the older ones recited the Westminster Shorter Catechism, hymns and religious poems."[3] Charles Blanchard was so grateful for his Christian heritage and the example of a godly life set before him by his parents that he never ceased to commend it in public addresses and talks to students.

No less significant than the influence of his mother in the shaping of Charles's character were the precept and example of his father. The younger man held the elder in great esteem, as a passage from the *Autobiography* recalling the Knox days attests: "Having put his hand to the plow, he never turned back. East and west, north and south he went, everywhere preaching the gospel of Christian faith and thorough culture...Young men and women flocked into the primitive town, and people who had houses and lands sold them or gave them for the founding of a college in the great valley. Along with these labors... with his Bible under his arm or in his hand he walked through summer heat and winter cold to humble cabins and little towns, speaking with individuals or addressing meetings, helping people everywhere to be reconciled to God...In those days a stream of young blood was constantly poured by Knox College into the channels of Christian ministry...those were wonderful days. I can remember them as a little boy remembers the shock and rush of great events which pass him uncomprehendingly."[4]

The historical highwater mark of the little frontier town of Galesburg occurred in 1858, when the fifth of the celebrated Lincoln-Douglas debates was held on the lawn of Knox College. Young Charles was there, about to witness an event he was to remember for the rest of his life. The day's events began with a parade down the main street, colorfully decorated with bunting, wreaths of flowers, and displays of political slogans. Galesburg had been founded as an abolitionist community and remained unwaveringly so; but the county was pro-slavery, having been settled by "Hoosiers." Along a dozen blocks people lined the street to watch the parade and shout their partisan sentiments as the wagons and floats rolled by with their streaming banners: "Honest Abe, the Rail Splitter." "Lincoln, the Giant Killer," "Hurrah for the Little-Giant," "Down with the Abolitionists."

The parade over and dispersed, the crowd drifted toward the Knox campus, there to eat their picnic lunches and await the appearance of their champions. Among those who assembled on the campus to the east of Old Main that memorable day was Edward Beecher, brother of Harriet Beecher Stowe and a warm supporter of Jonathan Blanchard during the stormy days at Knox College. Edward Beecher was the father of George Beecher, who would become a member of the first graduating class of Wheaton College. An ardent Lincoln supporter, Edward Beecher went home after the debate and wrote:

> There was a grandeur in his thoughts, a comprehensiveness in his arguments, a binding force in his conclusions which were perfectly irresistible. The vast throng was silent as death; every eye was fixed on the speaker, and all gave him serious attention. He was the tall man eloquent; his countenance glowed with animation, and his eyes glistened with an intelligence which made it lustrous. He was no longer awkward and ungainly, but graceful, bold and commanding.[5]

Charles Albert also had his memories of the occasion. He wrote: "The great Lincoln I heard in the Lincoln-Douglas debate when a boy of ten, and it has never passed from my mind. The tall, angular, loose-jointed, benevolent-looking man, inexpensively clothed; the short, well-dressed, polished-appearing opponent; the seething crowds, the bands of music, and the storm of flags. The evident appeal to conscience and humanity in the speeches of Lincoln, and the deft, cunning, clever twisting and turning of his opponent—a sense of these came to me as a child, and remained."[6]

Four months after Jonathan Blanchard left Galesburg for Wheaton in January 1860, the family followed him on a trip that Charles, then twelve, remembered vividly. "We journeyed all night from Galesburg in the low, smoky, dingy coaches of the Burlington Railroad. Sleepy and tired and dust-covered and cinder-covered and smoky, we disembarked on the morning of an April day in Wheaton." Through the eager eyes of youth the boy saw what was both forbidding and promising—"a little huddle of farm houses on the wind-swept prairie"; low ground "in and about the town on which the water stood the year round"; and on the hill a half-mile from the station "a single building, small, in ill repair and in every way forbidding, stood in the midst of a campus which was and is one of the most beautiful spots in the world."[7] All things together, however, "the town was unspeakably dreary."

Of his performance as a grade schooler, young Blanchard speaks with the frankness essential to a trustworthy autobiographer. "I was not a good student; it was not natural for me to like books." He did not believe his teachers liked him very well, but he was sure his "mind was ever wide awake." One redeeming quality he thought he had: if he became "interested in a subject, it was natural and easy for me to study concerning it until I had exhausted all the available sources of information. In this way I developed unevenly, knowing much more about some things than about others, lacking the symmetric development which is the great need of a child."[8] The following year Charles was transferred by his parents to the Academy, where his performance was little better.

Charles Blanchard was sixty-five when he wrote his autobiography, an age at which reflective people are likely to be unduly conscious of under-achievement in their earlier years. By his own testimony his college career was without distinction. "I often blush," he wrote, "as I think how poor it was, how much better it might have been." Nevertheless, he caught a "vision of the wide fields of knowledge" that stretched before him and was unfailingly thankful "to my heavenly father who gave me my being in a country and in an age like my own."[9]

During his senior year at Wheaton, Charles fixed his mind on entering Andover Seminary, like his father, to prepare for the ministry. He did not at that point have strong feelings against Freemasonry, but his father urged him to study the subject, beginning with a reading of Webb's *Free Masons Monitor.* The book impressed him deeply, persuading him that his father "was right and that the lodge contained in itself not simply folly but tremendous fundamental possibilities for evil."[10] In September 1869 he addressed an anti-lodge meeting in Kingston, Illinois, after a stranger approached and asked him to substitute for his father, then in New England. Young Blanchard prepared his lecture carefully in writing and delivered it without interruption. By the time he was graduated from Wheaton in June 1870, he had made sixty-five addresses on lodgery.

Like his father before him, who had left Andover Seminary to serve as an Anti-Slavery Society speaker, Charles began to lecture in 1870 as general secretary of the National Christian Association, which was opposed to secret societies. The only agent in the field, he was paid one hundred dollars a month plus expenses for his services. In the course of his speaking he traveled widely and met a number of eminent men. In Boston the celebrated abolitionist lecturer, Wendell Phillips, greeted him in his home on Essex Street. "I knew this great man for twenty or twenty-five years," Blanchard later wrote.[11] When Charles lectured in Oberlin, he was invited to dine at the home of Charles G. Finney, where the two engaged "in an hour or two of delightful conversation."

Young Minister

Charles Blanchard preached his first sermon in 1867, when he was nineteen, at York Center, Illinois, ten miles from Wheaton. It marked the beginning of a long career of preaching, much of it as a supply or special-occasion speaker. Though he did not hold a seminary degree, he was approved for preaching by the Aurora Congregational Association in 1875, and had the right extended by the Downers Grove Association after examination. While carrying on those duties, as well as his obligations at the College, he evidently pursued part-time studies at Chicago Theological Seminary. In May 1878, he was ordained pastor of College Church, where he served until 1883. While he sat in his home before the meeting of the ordination council, he tells us, he opened his Bible and placed his finger at random on a verse—a practice he did not generally follow and did not recommend to others. Nevertheless, the verse struck him forcefully: "What is my reward, then, that when I preach the gospel I may make the Gospel of Christ without charge, that I abuse not my power in the gospel." The verse was a sober warning "and my whole ministry has been guided by that verse (I Cor. 9:18)."[14] There were times, he said, when he could have sold the truth, but he never did.

Teacher

Blanchard had beautiful handwriting, at a time when artful penmanship was much admired. Before completing his baccalaureate degree he became a teacher of penmanship in the Academy. In 1874 he became the first professor of English language and literature on the college faculty, though he lacked specialized training in that field. The course was offered in the freshman and sophomore years, and was "based largely on ideals and methods derived from England by way of the eastern colleges." Charles's competence as a teacher of literature was strengthened by the trip abroad he took in the late summer of 1880. It was, he wrote in his diary, his "desire for many years to visit Europe, not so much for its natural scenery— though this I wished to see—as its people. And not the great but the common people." Arriving in Glasgow, he made his way to Ayr to visit the "humble cottage where Burns was born." In Westminster Abbey he sensed a "mingling of the grand, the beautiful and the quiet that came to mind and heart like a benediction."[15]

By 1880 he was listed in the catalog as professor of logic and rhetoric; English literature was assigned to another teacher. When he became president in 1882, he also assumed his father's teaching responsibilities as J.P. Williston professor of moral and intellectual philosophy. His versatility was not yet exhausted, however; in 1900 he became professor of psychology and ethics. Since he had no graduate training in those fields, Charles Blanchard, like many other college teachers of the time, was not a specialist. Rather, he was a liberal arts generalist in the best sense of the word. Clearly he felt no serious limitation, but taught with confident authority and to the profit of many students who attested to his effectiveness as teacher-friend.

The course in moral philosophy, offered at Wheaton College from 1860 to 1900, and taught by the president of the College, was a standard curriculum offering in American colleges in the late eighteenth and nineteenth centuries. In the senior year it usually took the place of classics and mathematics. The content of the course, in a broad sense, "included material from the fields of biology, and psychology, of politics and economics, as well as of religion and ethics," with the emphasis resting, as the title indicates, upon the last named.[16] An early American textbook of moral philosophy defines it as "that science which gives rules for the direction of the will of man in his moral state, such rules to serve for the guidance of the individual, the community and the nation."[17] Moral philosophy as a course was an import from England and Scotland, with much of the content based on the thought of philosophers and theologians of those countries; but in time the concepts of American thinkers were added.

Some teachers of moral philosophy were rationalistic, with an eighteenth-century cast of mind; in their hands the Puritan ideal of a God-directed, God-serving life was lost. Rationalists made the assumption that it was possible for man, through the discovery of nature's laws and the exercise of his own consciousness, to establish practical standards of right and wrong, and even to describe the nature of deity. Where such a moral philosophy was accepted institutions slipped away, sometimes quite noticeably, sometimes by almost imperceptible stages, from the Christian orthodoxy that had been the joy of their founders.

Many Christian teachers, including the Blanchards, believed that rationalism could be successfully resisted by the "common sense philosophy" of the Scottish realist Thomas Reid. Common sense philosophy, popular in the nineteenth century, held that the mind was naturally endowed with the capacity to perceive reality accurately, including moral truth, just as the senses comprehend the physical world authentically. Charles absorbed that philosophy both from his father and from James Barr Walker, his teacher in moral philosophy at Wheaton, as well as his pastor, for whom he had great respect.

For Jonathan and Charles Blanchard, moral philosophy, the capstone of the student's academic experience, was centered in the historic Christian faith and the pietistic heritage to which they pledged their lives and the destiny of the College. Moral philosophy was one of several means by which the leadership of Wheaton might preserve the intention of the Board of Trustees, in 1860, to found a college at Wheaton where the "institution and the influence of the institution shall bear decidedly against all forms of error and sin...and whatever else shall clearly appear to contravene the kingdom and coming of our Lord Jesus Christ."

As a young teacher, Charles Blanchard was gentle, patient, understanding, disposed to give the student credit for good intentions even when performance fell short of excellence. Child of the Puritan tradition, he was a hard worker who expected a similar response from others. Tall, and of commanding presence—some called him strikingly handsome—he evoked respect and confidence in students and associates alike. By precept and example he continuously set before his students the ideal of the Christian scholar who saw Christian higher education as the entrance to a satisfying and enriched life and a preparation for large usefulness in service for the Kingdom of God in the world of his day.

Family Life

In the fall of 1873 Charles Albert brought his bride, Margaret Ellen Milligan, to a modest home on a sloping hill just north of College Station.

They remained in this house until 1880, when because of a shortage of help in the main building of the College they moved there, and Ellen took over the duties of housekeeper and matron for a short while.[18]

The first child of the marriage was Jonathan McClead, who lived only a month. Charles's grief lingered long after the child's death. "I find myself missing him increasingly as years go by, thinking from time to time that if he had lived, he would have been a man, my companion and helper."[19]

When Charles became president of the College in 1882, he built a spacious home on twenty acres of land on north Howard Street, three blocks from the College. After twelve years of happy married life, Margaret Ellen Blanchard began to suffer severely from heart lesions brought on by childhood rheumatic fever. Her death came in the fall of 1884.

Left with four children and a heavy schedule of teaching, administrative work, and extensive travel in the service of the College, President Blanchard sought a new companion to grace his home and care for his children. He found a loving and sympathetic mate in Amanda Jennie Carothers, a graduate of Wheaton in the class of 1878, who had been dean of women at the College since 1880. Charles and Jennie were married on June 30, 1886, and to this union three children were born: Jane, Marie, and Mildred. Now the Blanchard household sheltered seven girls, though Marie died in 1891, when scarlet fever struck the Wheaton region severely.

Not long after Marie's death, Jennie began noticeably to decline in health. Her sister, Frances, a medical doctor and a graduate of the College, came from Des Moines, Iowa, to make an examination and request a consultation. A growth of suspicious nature now surrounded an area of her body that had been injured in a fall years before. An operation in Chicago, followed by patient and loving care by husband and children, failed to check the decline. Jennie died on February 10, 1894.

When Frances Carothers returned to Des Moines, she and Charles corresponded, first about family matters and then about the possibility of a future together. As Charles was now forty-seven and Frances thirty-six, a decision was not to be made lightly. The young woman lingered over her answer. It was a hard struggle for Frances Carothers to lay aside ambition to take on a new home and children. But in the end the call of the children won.

From their earliest years the Blanchard children took part in family devotions at the table after breakfast and the evening meal. Bible reading began with Genesis and continued day by day through the entire Scriptures, each person in the circle reading two verses. In this way the children learned to read, and when one could "read a couple of verses in the Bible at family worship without a mistake, she was to receive a Bible that was to be her very own." On severely cold mornings the family sat around a glowing grate-fire in the library while they read the living Word, sang, and prayed.

Some people felt that President Blanchard was away from his family too much. His work week was demanding: "It has been the custom of my teaching," he wrote, "to work twelve months in every year in some way, seven days of every week. When the teaching week was over, I have taken the train to go somewhere to represent the College in some way for the sake of securing students or money or both. The result has been that my home life has been deprived of many good and pleasant hours which I could myself have enjoyed. I surrendered this privilege for the sake of work—If I were to act again in the premises I should act as I have said above."[20]

A New Era

"A college presidency is not a profession,"[21] wrote one holder of the office. "A hundred years ago," adds George P. Schmidt, "it was an art, and was learned by doing. One did not prepare for it as one did for the ministry or even a professorship." In the nineteenth century most of the church colleges called their presidents directly from successful pastorates, as Jonathan Blanchard had been summoned from his church in Cincinnati to the leadership of Knox College. When Charles Blanchard was chosen in 1882 to follow his father in the Wheaton College presidency, he had served for four years as the pastor of College Church. Because his assignment at the College did not require him to give up his work at College Church, he chose to continue there, at least for a time. Unlike most college presidents of that era, Charles had some preparation for his new office as his father's assistant. As the two worked together, father and son by their presence indelibly minted the nature and character of the early Wheaton College. Charles lived in a time, perhaps advantageously for him, when small college presidents were free to act somewhat arbitrarily, without the counsel of others. President Blanchard, for example, in the early years, would not use caps and gowns at commencement. Later, as the College grew, he felt it necessary to conform to prevailing custom.

At thirty-three the young president found himself presiding over a financially stable institution, with a competent faculty and loyal student body. Among the thirteen faculty members listed in the 1882 catalog, two had been with the College since its founding in 1860: Oscar F. Lumry, professor of ancient languages, and A.H. Hiatt, professor of physiology and hygiene. These two were now teaching under their former pupil. J.B. Walker was acting professor of intellectual philosophy and belles-lettres, Herman A. Fischer served as professor of mathematics and natural philosophy, and his brother, William H. Fischer taught history and modern languages. Royal T. Morgan taught natural sciences. Young Darien Straw, who had been graduated the year before, was made principal of the preparatory school. Amanda Jennie Carothers, later Charles Albert's second wife, served as principal of the ladies' department. Under the direction of S. Wesley Martin, the Conservatory was a flourishing division with more than twice the number of students in the College. Art instructor Sarah Nutting for years kept in her studio a supply of trowels and pans which she urged students to use to rid the campus of dandelions.

Writing years afterward of some of his early colleagues, President Blanchard said of Dr. J. B. Walker that "he was the nearest specimen of pure intellect I ever saw. His body was frail and thin, almost to emaciation...So far as my intellectual life alone is concerned, he was the most satisfactory preacher I ever listened to."[22] Professor Lumry was a "patient, faithful, conscientious, hard working, true hearted man." But he "became a disciple of one of the strange leaders of our time"[23]—an unelaborated statement. A.H. Hiatt, physician and Wesleyan preacher, "was a natural orator and like other orators had ebbs and tides. When he was at his best, he was a remarkable speaker." For many years Hiatt was an effective and much loved teacher, as well as a generous supporter of the College.

In the twenty-two years since the founding of Wheaton in 1860, there had been little change in the number of students enrolled. The total in 1882 was 216, of whom only 29 were in the College; 6 were in the senior class. A choice among three degree programs continued as a student option: the classical course for which the B.A. was awarded; the Ph.B. degree was conferred for one year of classical studies and two years of selected work, including mental and moral philosophy; for a three-year course without Greek the student gained an L.A. degree, Laureate of Arts, the degree usually granted to graduates of the ladies' course. Apparently only the intellectually hardy survived the rigors of the B.A. program, heavily laced with the classics: Plato, Sophocles, Greek New Testament, Greek prose composition, Tacitus, Pliny, Horace, Cicero.

Among the patrons and graduates of nineteenth-century American colleges, the classical curriculum had its critics. "The kernels of classical wisdom and truth were imbedded in a hard shell of grammar and syntax," one observer noted, "and most students never learned to crack the shell. College classes rarely got to the point of discussing the ideas of the writers they were supposed to be studying but remained bogged down in the preliminaries of form and construction."[24] No doubt that judgment was unfair to the more scholarly professors and the most capable students. But breathes there yet a student of the classics who cannot remember a certain classic in which the highest adventure of the hour was the search for an elusive ablative absolute or passive periphrastic?

Whatever the reservations of others, Charles Blanchard did not waver in his loyalty to the liberal arts vision of education, with its undergirding of classical studies. "Why should we ask for the old paths?" he inquired in an address on the day of prayer for colleges. "Because the old are the best. The sun is old, the sea is old, the truth is old. Man's essential needs have not changed since the days of Adam. New circumstances will require change in form and mode of approach, but the great questions are reiterated in solemn tones throughout the centuries and again and yet again will demand answers from men."[25]

The American past had a solid splendor which Blanchard always admired and often appealed to; he knew how to identify the usable past. To a group of Congregational ministers meeting in Chicago in 1889, he said, in an appeal for support of the Christian college: "I plead today for a revival of the Puritan spirit concerning the education of our young people."[26] He was alluding to the early settlers' resolution to give sacrificially to that kind of education that would assure a dedicated and learned clergy. For him the purpose of education was "not to help men to get a living so much as to make men fit to live." College graduates knew, he was sure, that only upon "integrity, patience, self-denial, courage, and, above all, the Christian religion is a permanent national life to be built."[27] Besides those virtues, he frequently commended hard work, frugality, and compassion. Whether in the classroom, on campus, or in his far-ranging travels, he was a splendid exemplification of what he believed an educated Christian ought to be.

Newly established on the campus in 1882, and described in the catalog of that year, was the Wheaton Theological Seminary, founded by act of the Wesleyan Educational Society in October 1881, at Syracuse, New York. Of the fifteen founding board members, thirteen were from New York. With L. N. Stratton as president, the seminary was to be supported by the Wesleyans for the training of their own ministry. Wheaton had been chosen because there was a flourishing Wesleyan church there, the "thorough and reformatory education" to be had at the college would "stimulate piety," there was a commendable "absence of all saloons and pool-rooms," and the costs were low. Further, "opportunities for manual labor, at fifteen cents an hour, are afforded many students by the inhabitants of the place." For a cluster of reasons, therefore, young men "are looking hopefully to this School of the Prophets for instuction."[28] Announcements about the seminary quietly disappeared after the 1887 catalog.

With the 1886 catalog came important changes in the course of study. "The attention of friends of education is respectfully invited," the statement declared with muted pride, "to these revised courses, with the confident expectation that they will be found to compare favorably with those of any similar institution in the land. The faculty of the college have always been of the opinion that a liberal education includes more than a smattering of languages, a few formulas in mathematics and a few facts in the natural sciences . . . Wheaton College has never yielded to the clamor for short courses leading to cheap degrees which only serve to inflate the vanity of the possessors; but has afforded its students courses of study valuable not only for the information acquired but also for the mental discipline to be gained by pursuing them.[29] With that prelude the new scientific course leading to a B.S. degree was announced. Under the direction of

Wheaton College Faculty, 1882. Front row, l. to r.: Felecia Hiatt, Sara Nutting, A. J. Carothers, Oscar Lumry. Second row: W. H. Fischer, R. T. Morgan, H. A. Fischer, President Charles A. Blanchard, Darien Straw, J. B. Walker.

Class of 1888. Front row, l. to r.: James Parsons, Charles A. Blanchard, George Conrad. Back row: Arthur Northrup, W. L. Enlow, Clare Beach, Abram Stratton, F. F. Ames.

Royal T. Morgan, the course included geology, chemistry, physics, and astronomy. It differed little from the classical course; Greek, Latin, German, and French were still required. Two years later mineralogy and zoology were added to the scientific curriculum under the direction of Elliot Whipple, who in 1887 had begun what was to be a dedicated and extended career at Wheaton.

The tone of the catalog was optimistic: attendance was good, bills were being paid, the College no longer had paid financial agents. (To collect $5,000 the preceding year had cost less than $150. The old system of paying agents ten percent of what they collected, in effect since the beginning, was burdensome and had been abandoned.) Four thousand dollars had been subscribed for an east wing to what continued to be known as "the main building." When the building fund reached $10,000 work would begin. One other small building made up the whole sum and substance of Wheaton College, a frame dormitory "for young gentlemen." Library holdings "were increasing and would grow more if there were a place to put the books."

This illuminating catalog, recreating something of the tone of the College in the late '80s, notes that "in all classes text-books are used, and instructors give, from time to time, in the form of lectures, such additional information as may be required." Graduates "having two years of German, are expected to read, write and speak the language." For "rhetorical work, the President of the College meets the Freshmen, Sophomores and Juniors once each week. The plan is a complete and practical course in Oratory." For Bible study there were "eight classes every Monday morning." Expenses remained relatively unchanged, reflecting a stable economy.

The Last Years of Jonathan and Mary

When Jonathan Blanchard, then seventy-one, retired as president of Wheaton College in 1882, he resolved to spend his remaining years in the service of the National Christian Association, particularly in its unrelenting crusade to expose the evils of secret societies. In March 1883 he went to Washington to examine the new headquarters of the Association and to propose a number of projects to aid the cause, including the publication of a daily newspaper, the training of lecturers, the distribution of tracts through mission societies, and the sending of the *Christian Cynosure* to every minister in the United States.[30]

In May Jonathan returned to Wheaton feeling well, and expecting to take up his duties in Washington again in the fall. Toward the close of October, "escorted to the train by some two hundred students and friends,"[31] the Blanchards began the return journey to Washington. In October the American Party, closely allied to the National Christian Association, nominated Jonathan Blanchard as its candidate for the presidency to run against Cleveland and Blaine, in what had been expected to be a close contest. Shortly thereafter, however, Jonathan withdrew.

In March 1885 Jonathan was quite ill at his home in Wheaton, but by late spring had recovered and was delighted with the opportunity to preach the baccalaureate sermon at the College. He took as his text Daniel 12:4, "Many shall run to and fro, and knowledge shall be increased." That commencement was a special one for the aging president emeritus; it marked the twenty-fifth anniversary of his coming to Wheaton. Among the events of the week was a "special celebration on Wednesday under the auspices of the alumni and old students. Rev. L.S. Hand represented the former, and Major J.W. Powell, the intrepid, one-armed explorer of the Colorado Canyon, the latter."[32] J. Wesley Powell was a man whose daring explorations and scientific achievements had brought him wide renown. As a boy he had lived in Wheaton, his father being one of the first trustees of Illinois Institute. To his parents' disappointment, young Powell at first refused to enroll at the Institute because it offered no work in science. But after travels in the West failed to secure him a job opportunity, he returned home ready to cast in his lot with Illinois Institute and its newly established course work in science. Powell's biographer notes, however, that "Wes was officially connected with the school for only one term, in 1857-58."[33]

To escape some of the rigors of the winter, Mary, then in declining health, and Jonathan set out on January 6, 1890, the day before Mary's seventy-first birthday, to visit their daughter Sonora Caroline in California. Mary "remembered how her health had been benefited by her journey south, two years before."[34] When their train reached East Las Vegas, New Mexico, however, Mary became so ill that she was removed from the train for medical assistance. Three days later, on January 11, she died quietly. Funeral services were held in the college chapel with G.N. Boardman, an old friend and Middlebury graduate, officiating, followed by burial in the Wheaton cemetery.[35]

After the loss of Mary, Jonathan continued to live in the big house across the tracks, where he watched the brightness of spring come on and puttered in the garden. Surrounded and supported by the love of his children and grandchildren, he kept himself busy by writing for the *Christian Cynosure*, attending conferences, preaching occasionally, visiting the College frequently, offering counsel to Charles on administrative matters. For his eightieth birthday on January 19, 1891, friends, relatives, and the college family planned a gala occasion. Richard Edwards, a former Illinois State Superintendent of Education, was the principal speaker. For the celebration a poem was composed and read by Rufus Blanchard, a historian, unrelated to Jonathan. Congratulatory letters in great numbers were received. In the evening, family members, faculty, and a few friends gathered to hear the "Old President" read his autobiography, a slender twelve-page document.

On Saturday, May 14, 1892, with his loved ones nearby, and without evidence of pain, Jonathan Blanchard breathed his last. The valiant old heart was stilled; he had reached Home.

For the funeral in the college chapel on the following Monday, students formed two long lines outdoors through which Jonathan Blanchard's body was born into the chapel. Officiating at the service was Joseph Edwin Roy, one of Jonathan's students at Knox, and one of his many admirers. At the burial, in the Wheaton cemetery, Jonathan was laid beside his beloved Mary. Several days later the *Advance* said of him: "Tough minded though he was as one built of oak and steel, there was within a heart of sympathy and love which often gave him uncommon power as a preacher and college officer in drawing men to Christ."[36] The *Inter-Ocean* said editorially: "No one who knows the educational history of Illinois can feel other than profound reverence for the memory of Jonathan Blanchard."[37]

CHAPTER 4

The 1890s:
A Decade of Growth

W HEN THE FINAL DECADE OF THE NINETEENTH CENTURY
began, the President of the United States was Benjamin Harrison, an unin-
spiring figure, who had unseated Grover Cleveland and was himself to be
turned out after one term. The tarriff, civil service, and the authority of the
House of Representatives occupied Harrison's attention for much of his tenure in office—hardly matters to stir the impassioned interest of the country.
But while the Harrison administration occupied itself with the small gears of
national business, Wheaton's President Blanchard in the December 27,
1891, issue of the *Wheaton College Record* spoke boldly against much
deeper ills: "The danger to America," he wrote, "is a coarse, unintelligent,
unscriptural wealth. The need of America is that the intellectual and spiritual forces should be kept abreast of the tremendous advance of material
prosperity." It was a powerful indictment and great challenge. Charles Blanchard envisioned generations of self-giving young people marching out in
service to the church and the republic. Such a hope found vigorous expression in the pages of the *Wheaton College Record*.

Making its debut on March 15, 1890, the four-page newspaper was
printed on campus on an Aldine Job Press, the gift of Amos Dresser, Jr.,
"son of one of the heroes of the war against slavery." Edited by President

Charles Blanchard, it carried news of the College, announcements of administrative policy, personalia, occasional poetry, and a page devoted to the activities of College Church. Issue number one of the *Record* began by quoting approvingly from an editorial in the January 1890 *Century* magazine: "The country must have some men who will resist the temptation to devote their lives to mere money-getting, not because they would not like to have the freedom and power which money gives but because they love knowledge more. Our colleges alone can supply these men, and they are supplying them, and are thus of inestimable service to the Republic."[1]

Such sentiment captured the hearts of idealistic young men and matched President Blanchard's sense of individuality and self-reliance. Charles was interpreting his educational and social philosophy. Missing, however, from the pages of the *Record* in the early years are the day-to-day accounts of student life that would have fleshed out the chronicle of the years.

Under the title, "Colleges and Reforms," the second issue of the *Record* declared editorially: "Reformation always should follow malformation. If an abuse has become powerful, abusive and unquestioned; if it has become interwoven with the manners, customs, laws and opinions of the people, then there is a call for some one to break down, to plow up, to destroy this existing order, this abuse which has hardened into custom, and to establish on its ruins the true and the right."[2] Here was the spirit of Jonathan finding expression in the words of Charles. Here was a purifying, reforming mission for Wheaton—the tone is hardly less than that of radical activism. As he set down his thoughts in the *Record* of November 7, 1891, Charles's vision for the little college on the hill was large: "There is no place in the Mississippi valley where a blow struck for the honor of Christ and the good of men will tell more fully than here."[3]

To strike a blow from this cherished vantage point against the liquor traffic, Sabbath-breaking, and oath-bound secret societies, he never hesitated, even though it might cost him some friends and resources. "Wheaton might have been one of the largest denominational colleges," said James M. Gray, president of Moody Bible Institute, "had its president been willing to stifle his convictions on great public issues."[4] But Charles Blanchard had no wish to see Wheaton become a large institution. His ideal was a small, well-disciplined student body, and to that end he believed it essential to "scatter Christian schools over our land as flowers dot the fields or stars stud the sky."[5] He labored to fashion an institution that would honor God, educate dedicated young men and women, and in so doing contribute to the emergence of a just, humane, Christian society. "The many valued friends who are aiding us in carrying forward the work should rejoice,"[6] he wrote in 1896, "as those whom they aim to train shall contend against the evils of *their* age, and strive for the universal brotherhood which is to come in spite of all hindering causes."[7] Jonathan Blanchard had proclaimed that same social optimism and theological conviction for years.

The early College observatory, known to generations of students as the "Lemon," seen through Eastgate.

Williston Hall. First called Ladies' Hall, or Women's Residence, it was often known as the "Red Castle."

Wheaton's first gymnasium, acclaimed the finest in the area when it was built in 1899.

Schell Hall. Known as the Industrial Building when it was erected in 1898. Subsequently it became the Academy Building, the Graduate Building, and Buswell Hall.

Forward on Several Fronts

The last decade of the century witnessed a remarkable expansion of Wheaton's campus. Early in February 1890, the trustees authorized the additon of an east wing to the main building, in which would be located the "Cabinet, Laboratory, Library, Commercial instruction and two society halls." The cost was to be $12,000, of which $8,245 was quickly subscribed. By June the excavation had been completed, stone for the exterior walls began to arrive, and by October the walls were up and the interior was being finished. But there was still need for $3,000 to install a heating system.[8]

On October 1, the new "Alumni Observatory" was dedicated in a ceremony at which Judge O.N. Carter, an 1877 alumnus of Wheaton and judge of the Illinois Supreme Court, was the principal speaker. The observatory was purchased secondhand from L. F. Culver of Harvey, Illinois, for about $2,000 with funds supplied by alumni—half the original cost—and brought to Wheaton by two teams of horses. For transporting the observatory with its sixteen-foot dome and 800-pound telescope, as well as preparing the foundation and mounting the instrument, faculty and students raised approximately $1,000.[9] Known to generations of students as the "Lemon," because of its bright color and domed shape, the observatory housed a twelve-and-a-half inch Newtonian reflecting scope and a seven-inch refracting telescope, "together with celestial globes, charts and other items."[10] Once the object of great pride, the Lemon fell victim to the depredations of time and technological obsolescence. It succumbed finally in 1972, when it was purchased for $520 by the Honey Rock Camp Development Committee and was hauled to Wheaton's "northern campus" in Wisconsin.[11]

During the last decade of the century three new buildings were added to the campus: the Women's Building (also called the Ladies' Building) the Gymnasium, and the Industrial Building. Inspiration for the Women's Building came in 1894 from the offer of M. M. Brown, a Chicago realtor and one-time student of the College, to provide anonymously $30,000 for the construction of one or two buildings, as the trustees chose, if the College would raise a portion of the total cost. By trustee action the decision was made "to put $25,000 into a dormitory for women and $12,000 into another building to be planned later."[13] The College borrowed $6,000 to add to Brown's gift to complete the women's dormitory, Ladies' Hall, during the summer and early fall of 1895. The borrowed money was quickly underwritten by a number of friends of the College, including John Quincy Adams, a local citizen and descendant of the New England Adamses, David C. Cook, C. H. Chase, George B. Hopkins, and Mrs. A. F. Rider. Benefactor M. M. Brown was the contractor for the familiar Victorian Gothic edifice, with its rounded turrets, high peaks, and patterned brickwork, called by students in the beginning, and for many years after, "The Red Castle," but later named Williston Hall in memory of J. P. Williston, New England manufacturer, early donor, friend of Christian education, and counselor to Jonathan Blanchard.

For several years after the building was opened, the college catalog carried pictures of student rooms uniformly furnished with bureau, washstand, stuffed chair or sofa, bed, desk, rug, and window drapes—quite a contrast to the utilitarian plainness of modern college dormitory rooms. Singled out for special attention when the building first opened was its use of steam heat and electric lights, near luxury features, since Edison's light was first successfully demonstrated only in 1879, and the first electric street lights appeared in New York in 1882.

The dream of a gymnasium lingered over the years, though there were no concerted efforts to bring it to reality until the 1890s. Early in 1893 the Executive Committee of the College met at the Sherman House in Chicago and agreed, among other things, "to cooperate with the Excelsior and Beltionian Associations in case they should be willing to unite in an effort to erect a gymnasium and Society Hall. We have reason to hope that the plan will commend itself to the young gentlemen of the two associations and that in the near future a building, which will be a credit and a help to us all, will be erected."[14] Progress was clearly being made when President Blanchard and a small delegation of students went to Chicago in 1895 in quest of ideas for building a gymnasium. Their journey led them to make several specific suggestions: "The boards of the gym by all means," they said, "ought to be above ground, made of pine...the gym ought to be laid out by a gymnasium architect and have no pillars in the center of the room, the walls painted white, made by specialists."[15]

Finally, through the use of funds earlier contributed by M. M. Brown and through generous gifts from local citizens like John Quincy Adams and Judge Elbert Gary, the gymnasium was completed at a cost of $16,000, and dedicated on May 29, 1899. The three-story building contained the gymnasium proper, a running track, bowling alleys, and the two men's literary society halls. Many sports critics called the building "the best gym in this section of the country" and other observers heralded it as "the envy of many of the larger colleges west of the Alleghenies."[16] For the dedication of the gym the North Western Railway "contributed coaches to convey friends from Chicago and return after the exercises."[17] Special guests for the ceremonies were the Chicago Congregational Ministers Union, who were in charge of the program in the chapel.

The third addition to the campus during the 1890s was the Industrial Building (later the Academy Building), located at the corner of Franklin and Irving Streets, the gift of R. J. Bennett. It was intended to house such enterprises as the "printing office managed by E. W. Dresser, which had a payroll of over $200.00 a month and supported in part or in full fifteen students."[18] Housed in the Main Building, and providing a livelihood for two students at that time, were a barber shop and a bicycle shop, the latter offering repair services and new bicycles for sale. The student proprietor of the barbershop was W. W. White. The bicycle shop was managed by Oliver Stewart Decker, who took a full page in the 1897 Echoes to advertise his shop and himself as "The Hustler."

For the dedication of the Industrial Building, on October 24, 1898, students lined up in front of the Main Building and marched to the new site, where the Industrial Building "was handsomely decorated with flags and bunting." When the donor presented the deed to the College, "three cheers were heartily given for Mr. Bennett." President Blanchard responded by stating that Wheaton College stood "for the education of the whole man." It was committeed also to "a culture for all the people. Rich and poor alike are the work of God and all alike should have access to the means of education." Sentiments like those, added to the College's continually advertising itself as a "school for men and women," became the substance of a genuinely democratic philosophy of education, progressive for its time, and in the spirit of the egalitarian Midwest.

Wheaton College Echoes

Notable among student enterprises initiated in the 1890s was the first student annual. Named *Wheaton College Echoes*, it appeared for three successive editions: 1893, '94 and '95, when the name was shortened to *The Echo*. The last echo was heard in 1900, when the annual ceased publication.

College Echoes was printed on the college press, which had been publishing the *Record* for three years. Offered for sale at one dollar, the book was clothbound, measured 6 1/2" by 5", contained ten full-page photographs, and offered 100 pages of text, plus advertising. A tribute, in the 1893 issue, to Jonathan Blanchard, commenting on his death the year before, summarized his long career and praised his achievements. "At last after sixty years of courageous and successful warfare," the student writer concluded, "his wife and six of his children having preceded him to the better land, he fell asleep in Jesus, leaving to us the inspiration of his example."

Each book is a chronicle of the year's events, an enduring record of the pulse of the campus. In one volume there is the faculty picture, a circular photograph of each individual, with eight men ringed around the central figure, President Blanchard. Among the men, only W. H. Fischer was without beard or mustache. At the bottom of the page are the three women, with Mrs. Nutting in the center, her ribboned bonnet on her head. A biographical sketch was given for each, including birth date. A listing of the alumni, including home towns, and professions, revealed that by 1893 there were 200 graduates scattered from coast to coast. Of the male graduates forty percent had become ministers. As many as fifty percent of the graduates had come to Wheaton from farms, but the alumni catalog listed only five of the men as having returned to farm the land. Five physicians, twelve lawyers, and fourteen teachers are named. Only a few women are cited as having careers.

The senior class surveyed its history proudly and optimistically: "This is '93, the great year. It is just the time to launch out upon the Ocean of Life at flood-tide. This year marks the commencement of three most important and auspicious things, the World's Fair, the *College Echoes*, and 'The Class.' " "Most of the young ladies are skilled in domestic economy. A number of the

Aeliolian Literary Society, 1899. First row, l. to r.: *Cora Kimball, Mary Himes, Rachel Smith, Julia Blanchard, Stella Wakeman, Mary Phillips, Lottie Lonnon, Daisy Jones.* Second row: *Mrs. M. Fredenhagen, Ruth Ware, Mame Hall, May Carothers, Rachel Blanchard, Julia Cook, Ella Bowman, Cora Jean Bredenbeck, and Elizabeth Kellogg.* Third row: *Bessie Mullenix, Amelia Pierson, Winifred Smith, Ellen Kellogg, Jessie Wagner, Ellen Hall, Hannah Cook, Adeline Churchill.* Back row: *Florence Wheelcock, Ruth Himes, Laura Minnich, Ada Hednck, Frances Kellogg, Beulah Smith, Clara Blanchard.*

Beltionian Literary Society, 1900. First row, l. to r.: *B.B. Bingham, J.G. Marshall, E.W. Frye.* Second row: *R.J. Snell, J.E. Phillips, H.L. Kellogg, C.W. Dumper, G.T. Lloyd, H.K. Boyer, P.B. Phillips, S.H. Paine.* Third row: *W.W. Swink, H.H. Ferry, C.A. Ocock, H.S. Driesslein, C.M. Kremer, L.B. King, M. Wetzel, E.M. Leech, C.E. Ferry, and L.A. Royal.* Back row: *E. Parsons, C.W. Merritt, H.M. Callecod, J.H. Welsh, F.L. Fischer, W.B. Delancy, H.A. Fischer, A.C. Larsen, J.H. Snell.*

gentlemen are leaders in athletic sports, and several have taken prizes on Field Day." Half the class had expressed the desire to become missionaries or ministers; all the members of the class were Christian.

College Echoes, in summarizing student "religious work," reminded readers of their heritage as students of Wheaton College and of "the hallowed hour when the pioneers of the college knelt in the prairie grass and consecrated this spot to *Christian* education. The most reckless who came among us," the student writer continued, "perceive that this is none other than the house of God, and not a few find it the gate of heaven to their souls."[19] "Wheaton College may not be equal to some of her sister colleges in equipment, but she is second to none in spiritual influence."[20] Campus Christian activities included the Mission Band, a national student organization reaching out to most colleges and universities, the Y.M.C.A., Epworth League, Christian Endeavor, Noon Day Prayer Meeting, Students' Missionary Society, and Tuesday Evening Prayer Meeting. Prominent among those organizations was the Mission Band, formed in 1890 by a group of nine students and numbering thirty-five by 1893. Together, these activities did much to create a climate of opinion, an environment of commitment that was shaping the direction of the College and the lives of its students.

One of the memorable events described in the *College Echoes '95* was a debate between the Prohibition and Republican Clubs, held in the fall term of 1894, on the question: "Resolved, that the success of the Republican party in the recent election was necessary to the welfare of the country." Reported by Belle Blanchard, daughter of the president, the story tells how the evening began with "the Prohibition quartet" rendering "a parody on 'The Prohibition Ark' " and putting the people "in the best of humor to begin with." Mr. Stone, Miss Sleeper, and Mr. Anderson supported the affirmative side of the question, and Mr. Smith, Miss Pickney, and Mr. Peterson spoke on the negative. "Wit, wisdom, keen sarcasm, and weighty argument characterized the speeches. The ladies were not outdone by the gentlemen." While Florence Hoes entertained at the piano, the audience waited eagerly for the judges' decision; and then "the fateful papers were at last given and the decision rendered, two in favor of the negative and one for the affirmative."[20]

That the debate was held and that student response to it was enthusiastic suggests the degree of interest in politics in the 1890s. The 1895 *College Echoes* devotes six pages to three political clubs on campus, listing their officers, describing their activities, and projecting their goals. The Prohibition Club—often referred to as the Prohibs—appears to have been the most prestigious group, with a membership of thirty-five. Citing the particular interests of the club, student writer C. Petersen said: "The school has always been identified with reform. It is entirely fitting, then, that its students should be also. The prohibition of the liquor traffic, we consider the most pressing question of the day."[21] The Republican Club numbered thirty, and the Democratic Club struggled along valiantly with a membership of three—S. G. Barton, Addie May Green, H. G. Andrews—just enough to fill the essential organizational offices. *The Echo 1900* was the last in the series of eight volumes. The well-intentioned venture, which began with promise but declined markedly in quality, perished for lack of student interest in supplying copy and lack of funds. Not for twenty-two years was there to be another effort to launch a student annual.

Keeping the College Solvent

A frugal, conservative fiscal policy has always marked the management of Wheaton College funds. From the beginning of its history the Board of Trustees, college administration, and faculty have believed that Wheaton was brought into being and continues to be sustained by the providence of God, and that all resources received and used are a trust from him.

By the end of the century the annual financial report showed steady growth. Total resources were $208,937, including forty acres of land in Wisconsin valued at $120 and lots at Lake Minnetonka, Minnesota, worth $400. The large disbursement item was faculty salaries: $6,694, which was seventy-two percent of the expected wage. In 1900, salaries for the entire faculty were less than the salary of one teacher at the instructor's level today. There were three endowed chairs among a faculty of ten. For every need of the College there was continuing prayer among faculty members, students, alumni, and an increasing number of friends who believed in Wheaton's philosophy of Christian higher education.

Steady growth in assets was shown in the treasurer's report of 1905, establishing the institution's net worth at $266,678. Lawson Athletic Field, a full city block, situated in the center of a good residential area, was valued at $1,000. By 1918, Treasurer H. A. Fischer reported the net worth of Wheaton College as $528,638, with the worth of Blanchard Hall established at $120,000. The major holdings of the institution were in non-campus real estate, at a value of $203,954. In May 1925, the last full year of President Blanchard's leadership, Blanchard Hall was still valued at $120,000, but the worth of Lawson Field had risen to $3,000.

President Blanchard regularly used the pages of the *Wheaton College Record*, by 1898 a sixteen-page journal, to remind whoever might read it of their opportunities for stewardship. Appeals for assistance like this one were common: "The person who gives to the Christian College is sending into the world the ministers, missionaries, editors, statesmen, lawyers, and physicians who are to be most influential in determining the course of society. Five thousand dollars given to Wheaton College each four years send out six well-equipped men to do good in all walks of life. One who lives twenty years after making such a gift would have thirty men representing him."[22] At the end of the 1897-98 term the president could report that "a friend has promised so large a part of the cost of the gymnasium that we hope it may be erected this season"[23]—a hope that was realized.

By July 1898, readers of the *Record* learned of the trustees' decision to raise $100,000 for endowment, to be added to the then existing endowment fund of $50,000, enabling the College to "pay our instructors better than has been possible in these years when buildings have absorbed so largely the gifts of friends and the thoughts of laborers."[24] President Blanchard found it necessary to defend the use of an endowment for funding a college; for there were those who thought it encouraged indolence among instructors, and separated the institution from the people whose regular support was the means of survival. Rejecting those unsound fiscal notions, Blanchard pointed out that "a great school is a business enterprise" and no merchant wishes to carry on his business "depending upon today's income for today's outgo." He declared that a principal advantage of a "reasonable income, reasonably secure, is that teachers can be better housed, fed, and set to work when free from anxiety respecting their daily bread."[25] Some ascetics and martyrs had been great teachers, but the burden of "reason and Scripture is that the laborer is worthy of his hire." Blanchard, a faithful shepherd, was aggressively caring for his flock.

To build the endowment and to meet current financial needs, Charles Blanchard became an indefatigable traveler. With great frequency he rode trains to the East, where the sources of wealth were still centered and where evangelical Christianity had its strongest anchorage. He never lost his conviction that he was God's agent, doing God's will. Setting out from Wheaton on those journeys he always carried in an inner pocket a small, thin, black leather notebook commonly headed on its first page, in his meticulous and graceful handwriting, "Friends to be met in the East." One of those notebooks, undated, bears on the inside front cover these inscriptions: "My God shall supply all of your need according to His riches in glory by Christ Jesus.—Phil. 4:19." Charles A. Blanchard, Wheaton College, Wheaton, Ill. "Ask, and it shall be given you; seek, and ye shall find; knock, and it shall be opened unto you, Matt. 7:7."[26] As a young man Charles Blanchard had been hesitant in asking for funds for Christian causes; in later years he developed forthrightness in speakng of the needs of Wheaton College to old friends and new ones, made confident in no small measure by the assurances of his notebook verses.

From the listings in one little black book, the reader can almost follow the train—across the prairie and into the Alleghenies, with the first stop in Pittsburgh. Then on to Philadelphia and Germantown, New York City, Brooklyn, Jersey City, Boston, Newburyport, and clustered around Boston: Marblehead, Weymouth Heights, Brookline, Walpole, Dalton. On the way home to the Midwest President Blanchard may have called on the listings from Springfield (Massachusetts), Syracuse, Toledo, and Cleveland. Five residents of Toronto are also noted.

Among the Chicago names listed for attention in December 1888 are those of Philip S. Armour, John B. Drake, J. B. Blackstone, Jesse Spalding, Henry Field, Andrew MacLeish, W. H. Wanamaker. The name of George M. Pullman, maker of the Pullman car, appears three times, first with the notation, "call in one or two weeks," second with simply, "not at home," and finally, "Can't now. Perhaps in the Spring." On one of the early pages is the name of J. Pierpont Morgan, of Drexel and Morgan, Wall Street, but there is no indication of whether the suppliant from the Midwest ever saw the great financier. The little book does not record gifts or promises of aid; but there are brief notations like these: "Will think it over," "Won't say yes or no," "not now," "come again in two weeks," "not in," "see me about April 1." "Did not see him." Richard T. Crane's response was summed up: "Don't believe in colleges." William E. Hale declared, "give too much now;" H. B. Botsford declared bluntly, "We are a corporation. We have no souls."

Two other notebooks, undated, survive. One of them, under "Pittsburgh," lists the name of H. J. Heinz; the second one notes "H. J. Heinz, Deceased $100." Since Heinz died in 1919, the book probably represents a calling journey in about 1920. In Philadelphia the prospects included J. Howard Pew, president of the Sun Oil Company and William L. Austin, president of the board of directors of the Baldwin Locomotive Works (then the world's largest manufacturers of locomotives).

The charting of those odysseys, with their countless train trips, street car rides, lengthy walks through city neighborhoods, the climbing of steps to city offices, and patient waiting to see prospects, give some measure of President Blanchard's dedication to an ideal. The gifts he received both large and small—many of them made sacrificially by people who believed deeply in the Wheaton College vision of Christian education—gathered through the president's unwearying efforts, together with very modest student fees, were the foundation of the school's financial structure.

Tuition rates at Wheaton have always been modest, except in recent years, when spiraling costs have forced the institution to establish its fees at about the level of those of other small liberal arts colleges. In 1900 tuition was $8 a term in a three-term year. By 1905 the cost was $15, with half of the fee remitted for students who were children of ministers and missionaries. For 1910 the fee was $25 a semester; $40 in 1916 and $55 in 1925. Board was $108 a year in 1900, with a comprehensive room and board fee for women living in Ladies' Hall of $200 to $230. By 1920 board was $85 a semester and "electric lighted, steam heated rooms cost, for each occupant, from $15 to $34 per semester."

Scholarship grants have long been one of the means by which concerned donors have helped both the College and needy students. Early scholarship grants covering room and tuition were announced by the Board of Trustees in 1903, three given by Lucy M. Higgins, two by Mrs. E. B. Washburn, one by Timothy Hudson. Annual listing of these scholarship awards in the catalog shows how they increased steadily in number from six in 1903 to thirty-seven in 1925. The 1924 catalog notes that "the estate of La Verne Noyes provides ten scholarships to cover the tuition of students who served in the army and navy of the United States in the Great War or those who are descended from some one who has rendered such service. This is to be done without regard to differences of sex, race, religion or political party."

By 1919 thirty percent of the student body were "earning their living expenses" in whole or in part. "Under Opportunities for Self Help" there is in the 1925 *Bulletin* this encouraging word for the needy: "While we cannot promise opportunity for earning support to all who may desire it, there are means for helping a number in defraying or reducing their expenses. The janitor service of all college buildings is done by students. The churches, offices and residences about town furnish many with steady employment. A number of students can earn their living in homes, and some meet the expense of their table board by service at the Women's Building and at various boarding houses and restaurants. Besides, there is always more or less work of a promiscuous [that is, miscellaneous] nature to be had by efficient and energetic students."[28]

Athletics in President Charles Blanchard's Time

The first college athletic event, approved and supervised by faculty members, appears to have been an interclass track and field meet held in the spring of 1891. In the fall of that year, according to *Wheaton College Echoes '93*, a group of "from twelve to sixteen energetic and courageous youths" met to "discuss the advisability of bringing athletics into a more prominent position," persuaded as they were "that the greatest mental growth goes arm in arm with the best physical culture." The students organized an athletic association to finance a sports program, collecting dues and charging small fees to watch the games. With modest funds at their disposal, they "hired part-time coaches usually from off campus."[29]

Commenting in the *Record* on the second annual field day, June 11, 1892, President Blanchard wrote: "While we are not ambitious that our students should excel in athletics, certainly not so ambitious as to desire that they should spend time and strength in that line which belong to the more serious work of life, we believe in athletic exercises properly regulated and controlled, and are glad when our young men are able to do well without permitting other interests to suffer."[30] He reminded them that serious academic business was the essential concern of Wheaton College. "Good students only are wanted. Persons who wish to spend their time in sports or social recreations are advised to remain at home until they wish to study or go elsewhere. Our teachers wish to spend their entire strength on young people who value education and wish to obtain one."[31]

President Blanchard was not alone in his endeavor to maintain the delicate balance between a limited and guarded endorsement of athletics and an honest apprehension that sports were a waste of precious time that might be given to worthier pursuits. A former president of Princeton University, one Dr. McCosh, is quoted in the Feburary 18, 1893, *Record* as acknowledging the benefits "that could be secured from manly exercises when kept within bounds," nevertheless believing that they had at that time exceeded reason-

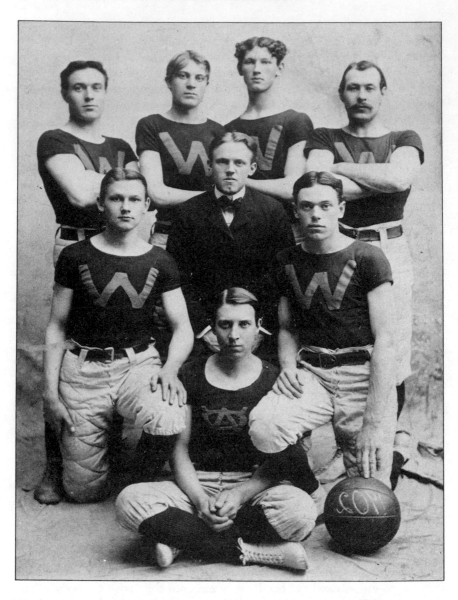

Basketball team, 1901–02. Front: *Herbert Hoisington.* Second row: *Howard Pinkney, J.L. Johnson, Alvin Schmidt.* Back row: *John Mainland, Del Lanon, Homer Hoisington.*

able bounds and "the enthusiasm of the student is in sports and athletic games and not in his studies."[32] Many college administrators had reservations, particularly about football, which they regarded as rough and dangerous, even though it had Ivy League auspices in a game between Princeton and Rutgers in 1869.

Despite President Blanchard's reservations about football, the game was tolerated in the beginning on a somewhat informal basis. The 1898 *Echo* indicates that there were occasional inter-literary society contests played on campus, as the section on athletics, written by Mary Belle Blanchard, suggests. "But football is not played? Oh no! Ask the one whose vest was left upon the field of conflict for the birds of prey to feed upon, if there was any such thing going on!... However, the sum of these answers would probably not convey the whole truth unless the question was asked of the one who had lain for ten whole minutes at the bottom of a mass of living humanity. Do they play football at W.C.? His answer would suffice."[33] As time passed, however, the risks in football were reduced through rule changes and the introduction of improved equipment. Dr. Blanchard recognized the changes in the game and, like others, was prepared to modify his earlier reservations.

Among all the collegiate sports "basketball has the longest consecutive record of Wheaton intercollegiate teams, with cage competition every year since 1901." That was only nine years after the game was invented by Dr. James Naismith in Springfield, Massachusetts.[34] Although there are references in the 1899 *Wheaton College Echo* to informal basketball games between the women's lits and an exhibition game by the men, the real beginning seems to have come in the fall of 1900. "The young men of the gymnasium class have selected from their class a basketball team,"[35] the *Record* briefly reported. The new sport was made possible by the completion of the College's first gymnasium in 1898, the third campus building. It was splendid for its time, the best in the area, but a cracker box compared with modern gyms. With a single ball for practice and games, baskets that were often makeshift, amateur officials, and two-handed shooting from the chest, basketball in those early years lacked much of the swish and polish of the modern game.

C. S. Byrne, imported from the Central YMCA Training School of Chicago, became Wheaton's first basketball coach. Byrne's new team was promptly defeated, 39-5, in its first competition game by his old charges, the experienced Central YMCA team. The humiliating defeat was owing, the *Record* editor said, "not so much to lack of team work as to defective basket throwing." Members of that first team deserve a lasting place in Wheaton athletic history: John Mainland, Del Lanon, Homer Hoisington, Howard Pinkney, Alvin Schmidt, Herbert Hoisington, and J. L. Johnson, Manager.

Later in the season the team defeated DeKalb Normal, 43-14, avenging a loss by the ladies to the same institution. Said a student reporter, quaintly, of this pair of contests: "The Ladies of the Normal, who had acquited themselves so well, were forced to stand by and see the young manhood of DeKalb chased over the floor in all directions, the ball flying, ever and anon, with fateful accuracy, to the Wheaton basket." Unwilling to accept a second defeat by DeKalb, however, the Wheaton women exerted themselves to the utmost and ran off—or walked off—with the contest on March 9, 1901, by a score of 8-4. "The Wheaton students were jubilant over the victory . . . the visitors, by their gentlemanly and ladylike actions, have merited the high esteem of the Wheaton people."[36]

The fall of 1900 marked the real beginning of football at Wheaton, with the Crusader team meeting the North Western Railway team, Batavia, and Geneva. The first intercollegiate contest for the Wheaton team was scheduled with North-Western College of Naperville, to be played November 24 on the new Lawson Field, named for Victor Lawson, publisher of the *Chicago Record*, who had given generously for the purchase of the land.[37] Enthusiasm was high among the students, and the game was eagerly awaited; but about noon heavy rain began to fall, and the game was moved to the college campus, thus depriving a number of visitors of the opportunity to see the new field. Outclassed, ill-equipped, and without a coach, the Wheaton team suffered a humiliating 31-0 defeat. It must be remembered, however, that there were only thirty-six men in the college department at that time.

Tennis was introduced at Wheaton when in 1890 Al Hiatt, Lucius Hiatt, and Frank Hawley built a court on the side of campus where the gymnasium was later to rise. By 1900 there were a half dozen courts and three tennis clubs. By faculty authorization five tennis courts were built on the northwest corner of the campus and continued in use until 1925, when Pierce Chapel was erected on the site. In 1920 Raymond Fischer and Ernest Shaw won the conference doubles championship at Peoria and the same year Wheaton defeated North-Western College twice.[38] The year 1925 saw an almost undefeated season with a single loss to Lawrence College.

CHAPTER 5

New Century:
A Time for War,
A Time for Peace

THE TWENTIETH CENTURY DAWNED ON A PROSPEROUS AND optimistic America. The *New York Times* declared editorially in its January 1, 1900, issue that the country was enjoying an "era of good feeling"; on the same day the *Chicago Tribune* noted "that men of commerce expect another year of prosperity." Both the *Times* and the *Tribune* gave extensive coverage to the Boer War in South Africa, where the British were suffering reverses, but the *Times* reminded its readers that the British Empire was not on the threshold of dissolution. The *Tribune*, then selling for two cents a copy, reported in the news of the day that John Alexander Dowie, a popular religious leader, had announced to his cheering followers that the "Holy City of Zion," now Zion, Illinois, would rise on the shores of Lake Michigan.

The 1900 Wheaton College catalog, a plain document for a momentous year ushering in a new century, was without illustrations (the 1899 edition had photographs of all the buildings, interiors of the library, dining room, a typical "society hall," and floor plans of the buildings). The faculty had grown to twenty-two. President Blanchard, having been granted an honorary degree by Monmouth College in 1896, could now add D.D. to his name. Long-familiar names appeared in the faculty roster of 1900 with the president continuing as J. P. Williston Professor of Psychology and Ethics. Ten faculty members had earned their Master's degrees, but no one held the Ph.D. Faculty organization was relatively simple compared with the modern maze of committees and long-range studies. The College functioned in 1900 with four committees, the nature of which makes clear that the administration had little disposition to share academic responsibilities with the faculty. The standing committees were: On College Campus and On Gentleman's Hall, Professor Smith; On Gymnasium, Professor Mullenix; On Rehearsals, Professor Straw; On Athletics, the President, Professors Smith and Mullenix.

At the January 1900 meeting of the trustees a faculty salary schedule and retirement program was agreed on, under which all faculty were to be classified as either A or B for purposes of salary determination. Designated as the A group were teachers "who own homes in Wheaton and maintain families." Others were classified B. If a B teacher purchased a home and maintained a family, he passed automatically into the A category. An instructor with A standing began at $600 a year, with annual increases of $100 until the level of $1,000 had been reached. Thereafter he was to receive $100 increases until the maximum of $1,400 had been achieved, without deductions of any kind. Those teachers who were given a B classification began at $400 a year and advanced at $50 a year to $700. A $100 raise every five years could bring the B faculty member to a maximum of $1,000. Obviously such an arrangement nearly always put women at a disadvantage.

When a professor reached age sixty-five, he could elect—provided he had had twenty years of acceptable service—to take a half load at half salary. If he had served acceptably for twenty-five years, he could elect to retire on one quarter salary. At age seventy, with twenty years' service, he was required to take a half load and half salary; with twenty-five years of service he could retire on one-quarter salary. Mandatory retirement age was seventy-five. Modern professors can be forgiven for wondering how their predecessors at Wheaton survived three-quarters of a century ago on such meager rewards for their efforts. The answer in part is that they kept gardens, cows, chickens, and preached for pay on Sundays. Appended to the new faculty schedule were the salaries of some faculty members in 1900: Blanchard, $1,800; Fischer, $1,400; Whipple, $1,200; Smith, $1,100; Mullenix, $1,100; Dow, $800; Cook, $700. When President Blanchard was asked to make a statement "in regard to the condition of the college" at a November 15, 1901, meeting of the trustees, he said, according to the secretary's summary, "that financially the college had been in better condition than at any time during his administration, and that for the first time in that period teachers had been paid in full."

The Washington Banquet

The second Washington banquet was held on February 22, 1910, in the college gymnasium. The first of these annual events took place on February 12, 1909, to mark the centennial celebration of Abraham Lincoln's birth; thereafter the banquet was always scheduled on or near Washington's birthday. In the beginning the emphasis was not on couples but on class activity, with seniors given the place of honor, and with the competitive freshmen and sophomores seated as far apart as possible. Students were permitted to sit with their dates if they were of the same class. Class rivalry was intense, both before and during the banquet, class speakers often being kidnapped before the evening began and taken out to the country for a lonely walk back. Bruce Hunt, '24, recalled such an experience: "I was cheer-leader for our class at the Washington Banquet, but some of the class above us kidnapped me and drove me into the country and dumped me in a roadside ditch. I used my cross-country experiences to get to the banquet just after the fruit cocktail had been served. My date, Alice Winsor, had to go by herself. Our class cheering was unusually boisterous that night."[2] Throughout the evening in the beautifully decorated hall "songs, yells, roasts, lemons, and bouquets were in order from any class at any time."[3] Year after year this event generated an intense enthusiasm that often got a little out of hand.

Not until the twenties, when the newly formed Student Council became responsible for the event and the evening was a couples' occasion, did a more tranquil atmosphere prevail. In 1923 for the first time seniors wore their caps and gowns and marched around the gym singing the *Alma Mater*, which gave rise to the tradition of seniors wearing their academic attire to each Friday chapel after the Washington Banquet until the end of the term. When the evening became a dating affair rather than a class-centered event, formal attire was expected, corsages were in order, the toastmaster was chosen from the senior class, and the highlight of the evening was the address by the president of the College. George and Martha Washington, usually a faculty couple, appeared in appropriate colonial attire, their identity kept secret until their arrival. For many years the Washington banquet was regarded as the one occasion when the whole College—faculty, students, staff—joined together in a social occasion. Precedent was broken, however, in 1938, when the banquet was held off campus at the Stevens Hotel in Chicago, marking the initiation of a financial campaign.

Through its general information section of the catalog, the College continually stated and refined its conception of Christian education at Wheaton. In 1910 it declared "that the great end of education should be to develop such genuine manhood and womanhood that all the powers of the individual will be devoted to the highest and best purposes. It seems to them an unspeakable misfortune when large intellectual gifts are devoted to trifling or ignoble ends. They find that in all spheres of human activity the essential thing is sterling character. They have, therefore, from the beginning, sought for the student earnest Christian faith and straightforward Christian life."[4]

The World War I Era

When World War I began with Austria-Hungary's declaration of war on Serbia on July 28, 1914, no one could have foreseen that the conflict would ultimately engulf nearly all the Western world, nor could anyone have anticipated the enormous cost in life and treasure. Political, cultural, and economic convulsions during and after the war would alter life in the West forever. In America prior to its entry into the conflict, however, life was prosperous, and, for a time, the people generally felt secure in the great expanse of the Atlantic Ocean and the promises of their leaders that America would not become involved.

Wheaton College shared modestly in the general prosperity of the prewar years. President Blanchard traveled widely in the interest of the College and of agencies with which he was associated: anti-secret society work, temperance, Sabbath-keeping, and the defense of orthodoxy against the inroads of modernism. Persuaded of the rightness of those causes, the student body, kept informed of their president's itineraries by the *Record*, prayed regularly for him as he left the campus for protracted absences. On one of his journeys he preached sixteen sermons, presided at five services in Philadelphia, delivered six addresses in Cleveland, two in New York, two in Boston, five in Springfield, and others along the way.[5] In 1915 he published his best-known book, *Getting Things from God: A Study of the Prayer Life;* in 1917 *Visions and Voices: or Who Wrote the Bible* appeared. Blanchard's varied activities won new friends for the College among evangelicals in many denominations and many others who supported the aims of Wheaton. The enlarging constituency represented a broad spectrum of business and professional people of wide geographical distribution (still with significant concentrations in the East), friends with substantial resources and friends who had little to offer except their prayers. In his autobiography, published in 1915, President Blanchard estimated that all gifts to the College up to that time had amounted to about $150,000 for buildings, $150,000 for endowment, and $100,000 for current expenses, including a contribution of $25,000 from Andrew Carnegie in 1911, all of which he saw as evidence of divine favor upon the institution to which he was giving unstintingly of his energies.[6]

Other significant advances in the history of Wheaton were achieved in the pre-war years. Notable among them was membership, in 1913, in the North Central Association of Colleges and Schools—although the approval was somewhat tentative, dependent on separating the Academy from the College and substantially increasing the endowment. During the following year the College and the Academy, then established in the Industrial Building, were separated in order to meet the North Central Association's requirement that students from the two institutions should not be enrolled in the same classes. No longer would sedate young ladies with long skirts and long hair walk the same pathways with little boys in short pants. But some of the Academy boys continued to be housed with the college men on the fourth floor of the Main Building. Until 1921 they were also permitted to play on college teams.

Inauguration of the Summer Session in 1916, with an initial enrollment of twenty-seven, permitted regular students to accelerate their program of education and students from area colleges to sense something of the spirit and quality of Wheaton College. Standards of admission and the quality of the work performed during the summer were for a number of years less demanding than those that prevailed during the regular academic term. After ten years the summer enrollment had grown to 173; after twenty years it had reached 419. Prodding from the North Central Association in the late thirties resulted in a considerable academic tightening of the program.

Another evidence of academic adjustment was the establishment of departments of study in 1917. The compartmentalization of learning had begun in the universities by the end of the nineteenth century. Such a division of subject matter was a recognition of the growing specialization, and the resultant diversity of knowledge. The old-time professor who could range through three or four subjects in different fields well enough to teach undergraduates had to narrow his interests. The ancient unity of knowledge was being fragmented, forced largely by the escalating search for scientific truth.

How to fit every course into a suitable department and how to name the departments was sometimes puzzling. Philosophy and Bible became Bible and philosophy, heading the alphabetical listing of the new departments. Since history professor E. W. Smith had died, his department, headed by Darien Straw, was called social sciences, and included logic and rhetoric, Straw's specialities, an odd arrangement that continued until 1925. Although the department was designated as social sciences, logic and rhetoric headed the list of offerings. Biology, previously listed under physical sciences, became a department of its own. Astronomy, physics, and mathematics were grouped together and might have led the listing of departments, except that Professor Hawley Taylor decided that mathematics, as the most important of the three, in his judgment, should be named first.

As departmentalization was developing in the universities, a new hierarchy of professors was emerging, a trend that was also a consequence of the proliferation of knowledge. Where one professor was once adequate to cover his field, several became necessary as knowledge accumulated; some order of authority among them seemed essential. Establishment of professorial ranks set off a competitive drive new to the academic community.

Many of the practices that had their origin in the universities filtered down, in time, to the smaller colleges. For more than a half century the regular teachers in the college division at Wheaton were designated in the catalog as "Professor." Not until the early twenties was the range of ranks used: professor, associate professor, assistant professor, instructor.

Wheaton's Response to the War

When war broke out in August 1914, many students found themselves confused about the complex issues that led to the outbreak of hostilities. Consequently, for the November 15, 1914, *Record*, President Blanchard wrote an editorial titled "Causes of the Great War," in which he declared that the enormous struggle then developing was a divine judgment for "grievous national transgressions." Belgium, which suffered frightful ravishment in the early stages of the war, had been guilty of gross cruelty in its exploitation of the Congo; Britain had forced the opium war on China; Germany in its devotion to higher criticism had compromised the Word of God; France had defied God's law in its ceaseless quest for pleasure. "Men must turn back to God," he concluded, "or they will be destroyed." "Proximate causes undoubtedly there are, but here is the actual reason for the horrors of this present time."[7] H. J. Ludgate, editor of the college paper, reflected student thinking about the conflict: "Mere words cannot paint the picture. It is too sad, too terrible, too devilish."[8] Writing again in the *Record* in March 1916 at student request, Charles Blanchard warned against the powerful munitions lobby, urging America to prepare for any eventuality.[9]

In spite of its desire to avoid engagement, America declared war on Germany on April 6, 1917, after unrestricted submarine attacks on the country's merchant shipping seemed to make any other course untenable. "The world must be made safe for democracy," said President Wilson to the Congress. Following the declaration of war, President Blanchard went to Fort Sheridan and then to Washington to secure for Wheaton College a unit of the Student Army Training Corps, thus indicating clearly that he was not a war resister. The S.A.T.C. established its barracks in the gymnasium in September 1918, and soon sixty students in uniform were parading the campus under an army lieutenant.

From the beginning the *Record* kept the student body familiar with the names of students who were entering army camps or being sent overseas, and frequently published excerpts from letters describing these former students' experiences in the services. Paul A. Thompson, on October 1, 1917, wrote one of them from Camp Grant, Rockford, Illinois: "We love to think of ourselves as students of Wheaton College because of that for which it stands. We, of course, are disappointed in not being able to continue our school work but this feeling is overcome by the importance of the task to which we have been called."[10] Under the heading "Our Boys in Camp and Field" appeared the "Student Soldier List." Among the men named were Larmon Smith, later editor and owner of the *Wheaton Daily Journal*; C. Wayland Brooks, son of a trustee, winner of the American Distinguished Service Cross and the French Cross of War, later a United States Senator from Illinois; Charles Farnham, son of Professor Henry Farnham; George Berrell, who served in the Canadian Army; and Arthur Twigg, John Conley, Harry Cork, Donald Ferris, Samuel Kellogg, and Clare Loveless. A listing of Wheaton men who served in World War I appeared in the September 1918 *Record*, where ninety-two assigned to various branches of the military are named; three were in the Canadian Army. Two Wheaton men gave their lives in the struggle: Russell R. Brooks, September 30, 1918, and Willis H. Cork, October 1, 1918. In memory of Willis Cork, Frank Herrick, whose verses often appeared in the *Record*, wrote a tribute which concluded:

Farewell, hero-heart that beat
Sweet music strong and brave,
Thine is the sacrifice complete
That Freedom's flag may wave![11]

Herrick, who was a city magistrate and a familiar figure on the streets of Wheaton for many years after his graduation in 1899, was known as "Judge" Herrick and was designated the city's poet laureate.

Record editor Effie Jane Wheeler, later a popular member of the English department, reflected the campus attitude toward the war: "It is with admiration and respect that we think of the 'old Wheaton boys' who have answered the country's call. America has answered the call nobly, and among America's colleges Wheaton ranks high for its unselfish offering."[12] Students were reminded that they could serve their country by going to war, farming, entering Red Cross service, economizing, and going to college; but if they were not called to active service, the best thing they could do was to stay in college. To further the war effort, local Wheaton homes were opened for girls to roll bandages for the Red Cross and to knit khaki-colored socks, gloves, and scarves for the soldiers in France. Everywhere there were knitters, boys and girls in the public schools, Wheaton students in chapel, in classes, and sometimes in church—though the last was frowned on.

Though the war was of intense concern to faculty and students, life on campus continued in most of its familiar patterns. The basketball team played out its schedule, the literary societies met and debated issues of war and patriotism, the usual quota of student pranks continued. Special events frequently engrossed campus attention, such as the "Billy Sunday Excursion" described in a 1918 issue of the *Record*: "Friday, March 29, was the occasion of much excitement at Wheaton when a large delegation of the college students and townspeople met at the North Western station, eager to be on their way to hear Billy Sunday. If the armbands and floating pennants failed to show that Wheaton College was aboard, the yells and songs did their duty in that line."[13]

A 1917 map of the College area shows the campus ringed by arborvitae, once thought to add charm and beauty to the location; it was in time removed, however, having provided too many convenient nooks for lovers. At the last wartime commencement, in May 1918, a class of twelve was graduated, nine women and three men, several other men of the class having been called to service. During the ceremonies Professor Darien Straw was granted an honorary LL.D. degree, "in recognition of his long period of successful service as teacher and his recognized activities in the field of Sociology and Political Science, besides other work in Philosophy and Education."[14]

Very early in the morning on November 11, the community and campus were aroused by continuous blasts from the town's fire siren proclaiming the joyous news that an armistice had been reached in the Great War. The guns were stilled on the western front. In the dormitories the word spread quickly, and alarms and bells of all kinds were set off. The tower bell clanged incessantly. Classes met until chapel time, for which a special program was quickly arranged. Judge Slusser, an alumnus, delivered the principal speech, followed by short patriotic talks by representatives of each class. Mrs. Stough sang "American for Me" and Mr. Morgan sang "A Perfect Day." The *Record* noted that "after the program everyone formed a parade, the Student Army Training Corps leading, followed by the faculty, seniors, and the other classes in order, with many flags in evidence. The parade marched downtown and returned, having exhibited joy and happiness in the greatest news of the world war."[15]

In September 1919, the largest class yet to enter the College made its appearance with seventy-six members, of whom fifty-two would form the largest graduating class, in 1923.[16] Among the entering class of 1919 was a young man named Enock Dyrness, who had been brought by his father from Chicago to enter the Academy in 1916[17] and who as student, teacher, and long-time registrar was to serve the College with distinction until his retirement in 1969—a fifty-three-year association with Wheaton. Tireless in his efforts, committed to high standards of quality, he played a large role in the academic development of the College.

Wheaton College Record

The October 15, 1900, *Record* announced in modest terms a significant change of policy. "As many who read these pages know," it said, "there was started among the students last June a movement which resulted in the transfer of the *College Record* from the faculty to the student body."[18] Many students had felt the need for a student news periodical, a need that the old *Record* did not meet. From 1890 until the appearance of this issue President Blanchard had served as editor; now the students had a paper of their own. After thanking the faculty for their show of confidence in turning the *Record* over to student management, the editor continued: "The paper is yours, alumni and students, and on you depends its success. Will you help us give to Wheaton College a paper of which it may be proud? With your help we shall succeed."[19]

Student editors for this initial edition of the ten-page paper, then selling for five cents a copy or seventy-five cents a year, were John S. Congdon, Editor-in-Chief; Marie Sephrene Burnham, Assistant Editor; and Fred L. Fischer, Business Manager. In a brief news item in the first issue of the paper, note was taken of the opening exercise in the chapel of the fall term, at which the Honorable O. N. Carter, an alumnus, and Mayor Grote of Wheaton spoke. The student editor commented: "It has been said that Wheaton, like "omnia Gallia" is divided into three parts—the college, the town, and the Golf Club. This gathering which was largely due to the happy inspiration of Rev. E. S. Carr, served to more firmly unite the first two of these parts." Since it operated on Sundays, the Chicago Golf Club, the first of its kind in America, located on the south edge of the town of Wheaton, was a source of distress to the college administration.

Gone from the new *Record* were the regular page of news of College Church, the President's frequent editorials on political and economic affairs (informative as they were), lectures by faculty members, and frequent appeals for operating funds. To encourage student literary effort the *Record* began to publish poetry, essays, and fiction. Student imagination expressed itself in such striking ways as the St. Valentine's Day issue of February 15, 1901, each page stamped with a red heart in the center, pierced with a Cupid's arrow.

Short story and poetry contests were frequently announced, with the winning entries being published in the spring issue of the *Record*. The June 1, 1904, issue of the paper was edited entirely by the women. "We have not attempted to do anything new or startling, but merely lighten the labors of the regular staff." The Wheaton-De Kalb baseball game was faithfully described by one reporter: "The game as a whole showed that our boys can play ball if they will tend to business, but delayed somewhat by disputes with the umpire, who couldn't see all the game without looking twice... The work of the Wheaton team in holding De Kalb on the bases is to be commended and, but for their good there and a couple of timely throws to the plate, the score would in all probability have had the majority on the other side."[20]

Fifty Years Old

The College's fiftieth anniversary, its jubilee year in 1910, was noted in the March issue of the *Record*, for which President Blanchard prepared a short history of Wheaton. He described the institution's relationship to the anti-slavery and anti-lodge movement, its material progress, its intellectual status, and made clear that "the religious life of the college has been from the beginning one of its principal interests. Men and women are not invited to its teaching staff who are not avowed Christians." One of the reasons for the "religious prosperity" of the College was that fraternities, "the centers of general demoralization," had never been countenanced. "The college does not favor dancing parties, card parties, theater parties. It favors lectures, or art exhibits and all high grade social pleasures. Acquaintance with literature, acquaintance with art, acquaintance with science, anything which rests the mind, strengthens the body, purifies the heart, ennobles the life is favored, and so far as conditions warrant, is aided by the institution."[21]

The semi-centennial weekend began with a meeting of the literary societies Friday evening in which old grads participated with short speeches. Speaking to an overflow crowd at the Gary Memorial Methodist Church in the baccalaureate sermon on Sunday, President Blanchard reminded his hearers that they were celebrating the College's Jubilee and that, in the words of Daniel Webster, "the past at least is secure." Early victories in the history of the College were achieved not because the founders and their successors were perfectly wise but "because the counsel and the work were of God, not of men; therefore they were not overthrown."[22] Class day exercises, typical of those held for many years before and after the jubilee year celebration, took place on Monday in front of the tower. The class history, poem, will, and prophecy, written and read with much seriousness, delighted the sympathetic audience. Phillip Fink "then made an eloquent speech in Latin as he presented the class gift 'to our beloved college President.' The President looked handsomer than ever in his cap, gown and hood, and responded in his beautiful and characteristic way to the senior class."[23] Concluding the day, members of the alumni association gathered in the gymnasium for their annual banquet, at which occasion they raised $14,000 to be added to the endowment fund.

Commencement, held in the chapel, was, as always, student-centered, with eleven orations delivered by members of the class on such subjects as "Woman's Influence," "The Price of Success," "Jesus in History," and "Good Citizenship."

Following the exercises, a picnic lunch was held on the lawn, when greetings were brought by personal representatives from Northwestern University, University of Chicago, Beloit College, Lake Forest College, North-Western College, McGill University, Moody Bible Institute, Chicago Theological Seminary, and McCormick Theological Seminary. In a preliminary announcement the *Record* had said: "Bring your picnic baskets, come early, and stay until the Senior Concert is over in the evening."[24]

Thus the *Record* remained a faithful chronicler of campus life, the primary source of much College history through the remainder of the Blanchard era, the first quarter of the century. The book-sized format of the paper continued unchanged from its beginning in 1890 until 1920, when the November 3 issue appeared in the tabloid form known to modern students and began bimonthly publication—followed the next year by the inauguration of weekly appearances.

The Tower

The faculty decision to terminate the publication of *Wheaton Echoes* after the financial failure of the 1900 edition was a great disappointment to students. From time to time during the following years they appealed for a new opportunity to demonstrate their competence and financial accountability. Finally, in 1920, the faculty gave its consent to an energetic junior class to publish another annual—the approval hedged with safeguards against any prospect of insolvency. Student editors willingly accepted the requirements "that all funds must be raised before the final closing of con-

The first Washington Banquet, 1909, held in the college gymnasium (called the Lincoln Banquet for that year only).

The first Homecoming gathering, 1923. L. to r.: Florence Cobb, Julia Blanchard, Carl Garlough, Herman Fischer, Julia Fischer, Martha Garlough, Harriet Blaine, Elsie Dow, Darien Straw, Edith Smith.

tracts."[25] "We believe that's fair," they said. To raise money they planned to sell refreshments at games, sponsor concerts, sell advertisements, and seek subscriptions among students, friends, and alumni.

By January 1921, with over $1,200 raised, the financial stability of the project was assured. Preparation of the book was well underway before the name *Tower*, submitted by a faculty member in a schoolwide contest, was chosen. Delivery by truck from Chicago and distribution of the first edition early in June 1922 was an exciting moment for students as they scanned its pages, read the text, and hurried to their friends for autographs.

The book is an excellent history of campus life in the early 1920s, with every faculty member, student, student organization, and college building pictured for posterity. Literary societies, music groups, athletic teams, and Christian service organizations, in their busy activities, are described in detail. The Christian groups included the Y.M.C.A., the Y.W.C.A., the Gospel Team, Student Volunteer Band, and the Ministerial Association. Organized in 1904 under the auspices of the Chicago Union of Volunteers, the Student Volunteer Band could say that by 1921 thirty of its members were "in foreign service in various parts of the world." Among the groups pictured in the *Tower* of 1922 was a company of thirteen veterans of World War I, most of them in uniform and all identified by their rank and area of service. A complete listing of the alumni showed that there had been, through 1919, a total of 494 graduates of Wheaton.

Writing in the June 1, 1921, issue of the *Record* about the eagerly anticipated delivery of the *Tower* within a few days, an unidentified student with impish tendencies concluded his story by observing that "it has been suggested that some moneyed person buy some extra annuals and mail them to members of the board of trustees who have never seen Wheaton College."[26]

In the *Tower's* early years of publication, the first copy was presented in chapel to the person to whom it was dedicated; that night the annual was viewed by the staff members at the home of the faculty advisor. Distribution followed the day after the chapel presentation.

Student Council

"Faculty Approves Student Council" was the page one headline story of the February 9, 1921, *Record*, marking the conclusion of a steady campaign by students for participation in campus government. It was a major achievement for students in the history of the College. For the first time they were to have a significant role in establishing some campus policies. In this concession Wheaton was responding affirmatively to a general trend in higher education. Powers granted to the council were considerable, including the right to represent the student body before the faculty, to manage all college and interclass functions, to elect the editorial staff of

the *Record* and the *Tower*, and to elect the officers of the Athletic association, glee clubs, Y.M.C.A. and Y.W.C.A.[27] Assigned to the council also
were such responsibilities as selecting choir leaders, organizing pep rallies,
electing the temporary chairman of the freshman class, and securing their
own finances by assessing each student twenty-five cents.

One of the council's earliest triumphs as a positive force on campus was
the organization of Wheaton's first Homecoming in the fall of 1923. For
three weeks prior to the event the *Record* carried stories that rang with
youthful exuberance, as students urged alumni near and far to return to
"the old school" and meet again some of the "old boys." The October 17
Record headlined the occasion, then one week away: "Homecoming
Draws Near; Large Crowd of Alumni Expected. Entire School is Looking
Forward to the Biggest Event of the Year." Students were promised "a bon-
fire pep meeting, novel stunts, new yells, songs, speeches, and a band."
Everyone was told: "Take your place in the band, on the team, or yell-
ing."[28] On Friday evening, October 23, excited students gathered at the
gymnasium to begin the weekend festivities with a parade, led by a band,
to the president's home, and from there to the center of Wheaton, after
which they returned to the field for a pep rally. Following the pep meeting
literary societies—Excelsior, Philalethean, Beltionian, and Aelioian—convened, with alumni as the welcome and admired guests for the evening.

Centerpiece for the Homecoming weekend was the football game with
North-Western College, which the Wheaton team lost 7-6, to the anguish
of the wildly cheering student body. The ever-loyal *Record* noted in covering the game that "Visitors, though Outplayed, Are Favored by the
Breaks."

At the Saturday evening gathering in the Women's Residence, or Ladies'
Hall, ("The Red Castle"), alumni, faculty and members of the senior class
exchanged reminiscences and enjoyed each other's fellowship. Clarence
Mason, speaking for the Student Council, greeted the alumni, Professor
Smith spoke of the value of school spirit, Coach Conley and Professor
Winsor expressed appreciation for both past and present generations of
students, and Wallace Graham '21 talked of the value of the Homecoming
experience. Vows were made to offer an even larger Homecoming the following year for old grads "to visit their Alma Mater."

Curriculum in Transition

When young Charles Blanchard came to the presidency of Wheaton
College in 1882, he had announced his allegiance to the classical curriculum and expressed his devotion to the good ways of the past. The curriculum was carefully prescribed, although students could choose between the
classical and scientific courses. By the turn of the century, however, five
elective courses were permitted.

The curriculum at Wheaton in 1915 offered students a choice among twelve majors: languages, sciences, history, social science, philosophy, and education. About three-quarters of the graduation hours were prescribed. All majors required courses in English, history, science, mathematics, foreign language, and Bible. Approximately forty-four elective hours were allowed in all majors.

How did the movement away from the prescribed classical curriculum toward a much more flexible system come about? When Charles W. Eliot became president of Harvard University, he rejected course prescription in favor of course election. In 1872 all subject requirements for seniors were abandoned. By 1897 only the freshman rhetoric course was prescribed. Few other institutions went to Harvard's extreme in adopting a completely "free elective" system, nor did Havard find the experiment altogether satisfactory. But new ground had been broken, and most colleges and universities abandoned rigid prescription, which infused new vitality into higher education at a time when many critics felt that American colleges were becoming more and more remote from society and its needs. A rapidly emerging industrial society called for a much greater diversity of preparation to meet the needs of the day and to harmonize with the spirit of the times. It was an era of optimism, of competitiveness, of William James's pragmatism. In the curriculum adjustments Wheaton made, it was responding to social forces it did not create and, in these matters, could not resist.

CHAPTER 6

Fashioning the College's Doctrinal Position and Other Aspects of Wheaton Life in the Twenties

FROM 1900 TO THE TIME OF CHARLES ALBERT BLANCHARD'S death in 1925, Wheaton College held steadily to the same spiritual and academic traditions it had pursued from the beginning. During the first quarter of the century most small liberal arts colleges charted their directions according to the vision of a strong, forceful president, such as Blanchard. To a marked degree the Christian causes with which Dr. Blanchard allied himself and the doctrinal convictions he held came to be those of the College as well. His written statements and public declarations both forged and reflected Wheaton College's developing Christian educational philosophy.

"The purpose of a college is to furnish men for home, church and state," Blanchard wrote. "So the college can have no joy unless those whom it instructs become powers in the world, working for righteousness."[1] Any impediments to those ends—a weak and uncertain theology, secret societies, intemperance, Sabbath-breaking—all were to be resisted as perils to the high ends for which Wheaton College existed. For Charles Blanchard a stable, Bible-centered theology was foundational for institutional leadership, social reform, and individual development.

One needs only to recall some of Jonathan Blanchard's thought to see how his son assimilated it into his own theological convictions. For the elder Blanchard "Jesus Christ was a model reformer,"[2] and every great social transformation stems from his teaching. The "enlightened Christian opposes and corrects laws, customs, and habits" that would in any way restrain the emergence of a righteous social order. It was therefore a Christian duty to "speak, write, vote, support public men and measures and sustain public papers on the sole principle of honoring God by rebuking sin and promoting holiness on the earth."[3] In that sense, both Blanchards believed, imperative Christian obligation lay close to patriotic, responsible citizenship.

Though not a revivalist himself, Charles Blanchard was a child of the revivalist era, and strongly believed in revival as an essential preliminary to personal and social reformation. Periodic revivals at Wheaton, following lengthy prayer meetings or a series of addresses by an invited speaker, were generally reported in the *Christian Cynosure*.[4] Blanchard was by no means alone in his conviction—millions of Americans cherished the thought, as well as some historians—that America had a special God-given role to preserve righteousness and freedom in a democratic order. The liberties assured in the nation's foundational documents were grants from God, and their preservation was the obligation of God's people; "religious democracy"[5] could be recognized in the spirit of the New Testament.

Under those convictions the younger Blanchard labored ceaselessly for the purification of society. "If I knew of a good cause, today," he wrote, "with which I had not been in some way associated, I should hasten to beg the privilege of saying, or giving, or doing something to promote it, for it is my conviction that every honest man should be directly connected with every movement for the glory of God and the good of his fellows."[6] That Wheaton College and other Christian colleges were called to labor in the cause of cultural, institutional, and political reformation continued as a strong emphasis in President Blanchard's pronouncements, up to the onset of World War I, even though he had much earlier been led to accept a premillennial interpretation of the Scriptures, a position viewed by some as pessimistic about the prospects of social advancement through human endeavor.[7]

In 1913 Blanchard published a premillennial study, *Light on the Last Days: Being Familiar Talks on the Book of Revelation*, and dedicated it to Emma Dryer, "the friend who first opened my mind to the Dispensational Teaching of the Word of God."[8] Emma Dryer, whom Blanchard had met while he was interim pastor at the Chicago Avenue Church and whom he had helped in the earliest efforts to finance D. L. Moody's Bible Institute, had been converted in 1870 under the ministry of William J. Erdman, "one of the patriarchs of American Premillennialism."[9] She herself notes that she then made a systematic study of the doctrine and found it to be "the key to the Scriptures."[10] Her influence on Blanchard's mind is clear not only from the prefatory statement of *Light on the Last Days* but also from other statements in that work. "For many years," he wrote, "I derived very little advantage from the book of Revelation. Since I began to study it twenty-eight years ago, it has continually grown on me as a book intended to accomplish real blessing for the people of God."[11] Though the dispensational premillennial doctrine matured in his mind over a period of time, he had made almost no public statements about it until the appearance of the 1913 volume.

Premillennialism was espoused by many respected churchmen across a broad spectrum of denominations, among them Robert E. Speer, revered secretary of the Presbyterian Board of Foreign Missions from 1891 to 1937, who was drawn to premillennialism during his student days at one of the Northfield Bible Conferences. Some years later he observed that "life seemed altogether changed for me in that hour." John R. Mott, a major figure in the Student Volunteer Movement, who made widely known the expression "the evangelization of the world in this generation," was also drawn to the premillennial view. The premillennial view of the future was generally acknowledged to be "an enormous catalyst to the missions movement." If history was moving rapidly toward its consummation with the return of Christ, as premillennialism taught, the urgency of world mission effort was clear.[12]

The Doctrinal Statement

For more than half a century Wheaton College trustees, administrators, and faculty members have been asked to accept the premillennial doctrine. Thus it is worth noting how this teaching, at first individually appropriated, became an institutional commitment.

Paralleling the premillennarian movement, and often merging with it, was the modernist-fundamentalist controversy. That controversy also influenced the direction in which Wheaton College moved, since President Blanchard, though not at the center of organizational efforts to stem the tide of liberalism, was significantly involved. Many students of the Bible associate the controversy primarily with the 1920s, when "American Protestantism was seized with a paroxysm of contention over the source of authority in Christianity, the validity of the theory of evolution, and the techniques of biblical criticism."[13] The roots of the controversy are complex, but the most evident cause was the rise of higher criticism in American colleges, universities, and seminaries—and subsequently within the major denominations—when those trained in the newer approaches to the study of biblical authority and analysis began to exercise influence within their denominations. As earlier noted, higher criticism was introduced into American institutions by scholars who had gone to German universities for their graduate study and there had become enamored of the new methods of biblical investigation. Clearly the tension began at the scholarly level. Only later did laypersons—the kinds of people who sent their sons and daughters to Wheaton—find themselves choosing between sharply divided camps in the controversy.

Though it is an oversimplification to suggest that people with a strong commitment to orthodoxy and a warm devotion to the Bible found themselves within the ranks of fundamentalism and those who lacked this anchorage drifted toward theological modernism, there is some accuracy in the generalization. Other efforts to characterize the participants in the struggle frequently ran into questionable generalizations that linger unshakably even today. Such a judgment, really a sociological explanation of theological change, was formulated by H. Richard Niebuhr: "In the social sources from which it drew its strength fundamentalism was closely related to the conflict between rural and urban cultures in America. Its popular leader was the agrarian W. J. Bryan; its rise coincided with the depression of agricultural values after the World War; it achieved little strength in the urban and industrial sections of the country but was active in many rural areas."[14] The tendency of some to associate fundamentalism with ruralism drew strength from the trial of John T. Scopes in 1925 on charges of teaching evolution in violation of state law in a public high school in Dayton, Tennessee, a rural area. In the eyes of many, the trial—conducted in an almost carnival-like atmosphere—was regrettable. Scopes was convicted, but his fundamentalist prosecutor, William Jennings Bryan, whose scientific knowledge was limited, was subjected to merciless ridicule for his biblical and anti-evolutionary views by Clarence Darrow, the scoffer, and by much of the press. Many Wheaton students and townspeople, reading about the events in Dayton, would have remembered the day in April three years before when Bryan, three-times unsuccessful candidate for the presidency, spoke to a crowded chapel in Blanchard Hall, telling his hearers that America's greatest need was "to get back to God." Ridiculing the theory of evolution, he called it "the greatest menace to the civilized world."[15]

Substantial support of the fundamentalist cause came from *The Fundamentals*, a series of pamphlets published between 1910 and 1915, twelve volumes in all, under the editorship of A. C. Dixon, and supported by a gift of $300,000 from Lyman and Milton Stewart.[16] Sent free to all Christian workers in the United States, the booklets carried articles by eminent evangelicals like G. Campbell Morgan, A. T. Pierson, Dr. Howard Kelly, Charles G. Trumbull, James Orr, B. B. Warfield, and W. H. Griffith-Thomas, all of whom rejected higher criticism and defended the fundamentals of orthodoxy. In 1923, Griffith-Thomas, who was professor of systematic theology of Wycliffe College, Toronto, was invited to head the department of Christianity and philosophy at Wheaton, but he declined the opportunity.[17]

Strategic to the history of Wheaton College was the founding of the World's Christian Fundamentals Association, which drew 6,000 people from forty-two states to its organizing convention in Philadelphia in 1919. To give stability and permanence to the association, five committees were appointed, one of which, the Committee on Correlation of Colleges, Seminaries, and Academics, was headed by Charles Blanchard. The committee, says Ernest Sandeen, "limited itself to denouncing the perfidy of Modernist colleges."[18] Another committee, much influenced by the positions taken in *The Fundamentals*, prepared a nine-point creedal statement, which included allegiance to the verbally inspired and inerrant Bible, and the personal, pre-millennial, imminent return of Christ. Frances Carothers Blanchard states in her *Life of Charles Blanchard* that her husband was called in to assist the committee after it had labored for some days and had experienced difficulty in making a clear, succinct statement. "Within a very short time President Blanchard had the difficulty solved" she says. "The order and wording he suggested was used and the Declaration of Faith, as he formulated it, was offered to the conference and unanimously adopted."[19]

At that time Wheaton had no clearly formulated doctrinal statement, but the need for such a document was becoming increasingly evident as the fundamentalist-modernist controversy intensified. What better way could there be of announcing a doctrinal position than to appropriate the nine-point statement of the World's Christian Fundamentals Association?

Though the faculty and trustees had no part in formulating the statement, President Blanchard gave them the opportunity to view it and to raise any objection they may have had. Only two replies survive, indicating that the faculty and trustees had complete confidence in President Blanchard's leadership in the formulation and wisdom of such a statement. Blanchard's letter to the faculty read:

> I am frequently asked these days whether our trustees and faculty believe in the fundamentals of the Christian faith. I always say as far as I have knowledge they do. In order, however, to be able to speak with authority I need to have a word with you. I am therefore enclosing to our people a few items which seem to me fundamentals of Christian faith.
>
> I shall be glad to know whether, so far as you have knowledge, you believe the things here stated, if there is any one of them which you do not believe, I should be glad to have mention made of the fact. What I want is to be able to answer this question.[20]

Professor of Greek George H. Smith sent back his signed statement with the comment: "This is in substance my belief." Trustee Fleming H. Revell, brother-in-law of D. L. Moody, responded in this way: "While I agree substantially with the outlines presented in the statement you enclosed, I do question the wisdom or the necessity of this proposition." What Revell perhaps could not have foreseen was the steady growth of the faculty and student body after Blanchard's death, making an instrument like the doctrinal statement an effective means of assaying a faculty candidate's suitability for the Wheaton environment. Historian Thomas Askew, '53, notes that the statement achieved two consequences: it "committed the school to a fixed theological position that guarded against philosophical change" and it was a means of preserving "Wheaton's continued orthodoxy after Blanchard's demise."[21]

At a meeting of the Executive Committee of Wheaton College on July 14, 1924, the members "voted that the printed platform of Wheaton College should be adopted and that the same should be presented to the trustees and faculty for their signature."[22] On March 3, 1926, at a meeting of the Board of Trustees at the LaSalle Hotel in Chicago, the "printed platform of Wheaton College," that is, the nine-point doctrinal statement prepared for the World's Christian Fundamentals Association, was adopted as the "testimony" of Wheaton College.[23]

Of the eighteen members of the Board of Trustees at the time the doctrinal statement was adopted, thirteen were clergymen and five were laymen. One of the laymen was Lewis L. McShane, vice-president of the G. C. Merriam Publishing Company; another was Fleming H. Revell, founder of the publishing house that still bears his name. The other laymen, all of whom lived in the Wheaton area, were attorneys, bankers, and merchants. Among the clergymen were John W. Welsh, pastor of College Church; P. W. Philpott, pastor of Moody Church; Paul Rader, then president of the Christian and Missionary Alliance; J. G. Brooks, a former pastor of College Church of Christ; and William McCarrell, pastor of Cicero Bible Church. These trustees had been elected to a ten-year term of a self-perpetuating board, a system that usually assured lifetime appointment.[24]

The doctrinal statement of Wheaton College has appeared in every catalog since it was first published in 1927. Part of the introduction declares that "it is not claimed that this statement, or any modern creedal statement, is inspired or authoritative except in so far as it correctly interprets the Scriptures."

The Statement follows:

1. We believe in the Scriptures of the Old and New Testaments as verbally inspired by God and inerrant in the original writing, and that they are of supreme and final authority in faith and life.

2. We believe in one God, eternally existing in three persons: Father, Son, and Holy Spirit.

3. We believe that Jesus Christ was begotten by the Holy Spirit, born of the Virgin Mary, and is true God and true man.

4. We believe that man was created in the image of God; that he sinned and thereby incurred, not only physical death, but also that spiritual death which is separation from God, and that all human beings are born with a sinful nature, and, in the case of those who reach moral responsibility, become sinners in word, thought, and deed.

5. We believe that the Lord Jesus Christ died for our sins, according to the Scriptures, as a representative and substitutionary sacrifice; and that all who believe in him are justified on the ground of His shed blood.

6. We believe in the resurrection of the crucified body of our Lord, of His ascension into Heaven and in His present life there for us as High Priest and Advocate.

7. We believe in "that blessed hope," the personal, pre-millennial, and imminent return of our Lord and Savior, Jesus Christ.

8. We believe that all who receive by faith the Lord Jesus Christ are

born again of the Holy Spirit and thereby become children of God.
9. We believe in the bodily resurrection of the just and the unjust, the everlasting blessedness of the saved, the everlasting punishment of the lost.

The doctrinal statement, known as the Statement of Faith, clearly grew out of an era of theological tension when many orthodox Christians earnestly believed that the foundations of their faith were being eroded. Alien teachings that dishonored Christ and his church were undermining many colleges and seminaries. The preservation of the statement as Wheaton's continuing affirmation of the historic Christian faith has helped to keep the College faithful to the values on which it was founded.

The College has never wished to convey the impression that its formulation of Christian doctrine is the only way in which those convictions can be acceptably expressed. For its own purposes and for its continuity and perpetuity as a Christian institution, Wheaton believes that the doctrinal platform is a good thing and consequently continues to ask the members of the faculty, trustees, staff, and administration annually to reaffirm their allegiance to the doctrines set forth in the statement.

The New Chapel

After Jonathan Blanchard had been president of Wheaton College for some years, he suggested the organization of the College Church of Christ in 1878 and gave it its name, believing that every church should bear the name of Christ in its title as an evidence of its dedication and orthodoxy. For many visitors to the campus over the years the name has proved to be a bit confusing; it seems to imply ownership and direction by the College, which has never been true, though many students and faculty have been members of the church. The church was organized along congregational lines because Blanchard believed that the Congregational Church was the least denominational of the American churches. For many years the College chapel adequately served as a meeting place for College Church, but as the community grew and the student body increased, there came a time when the church needed a larger meeting place.

When a new building was planned, with agreement that the church and the College would use it jointly, both parties resolved to raise an equal share of the $50,000 needed. The site chosen for the building was the northwest corner of the campus, where four tennis courts, some shade trees, and part of the arborvitae hedge that ringed the campus, were cleared for the groundbreaking in the early fall of 1924.

At the ground-breaking ceremony Dr. Darien Straw announced to the assembled company that though they were there witnessing the official breaking of the earth for a splendid new building, he had been at the site at five o'clock in the morning and been the first to turn over a spadeful of dirt. Thereupon a small girl in the crowd spoke up: "Oh no you weren't," she said, "because I was here at two o'clock in the morning and broke ground."[25]

On Thanksgiving morning a crowd of church members, faculty, and students assembled in front of the main building and marched to the scene of the excavation of the new chapel while a band played "Onward Christian Soldiers." President Blanchard rehearsed briefly the history that led to the construction of the building, after which Professor Herman Fischer deposited in the cornerstone a box containing college periodicals, the church manual, and other documents. On the cornersone was inscribed, "Wheaton College Church and Chapel. Erected A.D. 1924, for Christ and His Kingdom."

At the mid-November Sunday dedication service for the chapel, nearly 1,000 persons were in attendance at the College Church morning worship service. Dr. W. B. Riley, of Minneapolis, spoke on Micah 4:1-7: "The Future Kingdom of the Messiah." President Blanchard offered the dedicatory prayer, followed by the church choir's singing the "Hallelujah Chorus." The spaciousness and simple architectural lines of the building awed the worshipers that Sunday morning and filled their hearts with gratitude.

When the chapel became available for general college use, it seemed overwhelmingly large to the student body of the day and was not used at first for the daily chapel services. The building, however, was increasingly to be used for a variety of college activities. Here for thirty-five years, until the opening of Edman Chapel, students listened to noted Christian leaders, engaged in prayer meetings, dedicated their lives to the Lord's service, and, in many instances, resolved to go to the ends of the earth in obedience to God's call for them. Here, too, they thrilled to concerts of great music, a rare cultural experience for many a student from a remote area where such privileges were little known. Eager students filled the chapel to hear an intercollegiate debate or listen to a speech recital presented by one of the protégés of Professor Florence Cobb, a warmhearted and affectionate teacher from Maine, revered by her students and colleagues.

In 1925 Wheaton College possessed five buildings: the Main Building, after sixty-five years still known by that name only; the Women's Residence, which housed ninety students; the gymnasium; the new chapel; and the academy building, with its offices, laboratories, and classes. Besides those, the College had acquired three residence houses for women and two for men. Wayside Inn was originally located on the site later occupied by the academy building. It was at first a cooperative boarding club for men, but subsequently it was converted to house fifteen women.[26] Bent Cottage, located on Franklin Street between Irving Avenue and Adams Street, and accommodating ten women, had been owned by Joseph A. Bent, brother of Mrs. Jonathan Blanchard and a teacher from Illinois Institute days until 1872. When the need for a college infirmary became urgent, Bent Cottage was remodeled, and served for many years as a care center for students who were ill. Cork Cottage, at the bottom of the hill on Seminary Avenue, purchased in 1922, had been built by Hugh Cork, a member of the class of 1893, who became one of the pioneers in the Sunday school movement.

Bartlett Hall, accommodating twenty-two men, was first secured by the campus Y.M.C.A. for students who could not be housed in the Main Building, a financial undertaking that proved too great for the fellows. At that time Mr. and Mrs. Bartlett, of Elburn, accepted financial responsibility for this house, which became college property in 1921 and was then named Bartlett Hall. Located at Main and Union Streets, Bartlett, bulging at the seams with so many young men, was bound to be the center of many legendary escapades. Missionary Home, which had been acquired in 1916, housed twenty students, many of them children of missionaries. Other students found lodging in private, approved residences, often with faculty or staff members for whom housing students provided the necessary financial assistance they needed to purchase their homes. Students contrived their own names for the homes where they lived: The Friars was on east Lincoln Street, Grant's Tomb on Union, Barron's Castle on north Scott, Graham Cracker Box (owned by Mrs. Graham), the Hoss Stable (presided over by Mrs. Hoss), the Sandbox (Mrs. Sandberg), and the H.O.T. House, owned by Professor Hawley Otis Taylor.

The Alma Mater and College Motto

The Wheaton College Alma Mater was introduced to the student body by President Blanchard. He had brought it with him from Hedding College in the small town of Abingdon, near Galesburg, in western Illinois, where he had gone to speak to the student body. After hearing the tuneful Hedding Alma Mater sung, with its salute to the "Orange and Blue"—already Wheaton's colors—Blanchard asked the president of Hedding, scheduled soon to close, if Wheaton might use the song. The request granted, Charles Blanchard found that the lyrics lent themselves readily to the substitution of Wheaton for Hedding. The verses are a tribute to memories of "sacred halls and classrooms" to be cherished "through clouds and sunshine always."

For generations of students, who sang the song at athletic events, alumni gatherings, commencement, and other special occasions, the Alma Mater became an expression of devotion and loyalty to the school they had come to love. In days past, freshmen dutifully learned the words of the song as part of their orientation and sang them with something of the zeal they might bring to a rousing hymn, the chorus particularly:

O Wheaton! dear old Wheaton, live forever:
Brave sons and daughters true,
We'll e'er uphold thy colors
The Orange and the Blue.

Through the quarter century of his service as president, Dr. V. Raymond Edman loved to speak to the student body as "brave sons and daughters true." In recent years, however, the Alma Mater and its sentiments are little heard except at Homecoming, commencement, and alumni club gatherings, where its words still tug a bit at the heartstrings of the older grads.

The orange and blue colors of Wheaton had been chosen by Jonathan Blanchard because they were the colors of the Protestant Netherlands he admired and because he was inspired by the militant Protestant stand of Prince William, of the House of Orange.

The college motto, "For Christ and His Kingdom," expresses the kind of institutional dedication held and often expressed by Jonathan and Charles Blanchard, and their successors. Jonathan Blanchard's inaugural address at Knox College in 1846, "The Kingdom of Christ: And the Duty of American Colleges Respecting It," was an early elaboration of the theme. Years later, when he set down his recollections, he observed that he had come to Wheaton "still seeking a perfect state of society" and a college "for Christ and His Kingdom." The motto appeared on the masthead of the first issue of the *Wheaton College Record* in 1890 and continued to be used in that way until 1906. The earliest use of the motto in the college catalog appears in the 1907 edition: "It is the effort of the Trustees, Faculty, and friends of Wheaton College to make it stand firm and true 'For Christ and His Kingdom.' This is the college motto and the College is seeking to be faithful to it." The motto appears on the cornerstone of the eastern section of Blanchard Hall completed in 1890. The stone, with its inscription clearly visible, now forms part of the wall of one of the philosophy department offices. The motto is also inscribed on the cornerstone of the 1927 addition to Blanchard Hall and on the Eastgate entrance to the campus, given by the class of 1941.

Final Years of the Blanchard Era

During the last five years of his presidency, Charles Blanchard guided a steadily enlarging institution. Enrollment grew annually, so that there were 348 in the College by 1925; faculty were added to care for new students; the curriculum was broadened through the introduction of new courses in all fields. At the heart of the institutional purpose for President Blanchard was the luminous vision he had expressed many times through the years and restated at the opening of the 1924 fall term. "I think our friends all know that we do not consider intellectual training as an end," he wrote. "We look upon it as a means to an end, and the end for which we strive is the building up of solid Christian character. In this labor we have been wonderfully aided by our Christian students. They come to us from Bible schools, missionary homes, and other Christian colleges, and all parts of the world." He spoke with thanksgiving of student prayer gatherings which often brought together a hundred and fifty or more students—a real source of institutional strength, he believed. Through such gatherings students strengthened and encouraged each other.[27]

Student gospel teams and quartets journeyed frequently on brief or extended trips. Typical of such groups was the quartet that left campus in late December 1923, with William Jones, Harold Tiedt, Donald MacKay, and Alex Sauerwein scheduled to appear in nineteen churches and missions in the Boston, Pittsburgh, Cleveland, and Detroit areas. "The whole trip was manifestly blessed of the Lord," said the *Record.*[28] The following year the same group traveled to Dayton, Scranton, Philadelphia, New York, Boston, Buffalo, Flint, and Detroit, declaring before their departure that "we go out with joy, for we know that you, fellow students, and brothers and sisters in Christ, are holding us up daily before His throne in prayer."[29] Student religious groups such as the Y.M.C.A., Y.W.C.A., the Volunteer Band, and the Mission Study Class made strong, positive, optimistic contributions to the spiritual tone of the Wheaton campus. The Y groups, which had no affiliation with the national associations, performed many useful services, among them meeting all trains at the opening of the college year to welcome new students, and helping them find rooms and boarding places.

A good number of students from missionary families were always at Wheaton, many of them having resolved well before their arrival on campus to return to the fields of service from which they had come. Other young people found themselves being called to foreign service during their student days, sometimes through associations with the Volunteer Band, in chapel, during a reflective walk across the tree-lined campus, or in the quiet of a dormitory room. From 1920 to 1925 fifty-five graduates committed themselves to service in eighteen countries: fifteen in China, eleven in the Congo, and ten in Central and South America, to name only the most commonly chosen lands. From among forty-nine seniors, sixteen members of the class of 1923 went to the mission field; for the class of 1925 the figures were identical—forty-nine seniors, sixteen missionaries. Representative of the many who felt called were Elizabeth and Robert Ekvall, 1920, who went to Tibet; Mary and Earl Winsor, also 1920, who chose the Congo; Ada Sterns, 1922, who was led to India. From the 1923 class Harry Stam and Paul Stough left for the Congo, and Newberry Cox for Guatemala; the 1924 class sent Gladys Wright to the Congo, Albert Sanders to the Philippines, and Kenneth Landon, with his wife, Margaret, '25, to Siam. Other fields of service were represented when Mary Hunter went to Alaska, Thelma Nelson to Costa Rica, and Catherine and Ralph Varhaug to Brazil.

Many others became pastors, Christian workers, and teachers in Christian schools—all engaged in what President Edman liked so often to call "God's glad service." Undergirding the spiritual tone of the campus were the well-known fundamentalists who came frequently to speak in chapel and special services: James M. Gray, R. A. Torrey, T. T. Shields, J. Frank Norris, P. W. Philpott, Harry A. Ironside, and W. B. Riley.

Large interest was shown in those days in the activities of the debate teams, men's and women's. Much more frequently winners than losers— when contests were decided by a three-judge panel—Wheaton teams argued urgent issues of the day before large, engrossed student audiences. Some debates were decided by audience vote; others were open forums followed by audience discussion. Because membership on the debate team was recognized as a significant honor, usually twenty-five to thirty candidates appeared for team tryouts, seeking one of the coveted positions on the two three-man teams. Women's teams worked with equal diligence. "Debaters Work Hard; Fight for Team Positions," said the *Record*, as the 1924 team, coached by Assistant Professor of History A. M. Mintier, began in the fall to meet their opponents on the question: "Resolved that Congress should be empowered to override decisions of the Supreme Court which declare Congressional acts unconstitutional."

Usually the competition in debate was with area colleges. Occasionally there was a journey by train to the South or to the West, such as that taken by the 1925-26 team in the spring of the year to debate Luther College in Decorah, Iowa; Montana State College at Bozeman; Gonzaga at Salem, Oregon; College of the Pacific at Stockton, California; and Abilene Christian College at Abilene, Texas. By telegram and letter the debaters kept an eager campus informed of their progress as they carried the name of Wheaton before audiences who often had not heard of the College.

Music has always had a significant place in the life of Wheaton. The Conservatory sought to cultivate an enthusiastic response to good music by bringing to campus special performers, usually solo musicians, at a time when the College was not in a position to sponsor large groups such as the orchestras that were later to be a part of the famed Artist Series. In the early twenties the campus orchestra usually limited itself to local performances, but on occasion it made short excursions, such as when they played for 800 war veterans at the State Veterans Hospital in Elgin.[30] The same year the Men's Glee Club had the then-novel experience of singing at the Sears Roebuck-operated radio station WLS in Chicago, where they were "sandwiched in between a jazz orchestra and the Corn Huskers, an organization of doubtful worth."[31] In the following years would come the enriching trips for students of the musical organizations to the coasts, the Southeast, the Northeast, and the Northwest in Greyhound buses.

Athletics

Athletics has consistently been a controlled activity which trustees, administration, and faculty have not allowed to dominate the campus environment. Nor has there at any time been excessive recruitment or subsidization of players. Like other students, athletes in the twenties had work opportunities on campus and in the community, but no special privileges. They came to Wheaton through the encouragement and persuasion of alumni and friends, or because they had been drawn to Wheaton by its Christian commitment. Academically they were expected to meet the same standards as other students. Football, basketball, baseball, tennis, track, and cross-country were the college sports, with football and basketball always generating the major student interest and receiving the most coverage on the sports page of campus publications.

Between 1920 and 1924 Wheaton football teams compiled a record of eighteen wins, sixteen losses, and two ties. Scores ranged from a humiliating 60-0 defeat by the Chicago Y.M.C.A. in 1921, when the team won six and lost two, to a rousing 36-0 victory over Elmhurst in 1922. Of the defeat at the hands of the Y, the *Record* said, "Wheaton was piteously outweighed, about forty pounds to the man."[32] Statistics for that team show that on a squad of twenty-nine players, only two weighed as much as 183, one weighed 172, and the remainder were under 170, the lightest being Arnold Pent at 140. Great jubilation prevailed on the Wheaton campus when the 1924 team had the distinction of gaining the first victory over North-Western (later North Central), 13-6, a game in which Hicks and Wolstenholme scored the touchdowns. In that game Wheaton used only five substitutes (and averaged no more than three substitutes a game for the season). It was a day in which most players remained in the game for sixty minutes.[33] Competition in the twenties was generally with such teams as Elmhurst, North-Western, Augustana, Mt. Morris, De Kalb, Concordia, and Lake Forest.

Team travel to games was usually by train, a mode of transportation that was frequently slow and a bit uncertain. In 1921 the team traveled to Mt. Morris, a distance of seventy-five miles, leaving from the Wheaton station for West Chicago at five a.m., changing there for Oregon, and changing again at Oregon for the final destination. Bruce Hunt, of the class of 1924, remembered some of the adventures of the football team in his day, particularly when he made the 1922 team as a 150-pound guard, an era when guards were expected to be wiry and scrappy. "Our first game was against Illinois Wesleyan. We had an all morning train trip to Bloomington, and the train hit a car, delaying us an hour for Illinois Wesleyan's Homecoming game and dedication of their new stadium. Our coach had gotten us new jerseys for the occasion and they were yellow instead of orange and blue. Several of our team had never been in an intercollegiate game before; it was our first game and a hot day in September. We could afford to take only one sub. The home team had three full teams sitting on their bench, including two all-Americans."[34]

Basketball games in the twenties were quite different from the high scoring contests in the years following World War II. Low scores—Wheaton beat Loyala 14-12 in the 1922-23 season—were the result of several factors: shorter games, less skilled coaching, fewer trained players coming from high school, and a different ball structure, which sometimes caused an irregular bounce. Significant also was the tendency to make nearly all shots from a distance rather than from under the basket, and the practice followed by all players of shooting from the chest, which made blocking by the guards much easier.[35] One of the best games of the 1920-21 season was Wheaton's 20-14 victory over Crane College, the losers scoring only three baskets. In its only conference game of the season, Wheaton was defeated by Monmouth College, 36-16, the home team somewhat hindered by the loss of Vic Hicks, an academy student who was ineligible to play in a conference game, the rule against the use of noncollege students having been inaugurated that year.

In the 1922-23 season Wheaton defeated Loyola without committing a single foul; when the same team came to the Wheaton court, the home team lost, 11-4. That was an extraordinary game, in which a basket by Bill Gale and free throws by Vic Hicks and Orland Stockton were the only Wheaton scores. Of that game, Ed Coray observed that "one would have thought that if the coach had us throwing the ball in the right direction, it would have dropped in by accident more often than that."[36]

College baseball usually arouses only moderate student interest in comparison with football and basketball. At Wheaton the game had good student support in the twenties, but there have been few of the outstanding seasons known to the football and basketball teams. Yet there have been outstanding individual players, and team members are usually motivated by their love for the game rather than by cheering crowds. The 1923 team lost eight consecutive games; the 1924 squad won three and lost eight, but an 11-4 victory over Elmhurst resulted in "a clean sweep" in sports competition between the two schools that year.

In 1920 Wheaton joined the Illinois Intercollegiate Athletic Conference and entered four men in the conference track and field meet. Much of the track activity in the early twenties was limited to inter-class field days and inter-lit competition, although the College entered a team in a quadrangular meet in May 1924, in which Wheaton finished fourth behind North-Western, Mt. Morris, and De Kalb.

Wheaton teams have almost always done well in tennis. In 1922 the team of Raymond Fischer, Bill Jones, Bill Pickney, Clarence Mason, and Dave Myers won three matches and lost two. An exceptional record was compiled by the 1924 team of Henry Coray, Vic Hicks, Jim Schreiber, Dave Myers, and Ralph Noel when they won seventy-seven individual matches while losing only twelve.

During those years the athletic coach was responsible for all men's teams, as well as for part-time teaching. From the fall of 1919 to the spring of 1921 Rex Gary served as coach and taught mathematics. He was followed by Bob Woodruff, 1921-22, and Jack Conley from the fall of 1922 until the fall of 1925, both men teaching mathematics part-time. Turning in 1926 to one of its own, the college administration called Ed Coray, who had been graduated in 1923 and was coaching high school athletics in New Jersey, to return to his alma mater as coach of all men's teams.

Women's intercollegiate tennis was introduced in 1922, when the team of Margaret Mortenson, Elizabeth Conley, and Marguerite Stark defeated Lake Forest, 3-0, and lost to North-Western by the same score. In those days women appeared on the courts wearing long white skirts and white middies with black scarves. At the end of the season Margaret Mortenson, later

Mrs. Kenneth Landon and author of *Anna and the King of Siam*, and Elizabeth Conley were the first women in Wheaton history to receive varsity letters. In three years those two women won seven matches and lost three. The
1924 team of Margaret Mortenson, Ruth Nowack (both of whom played
regularly for four years), Gertrude Ekvall, and Lois McShane won four
matches and lost two. During the 1925 season, when the tennis courts gave
way to the new chapel building, they practiced on private courts.[37]

Not only baseball, tennis, and track occupied students' attention in the
spring. There was also the Annual Campus Day, to which many students,
freed from classes, looked forward. The 1924 event saw actual work done
not only by the "road and tree committees" but by "young ladies who
wielded rakes and hoes all day," their labors only briefly interrupted by "hot
dog" refreshments at ten o'clock provided by the residents of the "Red Castle."All workers were provided with a bounteous luncheon. The occasion
effected substantial savings for the College in service costs, provided fun
and exercise for the students, and brought a fresh and tidy look to the campus.

Controversy arises on every campus. Sometimes it is light and amusing,
sometimes serious; occasionally there is a fusing of both elements. Early in
1924 the *Record* editor noted that the *Chicago Herald and Examiner* had
carried a feature story with the headline: "Split on Hair at Wheaton," saying
that "the rock on which Wheaton College is split is a hair. A hair's length, to
be precise. Half the co-eds—the bobs—don't speak to the other half—the
unbobs." The *Record* had headed the story: "News Dailies Give College
Black Eye." The student writer acknowledged that there was some difference of opinion on the matter but that the story was distorted and greatly
exaggerated.[38] In an earlier edition of the campus paper the editor had commented on the tendency for some students to say "Oh, so and so had her
hair bobbed. She's fickle all right." Deploring the generalization he wrote:
"Is a girl any the worse afterwards than before? Do the shears sever her religion?"

Academic Tone

During the later years of his life, when he was often away from the campus, President Blanchard relied increasingly on the small, closely knit faculty for the effective operation of the College and the preservation of the
institution's unique environment. Numerous instructors came and went after a brief tenure at Wheaton. Others, like Professors Dow, Straw, Blaine,
and Smith gave the College a core of stability and continuity that did much
to establish Wheaton's distinctive character. Professor Herman A. Fischer,
long Charles Blanchard's closest counselor, had terminated his responsibilities as vice-president and professor of German in 1920, though he remained
as college treasurer. Known to all the students, the faculty were friendly and
helpful, but there was no organized counseling program to usher students

through their college careers; they were on their own, even in registration. Many a graduate of this era would later acknowledge, often with a measure of pride, that he went through college without a single counseling session. The faculty were devoted to their subjects, relied strongly on the lecture method, and published little, except in religious journals and denominational papers.

Many Wheaton students found their values shaped and their commitments stabilized through their exposure to the magnetic and imaginative teaching of professors like Elsie Dow and Darien Straw. Warm-hearted scholars of unusual perception, they had been serving Wheaton since the 1880s. Under their tutelage students learned for the first time to think in terms of large ideas, discovering how to enrich their lives through clear thinking, wide reading, and honest commitment to Jesus Christ. The world was never quite the same after one had studied Shakespeare and Browning with Dr. Dow and logic and rhetoric with Darien Straw. Once a young man who had been invited to teach a part term in history asked Dr. Dow if she thought he knew enough to teach. "Of course not," she replied, "no one ever does. But you can go on learning. The teacher should be the best learner in the class." Perhaps, only she was much known beyond the campus, a fact attested to when Lawrence College awarded her a Litt.D. in 1922. When she began her teaching at Wheaton a single course in literature was offered. By 1925 there were sixteen courses in English and American literature, most of which she taught by offering them in alternate years. With great devotion to her students, she taught at Wheaton for fifty-three years, retiring in 1942. Her sudden death occurred on the Sunday morning of Homecoming weekend in October 1944.

Professors Dow and Straw, together with Professor Smith, who taught Greek, probably made the program in literature, logic, and language the strongest in the College. Study in public speaking and expression with Florence Cobb was regularly in demand. In 1925 there were thirteen courses in Greek, extraordinary for a college of 350 students. In Latin, taught for many years by Harriet G. Blaine, there were also thirteen courses, indicating a continuing devotion to the classical liberal arts curriculum. French, German, and Spanish rounded out this rich program of language study.

From the earliest days of the College, Bible was taught more from a philosophical than doctrinal perspective. Students were required, as late as 1925, to take only one hour a semester in Christian evidences and Bible themes, courses for many years taught by Dr. Dow and Dr. Straw. In 1925 Edith C. Torrey, daughter of evangelist Reuben Archer Torrey, became the first full-time Bible instructor at Wheaton and, although she lacked advanced training in theology and biblical studies, was much admired as a teacher by many students. Under her direction such courses as Bible Survey, Life of Christ, Old Testament History and Prophecy, and the Apostolic Age made their appearance.

With the organization of departments in 1917, Bible was grouped with philosophy; and in the number of course offerings the two studies were given about equal attention. The work in philosophy, long carried by President Blanchard, was transferred in the fall of 1925 to Professor Hervin U. Roop, whose offerings were essentially surveys; courses in ethics and theism were senior requirements for over three decades. A course titled Present-day Philosophy introduced the student to such thinkers as Hegel, James, Dewey, Bergson, Royce, Bradley, Russell, and Croce.[39] Psychology was under the direction of the philosophy department. Until two years before his death, the course was taught by Dr. Blanchard, whose convictions led him to continued support of the outmoded faculty psychology, perhaps because it was theistic in viewpoint. He was fearful of some of the emerging behavioral sciences that seemed to minimize personal responsibility in human behavior. To confront some of those problems he was preparing a brief discourse on personal conduct, a work left unfinished at his death.[40]

The department of history was organized by Dr. Dow, whose conviction that English literature could not be taught without strong support in English history, is evident in that department's listings: two courses in European history, one in the history of civilization, four in American and six in English history, an imbalance that did not last long. History was offered together with social science, which then included elementary sociology, economics, and political science. Although Professor Earl Winsor's special training was in another field, he headed up the work in history in the early twenties until he was called to the mission field.

In the early years all of the sciences were grouped under the department of physical science: physics, mathematics, chemistry, astronomy, geology, and biology. Ultimately each of those disciplines was to achieve its own departmental status, but in the twenties there was a good bit of shifting about in departmental groupings, faculty assignments, and course structure. Perhaps that accounted for the fairly high turnover of instructors, particularly in chemistry. In 1923 biology and chemistry were under the direction of S. J. Bole. Listed in 1922 in a somewhat loose affiliation with science were three three-hour courses in agriculture—fruit growing, vegetable gardening, and farm crops—all terminated by faculty action in 1926.[41] With his appointment in 1919, S. J. Bole, who had a master's degree in science, brought strength to the work in biology by enlarging the course offerings and introducing a course designed to show the limits of evolution, a subject on which he gave off-campus lectures and wrote for the *Record*. Bole and his wife frequently traveled with student evangelistic groups in the summer, sharing their testimony and making new friends for the College.

Added to the science faculty in 1925 was L. A. Higley as assistant professor of chemistry, who, with a Ph.D. from the University of Chicago, was the first full-time faculty member to hold that advanced degree. Nearly everyone had an M.A. degree from an established university and six teachers had honorary degrees. Higley brought new strength to the work in science at Wheaton and encouraged the development of field work in geology and biology. J. W. Doolittle, professor of physics and astronomy, had joined the faculty in 1919, following his return from the mission field in China after his wife's death there. Mathematics, taught for many years until 1918, by Professor Herman A. Fischer, offered the familiar elementary courses and advanced work through calculus and differential equations.

The education department made noteworthy advances first under the direction of William F. Rice, a former school superintendent who had done graduate work at the University of Wisconsin and was appointed Professor of Education in 1916. Carl D. Garlough, who had come to Wheaton as a mathematics teacher in 1915, and also served as registrar following Dr. Dow, taught the psychology of learning. Enock Dyrness, of the class of 1923, with an M.A. in education from the University of Chicago, joined the faculty in 1924, bringing fresh ideas to the department.

The Death of President Blanchard

In 1925 President Blanchard was seventy-seven years old. Yet no successor had been designated and no search had been initiated to find one. When W. H. Griffith-Thomas, a widely known and much admired British Bible teacher, then living in Canada, had been invited in 1923 to join the faculty, it had been with the thought of his coming into the presidency; but he had declined. During November 1925, Dr. Blanchard was unwell and suffered a mild heart attack at home, from which, according to his physician wife, he recovered after a few days' rest. But he accepted no more out-of-town appointments.[42] On December 16 he went with Mrs. Blanchard to Chicago to have "sittings" for the college annual. Two days later he made his last chapel talk as students were preparing to leave for the Christmas holidays. Of that occasion one freshman student later wrote: "The President sat on the platform, an impressive figure with snow white hair and classic features but with a face that was filled with love for the students before him. He arose and began to talk to us about our conduct during the vacation days and particularly of the need for keeping close to God."[43]

Sunday, December 20, was clear and crisp; the Blanchards had a leisurely breakfast, after which they sang together "My Jesus, As Thou Wilt." Charles Albert excused himself from Sunday school attendance and promised to join his wife for church later, intending to prepare remarks for the funeral of Eva Lundgate, a missionary friend, who was to be buried that afternoon. When Mrs. Blanchard returned home, she found her husband lying on the floor. "At first glance I thought he was asleep, he looked so natural. Then I knew. It was his coronation day."[44]

Students, at home in various parts of the country for the holidays, learned of the death of their leader and friend by mail with a small white card edged in black: "It is with a deep sense of loss that we announce the home-going of our beloved President, Charles A. Blanchard, on Sunday, December 20th. Funeral services will be held at the New College Chapel on Wednesday, December 23, at 2 p.m." A telegram of sympathy to Mrs. Blanchard from R. A. Torrey, summed up what many friends and co-workers felt:

Deepest sympathy from Mrs. Torrey, Edith and me. Charles Blanchard was one of my dearest and most highly esteemed friends. He had a mind marvelously strong and keen, learning of unusual strength and fullness, a rare power of clear and forceful expression of his thoughts, singularly deep and well balanced piety and love for God and Man, seldom equalled.[45]

The funeral service was held in the new chapel, so recently completed and so much the consequence of President Blanchard's efforts, with College Church pastor John W. Welsh officiating. In spite of a December storm, a large company assembled to hear tributes and expressions of esteem from the City Council, the Business Men's Association, Northern Baptist Seminary, the Board of Trustees, and from the college faculty, read by Dr. Straw, who had joined the faculty in the same year Charles Blanchard became president. The congregational hymn was "My Jesus, As Thou Wilt." Speaking on the text, "For he was a good man and full of the Holy Ghost and of faith,"[46] Dr. P. W. Philpott, pastor of Moody Church, brought the message for the occasion. Dr. W. B. Riley, who had come from Minneapolis, also spoke in tribute to the memory of his gifted and beloved friend of many years, "a great Christian man." A faculty-student memorial service was held in the chapel on January 12, 1926, with Miss Edith Torrey offering the opening prayer. Professor Dyrness read several letters addressed to Mrs. Blanchard; and Henry Coray, president of the Student Council, read the resolutions of the student body. After brief tributes by a representative from each class, Miss Dow spoke on "The Inner Man."

And so for President Blanchard the journey was over, the stewardship was completed, the accounting had been made. A resolution of the Executive Committee of the Board of Trustees of the College observed that "in addition to his life-long ministry in the local community and college, there has been his nation-wide ministry, as author, Bible teacher, and executive. He served as president and secretary of the National Christian Association for many years; president of the Chicago Hebrew Mission; vice president of the Christian and Missionary Alliance; and faithful officer and friend of numerous missionary and philanthropic organizations."

A resolution of the college faculty adopted on December 21, 1925, declared what a multitude of students, alumni, friends of Wheaton College, and Christian leaders believed when it said in part: "Resolved, that we recognize in his departure the passing of one who, so far as human instrumentality is concerned, is chiefly responsible for bringing Wheaton College to its present condition of influence and usefulness in equipping young people for their largest values in this world."

A splendid bronze bust, sculptured by Holger Jensen and Helen Webster Jensen, '21, was presented to the College by the Alumni Association at Homecoming in 1948. For many years located in the lobby of Blanchard Hall, it now rests in the Nicholas wing of Buswell Library.

PRESIDENT JAMES OLIVER BUSWELL, JR., 1926-1940

CHAPTER 7

James Oliver Buswell, Jr., Scholar President

THE TRANSITION PERIOD FOLLOWING PRESIDENT BLAN-
chard's death was fraught with uncertainty. What was to be the direction of
Wheaton College after the passing of its revered, long-time leader? Would
the institution liberalize its doctrinal and cultural positions in order to attract a broader base of support at a time when Wheaton's financial structure
was somewhat insecure?[1] Some individuals who had watched the College's
growth over a number of years wondered if it would survive at all.
Wheaton, they said, was a product of the Blanchards' efforts, a family affair; the loss of that distinguished name was likely to prove a mortal wound.
The trustees, well aware of those expressions of alarm, made prompt decisions to assure continuity of leadership. Confident that God's providential
hand had guided the College up to that time as an institution dedicated to
his service, they were sure that his favor would not be withdrawn now.

Charles Blanchard had often prayed in effect: "Lord send me a successor
who will serve Wheaton College in my place when I am gone."[2] To meet the
immediate need for new leadership, the Executive Committee of the Board
of Trustees met at the LaSalle Hotel in Chicago on December 30, 1925, and
chose one of their own members, Dr. John Welsh, pastor of College Church,
to serve as acting president until a successor could be named. Shortly after
the students' return from their Christmas holiday, L. L. McShane, vice president of the Board of Trustees, presented Dr. Welsh to the student body in a

morning chapel service, urging them to give loyal support to their new leader. As evidence of their confidence, students rose to their feet before Welsh began his brief address in which he pledged to carry on the work and principles of Dr. Blanchard.[3]

On January 31, 1926, the minister of Grace Reformed Church in Brooklyn, New York, James Oliver Buswell, Jr., began a week of special services in the Wheaton College chapel. "He is a man of calm and deliberate thinking who is not given to emotionalism," wrote a student reporter midway through the week. "No one will be fanned into a burst of religious fervor under his preaching."[4] In the Friday morning chapel a request signed by many students was presented to the faculty urging that Buswell be invited to continue the meetings through a second week, a request graciously declined by the visitor, who had pressing business in Brooklyn. Buswell had made a strong impression on students and faculty alike. "His themes," said the *Record* the week after his visit, "were usually doctrinal, but not the cold, intellectual theology which clings about many preachers today. They were warm and vibrant with the practicality of a young man who knows what youth need."[5] While Buswell was on campus and during the days immediately following, several faculty members, particularly Dr. Elsie Dow, began to consider him as a person eminently prepared to become Wheaton's third president.

The Executive Committee of the Board of Trustees now moved swiftly to fill the office which had been vacant for only six weeks. Meeting at the LaSalle Hotel on February 16, 1926, they voted to invite James Oliver Buswell, Jr., to become president of the College. The decision was not unanimous. Acting president Welsh proposed Wendell Brooks, dean of Northwestern University, as a well-qualified candidate. When Welsh's recommendation found no support among the committee, he requested that his vote be recorded as negative.[6] Three days later the Executive Committee met in the president's office. Trustees present were J. W. Welsh, L. L. McShane, Nicolas Johnson, George W. McGill, and Howard Irwin. In addition, "Members of the teaching staffs of both College and Academy and Mr. Herman A. Fischer, Jr., Assistant Attorney of the College, were present by special invitation."[7]

Each of the trustees expressed his approval of "Rev. Buswell for President of the college—excepting Trustee Welsh, who declared that most of the Board of Trustees were not qualified to select the President," perhaps implying that among the nineteen trustees—bankers, merchants, publishers, and clergymen—there was not a single educator. The "leading members" of the faculty of the College and Academy, however, "expressed confidence in the judgment and ability of the Trustees and their willingness to support Rev. Buswell as President if elected."[8] At that point members of the faculty withdrew and the committee continued in executive session, at which it agreed to recommend to the Board of Trustees the election of James Oliver Buswell, Jr., within thirty days at a special meeting of the full Board. Acting president Welsh's proposal that the choice of a president be delayed for six months did not gain a second, nor did his next request for a six weeks' delay. The afternoon meeting concluded with the appointment of Trustees McShane, Johnson, and Irwin "as a committee to notify Mr. Buswell of the action taken."[9]

Since it seemed to the Executive Committee that Welsh was out of accord with the sentiments of the committee, they terminated his services as acting president of the College at a meeting on March 5. Probably to their surprise, Professors Dow, Smith, and Straw were designated to operate the College until the new president was chosen, a brief interim that proved to be less than a month. The full Board met in Chicago on March 3, 1926, to act on the resolution from the Executive Committee. Acceptance of the report was recommended by Trustee Welsh and the trustees unanimously agreed to call James Oliver Buswell, Jr., to begin his service on April 1, 1926. There is no evidence of extended discussions between the Board and the president-elect in which he was given a mandate to produce declarations of goals, statements of purpose, and plans for an exhaustive self-study—all dear to the hearts of contemporary boards and administrators.

Preparation of James Oliver Buswell, Jr.

James Oliver Buswell, Jr., was born January 16, 1895, in Burlington, Wisconsin, the son of a Congregational minister. The Buswell line had established itself in New Hampshire in colonial times after emigrating from Scotland. Following the familiar route through the Erie Canal and Great Lakes by steamer, the first family member to enter the Midwest was a school teacher who arrived on the shores of southern Wisconsin and claimed land a few miles west of Racine. To James Oliver Buswell, Sr., and his wife eleven children were born, one of whom was Wheaton's future president.

The elder Buswell had attended Hillsdale College, in Hillsdale, Michigan, and after graduation was ordained a Congregational minister. While engaged in evangelistic work, he had met and married Emeline Parker, daughter of a Congregational minister. In 1899 he moved with his family to Mellon, Wisconsin, an area little influenced by the work of the church, to begin home mission work. Saloon operators and lumberjacks frequently opposed the work, on several occasions even imperiling the lives of family members. Once while the father was away on an evangelistic trip among the lumber camps, an arsonist set fire to the family home, recently completed on a farm two miles from Mellon. The fire left the mother and eleven children homeless on a night when the temperature dropped to forty degrees below zero.[10] Sheltered temporarily by a neighbor, the Buswell family then moved into a former saloon, the only vacant building they could find in Mellon, and set about transforming it into a rescue mission.

The story of the family's plight as a consequence of the fire was so widely reported by the press, that many contributions were sent to support the home mission work in northern Wisconsin. Encouraged, the young minister labored with new energy to establish several churches in Mellon and the surrounding coutryside. Eventually the home mission work was taken over by the Presbyterian Church in the U.S.A., a body to which Buswell then transferred his allegiance.

James Oliver and Emeline Buswell's children included four sons and seven daughters. The eldest of the sons was Arthur, a chemist, at one time head of the Illinois State Water Survey, later a professor of chemistry at the University of Illinois. Second was Calvin, a medical officer in World War I, later a medical missionary in China. Youngest of the sons was Karl, who also went to China as a missionary, and later joined the Navy as a chaplain during World War II. While standing on the bridge of his aircraft carrier, Karl was killed on Christmas Eve 1943, having been hit by a wing fragment from a plane that crashed on landing.

Eventually the family left the rugged life of the north woods to establish an office for home missions work in Minneapolis. There young Buswell ran for the presidency of his senior class at West High, Minneapolis, on a "no dance" platform; and much to his amazement he won. His class yearbook of West High named him first as the most studious boy, second as the handsomest, and third as the most popular!

A family debate developed as to whether he should go to a nearby liberal denominational college or to the state university after his high school graduation. His father urged the university. In his "Reflections on My 'Liberal' Education," President Buswell commended his father's choice. Much later he wrote: "A pagan state university, where there is no reason for quibbling, provides a much more wholesome atmosphere for young men than a denominational college where Christian phrases and terms are used with non-Christian meanings."[11]

As a member of the Student Volunteer Band at the university, James attended a convention in Kansas City in 1914 where he resolved to become a foreign missionary, "though God, through ways known to himself, has kept me out of the foreign field."[12] From the middle of his freshman year until his graduation from the university, he served as a supply pastor, but also found time to make the varsity wrestling team in the heavyweight class. He was graduated from the University of Minnesota with an A.B. in economics in 1917.

The United States had become involved in World War I in the spring of 1917, and Buswell resolved to become a chaplain. He enrolled at the University of Chicago Divinity School during the summer, and in the fall he entered McCormick Theological Seminary in Chicago to continue his seminary training. On April 3, 1918, the Minneapolis Presbytery of the Presbyterian Church in the U.S.A. ordained him.

His training completed, he wasted no time in marrying Helen Spaulding, who had attended his father's church and had lived abroad for a number of years. The Buswells had planned to commit their lives to missionary work in Africa, but with the coming of the war, James requested commissioning in the National Army of the American Expeditionary Forces. The young chaplain was sent abroad in the fall of 1918, where he helped to initiate Bible classes, planned Sunday services, and began Sunday schools.[13] Of this period of his army service, Buswell wrote: "Just before the Meuse-Argonne offensive we were billeted in Camp Marquette for about five days. Everyone knew that we were going into a drive; the spirit of soberness was in the air. We had a revival there. . . . About thirty-five presented themselves for baptism, and in two days about a hundred and fifty men came to see one or the other of us, the two regimental chaplains, stating that they wanted to be known as Christian men."[14]

In the great Battle of the Meuse-Argonne, which began September 26, 1918, and became a turning point of the war, many of the men who had asked for Christian instuction were killed or wounded. Chaplain Buswell's own leg wound from shrapnel sent him to the hospital for three months. For bravery in the line of duty he was awarded the Silver Star and the Purple Heart and was eventually presented with the medals at a special ceremony for then President Buswell and other ex-servicemen, on March 17, 1934, at an evening gathering in the Wheaton College chapel, sponsored by the College History Club and the local post of the American Legion.[15]

Following the war Buswell served Perseverance Presbyterian Church in Milwaukee while continuing his theological studies at the University of Chicago and McCormick Theological Seminary. In 1922 he accepted a call to Grace Reformed Church in Brooklyn and continued there until his call to Wheaton College. In 1923 he was awarded a B.D. degree by McCormick Theological Seminary, and in 1924 an M.A. degree by the University of Chicago.

A New President for Wheaton

President Buswell arrived on the Wheaton scene at the end of March, beginning his responsibilities on April 1, 1926, a coincidence that he referred to as an April Fool's joke. He was warmly welcomed by the 377 students then enrolled. The family was established in a college residence at 620 College Avenue, where Mrs. Buswell set about making the fourth home of their marriage, for her husband and three children: Jane, 7, born in Minneapolis, James, 4, born in Milwaukee; and Ruth, 2, born in Brooklyn. John, the youngest, was to arrive a year later amid hearty congratulations to the parents from students and faculty, and the clanging of the Tower bell.

From the beginning the new young president impressed everyone with his friendliness, energy, and desire to strengthen the position of the College financially and academically, while preserving its historic Christian testimony. His handsome appearance and strong body, which he kept in good enough trim to occasionally take on members of the College wrestling team, were impressive. Whether striding across campus or through Blanchard Hall, he always moved swiftly—as if there were a genuine urgency to his mission. He enjoyed being a participant in student life, played in student-faculty basketball and baseball games, wore a green dink along with freshmen, led cheers at college pep rallies, and joined in the fun at Washington Banquets and on other social occasions.

Since Buswell's appointment as president carried with it the assignment of J. P. Williston Professor of Religion and Philosophy, his engagement with students at an intellectual level was assured. That academic chair, formerly held by both Blanchards, required him to teach one-hour senior courses in ethics and theism, both relevant to the times in their emphasis on faith and right conduct. His lifelong disposition to assess ideas philosophically was evident from the beginning. In his *Reflections on My Liberal Education*, Buswell offered a broad definition of theism as "that doctrine of God which regards him as a conscious self-determining personality, capable of willing and performing acts *in the physical world which are not determined by mechanical nature.* Anyone who does not regard God thus as a *Personal Original Cause* ought in honesty to refrain from calling himself a theist."[16]

James Oliver Buswell, Jr., was inaugurated as the third president of Wheaton College during commencement week ceremonies in 1926. On Tuesday afternoon, June 15, the trustees, college faculty, and twenty-four representatives from a number of colleges and universities—including Buswell's brother Arthur from the University of Illinois—formed a processional at Ladies' Hall and marched to the college chapel. From the community of Wheaton, Mayor M. J. Pittsford brought greetings. Lewis Sperry Chafer, of Dallas, spoke for the theological seminaries, E. G. Burritt, president of the Illinois Federation of Colleges, brought the congratulations of that group, and Don. O. Shelton, President of the National Bible Institute, New York, represented the Bible schools. From the faculty, Professor Darien Straw offered words of encouragement and support. Hamilton Sinclair, president of the senior class, assured the new president of student prayers and cooperation.

In his brief remarks Lewis Sperry Chafer spoke of Wheaton College as "one of the very few colleges which are as yet unspoiled by the blighting touch of rationalism and unbelief...I am convinced that Wheaton is just now coming to her greatest day of service and is about to harvest the seed-sowing of these many years."[17] President Buswell's inaugural address noted the loss of personal morality and the rise of hedonism since the war. Devotion to orthodox Christianity had waned in academic quarters, and among believers there was regrettable quarreling. "But if in the progress of events men prove incapable of discussing vital subjects without quarreling, shall we then cease to discuss such subjects? That were indeed a strange policy." He believed that unseemly controversy was not "characteristic of the conservative type of Christianity represented by Wheaton College." He stood resolutely for the whole testimony of Wheaton College. "Today I came with many misgivings as to my qualifications, to this position of responsibility and opportunity," he said. "No man living is sufficient in himself for such a task; least of all am I. But with the help of God and by the prayers of God's people, I shall keep the faith, that the light of Christian truth may shine forth in the earth, until He comes."[18]

The following day President Buswell presided at his first commencement, at which T. T. Shields of Toronto was the speaker. Recipient of an honorary Doctor of Divinity degree was Lewis Sperry Chafer of the Evangelical Theological College in Dallas, Texas. A year later Dr. Chafer invited President Buswell to be the commencement speaker in Dallas, when Wheaton's president received the first Doctor of Divinity degree granted by that institution.

Wheaton Achieves Accreditation

President Buswell recognized some of Wheaton's needs at once and moved quickly to meet them. At the first meeting of the Executive Committee of the Board of Trustees after his arrival the Board voted, with his urging, "that heads of departments be requested to furnish data necessary to meet the standards of Illinois, and the North Central Association, as accrediting bodies, this data to be furnished to President Buswell." They further voted that "the efforts of President Buswell to bring the college up to an A standing with the University of Illinois and the North Central Association be approved." With trustee authorization, the president initiated faculty studies and exchanges of correspondence with the University of Illinois. In August of his first year he was able to announce to donors and friends of the College: "I have good news from the Registrar of the University of Illinois. It has been the custom of the University of Illinois to subtract one credit out of fifteen from our students going there for graduate work, but I have assurance that in another year our credits will be accepted hour for hour." At the same time the constituency of the College needed assurance that recognition by the state university would mean that Wheaton could retain "without equivocation its fundamentalist doctrinal position."[19]

In 1928 President Buswell initiated a "Forward Movement" drive to secure one million dollars to be added to the endowment, which had never exceeded $600,000. The goal was achieved by December 1929, two months after the collapse of the stock market and the onset of the Great Depression, which wiped out the resources of thousands of Americans. The importance of the endowment in the accreditation process was seen late in 1926, when "it seemed that Wheaton College must send home about fifty students because of the endowment rule of the North Central Association"[20] (requiring a minimum sum of endowment for each student). A bequest from the estate of a Texas businessman, Ernest M. Powell, however, together with gifts from other friends, met the immediate need.

When Carl M. Garlough, professor of mathematics and registrar, died suddenly at Thanksgiving in 1927, President Buswell named Professor Enock Dyrness, then teaching education courses and serving as acting dean of the Academy, to become the new registrar and "to take whatever steps are necessary to secure full accreditation for the college."[21] Regional accreditation by the North Central Association had been granted in 1913. In 1927 the Class A rating by the University of Illinois promised President Buswell the year before was granted, and in 1931 inclusion in the Association of American Universities was won. Approval by the American Association of University Women soon followed, allowing Wheaton's women to hold membership in that organization.

One day while searching through the college archives, President Buswell came upon Jonathan Blanchard's original plan for the main building, at that time completed except for the east wing. He suggested that the proposal for a Blanchard Memorial Building, to be completed by November 8, 1926, in honor of Charles Blanchard's seventy-eighth birthday, be set aside. Instead, he urged that an east wing to be known as the Blanchard Memorial be added to the Main Building. Shortly before Christmas 1927, the work on the new addition was finished, opening nine new offices—one for each department—together with much needed classroom space.

The stately gray limestone building was at last complete, looking much like the structure Jonathan Blanchard had envisioned and had sketched for the 1868 catalog of the College. According to DeWitt Jayne, first chairman of the art department, the original plan for Blanchard Hall was drawn by Maria Blanchard Cook, Blanchard's daughter, and was a modified copy of the original Haskall Hall at the University of Chicago. On November 14, 1979, the State of Illinois and the United States Department of the Interior National Park Service listed Blanchard Hall in the National Register of Historic Places. The state commission, which made the recommendation for listing, noted that though the building was completed in five stages, it kept its architectural integrity. "Blanchard Hall," they further wrote, "is notable for its use of Italianate and Romanesque styles. Most college architecture was highly Victorian, Gothic, or classical in the 1850s and 1860s." The weathered tower of Blanchard, its American flag whipping in the breeze, is a symbol of the College to alumni and friends around the globe.

The entire Main Building soon became known as Blanchard Hall. Enlargement of academic facilities allowed for a steadily increasing student body in the College, even during the Depression. Enrollment reached 646 in 1930; 805 by 1935, and 1,085 in 1939, Dr. Buswell's last year. Early in his administration the president had once remarked: "I don't see any reason why we can't have a thousand students."[22]

George V. Kirk, an able executive from Moody Bible Institute, became President Buswell's assistant in financial planning and, as vice president of business administration, did much to bring fiscal stability to the College. In correspondence with Kirk, Buswell noted that "our salaries at the present time are low. Our heads of departments receive the maximum of "3,000 per year. My own salary is, I think, about that of the teachers on the Moody Bible Institute faculty."[23] Joining Kirk in the inner council of presidential advisors were Enock Dyrness, by then vice president in academic administration, and Wallace Emerson, appointed dean of students in 1932. Emerson left Wheaton in 1940 to become president of Trinity College, later Westmont College.

The Russell Study

Any college that aspires to become a quality institution will engage in continuous self-examination, both by its own administration and faculty members and by authorities outside the institution. In 1933 President Buswell, and a faculty committee, headed by Professor Enock Dyrness, with the approval of the faculty and the Board of Trustees, initiated a thorough institutional study under the direction of John Dale Russell, associate professor of education at the University of Chicago. Professor Russell, together with four graduate students, began assembling their survey data in December 1933, and made many subsequent trips to the campus to consult with administration and faculty and observe the academic process at work. The final report, 265 pages with thirty-five charts, was presented in May 1934, under the title, *Report of a Survey of Wheaton College.* Twelve areas were evaluated, including internal administration, faculty, program of studies, library, student personnel, services, revenues and expenditures, and endowment.

The report listed fifty-six points of strength at Wheaton and fifty-five areas of weakness. Ninety-seven suggestions for strengthening the College and its program were given. Among the points of strength were the *esprit de corps* of the faculty, the good physical facilities for much of the program, the fact that important steps were being taken to improve the educational and personnel services for students, the unusual drawing power of Wheaton's claims and objectives, and the promotional work of the president, faculty, student musical groups, and alumni. Among the weaknesses were administrative organization, physical plant equipment, arrangements for faculty advancement and growth, inadequate library space and insufficient annual book acquisitions, and inadequate endowment. Attention was called also to the average age of the faculty—"significantly higher" than in comparable institutions.

Many of the committee's recommendations were concerned with administrative supervision of the College's departments, and with responsibilities of the faculty members and benefits due them, since the College had no group insurance and no adequate pension plan. A new library should be given priority as the next building project—a recommendation that required sixteen years to fulfill. In the future—to conform with then-current practice—no faculty member should serve on the Board of Trustees, a proposal prompted, no doubt, by the fact that Dr. Straw had served as secretary to the Board for many years.

Some recommendations did not meet Wheaton's objectives, such as the call for a reduction of courses in Greek, Bible, and philosophy. Inappropriate, too, was the committee's urging that the training of elementary teachers be abandoned in favor of concentrated effort in the training of high-school teachers. In the years since the committee filed its report, Wheaton has trained over two thousand elementary teachers. In general, however, the report was enthusiastically received, and systematic efforts were begun to adopt many of the proposals. "We expect," wrote the registrar of the College, "to be working on the recommendations for several years."[24] Though it had a considerable way to go, Wheaton was determined to move toward quality performance through self-study and external prodding such as the Russell committee gave.[25] The improvements generated following the Russell study were among the numerous steps toward the widely acclaimed academic excellence Wheaton was to achieve.

Library Progress

Although the Russell committee saw the need for improved library services, the library had developed substantially since its beginning as a small collection of books, most of them owned by the literary societies, located in the back of the music room in the Main Building basement. Later it was moved to the back of the social science classroom, where poor lighting was hardly conducive to serious library use. For many years the librarian was appointed from among the faculty members, one of the early ones being the versatile Dr. Darien Straw. Growth was haphazard under a system by which the collection was enlarged mainly through gifts of books from the personal libraries of faculty members and friends of the College.

In 1889 the book collection numbered only 2,500 volumes, and the library was "open three hours every school day, that students may have abundant opportunity to use the books." In 1890 the library was moved to a larger, well-lighted room in the new addition of the Main Building, where it was possible, under the direction of Professor Elliot Whipple, for the library to fulfill its appropriate role in the college program. Through Whipple's efforts the library began to receive and classify government documents.

In 1912 Julia Blanchard, known to generations of students, faculty, and library staff members as "Miss Julia," became the first full-time librarian. By 1912 she had been out of college for eight years and was teaching in Plainfield, Wisconsin. During the summer she remembered her father saying to her, "Well, why don't you come into the library; that would be a change."[26] She quickly learned that in addition to supervising the book collection, then 6,000 volumes, she was required to buy the bookstore, a small operation in the rear of the building.

When the east wing was added to the Main Building, then renamed Blanchard Hall, the new area housed a number of faculty offices as well as the library. Named Frost Memorial Library, in honor of John Laurence Frost, his parents' gifts made possible an excellent reference library, supplementing the general collection.[27] In 1936, when crowded conditions in the stacks and reading room had become acute, the trustees assigned to the library the former Fischer Chapel and adjacent rooms located in the center of the building. The new arrangement lasted for more than a decade.

President Buswell's continuing effort to improve Wheaton's academic performance led in 1939 to inviting E. W. McDiarmid, one of the Russell committee members, to examine the library and make recommendations. Library expenditures were below desirable standards, reported McDiarmid; student rather than professional help was too extensively used; a system of direct student access to all books should be instituted; and the faculty was urged to study library resources in detail to make the library more truly the heart of the college academic program.

Varied Faculty Interests

During the years 1935 to 1940 a wide spectrum of academic interests engaged the faculty in their weekly meetings, all with a view to improving instruction and student-welfare programs. Reports, symposiums, and addresses highlighted the regular weekly faculty sessions. Instructors examined such subjects as trends in higher education; current trends in philosophy and psychology; Christian emphasis in literature, languages, writing, and the sciences; raising the general cultural standards; Wheaton's position on evolution; and the contribution of anthropology to Christian education. After a year of study by a faculty committee headed by Professor Lauren King, senior comprehensive examinations were introduced in 1938.

Another evidence of intellectual growth was the appearance of the *Faculty Bulletin,* under the editorship of Dr. Lauren King, the witty, popular professor of English. At first the *Bulletin* was a monthly journal of administration announcements, committee reports, book reviews, briefings on what other colleges were doing, and personal notes within the faculty family— "Dr. Wright reports that Marjorie (his firstborn) has begun kindergarten." Emphasis on the college community as a family, sharing concern for each others' needs, was still strong during the Buswell era.

In the first issue of the *Faculty Bulletin* a brief note from the editor declared: "The one aim of the *Bulletin,* as I understand it, is to stimulate us all to be better teachers. Since this cannot be accomplished without changes and soul-searching, you may expect that suggestions for change and soul-searching will appear from time to time." As the *Bulletin* passed from editor to editor through the years, particularly through the 50s and 60s, it became increasingly a scholarly journal, in which professors were encouraged to publish the fruits of their research. Gradually, however, interest in the publication waned; faculty members professed to be too busy to prepare articles; and the *Bulletin* expired in 1969.

For some time several members of the faculty and administration felt that a master's degree program should be initiated at Wheaton, especially for teachers, to give students the same quality of Christian graduate education they had had as undergraduates. Introduced in 1931, the program was short-lived; for a North Central Association evaluation committee, after several campus visits, issued a 29-page report in February 1937, concluding that the resources of Wheaton College—the library, science laboratories, teaching personnel—were not adequate for general graduate study.

Orlinda Childs Pierce Memorial Chapel.

President Buswell presiding at a morning service in Pierce Chapel. Student monitors in the aisles taking attendance.

CHAPTER 8

Through the Depression Years

IN ANNOUNCING PLANS FOR THE 1932 WASHINGTON BAN-
quet, at which Horace "Dit" Fenton, president of the senior class, was to
preside, the *Record* added: "In view of the depression and general lack of finances among students, the wearing of corsages is optional, but the classes
are advised to do away with them altogether." Small though the proposed
sacrifice was, it was a reminder of a darkening economic picture. Gone was
the vision of unending prosperity that with its hedonism dominated the
"roaring twenties". Instead, the country experienced closed banks, vast un-
employment—at one time as high as thirty percent—bread lines, ruined
businesses, dashed careers. People of large professional capability took me-
nial jobs in order to survive.

Not until the feverish effort of the Western nations to rearm in the face of
threats from Nazi Germany—and when the United States became a major
arms supplier—did clear-cut evidences of economic prosperity begin to re-
appear. Widespread adversity in the thirties caused the government to play
a much larger role in the lives of its citizens and many public institutions.
For Wheaton College those were sobering days, but many other liberal arts
colleges were more severely hurt by declining enrollments.

Students frequently had difficulty meeting financial obligations that
would seem inconsequential today. Faculty minutes for January 31, 1933,

note that "Professor Straw reported for the Committee on Student Accounts that a very large number of students were unable to register because they did not have the necessary funds for the $14.50 activities fee."[1] Students were given a three-week period of grace and "allowed to visit classes" until the fee was paid.

Although the College could hardly have anticipated the economic catastrophe of the 1930s, initiation of the Forward Movement Fund in May 1928 proved to have been a wise move. The successful completion of the campaign forestalled a severe economic crisis for the College. The original goal of the Forward Movement was $100,000; but in December 1928 the amount sought throughout the nation was raised to $500,000. Response from friends of the College came in cash, pledges, gifts of real estate, life annuity contracts, and estate promises. The trustees resolutely set their sights on securing a second half million dollars, much of which came from new friends of the College. Of thirty-six people who gave $5,000 or more, nineteen had never before made a gift to Wheaton. Many of those were undoubtedly drawn to Wheaton by its maturing academic capability and by its nationwide reputation as a theologically conservative institution.

During the thirties the budget showed remarkable financial growth. In 1930-31 the expenditures for the year were set at $270,835, which declined to $253,430 and $255,320 in 1933 and 1934. For the remainder of the decade the annual budget grew steadily and substantially, owing largely to the rapid growth of the student body, which more than doubled between 1930 and 1940. In 1935 the budget was $344,000; in 1936, $582,750; and by 1939 it had increased to $754,400. Finding themselves with a deficit in June 1939, the trustees initiated budget cuts of $40,000, achieved through reductions of campus services.[2] Coach Ed Coray remembers that there was only one stopwatch for men's and women's physical education and that his request for a second one was rejected.

As student enrollment grew, many facilities were severely taxed, the chapel among them. When the building was completed in 1925, there was a contractual agreement between the College and College Church that in the future the College might need to ask the church, after two years' notice, to find its own quarters. That the student body would outgrow the spacious chapel seemed a distant prospect; but in 1933, after only eight years of occupancy, the College gave notice to College Church that in 1935 joint occupancy of the building must end. The College agreed to compensate College Church for whatever equity it had in the building, and further agreed not to establish competing Sunday services in the building.

In the spring of 1935 a committee consisting of Carlton Fischer, for College Church, George V. Kirk, for the College and Allan Emery, as a third party, determined that the church's equity in the chapel building was $41,300, the sum to be paid in installments.[4] Balconies, each to seat 160 students, would be built on the north and south sides of the chapel, the work to be completed during the Christmas holidays. When Willis F. Pierce, a physician from California, offered to underwrite the cost of the balconies, Dr. Buswell agreed to name the chapel the Orlinda Childs Pierce Memorial Chapel, in memory of the benefactor's wife. Dedication services were held on Sunday, April 26, 1936.

Academic Emphasis

The quality of a college rests principally in the soundness and vigor of its academic program. Supplementary experiences enrich and enliven the students' days in academe; but learning, the stretching of the mind, responsible citizenship, and professional competence should be a college's primary concern. For a college like Wheaton, however, the foundation of learning has always been anchored in a Christian world and life view: of God, humankind, and nature.

Through the thirties Wheaton College kept unaltered its commitment to a liberal arts education, as it was then understood. The introduction of strictly vocational or technological courses was resisted, though one area resident offered to underwrite courses in printing. Administrators and faculty members contended that the liberal arts must prepare the student to enter a life that will have breadth, depth, and elevation—a life that, though increasingly dependent on technology, transcends technology's demands.

Departments of the College were grouped in six divisions in the thirties, an arrangement that continued for many years: Language and Literature; Bible, Philosophy, Psychology and Education; Music and Expression; Science and Mathematics; History and Social Science; Physical Education. Graduation requirements were intended to acquaint all students with the major fields of learning, giving them cultural enrichment that would serve them in whatever field they chose to enter. This, then, was the substance of a liberal education at Wheaton College: Bible, 8 hours; rhetoric, 6 hours; psychology, 3 hours; literature, 6 hours; science or mathematics, 14 hours (including one laboratory course); ethics and theism, 6 hours; history or social science, 6 hours; specialization in major field, 20 hours. The comparatively high requirement in science, instituted in 1932, represented an awareness of the increasing need for student understanding of scientific processes.

Four degree programs were offered: Bachelor of Arts, Bachelor of Science, Bachelor of Philosophy, and Bachelor of Music. The foreign language requirement was set by the various degree programs: two years of a modern language for science and philosophy, Latin for the arts. Except for the requirements in Bible and theism, the Wheaton curriculum was nearly identical with that of other small liberal arts colleges.

In English, students might choose from a rich diversity of twenty-five courses taught by a faculty of twelve. In history they could choose from sixteen courses taught by five professors. (In 1935 the history department had the largest number of majors.) In philosophy fifteen courses were offered, with Dr. Straw teaching logic and Christian philosophy. Forty-five courses were taught in science, divided among geology, chemistry, zoology, and botany. Education and psychology, with increasing numbers of students preparing to teach, offered twenty-eight courses with six teachers. Bible courses numbered only nine, but all students were required to take at least two of them. The newest addition to the curriculum, anthropology, listed thirteen courses, eight of which were taught by Professor Grigolia. The long-established foreign languages continued to be Greek, Latin, German, and French. For questing students asking "Where shall wisdom be found?" here was a perpetual feast.

During President Buswell's administration a substantial number of Ph.D.'s were added to the teaching staff. In 1925 there were five Ph.D.'s among the twenty-one faculty members, approximately 24 percent. By 1930 there were fourteen Ph.D.'s within the thirty-nine member faculty, or approximately 36 percent. By 1939, Dr. Buswell's last year, thirty-four Ph.D.'s among a faculty of sixty-nine brought the percentage to 49. One faculty member remembers having formerly approached the president of the College for a position while holding only a master's degree. "Go get your Ph.D. and then come to see me" was the response. The same professor, after having received his Ph.D, recalls having seen Dr. Buswell coming excitedly down the hall in Blanchard waving a set of papers and looking eagerly for Dean Emerson. He wanted to show him the credentials and letter of acceptance from Alexander Grigolia to teach at Wheaton[5] Dr. Grigolia had taught anthropology in Berlin and Paris and held a Ph.D. from the University of Pennsylvania.

In 1935, Dr. Buswell brought breadth of experience to the faculty by appointing eight new teachers to the College, trained at seven different graduate institutions: Dr. Henry Thiessen, Bible, from Southern Baptist Seminary; Dr. Joseph Free, archaeology, Princeton University; Dr. Lauren King, English, Ohio State University; Dr. Clarence Nystrom, speech, University of Iowa; Professor Clyde S. Kilby, English, University of Minnesota; Professor Lamberta Voget, sociology, University of Southern California; and instructors Ruth Berg, physical education, Northwestern University, and Angeline Brandt, mathematics, University of Michigan.

Faculty members have been drawn to Wheaton for a variety of reasons. All have believed that the College's commitment to Christian liberal arts is a sound philosophy of education; many have felt that the community is a good location to live in; others have been attracted by Wheaton's proximity to Chicago's cultural opportunities. Although salaries were not attractive in the 1930s, many teachers, seeing their service as a Christian ministry, were willing to live on a modest income. Some faculty members found a tuition rebate for their children a welcome benefit. Like other comparable institutions, Wheaton has had a normal faculty turnover, but many teachers have come to settle in for a long stay, a dedicated, hard-working group—giving unsparingly of their time to meet student needs—strongly interested in their own professional growth, and bringing distinction to the College by their writing and professional associations. '

"And Gladly Teach"

Of the Buswell faculty appointments twenty-four teachers completed more than two decades of service. Another ten stayed at Wheaton for more than a decade. Such long-term tenure helped to build institutional stability, allowed for effective long-range planning, and gave department programs continuity.

In 1926 Edward A. Coray, known to generations of students as Coach Coray, returned to campus, three years after his graduation from Wheaton, to take charge of all major sports. He coached successful basketball teams and served as athletic director during the substantial program development between 1926 and 1951. Subsequently, as executive director of the Alumni Association from 1951 to 1971, he was often referred to as "Mr. Alumni." On the alumni banquet circuit and elsewhere on campus, his wry humor, his devotion to Wheaton, and his Christian testimony are always evident.

Coming with a background of teaching and government service, Hawley O. Taylor joined the faculty as professor of mathematics in 1927. During his two decades at Wheaton, he taught mathematics, chemistry, and physics, and served as department chairman. In the same year Clarabelle Hiney began her work in education, later adding freshman writing to her responsibilities.

When Russell Mixter, '28, accepted an appointment to teach biology in 1928, it was the beginning of fifty-one years' service to his alma mater, many of them as department chairman. He also served as an auxiliary teacher of biology in the Wheaton West Suburban Hospital program, Oak Park. A believer in breadth of learning, Dr. Mixter liked to remind his colleagues, especially in the humanities, that his undergraduate major was English. As an early member of the American Scientific Affiliation, he became a specialist in the defense of the biblical view of creation and was long regarded as a campus authority on the subject. Except for Professor Straw, Russell Mixter had the longest teaching career of any instructor at Wheaton. Coming from the University of California, in 1935, Robert Cooke presided over the department of education in a time of expansion, when the demand for Wheaton-trained teachers brought job opportunities from all parts of the country.

Four long-termers arrived on campus in the fall of 1929: Paul M. Wright, '26; Effie Jane Wheeler, '19; Clarence Hale, '28; and Fannie Boyce. Dr. Wright taught both chemistry and geology at Wheaton, becoming head of the combined departments in 1944. When chemistry and geology were separated in 1963, he continued to direct the work in chemistry until 1969, one year before his retirement. Professor Wright was active in evaluation studies and had much to do with campus planning. With his encouragement, many students pursued careers in chemistry, geology, and medicine.

Clarence Hale, an outstanding teacher of Greek and French, served, as did several others, during three college administrations, retiring in 1975. Frequent trips abroad kept his French precise; diligent scholarship made him an effective teacher of Greek. Kindly, dependable, accurate—all are appropriate terms to characterize the academic performance, for thirty years, of Professor Fannie Boyce in mathematics. She was friend and counselor to many students.

Intensely devoted to her field of English literature, Effie Jane Wheeler, who as an undergraduate had been the first woman editor of the *Record*, had a vivacious personality and acknowledged teaching skill. Stricken with cancer at the end of her twentieth year as a Wheaton faculty member, she addressed a moving letter to the student body on Memorial Day 1949, two weeks before her death. "Please do not give a moment's grief to me. Think of me only happily, gaily as I think of you," she wrote. She assured the college family she would await their coming "in the Blessed Land."[6]

Fresh from completion of his doctoral studies in European civilization at Princeton, Joseph W. Free joined the faculty in 1935 and was to remain until 1966. Though he was employed to teach French, he soon moved into archaeology and established that department of the College. He and his wife Ruby initiated important archaeological excavations at Dothan in Israel in 1953, the first such effort undertaken by an American evangelical college. Clarence Nystrom, long-time teacher of speech and debate, and department chairman, another 1935 arrival, was a highly successful debate coach. Many of his teams won sectional and national honors, often competing against major universities. Lamberta Voget, hired first to teach German, soon moved into sociology, where she proved to be a stimulating teacher. She was a campus leader in encouraging interest in, and support for, minority groups. For many years she was the diligent and scrupulously accurate secretary to the faculty.

Clyde S. Kilby came to Wheaton, after graduate study at the University of Minnesota, to serve half-time in the English department and half-time as assistant to Dean Emerson. "Dr. Buswell and Dean Emerson were a great inspiration to me in those early years," Dr. Kilby later observed.[7] For sixteen years chairman of the English department, he evoked the admiration of students and the acclaim of scholars for his books and his work with the C. S. Lewis collection, later to be known as the Marion E. Wade Memorial Collection.

Ruth Berg, later Mrs. John Leedy, joined the faculty in women's physical education in 1935, after graduation from Chicago Normal College, and later from Northwestern University. As teacher, coach, and department chairman, she was an inspiring influence in the lives of a large number of Wheaton women. For her forty-one years' service to Wheaton, the new women's athletic field on University Place was named in her honor, and a brass plaque was affixed to a large boulder at the northwest corner of the field. The inscription notes that the plaque was placed "in recognition of a loved and respected teacher, counselor, friend and colleague" who "served Wheaton College with dedication and distinction." Angeline Brandt, professor of mathematics for thirty-three years, loved mathematics for its precision and its gratifying orderliness. Much as she loved her subject, she loved her students more, giving her time and energies to them unsparingly as counselor and friend.

In 1936, V. Raymond Edman arrived in Wheaton from Nyack Missionary Training College to teach history, little realizing that he was to play a larger role in the College's modern development. A popular teacher from the beginning, he moved to chairmanship of the department in 1939, then to the acting presidency of the College in 1940. Fred Gerstung, an able, friendly professor of German always retained something of the accent of his native Germany. Having arrived with his parents in Chicago as a boy of twelve, one month before the outbreak of World War I, he remained in the area all his life, teaching at Wheaton from 1936 to 1967. His courage, patience, and resolution were evident when he completed a second Ph.D. dissertation at University of Minnesota after discovering that his first topic had been covered by a graduate student elsewhere.

John L. Leedy, a faculty member for forty years, joined his father in teaching botany in 1937. The elder Leedy, John W., had come to Wheaton in 1929 at the age of sixty from the presidency of Marion College and remained for seventeen years. It was he who, with meager funds from the biology department, developed the long-familiar greenhouse next to the heating plant. In 1932 John L. Leedy and his father decided to take a trip. Uncertain as to whether they should go east to New Hampshire or west to the Black Hills, they resorted to a flip of a coin to establish their choice. West it was. On that trip they found the splendid mountain location which they subsequently recommended to Dr. L. A. Higley, then head of the chemistry department,[8] and which in 1935 became the Black Hills Science Station. The younger Leedy was a familiar figure on campus as he led his botany students around the grounds identifying trees and plants, or taught a popular noon-hour course often called "Lunch With Leedy."

With diligence and enthusiasm Robert C. Stone labored in the classical groves of Latin and Greek, undaunted by the knowledge that Latin was steadily declining in student favor on most campuses. Greek, however, at least at Wheaton, was holding its own, largely because of student interest in New Testament studies.

Other teachers who gave splendid service to Wheaton during the Buswell era included Orrin E. Tiffany, chairman of the history department, a fine scholar and academic leader. Born on the plains of the Dakota frontier, he came to Wheaton after teaching at Greenville College and Western Maryland, then serving as president of Seattle Pacific for ten years and Whitworth for three years. His wife, Katherine B. Tiffany, was an extraordinarily strong personality who brought a broad background of experience to her teaching in the English department. James B. Mack, a steady, competent scholar, came to the College in 1929 as chairman of the biology department.

Lauren King, a much respected teacher of literature, contributed to many campus efforts to encourage dedicated scholarship. Gordon H. Clark, soberly undemonstrative in all his ways, brought early distinction to the study of philosophy at Wheaton. DeWitt Jayne, '36, a fine artist, encouraged the College to accept art as a major contribution to a liberal arts education. Rebecca Price was praised by many devoted students as an unusually stimulating teacher of Christian education. Henry Thiessen skillfully directed the Bible department through a period of substantial growth in course offerings and was the first director of the Graduate School of Theology. Marian J. Downey, a 1923 graduate of the College, joined the faculty in 1934 and succeeded Dr. Dow as chairman of the Engish department. She left Wheaton to join Dr. Buswell when he became president of Shelton College. Peter Stam, an indefatigable laborer in many causes, commonly seen hurrying about the campus with armloads of papers, came to the College as manager of the student supply store. In 1934 he became director of the Conservatory, a post he held until 1948.

Internal Affairs of the Campus

Closely allied to salaries and service to the College was the retirement plan adopted by the Executive Committee of the Board of Trustees in 1935, and advocated by the North Central Association. Beginning in 1936 all college personnel were to retire at age seventy, though they could serve on an additional year-by-year basis by Board request until age seventy-five. Voluntary retirement was to be possible under a modest pension plan administered by the College. Several current elderly members of the faculty were exempted from those provisions: Dr. Dow, then 76; Dr. Straw, 79; Miss Blaine, 75.[9] In Miss Blaine's case the exemption was unnecessary; she had just resigned in 1936 and was given an annual pension of $750. The following year an improved pension program was adopted. It allowed retirees after age sixty-five an annual grant of $1,000, to be paid from an annuity fund to which the employee would contribute five percent of his or her annual salary and the College would contribute an equal amount.[10] Later in the year the trustees agreed to carry a $1,000 group insurance policy for each full-time faculty member, the amount to be reduced to $500 between the ages sixty-five and seventy, and to terminate entirely after age seventy.[11]

President Buswell was also constantly alert to ways of strengthening the administrative structure of the College, an area which, as the North Central Association had pointed out, needed improvement. In 1936 the Executive Committee approved his formation of a weekly executive council composed of Enock Dyrness, vice president in academic administration, George Kirk, president of business administration, Wallace Emerson, dean of students, and himself, the purpose of which was to facilitate the administration of college affairs.[12] President Buswell also suggested in the same year that "the officers of the college arrange with the officers of other colleges of similar size and circumstance to make exchange studies of the methods and practices followed in their respective institutions with a view of accomplishing improvements that would be helpful."[13]

Another of Dr. Buswell's innovations was the fall faculty retreat, held just before the opening of school, for academic discussion, instruction, spiritual fellowship, and recreation. The first was held on a rainy day in 1937 at Lake Geneva. One day was too brief a time, the administration readily recognized, and thereafter made the retreat a three-day event.

Meetings of the Executive Committee of the trustees, at which immediate problems were resolved and long-range policy was formulated for trustee approval, seem to have been quite congenial gatherings. The minutes of the sessions note that members often gathered in President Buswell's office "and after supper was served, the Committee was called to order by Chairman Fischer." Occasionally the routine was varied with a luncheon meeting at the Union League Club in Chicago or the Central Y.M.C.A. Sometimes daytime sessions were held in the Oak Park office of Robert E. Nicholas or at the office of Herman Fischer at Number 1 North LaSalle Street, Chicago.

At times the Executive Committee evaluated proposed grants to the College, offered with rather rigidly specified conditions. Such was a proposed but unaccepted contribution by a west coast friend in 1936. He required that if his gift were accepted, the College would not countenance any "doctrine contrary to the Scriptures of the Old and New Testaments, or to any doctrine expressly taught therein or to the doctrinal platform adopted by the Trustees of Wheaton College." If any violation of the agreement occurred, the sum of the grant was to be paid to the Moody Bible Institute. To give assurances to the donor that all conditions were being kept inviolate, the Reverend Harry Rimmer was to serve as Advisory Director of the endowment. Rimmer's duty was "to examine annually the soundness in Christian doctrine of the teachings of Wheaton College" and to report his findings to the donor, to the president of Wheaton College, and to the president of Moody Bible Institute.[14]

Members of the Executive Committee were always scrupulously careful keepers of the treasury. They set faculty salaries according to the president's recommendation and without a salary scale, fixed tuition, authorized expenditures for campus upkeep, and insisted on economies. One resolution in the minutes of July 21, 1936, recommends "that the Insull Utility Investments bonds, carried at $5,000 in the Endowment Fund, be written down to $1.00 and the loss be charged to Endowment Fund Surplus," a curious echo of the collapse of Samuel Insull's two billion dollar Middle West Utilities empire, with repercussions throughout the nation.[15] The minutes of the Executive Committee and the Board of Trustees, show clearly how these bodies were responsible for shaping the general policies of the College.

Minutes of the faculty give evidence of the development of the academic policy of that group. They suggest the range of concerns of the faculty, whose weekly meetings—preceded by tea—were always opened and closed with prayer. Occasionally there were unusual concerns, as indicated by faculty action in February 1933, requesting Governor Horner to enforce the Eighteenth Amendment, then being widely violated while the process of repeal of the Eighteenth Amendment by the Twenty-first Amendment was moving through the state legislature. Faculty members requested local merchants not to sell beer, and compiled a list of approved stores where beer would not be for sale.[16] That action aroused antagonism between the College and some community businesses; but before long, by local referendum, Wheaton chose to be a dry city, and at this writing continues to be.

The regulation of student conduct included the right of the faculty to approve a student's request to marry before completing college. Such requests, usually presented several times a year, were rarely denied. On October 25, 1932, one student asked for permission to marry but withdrew the request on December 13 "for economic reasons"—probably a casualty of the depression.

There were, of course, the lighter sides of otherwise serious business. In April 1938, the minutes note that the faculty meeting was opened with prayer by President Buswell, and the minutes were approved. A single item of business followed: "Dr. M. A. Stone moved that the meeting be adjourned to go to the baseball game. seconded by Dr. Higley, and carried."[17] Faculty members had their own social life, with seasonal parties, dinners in lower chapel, and year-end picnics. The fall faculty reception for freshmen and new students was a formal event, generally enjoyed by all, though the long reception line was sometimes a bit wearying. Prayer and praise services at Thanksgiving were part of a long tradition. In January 1938, the Faculty-Staff Dinner was announced at "75¢ per plate."[18]

Student Activities

Their financial resources severely limited, students for the most part stayed close to the campus in the thirties, participating in college activities for their fun and social life. Like generations of Wheaton students before them, they gave their enthusiasm to the literary societies, writing for the *Record* and *Tower*, taking part in musical groups, debate, athletics, oratorical and short story contests. They went to games and concerts, listened to lecturers, committed themselves in large numbers to the Christian concerns of the campus religious organizations. In the fall of 1935 the *Record* reported that "Wheaton's social life started with a 'bang' as the men staged their annual stag party sponsored by the League of Evangelical Students, while 'the women frolicked in the hay loft of the Stanton Stables,' an event promoted by the Women's Athletic Association."[19]

A triumph for the enterprising *Tower* editors was their bringing the United States Marine Band to campus in October 1938. "It is the biggest musical event that has ever taken place in DuPage County," said the *Record* editor, with youthful pride, "and Wheaton is the smallest city the band will visit on its tour." That this was to be a splendid occasion was suggested by the writer's opening paragraph: "In a blaze of scarlet glory and with a blast of trumpets the United States Marine Band will arrive in Wheaton at 1:00 at Roosevelt and Main. After the parade through the town the band will conduct its concerts at 3:00 P.M. and 7:45 P.M. in Pierce Chapel." The Marines returned to campus many times following their initial performance. Before the 1939 concert, the band leader was requested not to include any jazz among the encores; but the audience warmed up so enthusiastically to the music, the director later explained, that "Alexander's Ragtime Band" just popped out. One faculty member was seen to leave when the number began, but the lively music set many feet tapping, including those of several faculty members. Students loved it.

In another student-sponsored activity lecturers came with their stories of intrepid adventure in distant lands. In 1930, when nearly everyone had heard of Admiral Richard E. Byrd's Antarctic expedition, Larry Gould, Byrd's second in command, spoke of the largely unexplored region at the South Pole. Two years later Sir Hubert Wilkins showed moving pictures of his Arctic explorations.

Many candidates auditioned in the fall for a place in the Glee Club, but only the number necessary to complete the desired size for the organization was accepted. Beginning in 1932 through student initiative, the men's and women's clubs each made two trips a year, one at mid-year and one at spring vacation, singing at schools and churches, urban and rural. They were goodwill ambassadors for the College and for the cause of Christ. Each club presented a spring concert, still a campus highlight, and each had its year-end formal banquet.

In 1936 an informal debate arose on campus over the merits of the modes of travel students would use—car, bus, train, plane—when traveling home for Christmas vacation. Champions of the train, led by Harold Lindsell, seemed to have won, 2-1, contending that trains were cheaper and safer. Everett "Doc" Frohock, however, set forth the advantages of plane travel. "This is only the beginning, my friends" he declared. "Although I am beaten now, I will never admit defeat. Lindsell may have the upper hand today and in this generation; but this is a feud and in years to come, when America becomes air-minded, the name of Frohock will triumph." One unnamed student announced his intention to fly home.[20] One can understand Lindsell's faith in the railroad. The thirties were the age of the train; Chicago was the rail center of the nation, daily dispatching hundreds of trains to all parts of the country. Most Wheaton students who journeyed long distances home for Christmas 1936 spent the night in the day-coach.

Wheaton debate teams in the same year compiled an enviable record, as they did in many other years. In March 1937, for the second consecutive year, the men's team won the Illinois Intercollegiate Debating League championship against thirty-six teams from eighteen colleges. Coached by Professor Clarence L. Nystrom, the affirmative team was represented by Harold Lindsell and Thomas Lindsay, the negative by Ken Taylor and Roger McShane.[21] For four years Don Hoke and Abe Van Der Puy debated together as a successful team.

The women's team traveled more than 2,000 miles during the season, and finished third in the state. Debating the subject: "Resolved: that the extension of consumer cooperatives would contribute to public welfare," the women won twenty-nine contests while losing thirteen. Wanda Simpson and Margaret Meredith for the affirmative, and Grace Vander Poel and Delle Mackenzie for the negative were coached by Florence Cobb.[22]

The Washington Banquet of 1938, held at the Stevens Hotel in Chicago, was attended by 1,000 students, faculty, trustees, alumni, and friends. President Buswell had earlier suggested that the banquet committee invite Ex-President Hoover as the speaker for the evening. When that effort failed, W. J. Cameron, popular radio speaker on the high quality Ford Sunday Evening Hour, was invited. With Roger McShane as toastmaster, the evening was filled with speeches and music. It was also the occasion for launching the alumni campaign to raise $200,000 for the construction of an auditorium-physical education building. The faculty and student part of the campaign was to raise $35,000 for the swimming pool. Simultaneously, dinners were held in seventeen cities from California to Massachusetts and from Florida to Minnesota. In 1940 the banquet was omitted, at the urging of Acting President Edman, and students were encouraged to contribute what they would have spent on the banquet to a Christian Relief Fund for Finnish and Chinese Christians in war areas. An informal program was held in Pierce Chapel, with Walter A. Maier, widely heard speaker on the Lutheran Hour, as guest of the evening.

Spring activities followed an annual pattern of events that students eagerly anticipated and treasured in their memory long afterward: the issuance of the *Tower*, the senior "sneak," junior day, class day, commencement, and the hunt for and digging up of the senior cake. Sometime early in the senior year members of the class buried a large fruit cake sealed in a tin container somewhere on campus, challenging the juniors to find it. If the juniors failed to discover the cake, they were expected to attend the digging-up ceremony on class day and cheer for the seniors. If the seniors retained the cake, they ate it in triumph at the alumni banquet. On the sidewalk at the southwest corner of Blanchard Hall a small brass plaque reads: "Senior cake found here by the Class of 1939."

For the senior sneak in the thirties the class left the campus late in the spring for a weekend of fun and inspiration at a resort or state park in one of the nearby states, Turkey Run State Park in Indiana being one of the favorite spots. Inaugurated in 1922 when the seniors sneaked away from campus, boarded the Aurora and Elgin electric railway, and spent the day in St. Charles along the Fox River, canoeing, playing games, and picnicking, the one-day excursion soon became a week-end retreat. It also became for many students the social and spiritual climax of their four years at Wheaton. Far from the hectic rounds of academic life, Wheaton seniors found time to relax and laugh, to become better acquainted, and to worship together. They sang favorite hymns as well as popular songs, "Moonlight and Roses," "Let Me Call You Sweetheart," "Down by the Old Mill Stream." Returning on Monday morning they sang with gusto a song they had composed declaring the undisputed superiority of their class. Many students captured, with their cameras, the treasured moments of the sneak.

On Junior Day, when the seniors had left the campus for the sneak, juniors occupied the senior chapel seats and assumed other privileges until then belonging exclusively to seniors. Class day activities supervised by the seniors offered humorous skits or stunts by each of the classes, the reading of the senior class history, prophecy, and will—all filled with more than a little levity—and the planting of a class tree. The annual ceremony of the class tree helped the Wheaton campus become a veritable grove of academe, although the Dutch elm disease would later destroy most of the historic and graceful giants. Campus gardener Al Karnstedt noted in 1983 that when he had first arrived in Wheaton there were 129 elm trees on campus, of which only 7 then remained. To replace the stately elms eleven other varieties of trees have been planted, including maple, ash, oak, and sycamore.

Faith Alive

To coordinate Christian activities of Wheaton students on and off campus, the Christian Council was organized in 1938. The Tuesday evening prayer meeting was already established, having begun in the days of the Illinois Institute in 1854. Students voluntarily attended and found the time of worship to be an important factor in their spiritual growth. In addition each dormitory or house had its own prayer time, as did some campus organizations, many of which, like the four classes, had a prayer chairman. The Foreign Missions Fellowship, meeting on Monday nights throughout the year, had a large membership, since many students dedicated themselves to serve on a foreign field. F.M.F., after a presentation by a missionary guest speaker, would divide into bands to pray for particular mission fields around the world.

In 1931 a group of students decided to distribute copies of the Gospel of John to football fans at Northwestern University and the University of Chicago games. This modest beginning was to lead to the formation of the Scripture Distribution Society, instrumental in the distribution of more than a half million copies of a specially printed Gospel, on American campuses.[23] The Society, directed by Carl Anderson and his team, was supported by the prayers and generous gifts of students.

Gospel teams of three to five students left the campus nearly every weekend to participate in Sunday services at urban and rural churches. Other students served in rescue missions, Sunday schools, hospital visitation, jail ministries, street meetings, and youth work. Of particular interest were the weekly visits to the Moosehart Orphanage and the Geneva State Training School for Girls, where students befriended young people, planned activities for them, took gifts at holiday time, and witnessed to the transforming power of Jesus Christ.[24] Each summer, gospel teams, often consisting of a brass or vocal quartet and a speaker, made extended trips throughout the United States. In the summer of 1934, the Gospel Messengers went to Northern Michigan and the Upper Peninsula, while the Gospel Heralds and the Quintet toured the East and Northeast. The following summer the Crusaders appeared in Kansas, Nebraska, and California. These groups financed their own trips.

Evangelistic services, a part of Wheaton life from the founding of the College, were especially meaningful during the depression. In anticipation of those services, at the beginning of each semester, the Christian Council, together with the Student Council, organized a day of prayer when students gathered by classes, majors, dorms, or spontaneous and informal groups for prayer. Faculty members had their own prayer times or met with student organizations with which they had a relationship. Among the speakers who came for the week of evangelistic services were such well-known fundamentalists as Dr. Harry A. Ironside, of Moody Church; the Reverend Will Houghton, of New York's Calvary Baptist Church; and Dr. R. C. McQuilkin, President of Columbia Bible College. The emphasis of the meetings was on a personal relationship to Jesus Christ and spiritual growth, together with frequent appeals to commit one's life to missionary service. Calls for action to ameliorate great social evils were rarely heard; such appeals were thought to be tinged with liberalism.

For the mid-year evangelistic services in 1936, Dr. Robert McQuilkin was the speaker, assisted by Dr. Howard Kelly, seventy-eight-year-old world-renowned surgeon from the Johns Hopkins University Medical School. On Tuesday evening Dr. McQuilkin was stricken with influenza and confined by Dr. Kelly to the college infirmary for the remainder of the week. After substitute evangelist Dr. Walter Wilson, of Kansas City, had spoken on Thursday morning and song leader Homer Hammontree rose to dismiss the meeting, one of the senior men asked what Christian students who loved the Lord were to do to receive the fullness of the Holy Spirit's power.[25] Thereupon the whole student body knelt in prayer, which they followed with a time of confession and testimony. Most of the students remained in he chapel for an all-day prayer meeting that continued until the evening service. "It was a rebuke to our faith," said President Buswell, "that those we counted on most to bring revival blessings were all laid aside, so that when we might least expect it, the Lord sent us great blessings."[26] Dr. Buswell himself had been called to be a witness at a church trial in Chicago during the week.

A new form of college outreach was initiated in October 1939, when a daily radio program was broadcast from a studio in Pierce Chapel and aired by Station WMRO, Aurora. Heard five days a week from 7:45 to 8:00 A.M., the program featured music by student groups and a devotional talk, often given by President Buswell. Supervised by Public Relations Director Edward Cording, with Al Smith as announcer, the program was intended to "carry the distinctive Christian message of the College to Chicago and the surrounding area." In 1941 the station began to send recorded Wheaton programs to over 100 stations throughout the country. Thus the College recognized early the value of radio ministry. Students who owned and listened to radios in their rooms were required to have a permit from the dean's office. They were also obligated, if they listened between 7:00 and 10:30 P.M., to do so by earphone only.

Church and Chapel

Though the students were not required to go to church, most of them were faithful in attending Sunday worship services at local churches. Some continued, loyally, to attend the denominational church from which they had come; but the two churches nearest the campus, Wheaton Bible Church and College Church of Christ, usually drew the largest number of students. Often college students served as youth leaders, Sunday school teachers, or choir members in local churches. From time to time the young men and women were reminded, as they were by Dean Corrine Smith in *Traditions*, (a small, locally published handbook of campus customs) "that for some years it has been tacitly understood that when a young woman and her escort attended a Sunday morning church service on Wheaton College campus or at one of the churches frequented by students, they proclaim serious interest in one another, if not an engagement "[27]

When President Buswell was on campus, he was often the speaker at daily morning chapel, frequently expounding one of the Psalms or a passage from the Epistles (using his Greek New Testament). Faculty members and invited guests also gave messages and reports of church, educational, and missionary activities, along with biblical expositions—all intended to deepen their hearers' spiritual perceptions. These daily gatherings were opened by the president leading in the singing of the Doxology. Old hymns and gospel songs, like "Wonderful Grace of Jesus" and "When Morning Gilds the Skies," were sung with wholehearted fervor by students and faculty. Visitors to the morning chapel invariably commented on the moving experience of hearing the Wheaton student body sing. One young man, Edward Groesbeck, '37, visiting from Whitewater, Wisconsin, later told a friend that it was during the chapel singing that he resolved to transfer to Wheaton. Years afterward Groesbeck became registrar at the University of Michigan and was immensely helpful in introducing Inter-Varsity Christian Fellowship to American campuses.[28]

Chapel was not used for academic lectures; but occasionally it served as an appropriate time for examining intimate moral and ethical concerns. Such occasions included the divided chapels in which Dr. Buswell spoke to the men and Dean Shapleigh to the women on man/woman relationships— what a few students called "chastity problems."[29] In other divided chapels

Dean Wallace Emerson counseled the men and Dean Corrine Smith the women on courtesy. Some of Dean Emerson's thoughts were included in *Traditions*. "It is possible for a person to be morally sound and socially crude," he declared. . . . "Certain things on Wheaton campus have been frequently commented upon as not embodying either the form or the spirit of courtesy. The failure to make way for the President or the professors; the crowding of guests in line; noisy, obtrusive and sometimes crude dining hall manners . . . discourteous remarks with reference to visiting teams; 'booing'; failure to greet either fellow students or faculty; a failure on the part of a few to recognize the presence of women by lifting the hat—all of these things are reflections on one's state of grace, his home background, and the spirit of the college."[30]

In chapel, men and women were seated separately, an arrangement that students of the thirties and forties had no urge to challenge or resent. Daily chapel and the long-observed practice of a brief devotional time before each class did much to preserve a steady campus commitment to "Christ and His Kingdom," to preserve the historic Christian beliefs on which Wheaton was founded.

Literary Societies

Central to the students' social and cultural life in the thirties were the six literary societies. For men there were Beltionian, Excelsior, Aristonian; the women's societies were Aelioian, Philalethean, Boethallian. In 1935, two new lits, made necessary by the growing student body, were authorized by the inter-lit council and approved by the faculty—for the men Naitermian, known as "Knights," and for women Ladosian, generally referred to as "Ladies." All the societies had idealistic mottoes; Excelsior's motto was "Ever Onward and Upward." Philaletheans challenged themselves, "From Possibility to Achievement." Officers of the societies regarded their selection as a high honor. Besides the conventional officers for each society, there were three critics, three sergeants-at-arms, a parliamentarian, and a cheerleader.

Throughout their long history on the Wheaton campus, literary societies were to give students opportunities to develop literary appreciation, and to gain confidence in public speaking through debates, orations, story and poetry readings, and to develop close friendships. Many students regarded their experiences in the societies as among their best in their four years at Wheaton. Most alumni of the lit era recall their devotion to their chosen society with great affection. Once meetings had begun, *Roberts Rules of Order*, a classic manual owned by many students, guided the evening's procedures. Prior to the meeting the sergeant-at-arms would go to the society's assigned room in Blanchard Hall or elsewhere on campus, hang the society's drapes and set up the group's seal to transform a classroom into something a bit more glamorous.

At special "informal" society meetings early in the fall, open to everyone, members introduced their younger brothers or sisters, or students new to campus, inviting their membership. Often carefully planned during the summer, those open meetings were quite elaborate, featuring, with appropriate settings, such programs as "Arabian Nights," "The Royal Road to Romance," "A Child's Garden of Books," and "Sons of the Forest" (exploring Indian legends). *Tower* pictures of the informals reveal how student enthusiasm and ingenuity could turn a drab lower chapel into an exotic land for one enchanted evening. Each men's society was paired with a women's society—Aels and Belts, Bows and Arrows, Celts and Phils, Knights and Ladies—and they often held informals on the same evening or presented joint chapel programs.

The informals over, each society having made its best effort to win the favor of new students, members waited eagerly to see what choices would be made. In one representative year, 1936, the women's societies accepted 100 members: Phils 32, Bows 30, Aels 25, Ladies 13. The men inducted 40 members: Arrows 17, Knights 14, Celts 7, and Belts 2, a bad year for the oldest lit on campus. Popularity among the societies shifted from time to time, no society always winning the highest number of new students. No student was excluded from the lits if he or she chose to join one. Meetings began promptly at 7:30 on Friday night, when the president of each society, wearing a black academic robe, pounded the gavel for order and formally opened the session.

Carefully kept minutes of a Knights' meeting take note of such items as musical numbers by John Brobeck; an extempore, "Knighthood's Gift to the 20th Century," by Carl Henry, Wilbert Norton reading a short story, Kenneth Taylor reading his own poem; music by Robert Carbaugh, accompanied by Helen Dobbins; and a discussion on "how to find the girl of your dreams, led by Dr. Emerson." Following that momentous discussion "the assembly was resolved into a quasi-committee of the whole in order to facilitate a discussion on Wheaton's dating system."[31] Frequently Knights' meetings closed with a recital of the society's creed: "I believe in the highest standards of Christian knighthood. I propose to hold high the shield of faith with the message of purity and sacrifice which its colors symbolize. True to Naitermian, I shall be a dweller on the heights in every realm of experience."

Each society conducted a regular prayer meeting, weekly at first, then monthly when the Christian Council won greater support for the regular Tuesday night prayer meeting. Highlights of the year were the annual banquets given by the men's societies on the Friday of commencement week, to which women lit members were invited. In the early days, dating back to 1889, there were dish committees, chair committees, waiter committees, and on one occasion a lemonade and strawberry committee. By the thirties, however, the banquets had become formal and were held at hotels, country clubs, or church halls.

A very special event for the women's literary societies was the annual crowning of the May Queen, with a crown bearer, usually a small child, and the societies' presidents as ladies-in-waiting. In a setting of beautiful gowns, spring flowers, and graceful music, Lois Dickason was named May Queen for 1937, with attendants Enid Dresser, Dorothy Kellogg, Polly Allen, Irene Ackerman, Donna Ruth Breining, Helen Stephens, Eleanor Loizeaux, and Inez Hulting.

Honor Societies

Dr. Orrin E. Tiffany urged upon the faculty on November 1, 1930, the need for a campus society to stimulate scholarship of a superior quality, the kind of excellence known to characterize Phi Beta Kappa chapters. Having "brought with him a rich experience in Christian living and scholarly achievements" as president of Seattle Pacific College and Whitworth College, Dr. Tiffany was a good choice to head a committee for the organization of a Scholastic Honor Society.[32] He and Professor Enock Dyrness worked out the structure and the statement of ideals for the society, so that, in the spring of 1931, the faculty was ready to elect the first group of students to the Wheaton College Scholastic Honor Society. The Constitution declares that "the object of the Society is the promotion of scholarship, Christian culture, and helpful activities." By faculty action on May 27, 1931, the following students became charter members: Lucille Swanson, Natalie Ann Morris, Florence Vouga, Charles Baker, Dorothy Lains, Inez Larson, Harriet Jameson, and Willard Aldrich. President Buswell was the first honorary member.

The initial dinner gathering of the Scholastic Honor Society was held at the local Court House Tavern, a respectable establishment in spite of its name, on June 16, 1931. Each member was expected to make a speech. Since its founding the society has grown, by 1983, to a membership of over 1,350 around the world. The society makes annual grants to seniors planning to enter graduate school.

Among the thirteen students elected by the faculty to the Honor Society in 1938 was an extraordinary quartet of scholars: Samuel Moffett and Harold Lindsell, both graduated with highest honors; Kenneth Taylor and Carl Henry. Since his student days Samuel Moffett has been a widely-known missionary to Korea; Harold Lindsell has served as a seminary teacher, as editor of *Christianity Today*, and as the author of numerous books. Kenneth Taylor is internationally known as the paraphraser and publisher whose Tyndale House has distributed more than twenty-five million copies of *The Living Bible*. Indefatigable is the word for Carl Henry as prolific writer, seminary teacher, lecturer, scholar-at-large, and now elder statesman among evangelicals. After his graduation Henry worked briefly in the college news bureau and taught journalism; later, as a visiting instructor, he offered courses in philosophy and theology. He was also a member of the founding faculty of Fuller Theological Seminary and the first editor of *Christianity Today*.

Members of the Honor Society, limited to five percent of the graduating class, distinguished alumni, and a few faculty members, are each given a certificate and a gold key. An early expectation that initiation of a local honor society would be preliminary to the establishment of a Phi Beta Kappa chapter has never been realized because there have not been enough Phi Beta Kappa members on the faculty. Other Wheaton honor societies were established in specific disciplines. Pi Gamma Mu, a social science society, was founded at Wheaton in 1930, with the motto: "Ye shall know the truth, and the truth shall make you free." Sigma Pi Sigma, national physics honor society, installed a chapter at Wheaton in 1931. With the motto "Investigation, the forerunner of knowledge," members discussed scientific problems and read papers, later published in *Wheaton Radiations.* Alpha Delta, national journalism society, was organized at Wheaton in 1933, to advance practical journalism by holding contests, making awards, and publishing the *Reviewing Stand.* Pi Kappa Delta, 1930, is intended to promote excellence in debate, oratory, and extempore speaking. Its motto is "Persuasion, Beautiful and Just." Chi Sigma Theta, founded at Wheaton in 1933, is a national Christian education honor society with the motto, "Christ, the Wisdom of God." Added to these later were Lambda Iota Tau, national honor society for students of English and foreign literature, and Eta Beta Rho, a national society honoring students for achievement in the Hebrew language.

Athletics: Soccer, Football, Basketball

Soccer has perhaps been the sport in which Wheaton has most consistently fielded winning teams. Many of the players in the early years, the sons of missionaries, had grown up with a soccer ball; others came from eastern high schools where soccer was more generally played than in the Midwest. The first Wheaton team was organized in 1935 by James McKellin, who, after his graduation, accepted the position of superintendent of grounds with the agreement that he could organize a soccer team without obligating the College financially.[33] Lacking official uniforms, the team that season nevertheless completed a four-win, three-loss record in a schedule that included games with the University of Illinois and the University of Wisconsin.

The first soccer squad included sons of missionaries from Scotland, Korea, Iraq, Ireland, China, Japan, India, Canada, and Egypt. In the early forties the soccer team was making trips to the east coast, there to play such teams as Haverford, Princeton, Army, St. John's, and West Chester. Wheaton lost to Princeton, eastern intercollegiate champions, 2-0, and to Army, with its squad of 150 players, 4-1.[34]

Swimming got off to an uncertain start at Wheaton in 1936 when student Edwin McCausland urged Coach Coray to organize a team and investigate the possibility of using the North Central College pool for practice. In the team's first meet, with North Central, they were losers by only four points. In 1938 Wheaton finished fifth among nine schools in the first meet of the newly organized Illinois College Conference. The following year the adoption of an austerity budget, made necessary by the protracted financial depression, resulted in the elimination of intercollegiate swimming, not to be restored in the college athletic program until 1967.

A decade of football in the thirties produced twenty-five wins, forty-one losses, and eleven ties. Of those ten years only the 1932 season, with four wins and three defeats, and the 1936 season, with three wins, two losses and two ties, were winning years. Nevertheless, there were many hard-fought games in which Wheaton, though the loser, gave a good account of itself. Whether in fortune or adversity, the football teams never wanted for strong support from the student body, the sports writers of the *Record*, and many of the faculty.

From 1920 to 1939 more than 200 players gave their best efforts to Wheaton football. Many of them later became business and professional men, pastors, and missionaries serving around the world. These team members were coached by Vic Gustafson, Wendell Smith, and Fred Walker.

Coach Fred M. Walker came to Wheaton in 1936 on recommendation of Trustee McCarrell, who had met him at his Cicero Bible Church office. Walker's credentials were impressive; he had served as an assistant in football to Alonzo Stagg at the University of Chicago, and had further service in Texas. In his first year at Wheaton, Walker's team won five, lost three, and tied two. Voluble and enthusiastic, Walker persuaded the college authorities, before the football season was over, to let him coach basketball. Before the conclusion of the basketball campaign, he managed to have himself named baseball coach.

For the football banquet held in January 1937, Walker invited as speaker his friend Dizzy Dean, colorful St. Louis Cardinal star pitcher and later Hall of Famer. The irrepressible Dean, whose language was usually characterized as an English teacher's nightmare, had strolled about campus in the afternoon regaling students with his admiring comments on Wheaton College.

Basketball was a very popular sport and regularly drew enthusiastic crowds to what, by the thirties, was coming to be known as a cracker box gym. For the greatly expanded student body, it was hardly adequate, though when it was built, at the turn of the century, the gymnasium was the finest building of its kind in the region. Through the depression decade the team posted 81 wins and 106 losses. In five of the ten seasons the team either had more wins than losses or broke even. Traveling by car, the 1933-34 team covered 2,000 miles in playing nine games in the East, the longest trip by a Wheaton team since the basketball team had journeyed to Salt Lake City in 1905. By contrast, the 1934-35 team traveled eastward by Pullman on a six-game trip.

In Fred Walker's first year as coach the team won nine and lost nine. Walker's style called for the use of large, rugged men for aggressive rebounding, and the frequent use of substitutes. Severe problems for the college administration and accumulating difficulties for Coach Walker, who had reason to fear that his services would be terminated at the end of the year (see Chapter 9), may have affected the team's 1939-40 record of four wins and ten losses, the poorest showing of the decade.

Athletics in the Spring

By winning the Northern Illinois College Baseball League championship in 1932, the baseball team brought acclaim as well as a handsome trophy to the College and community. The faculty seemed to be especially supportive of baseball, particularly on warm spring afternoons. On May 13, 1938, a special faculty meeting was called to resolve a conflict between the scheduling of comprehensive examinations and the North Central baseball game. Examinations were delayed one day to make way for the game, but Wheaton lost on North Central's rain-soaked field, 5-1.

Tennis, track, cross-country, and wrestling usually generated less attention than other sports, but those who participated in them submitted to the same rigorous training regime and time commitments as other athletes. They played or ran or wrestled with the same devotion to Wheaton and with the same desire to win that motivated all enthusiasts who wore the Crusader colors.

During the spring of 1932 the tennis team won ten matches and lost only to Milwaukee Teachers College. In his number-one position Captain Wes Carlson won all ten of his singles matches, including victories at the Universities of Kentucky, Purdue, and Vanderbilt. The 1936 team, with Howard Fischer and Maurice Dobbins as co-captains, won nine matches and lost three. Nine victories in the 1937 season gave Wheaton a remarkable undefeated record, with Howard Fisher winning nine of his eleven matches. In doubles the Moffett brothers won the sectional conference tournament.

No other Wheaton team has equalled the women's tennis teams in consecutive victories—they went undefeated in dual matches through seven straight seasons from 1928 to 1934, a streak that came to an end when the team lost to North Central in 1935. In 1938 Beth Blackstone, who had grown up in Nanking, defeated Tari Takati to win the Illinois State Tennis championship for women at Millikin University. Said the college *Record:* "China defeated Japan Saturday."[35] Beth repeated her stellar performance to win the state championship again in 1939.

In track Wheaton produced many fine runners, but the teams of the thirties had little success in winning major conference meets, often for lack of strength in field events. Among the conference teams that Wheaton regularly met, North Central was a dominant power for a number of years. Wheaton runners were undoubtedly at a disadvantage in competition because of the poor quality of the local track on which they trained.

Cross-Country, Wrestling, Hockey

In cross-country running Wheaton did well in dual meets with the regional schools they generally met in other sports. Winning five out of six dual meets in 1931 and placing second in the midwest invitational, the team had a fine season. For the next two seasons Professor Clarence Hale was persuaded to serve as coach. For home meets the cross-country course ended at the football goal posts, an arrangement that brought rousing cheers from the crowds—since the races were scheduled, when there were football games, to finish at half time.[36]

Wrestling began during the winter of 1928-29 with makeshift equipment in the basement of the old gymnasium, now a part of the bookstore. President Buswell, who had wrestled at the University of Minnesota, gave strong encouragement to the sport, once engaging in an exhibition match at Homecoming with Irving Pett, a student wrestler and early coach.[37] In 1933-34, with John Player, a local businessman and former Big Ten champion wrestler as part-time coach, the team won eight of eleven matches, losing only to the University of Illinois and twice to Northwestern University.

Since success begets success, many candidates for wrestling appeared regularly, making it necessary in 1935-36, for example, to limit the squad to forty men.[38] In that year Wheaton won twelve dual meets against one loss. Captain Les Malmquist, during his career, won thirty-five of forty-two matches and was never pinned. The following year Jack Dawson, a friend of the College, offered an inscribed cup to be given to the wrestler scoring the most points during the season, the first winner of which was Howard Schoon. One of wrestlings' best friends on campus was Professor George Smith, sometimes known as "Greek" Smith. He was rumored to have favored wrestlers in issuing grades because, he held that wrestling, practiced by the Greeks, was the most ancient of sporting contests.

Field hockey for women, which began as an intramural sport before Wheaton entered intercollegiate competition, was introduced in 1936 by Ruth Berg, who in 1934, had joined the faculty as instructor for women's physical education. Intramural games, often between societies, provided fun and exercise in basketball, tennis, and soccer, the last played by the young women on the spacious lawn in front of Williston Hall. A more extensive program in women's athletics lay ahead.

In 1939 Dr. Clarence Wyngarden, of the class of 1932, became team physician. For many college generations, until his retirement, he was a familiar figure at football and basketball games. In tribute to him, and in recognition of his long service to Wheaton, the new college health center, completed in 1957, was named for him in June 1976. In the old college infirmary on Franklin Street, which stood next to the graduate building, Dr. Wyngarden and Ada Rury, faithful and efficient nurse, later Mrs. Earl Winsor, had for many years assisted students through injury and illness.

To encourage good sportsmanship and to discourage inconsiderate, careless actions, the Student Council in 1937 had printed and distributed to every student a copy of a "Wheaton Code of Sportsmanship." The preface read: "Believing that athletics on our campus can be used to build strong bodies and alert minds, can strengthen character and develop personality, and can be used as a means of witnessing for our Lord and Savior . . . the Student Council offers this Wheaton code of Sportsmanship." Article two read: "Until I become infallible myself, I will not boo or criticize a referee for mistakes which I think he has made. Even if I should be right, and he wrong, I will remember that the breaks of the game even up in the long run."[39]

For a complete account of Wheaton College athletics, the reader is urged to consult Edward A. Coray's *Through Clouds and Sunshine*, a lively, anecdotal history.

CHAPTER 9

Strong Wills
in Tension

THE EARLY MORNING AIR WAS FRESH WITH THE DELIGHTFUL fragrances of spring. Shortly before eight o'clock, from the fourth floor of Blanchard Hall and from Pierce Chapel, came the clear, vibrant sound of trumpets played by Ralph Powell and Walton MacMillian, and the trombones of Adrian Heaton and John Brobeck. Following an old German custom of announcing important events by playing carols from the tops of public buildings early in the morning, instrumentalists were initiating a day of celebration honoring Dr. Buswell on the tenth anniversary of his presidency. The day, April 23, 1936, was also to mark the formal opening of the newly named Orlinda Childs Pierce Memorial Chapel built in 1925 and enlarged in 1935 by the addition of balconies.

With the theme "Ten Years of Progress," and the message of Psalm 127:1, "Except the Lord build the house, they labor in vain that build it," the day's program began with the chapel service under the direction of the Student Council, led by Charles Troutman. At an early evening banquet President Buswell was the guest of the trustees, faculty, staff, friends of the College, and student representatives from the four classes and literary societies. Following the dinner, at which George V. Kirk, vice president in business administration, presided, the company moved to the upper chapel, with its commodious new balconies, for the climax of the day's activities.[1]

Principal speaker for the evening celebration was Trustee Peter W. Philpott, former pastor of Moody Church, who was presented to the college community by Herman A. Fischer, president of the Board of Trustees. "Personally I thank God for every year of Wheaton College," said Dr. Philpott. "I thank God for its president, Dr. Buswell, for his ability, for his leadership, and for his courage in these days. I thank God for the faculty of this great school."[2]

For the president, one of the gratifications of the day was the gift to him of the keys for the new presidential home at Washington and Union streets, a home purchased from the Oury family and subsequently known as Westgate.

In the summer of 1936 great progress was made at the Black Hills science station, located twelve miles west of Rapid City, South Dakota. Using Camp Tamalen at Hisega as a base, Professor John W. Leedy, camp director, offered work in botany, and Professor L. Allen Higley directed the field work in geology. Wives of the two men assisted in the supervision of the camp, and John L. Leedy, then a graduate student at the University of Minnesota, assisted his father in the field. "There is probably no area of similar size in the world," the college announcement noted, "which holds the wealth of minerals and plant specimens that is found in the Black Hills. It abounds in plant life, and all but two of the known minerals are found in its ranges."[3]

Later that year the College sponsored an Open House, when citizens of Wheaton and the neighboring community of Glen Ellyn were invited to visit the campus and enjoy special events scheduled between December 1 and 13. The plan had been initiated the year before, an effort to create amity between town and gown, for in some segments of the community a measure of animosity was felt toward the College, generated in part by the firm stand the Blanchards had taken against secret societies. There were also those who resented the College's tax-free status and saw the institution as a self-contained economic unit. Still other local residents were not in sympathy with the fundamentalist position of the College. All of these, the planners felt, might come to a warmer understanding of the folks on the hill if they could see that they were a group of friendly, earnest, hard-working, talented people. Of course, there always had been many friends in the community strongly in sympathy with the work and commitments of Wheaton.

Only four days earlier, sixty-seven women students had moved into the first unit of the new women's dormitory, completed at a cost of $80,000. The building was of Georgian architecture and faced westward in anticipation of a quadrangle of buildings to be completed at some future time. The south end wing was the second unit to be completed, made possible by an anonymous gift of $50,000. Later an addition, attached to and extending northward from the first unit, would be completed and would house an equal number of women. The two buildings were simply called North Hall I and II. Completion of the women's dormitory had been made urgent by the increases in enrollment during the preceding years: there were more students enrolled than rooms available on campus and in private homes. For at least twenty years longer a considerable number of students would be lodged in private residences, frequently faculty homes.

It was a good year, 1936. Administration, faculty, and students could survey a spectrum of improvements: increase in enrollment, modest gain in the endowment, new faculty strength, curriculum enrichment, an attractive addition to the physical plant, and a growing constituency of supportive friends. All of this had come in the midst of the great financial depression. Before the academic year was over, President Buswell was granted a Doctor of Laws degree by Houghton College, where Stephen Paine, a graduate of Wheaton, was president.

No one was more pleased with Wheaton's advancement than President Buswell; yet for him, the year was not without disquietude. For one thing, friends of the College feared that a too rapid expansion of student enrollment would inevitably create a financial deficit during times of depression. Another matter of concern was the president's controversy with the Presbyterian Church in the U.S.A.

President Buswell and a Church Controversy

Except for the four years James Oliver Buswell, Jr., served as pastor of the Grace Reformed Church of Brooklyn, he was a lifelong Presbyterian, strongly committed to that denomination's theology and ecclesiastical polity. When tensions between modernism and historical Presbyterian orthodoxy began to develop, he expressed himself forthrightly whenever he perceived evidences of liberalism. One area in his denomination where he believed there was a serious erosion of orthodoxy was in the Presbyterian Board of Foreign Missions. J. Gresham Machen, of Westminster Theological Seminary, as well as others, agreed with him.

To assure doctrinal honesty in the calling, sending, and support of missionaries, Dr. Machen, Dr. Buswell, and their associates established the Independent Board for Foreign Missions in June 1933. In response to this action the general assembly of the Presbyterian Church in the U.S.A. requested that the members of the Independent Board resign from the organization or face disciplinary action through ecclesiastical trial. Dr. Buswell contended that the command from the general assembly was without constitutional authority and refused to comply with the mandate.

In June 1935, Dr. Buswell was placed on trial by the Chicago presbytery, where he was told by the trial chairman, Dr. E. E. Hastings, that the case was a constitutional one with no bearing on "religious beliefs." The question at issue was whether Dr. Machen, Dr. Buswell, and others were to obey the laws of the church.[4] At a subsequent meeting of the trial commission in July, Dr. Buswell challenged the right of two of the commissioners to hear the charges. He called Henry P. Chandler, a Chicago lawyer and former president of the Union League, a "Communist sympathizer"—a designation that

Chandler admitted in cross examination[5]—and declared that Dr. Federick L. Shelden, a signer of the Liberal Auburn Confession, could not be regarded as an unbiased judge. The case was dismissed when the trial chairman declared that all charges against a defendant must be specific. Those against Dr. Buswell were only general.[6] The charges were dropped, but when the Chicago presbytery in September 1935 brought charges again they specifically accused Dr. Buswell of insubordination, diverting funds from the denominational board to the Independent Board, and violating his ordination vows in disturbing the peace of the church. The commission met intermittently and, as the *New York Times* reported, found Dr. Buswell "guilty of insubordination and conspiracy to undermine The Presbyterian Church."[7]

The commission chose the lightest of five possible sentences, admonishing the defendant to "desist from this course," and explaining that the mild censure was selected because the commission believed that although he was "clearly misguided," he had acted sincerely and without conscious wrong.[8] Stories of tensions over the creation of the Independent Board and the trials of the central figures in the establishment of the board were carried by the wire services to major newspapers, and were covered by religious journals as diverse as *Moody Monthly* and *Christian Century.*

Concerns Beyond the Campus

To more than a few friends and alumni of the College, these controversies were an embarrassment, a source of unfavorable publicity for the College. A good many students, parents, and alumni who were members of the Presbyterian Church in the U.S.A. were little inclined to concur in Dr. Buswell's judgments in these ecclesiastical matters. The trustees were quite aware of a developing problem. At a meeting of the Executive Committee on June 22, 1936, "with a view of guarding against misunderstanding on the part of friends of the college, Trustee Nicholas moved that a letter by the chairman, Herman Fischer, in tentative form and subject to further study by the President and Chairman, be sent to the mailing list of the College."[9] At their meeting in January 1939, the trustees again expressed concern over "President Buswell's church relationships."[10]

As the months passed, the College's two other principal officers, Enock Dyrness, vice president for academic affairs, and Wallace Emerson, dean of students, were finding it difficult to work with the president in full accord and amicability. From the field men came reports of churches threatening to withdraw the support they had been giving to Wheaton College.[11] By June 1939, the financial deficit had grown to over $200,000, in spite of several years of rigorous economies that left many faculty and staff with a continuing fear that their positions were in jeopardy. However, by June 14, 1941, Trustee Thomas Crofts was able to report to his fellow Board members "that much progress has been made in the last three years in reducing the current deficit in operations from over $200,000 to less than $100,000."[12]

Early in May 1939, Torrey Johnson, president of the Alumni Association, then living in Chicago, and Hamilton Sinclair presented a petition to the Executive Committee which they claimed had been signed by eighty-one students, though there were no signatures attached. The petition called for an investigation of the institution through consultations with "administrative officers, faculty members, students, and alumni." Such an investigation would reveal widespread dissatisfaction, the signers claimed. When the petition was transmitted to Dr. Buswell, he quizzed several students, some of whom said they had "very different ideas of the impact of what they were signing."

Responding to the challenge, President Buswell prepared an evaluation form, which he asked the faculty to check and mail to his office in addressed, stamped envelopes he had paid for. To the first question, "Are You Dissatisfied with the Work of the President of the College?" thirty-four said "no," six said "yes," and five declared themselves "neutral." The second question asked the faculty to grade the work of the president on a scale between 95 (excellent) and 50 (failure). Scoring gave the president an average of 89.43, based on forty-four replies. The fact that twenty-three faculty members did not reply left the validity of the results somewhat in doubt.

Another problem confronting President Buswell in 1939 concerned Coach Fred Walker, who by then had completed three years as head coach of football, baseball, and basketball. Walker worked in Chicago, lived in Oak Park, and came to the campus only for practice sessions and games. Consequently, he was less well known to faculty and students than other campus figures. He was a large man, aggressive, strong willed, somewhat loud, a hard driver of his men, who expected players to give their utmost to win.[13]

Walker came to the College at a time when Wheaton's athletic fortunes were low, and it was hoped that he could turn adversity into good fortune. Impatient with institutional routines that required approval by his superiors for his actions, he sometimes ordered athletic equipment without authorization or planned team transportation without consultation.

In the Executive Committee meeting in January 1939, George Kirk, Dean Emerson, and Dr. Dyrness recommended that "Mr. Walker's services be discontinued,"[14] though no action to that effect was taken. A week earlier Dr. Buswell had urged that James R. Graham, a former missionary to China, who had had an athletic career in the marines, be appointed for the year 1939-1940 to teach Bible and serve as assistant dean of students, and be responsible for the entire athletic program.[15] Though the latter suggestion prevailed, Coach Walker was still on duty as the new football season opened in the fall.

In almost all of his adversities Walker had strong support from President Buswell, who wanted a successful athletic program, believed Walker could deliver it, and wished to be loyal to a man he himself had recommended for appointment. In backing his coach against others' criticism the president aroused additional criticism of himself by some faculty, students, and alumni. In all of this controversy the won-lost record of Wheaton Crusader teams was not at issue; nor was there ever any question raised about Fred Walker's integrity.

At the meeting of the Board of Trustees on January 20, Trustee Emery moved that Coach Walker be notified that his services would be terminated at the end of the baseball season. The motion carried, but Trustees Fischer and Nicholas abstained, and Trustee McCarrell voted no. Before it could be announced officially that Walker had been dismissed, he released a statement to the *Wheaton Daily Journal* stating his intention to resign as head coach at the College following the baseball season. Walker spoke of his players as the finest group of boys he had ever worked with and praised their loyalty to the College and to himself. In the same issue of the *Journal* there was a statement by Dr. Orrin E. Tiffany, professor of history and a member of the faculty athletic committee, who declared: "My personal relations with Mr. Walker, both as a faculty member and as a member of the board have been pleasant and I hold him in high esteem.[16]

A Turning Point in Wheaton's History

When the Board of Trustees convened at eleven A.M. on January 20, 1940, no one among those present knew the end to which the long day's business would bring them. No prior caucus of the Board had arranged the events for the day. Years later, Trustee David Otis Fuller acknowledged that the outcomes of the meeting were a "complete surprise" to him, as he believed they were to others assembled in the president's office. The trustees addressed themselves "to the principal problems before the Board," the first of which was the reading and discussion of the "communication from ten Chicago Alumni." Following lunch a number of letters from faculty members were read, during which President Buswell and Mr. Kirk were asked to retire. Letter writers were professors Eavey, Kilby, Mixter, Straw, Edman, Thiessen, Graham, Mr. Stam, and Mr. Strombeck. At earlier faculty meetings Dr. Buswell had invited instructors to express themselves candidly to the trustees, if they chose to, about the climate of opinion on the campus. The minutes made no comment on the content of those letters.[17]

When President Buswell returned to the meeting, he told the trustees that it seemed to him they had three courses of action open to them: to dismiss the president and establish a new administration; to give the president a vote of confidence; to continue the present situation. He further proposed a program that would terminate Coach Walkers's association with the College in September, reaffirm the economy plans, and give the president a vote of confidence. Following those proposals Dr. Buswell and Mr. Kirk were again asked to withdraw during the ensuing discussion, which lasted, without a vote, until 5:50 P.M., at which point President Buswell and Mr. Kirk were again asked to join the group.

Trustee Ironside stated that the Board could not grant the requested vote of confidence. One trustee asked if the president would be willing to submit his resignation. He replied, as reported by Professor Straw, long-time secretary of the group, "that he would not,—that he had considered his work here one to which he was called, that he did not consider it completed, and that if it was to be terminated, the trustees would have to take the responsibiltiy for that termination." Trustee McShane than declared that it was the consensus of the Board, without a formal vote, that the president's services should be terminated at the end of the year. The Reverend Mr. McCarrell then asked if the president's services were not terminated at that point, if it would be possible to resolve differences by June. To him it seemed "unthinkable that a body of Christian men could not find a solution."

To this suggestion President Buswell responded that such a plan would only perpetuate conditions as they were. If his services were to be discontinued, better it were sooner than later and by trustee vote. Thereupon Robert Nichols moved and Lewis McShane seconded a motion that the president's services be terminated at once, and that he be allowed his salary and the use of his home until September 1940.

The motion passed by a ballot vote, nine to three. At this point trustees adjourned for dinner, agreeing to reassemble at 7:30, the third session of the day, to which Dr. Buswell did not return. In presenting a set of options to the trustees, the president had forced the issue and may have been stunned by the consequences. Whatever vision he may have had of Wheaton's advancement into the future with sturdy confidence through his leadership had been shattered.

After an informal discussion among the trustees as the evening session began, Chairman Fischer, at the request of the others present, telephoned Dr. V. Raymond Edman, chairman of the department of history and political science, to come to the meeting of the Board in the president's office. Dr. Edman was at home playing ping-pong with his son David, had no knowledge of what had happened at the trustee meeting, and did not guess why he was summoned.[18] In calling Professor Edman, whom they were now prepared to name temporary president, they knew they were turning to a popular history teacher, a peacemaker among dissident elements, an effective department chairman, and a potentially strong leader for Wheaton College.

Surprised by the commission now laid on him, but encouraged by assurances of the Board's full support, V. Raymond Edman, with some hesitancy, agreed to serve as temporary president of Wheaton College. The trustees then called in Dean Emerson, Professor Dyrness, and George Kirk, reminding each that a new team was now to take the field and they were expected to work harmoniously together.

The Days Following President Buswell's Dismissal

On Monday, January 22, the following statement was issued:

The Board of Trustees of Wheaton College, at the quarterly meeting held Saturday, found certain difficulties in administrative cooperation, which in the Board's opinion, necessitated a change in the presidency.

Dr. James Oliver Buswell, Jr., was called to the presidency of the college in 1926. Under his administration the student body has more than doubled, the plant has been modernized and the curriculum expanded.

He is esteemed by the Board as a Christian leader and as an able minister. It was his preference that the change take place now, rather than at the end of the year.

The Board appointed Dr. V. R. Edman, head of the department of History and Social Sciences, as acting president.

The Board is carrying out plans for reducing annual overhead, mainly along the lines recommended by President Buswell.

Later in the day Dr. Buswell issued a short statement urging "all parties to be loyal to the College and to Dr. Edman, in his difficult position."[19]

Carried as a 110-word dispatch by the Associated Press, many newspapers throughout the country published the story of Dr. Buswell's dismissal on an inner page. Headings for the story varied greatly. "Ousted as Wheaton Head," the *New York Times* said; "Wheaton College President Fired," the *Pittsburgh Post Gazette* declared; the *Los Angeles Times* headed its story: "College Head in Row Dismissed by Board." The *Wheaton Daily Journal* said in a seven-column headline: "President Buswell Dismissed."

When news of the trustees' action reached the faculty and students, they were stunned. They came quietly to the Monday morning chapel service, where the esteemed Professor Darien Straw—commissioned by the trustees to do so—announced the appointment of Professor V. R. Edman as acting president. In his fatherly way Dr. Straw, then eighty years old, spoke to the students on the theme, "Fear not, little flock; for it is your Father's good pleasure to give you the kingdom," after which Dr. Edman made the closing prayer and announced a brief faculty meeting, following chapel, to ask for God's blessing on Wheaton College and on himself as he began his new responsibilities.[20] At a faculty meeting the following day Board chairman Herman A. Fischer addressed the group on "The Dignity of the Teaching Profession" and asked for the earnest cooperation of the entire faculty.[21]

That the alumni and friends of Wheaton might know of the change in command, the trustees' statement was published in the February 1940 issue of the *Bulletin of Wheaton College*. Herman A. Fischer added a clarifying word under the heading: "The change—what it does and does not mean." It did not mean that there was any question about Dr. Buswell's faith or scholarship, nor call in question his efforts to uphold clarity of faith and purity of life in the groups with which he was associated. It did mean that sometimes "differences of viewpoint arise" and "men of principle may find cooperation difficult." It also meant that the action taken was done with regret "but with a firm belief that a work, founded by God and continued by Him, will not fail."[22]

A number of individuals wrote to the College to say that the newspaper stories of President Buswell's release were somewhat cryptic and left them ill informed. What indeed had happened, and why? Had the Board yielded to alumni pressures, had the church quarrels been the president's undoing, was Wheaton moving toward liberalism and dismissing its indefatigable fundamentalist leader? One alumnus, who had been graduated from Wheaton in 1933, and was, in 1940, a pastor in South Dakota, wrote: "Why can there not be a clear statement of the reason that Dr. Buswell left an institution which has been greatly blessed during his presidency?"[23]

To this letter Chairman Herman Fischer responded with an even-tempered statement of a page and a half. "For some two years," he wrote, "President Buswell and the three officers immediately under him have been having repeated disagreements and differences." It was "simply a situation where good men could not get along together and could not cooperate." Their differences "did not arise over matters of principle." With reference to the alumni communication, Fischer wrote that he "was not sure that the group was right in its conclusions and felt definitely that in respect to a number of details in their communication, President Buswell was not at fault." The alumni memorandum was read to the trustees but, Fischer continued, "I do not think it was so much as mentioned in their later discussion, and I am sure the Presbyterian situation was not mentioned. I very much doubt if these matters weighed materially with the trustees in their decision."[24] If, then, we are to accept Chairman Fischer's analysis, the crisis arose and was beyond resolution because of the president's inability to work harmoniously with his three principal administrators. But it also seems necessary to conclude that much of the disharmony was prompted by Dr. Buswell's supplementary activities.

In Appreciation of President Buswell

Some of the others who wrote to the trustees asking for illumination, especially those who had been students during the Buswell era, expressed appreciation for the president. "It was my pleasure and privilege to graduate from Wheaton during the leadership of President Buswell," wrote Martha Johnson. "I believe that it has been his courage and fine faithfulness to God that have helped to build the greater Wheaton, whose foundations were so nobly laid by his two predecessors."[25]

Within two weeks of the termination of his services, Dr. Buswell accepted an appointment as professor of systematic theology and apologetics at Faith Theological Seminary, to begin the following September. On February 2, 1940, he released a somewhat lengthy statement for publication in the *Christian Beacon*, edited by the Reverend Carl McIntire, in which he praised his successor and declared that "the greatest good for the College will come through a genuine rallying in support of Dr. Edman." He also offered a brief defense for his conduct as president and spoke of a lack of cooperation from a few persons, though he made clear that Dr. Edman was not one of these.

Dr. Buswell served as president of National Bible Institute, renamed Shelton College, from 1941 to 1955. In 1956 he moved to St. Louis, where he was associated with Covenant Theological Seminary from 1956 to 1970, when he suffered a paralysis of his left side and retired with Mrs. Buswell to the Quarryville Presbyterian Home, Quarryville, Pennsylvania.

No matter what the difficulties of President Buswell's last years at Wheaton his lasting contributions to Wheaton College stand undiminished. He was a courageous leader, fine scholar, vigorous champion of academic excellence, unyielding defender of Christian orthodoxy, devoted family man. When he came to the presidency in the mid-twenties, although the tides of theological liberalism were running strong, he held steady against their engulfment. His effective drive for accreditation led to academic maturity for Wheaton College and the development of a national reputation. What he regarded as a crowning achievement among his many writings, *A Systematic Theology of the Christian Religion*, demonstrates the penetrating and comprehensive quality of his mind.

For the *Wheaton Alumni News* of April 1940, Elsie Storrs Dow wrote an article entitled,"He Was Sent Among Us." Dr. Dow had retired the year before at the age of eighty, after fifty years of teaching literature at Wheaton; and through all the years of the Buswell regime, she had been one of the president's most enthusiastic supporters. Her concluding words of tribute were: "These fourteen 'beautiful years' have passed into history and are imperishable; our possession forever. If Wheaton is to survive, future success will owe a heavy debt to this inheritance."

Some of the students Dr. Buswell had helped to train through his classroom teaching later became presidents of Christian institutions. Among them: Stephen Paine, Houghton College; Percy Crawford, The King's College; John Walvoord, Dallas Theological Seminary; Edmund Clowney, Westminster Theological Seminary; and Robert Rayburn, Covenant Theological Seminary.

Dr. James Oliver Buswell, Jr., died on February 3, 1977, at the Quaryville Presbyterian Home at the age of eighty-two. At a memorial service on April 12, 1977, in Edman Chapel, James Oliver Buswell III, then professor of anthropology at Wheaton College, spoke of some of his father's non-academic interests. For several years he sang the bass solos in the college performance of the *Messiah*. He owned a ukelele and loved to play and sing songs from his courtship and army days. He loved to hike and was a serious gardener. "I remember how excited he got when I caught my first fish," his son recalled; "how he taught us to swim, and to play a decent game of chess; how to handle a canoe with a sail in a brisk wind; how to patch an inner tube; how to follow the bass line in a quartet; and how to turn bitterness into tolerant forgiveness."

Building on the achievements of his predecessors, Jonathan and Charles Blanchard, who had guided the College through other troubled eras, President Buswell set a pattern of scholarly dedication, integrity of life, and commitment to the service of Jesus Christ that has prevailed at Wheaton through the succeeding years.

PRESIDENT V. RAYMOND EDMAN, 1940-1965

CHAPTER 10

V. Raymond Edman and the World War II Years

D<small>URING THE YEAR</small> V. R<small>AYMOND</small> E<small>DMAN</small> <small>SERVED AS ACTING</small> president of Wheaton, students dedicated the 1941 *Tower* to him. An inscription, written by David L. Roberts, read: "Dedicated to Dr. V. Raymond Edman, who is loved by the Wheaton campus for his genuine humility, deep spirituality, profound understanding, godly wisdom, sweet simplicity, appropriate humor, adept leadership." Popular with students and colleagues alike, Dr. Edman came to his new office supported by a foundation of goodwill.

From the time of his arrival on the campus in 1936 until the Board of Trustees chose him for larger responsibilities, Dr. Edman had given evidence of superior capabilities as teacher, pastor, counselor, and committeeman. Though he lacked administrative experience, his strength of mind and character quickly demonstrated that he was adequate for his tasks.

V. Raymond Edman was born to Swedish parents, Anders and Alma Edman, in Chicago Heights, Illinois, May 9, 1900. In 1918 he was graduated from Bloom Township High School, where he had been a member of the football and basketball teams, editor of the yearbook, a member of the Forum, and president of the senior class. In the summer of 1917 he went on a camping trip to Saskatchewan, an experience that drew him close to the vast expanses of prairie and mountain beauty. As a senior in high school he accepted Jesus Christ as his Savior at a union service held in a wooden tabernacle built for the meetings.

Patriotic fervor was strong in the summer of 1918; the Allied victory in Europe was not yet assured. Fresh from high school, Raymond Edman joined the Army and went overseas on the *S. S. St. Louis,* his unit landing at Brest, France, where he was attached to the First Division.[1] Because the First was a reserve division, Edman engaged in no combat. Instead, when the war was over, his unit was assigned to occupation duty in western Germany, where the lonely soldier spent his first Christmas away from home. The days were not without reward, however; he learned to write and speak German with considerable skill, on several occasions serving as translator at company headquarters.[2]

Encouraged by his father, Raymond had joined the Pocket Testament League, promising to read a passage of Scripture each day, a practice he faithfully observed throughout his service abroad.[3] His view of life and the world was profoundly influenced by his army days, which were concluded with his return to the United States in September 1919. From his experiences in Europe, he drew many illustrations for his chapel talks to students, especially on patriotic occasions.

In *Out of My Life,* a series of autobiographical sketches published in 1961, Edman tells of entering the University of Illinois in the fall following his release from the Army. At the end of his sophomore year, feeling the University of Illinois was not preparing him for the missionary career he envisioned, he decided to enter the Missionary Training Institute operated by the Christian and Missionary Alliance at Nyack, New York. His twenty-two hours of biblical studies there in 1921 comprised his only formal training in the subject.

During a conference at Park Street Church in Boston in the fall of 1921, he met the Reverend E. Joseph Evans, who remained his close friend and counselor throughout his life. Superintendent of the New England area of the Christian and Missionary Alliance, he became "Uncle Joe" to Edman. At the same conference Edman was much impressed by a gracious young Swedish woman named Edith Olson, Evans's secretary. She had played the piano that evening, and had recently graduated from a two-year course at Nyack in preparation for missionary service in Indo-China. Much later, at the inauguration of V. Raymond Edman as president of Wheaton College in 1941, Edith Olson Edman told how after her graduation, at the family summer home in Old Orchard, Maine, she acknowledged to God her willingness to go wherever he would lead.[4] Not long afterward she met her future husband.

When young Edman completed his year at Nyack, he enrolled in a summer program at Columbia University studying Latin American history and Spanish. At Nyack he had sensed a growing conviction that he was being called to missionary service in South America. In the fall he accepted an invitation to live in the Evans home in Somerville, Massachusetts, where he remained, performing light services, for two years. He completed his A.B. degree at Boston University with a major in Spanish. On graduation day in June 1923 Raymond Edman and Edith Olson announced their engagement, planning a wedding after a period of separation, during which they could clearly determine if it was God's will for them to serve together as missionaries in South America.

Ten days later Raymond boarded the liner *Santa Teresa*, enroute to Ecuador, which he called "that interesting and colorful republic astride the equator in western South America."[5] There he began to work among the Quichua Indians, whose language he found difficult though fascinating. He also worked to adjust his academic Spanish to the Ecuadorian idioms. A small black notebook begun at this time is filled with outlines, half of them in Spanish, for sermons and short talks. Interspersed are quotations from Browning and Bunyan, and, neatly typed in its entirety, Kipling's "If," a favorite poem in those days for idealistic young men facing life's rigors. Edman experienced much loneliness but when a mission rule requiring two years' residence on the field before marriage was waived for him, he was granted permission to marry Edith. The wedding took place at the mission headquarters in Quito on June 19, 1924. Edith's gift to her husband was a beautiful bay horse, a necessity for transportation to the mission's outposts.

The Edman's first child, Charles, was born in May 1925 at Ambato, Ecuador. The following month the new father was seized by typhus fever and, after examining him at a hospital in Guayaquil, the American doctor said that Edman's death appeared imminent. A coffin was made, and Edith Edman was advised to dye her wedding dress black for the funeral. Meanwhile, in Boston, Joseph Evans sensed an urgent need for prayer for Ray, though at that time he did not know of his young friend's grave illness. At a Bible conference in Attleboro, Massachusetts, Evans requested prayer that God would spare the life of the young missionary. In Ecuador the crisis eased. Raymond began to hold his own, then rally, though he did not recognize his wife until ten days later. Recovery was slow, and in February 1926 the mission director urged him to return to North America with his family to speed his recuperation. In Boston, Joseph Evans provided quarters for the Edmans in Jamaica Plains and secured a position for Raymond in the small Boston Bible Training School in Roxbury. The couple's second son, Roland, was born in Jamaica Plains in October 1926.

Following the spring term at the Roxbury school in 1927, the Edmans returned to Ecuador. But Edman was soon stricken ill again, this time with amoebic dysentery, which left him extremely weak and reduced from 165 to 120 pounds. Doctors advised him again to return to the United States, a journey he made with young Charles in the summer of 1928 while Edith remained at the mission station.

After a thorough examination at the Department of Tropical Diseases at Harvard Medical School, Raymond was advised that his survival hinged on his abandoning plans to return to the tropics.[6] That sad news reunited the family in Chicago, where Raymond found an apartment. They remained there until February 1929, when they left for Worchester, Massachusetts, where Raymond was to serve as pastor of the Alliance Tabernacle. Shortly after his arrival the young pastor was ordained in Boston by Joseph Evans and Fred Hayes. Then, in the fall of 1930, he began graduate study at Clark University, completing an M.A. in American history in 1931 and a Ph.D. degree in Latin American history and international relations in 1933.

With the arrival of David in 1930 and Norman in 1935, their family was complete. In later years the president of Wheaton College often, and fondly, referred to his sons as "the Four Horsemen."

V. Raymond Edman Comes to Wheaton

Edman described the two-year period following the completion of his degree as a time of "silence in which no one made inquiry as to what we were doing, or desired to have us help them in Christian work."[7] The silence was broken, however, when he was offered an opportunity in April 1935 to teach history at the Alliance Missionary Training Institute at Nyack, New York. It was a happy and busy year for the Edmans in the small community of Nyack overlooking the Hudson River. At that time Edman began to prepare for his teaching and preaching obligations by rising at 5:00 A.M., sometimes earlier, a practice he continued throughout his life.

In March 1936, he received a letter from President J. Oliver Buswell inviting him to become a member of the Wheaton College faculty as an associate professor of political science at a salary of $2,500, less the ten-percent temporary reduction then being accepted by all faculty members as a depression emergency measure. After much family prayer, and encouragment from Joseph Evans, Edman wrote to tell Dr. Buswell he would come to Wheaton for an interview. As he came by train from Chicago to Wheaton, he felt that God was urging him to "be a shepherd to my people at Wheaton."[8] By the end of March his acceptance was in the mail, with the original salary offer raised to $2,800. The family moved into a home at 330 East Franklin Street, a block from campus, where they remained until 1940, when they moved to Westgate, the president's home on Washington Street, directly across from the campus.

When Associate Professor Edman took up his teaching duties in September 1936, his course assignments included early European history, political science, American government, international law, and American political theories. As a teacher he was well prepared, thorough, inspiring, and patient. His witty style—with puns as a ready resource—helped to establish him as a professor whose courses had substance enlivened with humor. In the spring of 1938, to give his students in political science an opportunity to observe the national government at work, he took a group to Washington, initiating an annual study tour of the nation's capital for Wheaton students.

When Dr. Orrin Tiffany retired at the age of seventy in 1939 from his administrative responsibilities, he recommended Professor Edman as his replacement in the chairmanship of the department of history and political science. Though he was aware that President Buswell was having administrative difficulties, Edman took no part in the controversies. Life in Wheaton for him and his family had begun to seem quite comfortable.

Then came the unexpected call from the chairman of the Board of Trustees on the night of January 20, 1940. When Edman was informed of the termination of Dr. Buswell's services and of his own election by the trustees as acting president of the College, the tranquility he had known for three and a half years was ended. The burdens of the office he was being called to accept would exceed anything he had known before.

In the days that followed, he quickly recognized the magnitude of his responsibilities. There were wounds to be assuaged, fractured relationships to be restored, disaffected alumni to be restored to relationship with the College. He must have sensed that God's providence had brought him to the leadership of what was now the largest liberal arts college in Illinois. Edman was deeply conscious of the influence of its three former presidents, who together had guided Wheaton for eighty years.

Dr. Edman came to the presidency with the College fully operative. The second semester had begun; the faculty was complete; committees were at work; the budget was set for the present year; students were too busy to be overawed by the transition from one presidency to another.

Dr. Edman's first major obligation as president was to prepare the budget for the 1940-41 fiscal year. In *Out of My Life* he tells of that experience. The budget committee had met in the president's office. "The committee members departed and I took a few moments to close all the books which had been left on my desk. Then with a prayer of thanksgiving to the Lord, I put out the lights, walked down the hallway to the Tower stairs and out through the Tower door to the campus. I turned westward and walked slowly toward home. There was a deep sense of human inadequacy. I repeated over several times. '760,000.00' . . . The amount staggered me." He walked down through the double row of maple trees leading to the limestone gates, the gift of the class of 1938. There, after prayer, he was assured "from far beyond those lovely stars the Most High had heard my request and would answer in His own time and way." To his mind came the words of Jeremiah 33:3: "Call unto Me, and I will answer thee, and show thee great and mighty things, which thou knowest not." The financial needs for that year were met, as they were two decades later when the president and his associates were struggling with budgets of well over three million dollars.[9]

President Edman's Inauguration

While V. Raymond Edman performed his duties as acting president during the spring and fall of 1940, the trustees made no systematic effort to search for other candidates for the presidency of Wheaton College. They did, however, sense that Dr. Edman was pleasing the alumni, faculty, students, and the trustees themselves. Consequently, few were surprised when, at their meeting on January 11, 1941, the trustees unanimously elected him president. The action seems to have been unplanned; the minutes of the meeting note that "Chairman Fischer read letters from Trustees Emery and McShane, who could not be present, stating that they felt it seemed evident Dr. Edman was the Lord's choice for the leadership of the College and that they felt the time had arrived for electing him president."[10]

For his inaugural day, President Edman chose his forty-first birthday, Friday, May 9, 1941—a date in one of the loveliest months on campus, with the great elm trees in full leaf, the lawns bright green, the early flowers rich-hued. The day's activities began with the playing of the Anders V. Edman memorial chimes, given by President Edman's mother in memory of her husband, who had died the year before. For students, faculty, and representatives of seminaries and Bible institutes, a morning convocation was held in Pierce Chapel at 9:30, with Edgar F. Dival, of the Board of Trustees, presiding. The address of the morning, "Forgetting—and Pressing Forward," based on Philippians 3:13, was presented by Dr. Harry A. Ironside, pastor of the Moody Church and a trustee of the College. Greetings were brought from the faculty by Professor Elsie Storrs Dow, from the student body by Abe Van Der Puy, from the alumni by Kenneth Gieser, and from the trustees by Edgar Dival. Dr. Edman's friend, Dr. Ernest Wadsworth of the Great Commission Prayer League, gave a prayer of dedication. Dr. Edman's brief remarks, which he titled "Brave Sons and Daughters True," encouraged students to live out their days in confidence, knowing they did not walk alone.

In a brief ceremony at 11:30 President Edman turned over the first spadeful of earth for the new, long-hoped-for gymnasium. Following the ground-breaking a luncheon was served in lower chapel at noon for visiting delegates who had come to participate in the inauguration ceremonies. After lunch the new memorial chimes were again played for a quarter hour, followed by an organ recital by Professor Lester Groom. At two P.M. the colorful academic procession began the short march from Blanchard Hall, through a court of honor formed by students, to Pierce Chapel, where the 152 delegates from colleges and universities and the 20 representatives of learned societies would take their assigned places. Seniors, in their caps and gowns, joined the procession, led by Ed Rosser and Robert Spiro, later also a college president.

From Dr. Guy E. Snavely, executive director of the Association of American Colleges, came the academic challenge of the afternoon: "The Liberal Arts College in an Upset World." He noted that the intensifying European war was likely to involve America much more fully than it had so far, and that if military involvement came, the colleges would have a major role to play.[11] Following an anthem by the Men's Glee Club, "O Praise the Name of the Lord," Stephen Paine, president of Houghton College, a Wheaton graduate and grandson of Jonathan Blanchard, addressed the assembly on "Service That Lives." The induction of V. Raymond Edman as the fourth president of Wheaton College was presided over by Herman Fischer, who said in his charge: "We depend on you to guide the institution in paths of learning and of truth, but to follow them in humble reliance on the Giver of all Truth. We expect the college to impart to its students knowledge of all that can be learned of earth and life and men, but, beyond that, of the Creator of earth and life and of the Savior of men."[12]

Dr. Darien Straw presented the seal of the College to the new president. Responding in his inaugural address, "For Christ and His Kingdom," President Edman noted that Wheaton College had come into being on the threshold of the Civil War, days as troubled as those of 1941; it had witnessed in the intervening generations "tremendous changes" and sometimes "fierce struggles between divergent interests." He reaffirmed the College's devotion to democracy, to liberal arts education, and to its Christian heritage. "We pledge ourselves to represent to American young people," he concluded, "the best of human thought and achievement as well as the unsearchable riches of Christ, without Pharisaism or fanaticism, but rather in humble devotion and dependence upon Almighty God."[13] The benediction was given by Dr. Lewis Sperry Chafer, president of Dallas Theological Seminary.

The inauguration day issue of the *Record* carried a column by editor John Witmer in which he wrote:

> Dr. Edman answers to many names—interesting teacher, inspirational preacher, understanding counselor, convivial companion, warm friend, spiritual father, human exemplar. His calm confidence, his industrious scholarship, his innate humbleness, his Spirit-filled Christian life has made him the ideal after whom many Wheaton students try to pattern their lives. He teaches character by what he does, not by what he says.[14]

Alumni Gymnasium

On inauguration day the ground-breaking ceremonies for a new gymnasium marked the first of many building projects that would characterize the expansionist era over which President Edman was to preside. The old gymnasium had become increasingly inadequate, especially for intercollegiate basketball. A campaign in 1937 to raise funds for a gymnasium and swimming pool had fallen short of the goal and had been laid aside. Consequently, in 1940 Dr. Edman suggested to Edward Cording, director of public relations, Ed Coray, who was to do much of the solicitation for funds, and Harvey Chrouser, just returned to the campus as football coach, that they work for a more modest building than the 1937 plans called for, a gymnasium-auditorium without a swimming pool. During a soccer trip to Western Maryland College, where he had gone as substitute for the regular coach, Chrouser saw a gymnasium that seemed like a model to meet Wheaton's needs. Never hesitant in advancing the cause of Wheaton, Harvey asked for, and was given, the plans for the building to bring home.

President Edman was impressed with the drawings and invited Chrouser and Coach Ed Coray to present their ideas to the Board of Trustees in February 1941. When asked by Trustee Robert Nicholas *who* would pay for such a building, Chrouser replied with confidence that the alumni would—his assurance based on talks with alumni at recent banquets where he had represented the College. Coray and Chrouser had also the enthusiastic support of alumni president Russell Mixter. The Board granted permission for the initiation of a new fund campaign and specified that if $75,000 could be raised by May 1, ground-breaking could take place on May 9. By the established date $85,000 was in hand, or pledged; architectural plans for a modified Georgian colonial brick building, to match the new women's dormitory, had been sketched by Herbert Brand of Chicago. Steel for the building—completed at a cost of $160,000—was procured the day before a freeze was put on such uses of steel by the War Resources Board.[15] On completion of the building the old gymnasium would be used for women's physical education classes and intramural sports.

The cornerstone was laid at Homecoming on October 11, with President Edman, Trustee Fischer, Professor Russell Mixter and the Reverend Torrey Johnson, present and past alumni presidents, and Tom Parks, Student Council president, participating. A copper box placed in the cornerstone contained a copy of the *Record,* the *Wheaton Daily Journal,* a college catalog, a student directory, and a copy of the Homecoming program.[16] The first event held in the new gymnasium-auditorium was a long chapel on May 29, 1942, marking the fulfillment of a dream for which many had worked and prayed. The building was dedicated on the Sunday afternoon of commencement weekend, June 14, when the combined men's and women's glee clubs sang before an assembly of 2,200 people, many of them awed by the size of the building and the realization that a dream had been fulfilled.[17] For a good many years the building was known simply as Alumni Gymnasium; but in 1968, in honor of Coach Coray's long service as athlete, coach, athletic director, teacher, alumni director, and friend to countless Wheatonites, the trustees fittingly renamed the building the Edward A. Coray Alumni Gymnasium.

The Alumni Association

Wheaton College alumni have always been strongly supportive of their alma mater, as the Alumni Gymnasium project indicates. Legend has it that the first gathering of Wheaton alumni occurred when a few of them met at the North Western station in Wheaton in 1862 and decided to have a friendship gathering. In time these alumni meetings became an annual banquet on campus at commencement—the only alumni activity—at which the entire senior class were guests. Gradually, however, student interest in this activity waned, and the alumni withdrew their largess.[18] In 1929 *The Alumni Quarterly* made its appearance, with Alex MacLeod, '23, as editor, and was offered at a subscription rate of one dollar a year.

In 1944 Ted Benson, '38, director of public relations, proposed the establishment of an alumni association with a paid executive secretary and office staff. The suggestion met with approval, and Benson was invited to become the first full-time secretary of the association, chartered in 1944 by the State of Illinois. Ed Coray succeeded Benson as executive director in 1951 and served until 1971, when he was named senior director, a position he held until 1981. John Taylor, '45, directed the affairs of the association from 1971 to 1974. At Coray's suggestion the first Alumni Day, intended to bring Wheatonites back to campus for class reunions at five-year intervals, was held in 1956. Lee Pfund, a member of the physical education department and successful basketball and baseball coach from the time of his arrival on campus in 1949, followed Taylor in the leadership of the association in 1975 to the present.

The Alumni Distinguished Service Award to Alma Mater was established in 1953, the first recipients being Mignon Bollman Mackenzie, '33, professor of music, and Enock Dyrness, '23, registrar, who had served the College in several administrative roles. The first winner of the Alumni Distinguished Service Award to Society in 1953 was John Brobeck, professor of physiology at the University of Pennsylvania.

Senior Scholarship Awards, announced annually at the spring honors convocation to a junior man and woman, based on citizenship, Christian character, and contribution to college life, make a substantial contribution to those two students' senior year tuition. Small unannounced grants are occasionally made to needy students and to projects that might not otherwise find support.

Long housed on the first floor of Blanchard Hall, the Alumni Association moved in 1980 to attractive newly furnished quarters in Westgate, the home of Wheaton College presidents from 1936 to 1980.

By 1983 there were 32,300 Wheaton alumni around the world, and eighty alumni clubs in the United States and abroad, meeting from time to time for fellowship and to hear Wheaton news from a college representative. The large turnout at these gatherings is an eloquent witness to the affection Wheatonites have for their alma mater. For many years Wheaton has been among the top ten colleges of its size in the nation in the number of alumni donors, the amount of money given, and the percentage of contributing association members. In four of these years the Wheaton Alumni Fund was first in alumni giving among all large coeducational colleges in the nation.

From its resources the Alumni Association has given generously to the faculty salary program begun in 1952. For the ten years following, $455,000 was contributed, and $1,373,000 between 1970 and 1983.[19] Through its plan of Alumni Study Grants, begun in 1946, the Association has subsidized many leaves of absence for faculty members for study and writing. For this purpose $422,000 was given between 1970 and 1983. Since Wheaton did not have a sabbatical program prior to 1982, these Alumni grants were immensely helpful in contributing to faculty growth in scholarly competence.

The Association, as an autonomous corporation, tries to maintain an objective view in its efforts to be constructive in its service to Wheaton College.[20]

Edward A. Coray,
Executive Director of the Alumni
Association 1951–1971; Director of
Physical Education 1926–1951.

Edward A. Coray Alumni Gymnasium.

On the Threshold of War

When the fall term opened in 1941, the beginning of Dr. Edman's first full year as president, 1,193 students were enrolled. They came knowing the perilous state of the western world: France and the Low Countries were prostrate, Britain was severely bruised after the retreat from Dunkirk and the devastating aerial attacks. The German Third Reich dominated Europe. There was no sure foreshadowing what was to come by year's end, changing lives and drastically altering the world.

Students came from every state except Nevada, Vermont, and New Hampshire and from thirteen foreign countries. Among the new arrivals those warm September days were over 400 freshmen. Many of them had gotten their first glimpse of the historic Tower as their train passed the edge of the campus to the south of Blanchard Hall. They were welcomed by college officials and "big brothers and sisters," taken on a tour of the campus, established in their living quarters—and did the bidding of upperclassmen: carried their books, ran errands, stood in their presence.

Enrollment in 1941 exceeded that of the preceding year, even though a number of young men had entered the armed services during the summer. Football coaches Chrouser and Nelson noted that the military draft, at least for the present, had not seriously cut into their squad; they looked forward, with Captain Valdo Oleari, to a successful season. During the fall only four athletes were drafted. The Homecoming committee, in the annual fall rite, presented the traditional activities. In addition it sought to reach widely scattered alumni through a one to two A.M. broadcast from WMBI, the Moody radio station. Featured on the program was J. Wesley Ingles, '25, author of the popular novel, *Silver Trumpet*, which by then had sold 30,000 copies in sixteen printings. Begun after Ingles's graduation from Princeton Seminary in 1929, the story was intended to be a contrast to the popular "flaming youth" novel of the twenties. The main character, Randall Mac-Rae, well-to-do socialite and jazz trumpeter, is converted at an evangelistic meeting, comes to Wheaton, falls in love with Fay Thurston, and dedicates his trumpet to the Lord's service. MacRae is greatly inspired by Dr. Blanchard, Dr. Dow, and Dr. Straw, who appear under the names of Brainerd, Dawn, and Stow. Though the book is now little known, it was still being read in the 1950s, and a number of students attributed their conversion and subsequent matriculation at Wheaton College to reading *Silver Trumpet*.

In September 1940 a young man from North Carolina named Billy Graham entered Wheaton as a transfer student from Florida Bible Institute. The following year he became pastor of the United Gospel Tabernacle, an independent church, meeting in the Masonic Hall in downtown Wheaton. Graham succeeded President Edman, who had served the church since 1938, but now, under the press of this new duties, felt the need to resign. In 1942 Graham was elected by the student body to the presidency of the Christian Council. Commenting on his vision for the work of the council, he said:

Alumni line up at Blanchard Tower for parade of classes.

The Stupe. Popular student center in the old gymnasium building during the 1940s.

"We want to stress a spirit of evangelism next year that will put the whole campus on a mass production basis."[21]

The autumn days, always ornamenting the campus with red and yellow leaves, moved swiftly by. The Marine Band came again, with their shining brass and dazzling scarlet and blue uniforms; the football and soccer teams played out their games before excited crowds; the lits met weekly for fellowship and challenging programs. The second annual Mothers' and Dads' Day came and passed, and was accounted a success.

To meet a friend, make a date, or simply relax over a coke, students made the "Stupe," a name derived from Student Union and physical education, the popular center of the campus. Located on the ground floor of the women's gymnasium in a single large room were the bookstore and a refreshment counter, with a few tables and chairs. In the hallway was the student post office, daily a center of expectations, greeting, and animated conversation. Often President Edman would announce that he and "Friend Wife" would be at the Stupe at four o'clock that afternoon for a coke date and invited students to join them. The cooperative refreshment center was run entirely by students.[22]

The war in Europe led Americans to accept voluntary restraints on many activities, among them unnecessary travel, since American army trainees were continually in transit on public transportation facilities. To restrain student travel at Thanksgiving, President Edman announced in 1941 that only Thanksgiving day would be a holiday, a none-too-popular move, though the practice continued throughout the war. The day began with a chapel service, followed by a football game with North Park College, won by Wheaton, 27-13. So that all students might have Thanksgiving dinner at the same time, the food service made use of the two dining halls and lower chapel, gracefully decorated for the festivities. Games, exhibitions, and an evening musical program completed a memorable occasion.

World War II Begins

Although there had been exchanges of threatening diplomatic notes between the United States and Japan in late November and early December 1941, there was no reference to those ominous events in the *Wheaton Record* of December 5. The lead story announced: "Dobbins Conducts Band in Concert of Light Numbers." Students, however, were not unmindful of the vast struggles in the European theater of war, nor did the College fail to remind them that Nazi barbarism threatened to destroy western democracy. Class instruction, evening lectures, and *Record* articles by faculty members helped interpret the cataclysmic struggle.

Wheaton College students were as shocked as other Americans when they learned on Sunday afternoon, December 7, of the Japanese attack on Pearl Harbor, even while diplomatic negotiations in Washington were in progress. Days were to pass before the country would know the devastating extent of the attack on the American naval base in Hawaii. On Monday morning,

December 8, the *New York Times*, in its major headline, summed up what had happened: "Japan Wars on U.S. and Britain; Makes Sudden Attack on Hawaii; Heavy Fighting at Sea Reported."

Students and faculty assembled to hear a radio broadcast of President Franklin D. Roosevelt's address to a joint session of Congress in which he requested from them a formal declaration of war. "Yesterday—December 7, 1941—a date that will live in infamy," he said, "the United States of America was suddenly and deliberately attacked by naval and air forces of the Empire of Japan." In resolute tones the President assured the nation of ultimate victory: "With confidence in our Armed Forces, with the unbounding determination of our people, we will gain the inevitable triumph. So help us God."[23]

Coach Ed Coray, from his place among the faculty on the platform of Pierce Chapel, watched the faces of students as they listened to the solemn words of President Roosevelt. "On this historic winter morning in 1941," he later wrote, "I looked at faces of strong young men, many of whom I had been associated with in athletics or in classes. I wondered how many would soon be in the military forces and which ones would never come back. I looked at the faces of the fine young women, some engaged to be married, and many with boy friends. I wondered how the war would change the course of many of their lives."[24]

President Edman then spoke to the students, reminding them that their patriotic obligation for the present was to perform their routine duties to the best of their abilities. He urged them to continue with their college work a semester at a time; there was no need for immediate military enlistment. "We should prepare ourselves," he said "to make sacrifices in the real sense of the word. We can begin by saving time, energy and materials." There would soon be need for sacrifice and service among the college women, as well as the men.[25]

For the students, war had suddenly became real, as John Witmer declared in the *Record:* "We college age Americans have never lived through a war before. It was always something remote, ghostlike, that haunted other nations of the world; but it never touched our nation with its lightning fingers of invasion."[26] In the classroom, over coffee and cokes in the Stupe, in sober dorm discussions, everywhere on campus the war was the focus of concern. What could Wheaton College do to further the war effort? Was the war a threat to the survival of western civilization? What was the Christian's responsibility? Asked by the *Record* what their attitude toward conscientious objectors was, most students were tolerant of that position, but few held it as their own. Senior Floyd Northrup of Oneonta, New York, expressed a typical judgment: "Admitting that war itself is not a Christian policy, nevertheless, in my opinion, it is the duty of the Christian steward to remain faithful in war or peace. If our nation calls, an answer could well be given in Christ's own familiar words: 'Render to Caesar the things that are Caesar's, and to God the things that are God's.' "[27]

Early in January 1942, President Edman was called to Baltimore for a series of conferences of college presidents to discuss with representatives of the national government the role of the colleges in the war. In the same city, he also attended the annual meeting of the Association of American Colleges, which passed a number of resolutions, among them one recommending that colleges accelerate their educational programs in order to help many students complete their training before entering service. In compliance with that proposal Wheaton instituted, in January 1943, graduation convocations in January and August, a practice that continued throughout the war and for several years after.

Wheaton's Contribution to the War

Wheaton's immediate response to the war was to organize campus energy and resources for a victory effort. Professor Enock Dyrness was appointed advisor to students considering the opportunities for military service. Red Cross classes under the direction of campus nurse Ada Rury and Coach Del Nelson were begun at once. Defense stamps and bonds went on sale at the college post office, stamps for ten cents each and bonds for $18.75. Nearly every student carried a small booklet in which savings stamps could be pasted, the booklet to be surrendered, when filled, for an $18.75 war bond, worth $25.00 at maturity. At the suggestion of the Student Council, President Edman appointed a Victory Committee to coordinate all campus war-related activity, made up of the Faculty Advisory Board under the direction of Harvey Chrouser and the Student War Board, both groups working closely with the local office of civilian defense.

Quickly a dozen red-white-and-blue collection boxes were placed on campus, where students might deposit empty tooth paste and shaving cream tubes, old razor blades, books and magazines, and waste paper, a small but useful initial effort. Many students and faculty took Red Cross first-aid training and prepared bandages and surgical dressings. Sponsored by the American Red Cross, a Blood Donors Service was established and directed by the Pre-Med Club, under the leadership of Carl Johnson.

Hung in Pierce Chapel, shortly after the war began, was a large service flag with a red border, a white satin field, and in the center a blue star in which periodically the number of Wheaton students and alumni in the service was shown. The number 56 appeared in the star when the banner was first raised, with student Marshall Weatherby making the dedicatory address.[28] The first gold star was in memory of Neal Curtis, killed in a training flight in Sumter, South Carolina. His wife Kathleen Peacock Curtis, ex '44, became Wheaton's first war widow. Ensign William Lloyd, '39, killed aboard the Oahu near Corregidor in May 1942, was later honored by the launching of the U.S.S. Lloyd, a destroyer escort, at the Charleston Navy Yard. Lloyd's mother looked on and Harold Lindsell, a recent graduate of the College stood nearby. Wheaton's first war hero, according to the Re-

cord, was Lieutenant David D. Kliewer, '39, who bombed and sank a Japanese submarine off the coast of Wake Island five days after Pearl Harbor. Later he was made a prisoner of war by the Japanese and held for the duration of the conflict.

Lists of former students and alumni in service, together with their rank, unit, and location, appeared regularly in the *Record* so that those who remained on campus could write to them and pray for them. Shortly after the conflict began, the Inter-Service Prayer Fellowship, directed by Ken Hammonds, was organized to pray for the men in service and to keep them in touch with one another through a circular letter.[29] A full day of prayer was held several times during the war. In April 1943, at the suggestion of Billy Graham, speaking for the Christian Service Council, students began the practice of ringing the tower bell each evening at five o'clock, calling everyone to pause and remember the men of the college family in the armed forces.

To keep the campus and the community informed of the many phases of the war effort, the college faculty organized a War Lecture Series, in which more than twenty faculty members offered their service to public schools, women's and service clubs, and campus groups. Talks on such subjects as "Ships at Sea and in the Air" and "Sky War," given by Dr. Hawley O. Taylor, "Our Government Organizes for War," given by Dr. S. Richey Kamm, "Wartime Censorship" by Dr. Joseph Free, and "If Bombs Fall in Your Community" by Dr. Paul Wright, provided practical information. Courses like bacteriology, physiology, American government, social psychology, and astronomy were adapted to give them some immediate war usefulness. New courses, such as chemical warfare and economics of war, were added to the curriculum as the second semester began.[30] For area residents engaged in war industry, night courses, in cooperation with Illinois Institute of Technology, and under the Engineering Science and Management War Training Program, were introduced in statistical methods, personnel management, and production management. During the first summer of the war Wheaton trained a group of Naval Cadets in their primary flying program, and prepared for other campus service programs that would be assigned to Wheaton.[31]

Academic departments were asked to examine their offerings and make an accounting of their services to the war effort. For departments like the sciences, mathematics, foreign languages, history, and physical education the contribution was readily evident. Other departments found their efforts less direct and visible: Dr. Henry Thiessen said for the Bible department, "War conditions have had little effect on this department"; Professor Peter Stam said for music that the department was "supplying music for many patriotic meetings and general morale": the English department, Professor Marian Downey declared, "expects to continue warfare offensive and defensive, for the purity, protection, and preservation of the English language."[32]

Army Specialized Training Program

The first Chicago area blackout was held on August 12, 1942, at 10:30 P.M., when sirens, whistles, and air-raid warning alarms sent students hustling to their pre-assigned dorm basement shelters. Fourth floor Blanchard men fled down four flights of stairs in the darkness to the east end basement rifle range. Many such groups held prayer meetings during the blackout.[33]

In the summer of 1943, 250 soldiers, who had completed basic training, arrived from all parts of the country to begin their assignment in the Army Specialized Training Program 3672, known to students as ASTP. With headquarters in the Women's Gym, the men were housed in Hiatt Hall, Plumb Studio, Bartlett Hall, and Howe House. Meals were served in lower chapel. The rigorous program consisted of three twelve-week terms, with a weekly schedule of twenty-four class hours, twenty-four hours of supervised study, six hours of physical education, and five hours of military science. Academic work was offered by members of the college faculty—Professors Taylor, Wright, Kilby, Kamm, Winsor, and Jayne—with Ed Coray supervising physical education.

Commander of the Wheaton ASTP was Major Joseph J. Peot, who had been sent to the local campus from the University of Wisconsin. Interviewed shortly after his arrival by a *Chicago Tribune* reporter, Peot said: "The men like it here. We are being given fine cooperation from both the college and the town."[34] When he was informed that the College would not relax its behavior standards for the soldiers while they were on campus, and that the army in negotiating the contract had accepted the limitation, Major Peot was understanding and cooperative.[35] Through the influence of Wheaton students and the general atmosphere of the campus, a number of the young soldiers became Christians. The ASTP unit, which remained on campus until it was withdrawn in April 1944, was granted to Wheaton in place of the U.S. Air Force unit promised early in 1943 but cancelled when no adequate air strips could be found in the area.[36]

With the arrival of the ASTP, the Student War Board, under president Dick Strom and faculty advisor DeWitt Jayne, intensified its efforts, both to entertain the young soldiers and to encourage campus participation in war-related activities. As he began his responsibilities Strom said: "We hope to have every Wheaton student well informed about the war, with the hope that this will lead to willing sacrifice in every way to insure speedy victory."[37] Entertainment included concerts, public readings, and special events like Phil Foxwell's mystifying magic show. News films were a regular weekend feature, as were *Record* columns such as "Onward Christian Soldiers" and "Off the Record"; Red Cross blood drives were sponsored quarterly; and from time to time special projects were undertaken, such as organizing students for routine jobs on campus and in the community.[38]

A typical blood drive, like the one announced in the *Record* and promoted in various ways on the campus in December 1942, produced 263 pints of blood. For their gifts of blood that would save lives on the battle-field or in a hospital, students were awarded a blood donor medal by the Red Cross.[39] On another occasion a well-publicized "Buy a Jeep Week," sponsored by the Student War Board and intended to arouse interest in the sale of war stamps, produced excellent response. With the cooperation of the U.S. Army, a small new reconnaissance jeep, costing $600, was brought to campus and its "rideability" publicly demonstrated by President Ed-man.[40] Contributions toward the purchase of a jeep helped to send the War Bond and Stamp drive, begun in October, over the top for $2,500 by No-vember 15, 1943. A March 1945 bond drive was stimulated by auctioning President Edman's "Old Gray Hat," sold by auctioneer Bill Standridge to student Axel Anderson for a pledge of $768.[41]

Spiritual Impact of the War

During times of war there is a heightened sense of life's transience, the need to examine priorities, and to review one's relationship with God. Wheaton students were seeing their young friends called into service in in-creasing numbers in 1943, the year in which the western Allies began to hold their own against the enormous war-making capacity of Nazi Germany. So-bered by the growing number of gold stars on the service flag hung in Pierce Chapel—seven by 1943—they were ready to listen intently when the Rever-end Harold P. Warren, pastor of the North Baptist Church, Flint, Michigan, came to speak at the mid-winter services, February 7th to 14th.

Throughout the week students and faculty were conscious of an unusual moving of the Spirit of God in their midst. At the first meeting several hun-dred persons responded to Pastor Warren's invitation to accept a deeper re-lationship with God.[42] Tuesday was declared a day of prayer, classes were suspended and students assembled by classes, dormitories, lits, and other groups to seek the blessing of the Lord for themselves and the country. At the Thursday chapel the captain of the cross-country team confessed that he had led his men in a Sunday race without the knowledge of the administra-tion; he asked forgiveness.[43] Dr. Edman then said, "If there are others who have need to confess their wrong-doing, they may do so now." At once, in all parts of the chapel, students began to stand and acknowledge their desire for cleansing from unconfessed sins. Long into the night the confessions con-tinued. Classes were suspended, and the Spirit of God moved quietly among the gathered students and faculty. On Friday the revival continued often with as many as a hundred standing, waiting to speak. The spirit of revival was also carried by a number of student pastors to their own churches.

Frequently on a Saturday night as many as a hundred students took the train to Chicago, some to sing or play in the Youth for Christ band, some to attend the rallies. Such rallies, begun in New York during the war as a wholesome way for youth to spend Saturday night, spread quickly through-out the country. In Chicago they were especially successful under the direction of Torrey Johnson, '30, one of the early leaders of Youth for Christ, and his associate Bob Cook, '34. Held first in Orchestra Hall, they soon moved to the much larger auditorium of Moody Church; and early in 1945 they drew a crowd of 30,000 to a giant rally at the Chicago Stadium, with many Wheaton students attending.[44] Billy Graham was the first field representative of the Chicago Youth for Christ. Other Wheatonites who gained early experience with the organization included Bob Evans, '39, founder of Greater Europe Mission and Paul Freed, '40, organizer of the Far East Broadcasting Company.

From the Wheaton classes graduating immediately following the war years, 169 students committed themselves to foreign missionary service. A number of these were former servicemen who in their military assignments, particularly in the Far East—Japan, Philippines, New Guinea, Okinawa— had seen the urgent need for the gospel in those lands. There were times of fellowship, too, when Wheaton men encountered each other in many parts of the world. David Roberts, '41, remembers how, in 1944, seven of these men, each from a different branch of service, met in Okinawa, sat on the floor to share their simple rations in a bombed-out building, and sang and prayed together in reunion and thanksgiving.[45]

Homecoming in 1943 was typical of those events during the war. Using the theme A.W.O.L.—"At Wheaton on Leave"—Wallace Greig and his student committee focused on the many soldiers already on campus and a contingent of Wheaton Navy men on leave from their station at Mt. Pleasant, Michigan. Arriving on campus, they saw a row of large wooden letters in front of Blanchard Hall announcing the theme. On President Edman's lawn was a picture of him, in his buck private's uniform of World War I, and son Charles, in the Seabees blues of the present, with the legend "Like Father, Like Son."[46]

Wheaton College and the local community were gratified when they learned that a Victory ship, the S.S. Wheaton, was to be launched on March 22, 1945, at Terminal Island, California. The *S.S. Wheaton Victory* was one of the series of Victory ships named for America's oldest educational institutions with student bodies over 500, the order of assignment following the chronological order of the founding of the colleges. Present at the launching were Stephen D. Bechtel, whose company had built the ship, and to represent Wheaton, the Reverend John Shearer, '39, pastor of the North Hollywood Presbyterian Church.

Rejoicing on campus, together with prayers of thanksgiving for victory and peace, marked the coming of V-E Day (Victory in Europe) on May 8, 1945. V-J Day (Victory in Japan) was not to be achieved until August. By the end of the great conflict the service flag in Pierce Chapel showed that 1,485 Wheatonites had entered the services. In the white satin field of the banner, edged with red, were thirty-nine gold stars. The *Armed Forces Tower*, a supplement to the regular 1945 *Tower*, published a complete Honor Roll of the Wheaton men and women who had served their country, with pictures of all those who had given their lives in the conflict.[47]

A WETN broadcast in 1949. At the piano, Virginia Erickson Heck, station manager Richard Gerig at the microphone, quartet members: James Wroughton, Juliana Sieker Asbrink, Virginia Piepgrass Loptson, Eugene Nelson.

Breyer Chemistry and Geology Building.

CHAPTER 11

Post-War:
New Visions
Of Service

A CENTRAL CONCERN OF THE CAMPUS DURING THE WAR years was to contribute to the successful outcome of the conflict. But there was also thoughtful planning for the days after the war's termination. At an early fall faculty meeting in 1943 Dr. Edman outlined his vision for the campus building needs. Wheaton urgently needed a student union, a modern dining hall, completion of the North Hall women's dormitory complex, a conservatory of music, men's residence halls, a science building, an enlarged health center, and a new academy building.[1] Later he shared his hope with the alumni in an open letter and requested their prayers and thoughtful stewardship.[2] Overwhelming as those expectations may have seemed at the time, they were to be fully realized.

A faculty planning committee, headed by Dr. S. Richey Kamm was formed in 1944 after a small faculty group urged President Edman to seek faculty assistance in exercising more effective administrative leadership. During the summer of 1944 the group divided and journeyed east to visit colleges and universities—among them Antioch, Haverford, Swarthmore, Bryn Mawr, Dartmouth, Oberlin, Princeton, Pennsylvania, and Indiana. During the school year, visits were made to Beloit, Lawrence, Hope, Grinnell, Iowa State, and the University of Wisconsin. Committee members, as they traveled, found themselves amazed "at Wheaton's having been able to carry on so high a type of work as she has done in such unbelievably cramped quarters."[3]

The committee's purpose was to make recommendations, "to strengthen the intellectual, spiritual, and social life of the campus that we shall be adequately prepared to carry on the training of our present study group in a way pleasing to God and in harmony with the standards of the school."[4]

In the beginning, the committee found that "we have been too slow in recognizing our increased responsibilities as a Christian college in this day, and that our present system for the formulation and execution of college policies is very frequently hampered by indecision and lack of properly coordinated effort among trustees, administration, faculty, and alumni."[5] The committee proposed to identify, describe, and eliminate deficiencies through a series of constructive proposals and to keep the faculty informed of the progress of its work by weekly reports.

The committee began its study by strongly urging that the student body not exceed 1,200, the maximum number that could be seated in Pierce Chapel, until there were more adequate residence and dining facilities. But like the adolescent boy who persists in outgrowing his trousers, the enrollment did creep upward as the College tried to reduce the number of highly qualified Christian young people denied admission.

To the disadvantage of the College, Wheaton was often without a chief executive officer during long periods of the summer. The College also needed someone to formulate and administer the curriculum, the person now known as the academic dean. Nor was anyone designated to orient new faculty members and assist them as they settled in. Administrators charged with overseeing student activities and student discipline were in need of more training and authority.

The library was in two locations on the second and third floors of Blanchard Hall—one called Frost, the other Fischer—and thus was burdened with logistical hindrances to efficiency and comfort. Its growth rate in volumes was regarded as commendable, with holdings of 87,000 volumes in 1945, increasing by 4,500 accessions a year. The librarians were recommending a new emphasis on quality of holdings, yet the urgent need for a new library building was acknowledged by everyone.

"Teaching is the main business of a college," the committee declared. It is "around instruction that all other phases of the educational process in an institution must center." "Where the fundamental philosophy of the college is most manifest is in the teaching process; here in an institution like Wheaton the Christian view of life must emerge clearly. Excellence in teaching can come only from a good faculty, clearly committed to scholarship as a Christian calling."[6] "No excellence of administration, no abundance of buildings, no amount of physical equipment, no success in athletics, not even a strong spiritual life can make up for a poor faculty." Wheaton had been attracting competent faculty members, but better salary inducements were necessary, and the College needed to draw its instructors from a wider range of institutions and backgrounds. Progress had been made in reducing the average age of teachers, a correction urged by the North Central Association a decade before. In 1934 there were twelve very capable professors aged seventy or over; in 1944 there were none.[7] The retirement plan had made that adjustment possible.

Wheaton was unique among American colleges, the committee held, because it had no denominational support and no regularly organized clientele—though it had never disparaged denominationalism. In 1945 it drew its largest number of students from three groups: Baptist, Presbyterian, and independent. An economic study indicated that Wheaton families were a fairly well-distributed sampling of American middle-class society. A combination of factors usually influenced a student to come to Wheaton College, but two-thirds of the students were most influenced by other students, past or present (many of them their parents or pastors). Occasionally students were influenced in their decision to come to Wheaton by their experience in a summer session, enrollment in which in 1945 had grown to 727 from 16 in the first session of 1916.

According to the faculty planning committee the objectives of the College for students could be reduced to a brief list: (1) liberal education in the arts and sciences; (2) study of the Bible as the foundation of a liberal education; (3) intellectual and aesthetic development; (4) development of a philosophy of life based on Christian values; (5) physical, mental, and spiritual health. The committee, however, believed that these values needed to be reconsidered; they did not assure students adequate counsel in vocational choices, preparation for marriage and family life, integration of faith and learning, or education for citizenship, world and national. Samplings of student opinion through the senior questionnaire, given annually at the end of the year, and alumni surveys indicated that a broader understanding of objectives was necessary, with consequent improvement in instruction to assure the realization of the objectives.

Wheaton, reluctant to be a trend setter, had been hesitant to move forward along as yet uncharted academic pathways. Fear of the disapproval of a conservative constituency was often a restraining factor. But the work of the planning committee encouraged many segments of the College to realize the need for freedom to act independently to achieve more effective programs.

The academic planning committee suggested the need for reexamining Wheaton's program in general education, a kind of study begun by many colleges during the late war years, prompted in part by the appearance in 1945 of the influential Harvard report, *General Education in a Free Society.* The report noted that the free elective system in many institutions—this was not true at Wheaton—had fragmented students' education to such a degree that there was no longer an essential core of knowledge. Further, it declared, the war had caused many educators to realize that a free society must have a cluster of essential values, for the preservation of which it is ready to sacrifice life and treasure.

With the report of the academic planning committee in the fall of 1945,

Dr. Kamm's group completed its work and was succeeded by the newly formed North Central Committee. One of the immediate outcomes of the academic committee's work was the appointment of Dr. Roger Voskuyl, professor of chemistry, in the fall of 1946 as academic dean, a move that was to bring new strength in institutional leadership. The work of the academic planning committee was perhaps the most thoroughgoing self-study in the history of the College. It set numerous faculty committees to work, established a pattern for institutional self-study that was to be a model for years to come, and inspired individual studies such as Professor Earle Cairns's *A Blueprint for Christian Higher Education*.

The Building Boom

The campus planning committee laid out a comprehensive, long-range building plan based on (1) its experience in visiting other institutions, (2) the land area available for expansion, and (3) the counsel of a committee of trustees, alumni, and faculty, headed by Robert Walker, '36, who was then a teacher of journalism at the College and an editor. A Wheaton Centenary Plan for buildings was presented, setting the Charles Blanchard 100th anniversary in 1948 as the completion date for the Memorial Student Center. For the 100th anniversary of the founding of Illinois Institute in 1954, the completion of all the necessary dormitories was proposed, and by the centennial of Wheaton College in 1960, the completion of science, library, and conservatory buildings.[8]

At all of the colleges visited by the campus planning committee, they found, on the average, two to three times as many buildings per thousand students as Wheaton had. The committee projected a decade of growth within a quadrangle north of Franklin Street, bounded on the east and west by Adams and Irving streets and on the north by Kenilworth. At the north, and running along Kenilworth and facing south, would be the Memorial Student Center, long needed and much talked about during the war as a suitable tribute to Wheaton men and women who had served their country. The Memorial Center had been authorized in the fall of 1943 by the trustees, who proposed, then, the securing of a fund of $250,000 for the building, "to contain a dining room, the department of home economics, a student lounge, student services, and such other activities as seem appropriate."[9]

With the approval of the trustees the campaign for funds was initiated by the Alumni Association under its secretary, Ted Benson, who drew Coach Ed Coray into the effort. During the planning stages for the building, controversy arose over its location: the planning committee and students favoring a site north of Franklin Street, others feeling that the Center should be placed on the lawn between the Stupe and Williston Hall. An informal poll of students found them favoring, ten to one, the northern location.[10] Nevertheless, the location between the Stupe and Williston Hall was chosen on the recommendation of Porter Butts, a University of Wisconsin authority on

Student Union buildings, his argument being that the center would be most useful at the point of largest student traffic.

A second controversy developed over the design of the building prepared by local architect Robert Salisbury, but Salisbury readily agreed to numerous modifications and improvements suggested by art professor Karl Steele.[11] With $120,000 raised from all sources, ground-breaking took place at Homecoming in October 1949; the cornerstone was laid during commencement in June 1950. With its graceful Georgian lines and handsome furnishings, the Memorial Student Center evoked many expressions of thanksgiving during the dedication ceremonies, at which President Edman presided on June 11, 1951.

In the lobby of the building is a bronze plaque bearing the names of the thirty-nine Wheaton men who gave their lives in World War II. On the second floor of the building is the Gold Star Chapel, a place for meditation, individual prayer, group worship, and small weddings. When the new building opened, the administration and student leaders urged that a new name be found for the dining and snack area, something more aesthetic than "Stupe." But the old name was comfortable and familiar, so "Stupe" it remained.

While the trustees were discussing plans for the Memorial Student Center in 1944, they were also sensitive to the urgent need for student housing. Rejecting suggestions for temporary accommodations, they authorized the building of two men's units at President Street and College Avenue, and the extension of North Hall. Buildings at both locations were completed for occupancy in the late fall of 1946, the two men's dormitories at the cost of $120,000 each, one half the cost per student of the North Hall construction. The President Street dormitories were cheaply and hastily built under wartime stringencies of materials, money, and labor.

With the prospect of a large number of returned veterans appealing for admission to Wheaton under the GI Bill of Rights, which provided tuition for service men and women, the faculty recommended to the trustees in February 1946 that enrollment be increased to 1,500, a request promptly approved.[12]

Wheaton and Federal Aid

The press for admission of students far in excess of the institution's capability to accept them was a common experience throughout the country, for universities and colleges alike. Most of these institutions lacked the resources to build the dormitories and other necessary elements of the educational complex and gladly accepted the federal government's offer to provide funds for new buildings and programs. Wheaton, however, with a few others like Rockford College, chose not to receive government funding, but to finance its growth through private efforts only. Wheaton's resolve won acclaim in the press and in conservative financial circles; some donors assisted Wheaton out of admiration for what they believed to be a courageous stand.

Without compromise or variation, the resolution of Wheaton College to meet all its needs by private funding was maintained throughout the Edman and Armerding administrations. In the spring of 1980 President Armerding issued a brief statement, published as a leaflet and widely distributed called "Here We Stand..." It cites several government regulations which would compromise Wheaton's commitment to biblical morality if the College were forced to comply with them. The leaflet sums up institutional policy by declaring that "because government assistance usually leads to government interference, Wheaton College steadfastly guards its independence from federal funding."[13]

In May 1934 the Russell Committee's *Report of a Survey of Wheaton College* had suggested that an adequate library should be the first among new buildings planned by the College. But with the intervention of World War II and its consequences, other matters received priority. Nonetheless, Dr. Edman and the faculty continued to cherish the dream of a spacious library worthy of Wheaton's aspiration to maintain an institution of superior quality. Consequently, it was with great joy that President Edman was able to announce in chapel on January 6, 1950, an anonymous gift of $250,000 for the building of a new library that would seat 600 students and have shelf space for 150,000 books. The anonymity of the donor was well kept for a while, but he was ultimately known to be Robert F. Nicholas, a trustee and realtor from Oak Park, Illinois. Together with his wife, he had made the gift with the specification—accepted by Dr. Edman—that no additional funds be sought from alumni and friends, who had already been solicited for several projects through the 1940s.

Ground was broken for the library at commencement in June 1950; the cornerstone was laid on Sunday, December 10. Standing beside Dr. Edman for the ceremony was Miss Julia Blanchard, '99—daughter of Charles Blanchard and granddaughter of Jonathan Blanchard—librarian for forty years, who was serving at the time as college archivist. President Edman said: "As we lay the cornerstone, we remember that our Lord and Savior is called in Scripture the Chief Cornerstone, and we are all 'living' stones in the building."[14] On December 5, 1951, librarian John Kephart and his staff moved more than 95,000 books from the Frost and Fischer libraries in Blanchard Hall along a chain of student hands across the campus to shelves in the new library.

In the midst of the aggressive building program, the trustees made the dramatic announcement that Fred McManis, Sr., of Houston, Texas, son of a Methodist circuit rider, had named Wheaton College the recipient of a munificent gift, a half interest in the W-K-M Company, which he had founded in 1918. The College was to buy up the outstanding stock of the company, valued at $5,000,000, at $250 a share through the use of earnings from the company's oil field equipment business.[15] The other half-interest in the com-

Memorial Student Center.

Ground-breaking for Nicholas Library, Commencement 1950. L. to r.: Trustee Robert Van Kampen, Harold Mackenzie, Dr. Merrill Tenney, President Edman, Julia Blanchard, Dr. Paul Wright.

pany was given to Southwestern University, Georgetown, Texas, whose president had been a former pastor of the McManis family church. Realizing that they did not have the managerial skill to run the W-K-M Company, the two institutions sold the firm to the American Car and Foundry Company in 1954 and added the money to their endowments. Fred McManis had been told about Wheaton College by his cousin, Cary Weisiger, on the day of the stock market crash in 1929, when McManis was in Chicago in search of capital for his company.[16] If he had the resources to do so, Cary suggested to McManis, he should remember the needs of Wheaton College. The Texas businessman, who had professed faith in Christ "through the influence of the courageous life of his God-fearing, widowed mother," visited Wheaton several times, and was impressed with the Christian standards of the College.[17] At commencement of 1956, the south section of North Hall, the women's residence, was named for Carolyn McManis. A brass plaque in the lounge speaks of her as "the gracious and Godly wife of Fred McManis, Sr." On the same occasion the north section of the residence hall was dedicated to the memory of Alice Evans, the "Godly and gifted" wife of Dr. E. Joseph Evans, trustee of the College and long-time friend of President Edman.

In December 1951, Robert C. Van Kampen, chairman of the building committee of the Board of Trustees, announced plans for a new dining hall, a two-story building on Adams Street to accommodate the entire student body in two sittings. The initial cost estimate of $250,000 was raised to $350,000 by the time of ground-breaking on May 9, 1952. Students cheered the prospect of an end to the long lines they formed waiting for food service on the first floor and on the lower level (an economy dining room) of Williston Hall. Plagued by weather and strike delays, the building was finally ready for use when students returned from the Christmas holidays in January 1953. An open house for the community, faculty, and students on January 3 drew 1,000 guests.[18] When Williston Hall was no longer used for dining, the spacious front porch was removed and the exterior brickwork painted to match other campus buildings.

For many years the science departments had operated with inadequate laboratory facilities in the west end of Blanchard Hall. Little wonder, then, that there was great joy among the science faculty when, in 1951, announcement was made that Dr. John H. Breyer, of the class of 1905, a physician in Pasadena, California, was contributing a substantial portion of his resources to his alma mater for the construction of a science building. At the cost of more than a half million dollars, the structure to house the chemistry and geology departments was completed in 1955. Breyer Hall (designed by Warren S. Holmes Co. of Lansing, Michigan), was dedicated in honor of John H. Breyer and his wife, Georgia Allen Breyer (who had been graduated from the academy in 1901), at the fall Homecoming, with President Edman and Dr. Paul Wright, chairman of the chemistry department, presiding. Both Breyers were then living but were not present at the ceremony. Set in the brick wall on the west side of Breyer Hall is a large gray stone bearing the words: "In the beginning God created the heavens and the earth."

The transfer of the chemistry department from Blanchard Hall left desirable quarters on the first floor of the west end of the building for someone to claim. Dr. Clyde Kilby, chairman of the English department, acted quickly to win the space for his scattered colleagues. Of the move, student writer Joy Rice observed: "An old tradition on Wheaton's campus disappears this year as the English department invades an area long claimed by scientists—the west end of Blanchard. The staid English teachers, formerly known as East Enders, have abandoned their broom closets and settled in a seven-room suite of offices. . . shelves once filled with bottles of sulphuric acid and ammonium hydroxide have been replaced by bookshelves containing the works of Shakespeare, Milton, C. S. Lewis, and Dylan Thomas."[19] The move made possible, within the English department cluster of offices, the restoration of the office of Jonathan and Charles Blanchard, with the original desk, chair, and bookcase used by them.

The cornerstone of the long-needed new Health Center was laid at commencement in 1957. The attractive, well-equipped building, with twenty-five beds, was dedicated on October 20, 1957, as part of Homecoming. Now more complete diagnosis and medical care were possible than the old facility could offer.

The extensive building program in which Wheaton engaged following the war substantially increased the assets of the College—from $3,625,000 to $12,098,000 by 1959; during the same period the endowment rose from $706,000 to $4,650,000. The post-war decade was thus one of unprecedented growth in the history of Wheaton College.

Troubled Times and Recovery

The veterans who came to Wheaton after the war—many of them in their early twenties to begin their freshman year, some returning to college in their mid-twenties—were a serious minded group. Matured by travel and peril, by tough discipline, and by their awareness of the value of an education, they were eager to compensate for the lost years. In many classes they outnumbered students who had come to college directly from high school. Crowded conditions nearly everywhere on campus and the need for veterans to find housing in private homes were of small concern after what they had endured. Student initiation rites, which sometimes required newcomers to wear their clothes backwards for a day, or to drag a five-gallon tin attached to one leg, seemed foolish in that more sober age and disappeared for a while.

The administration and faculty recognized that the maturity of the veterans significantly affected the way many courses were taught. Progress in strengthening the college program was noted in committee reports at the faculty workshop at Winona Lake, Indiana, in September 1946. Dr. C. Gregg Singer, professor of history, challenged the faculty to leadership in the formulation of a Christian world and life view and to apply it to the development of a Christian philosophy of higher education. Many influences at work in American life and culture in the post-war years militated against a philosophy of Christian education: materialism, relativism, secularism, naturalism, humanism, and aspects of the pragmatic philosophy of education of John Dewey, the time's most influential educator. The old moral and ethical verities of pre-war American society were under steady attack. In their place, science and reason could be counted on, many educators believed, to formulate new systems of values and behavior appropriate to the realities of the mid-twentieth century.

Valiant efforts were made by educators like Robert Hutchins, Mortimer Alder, Norman Foerster, and Mark Van Doren to challenge pragmatic materialism through the advancement of the new humanism. The new humanists envisioned a reconstruction of society through the recovery of intellectual and moral values derived from classical and medieval philosophy.[20] They also cherished the Renaissance concept of man and human nature. The movement had merit but it was not Christian at its heart. It exercised significant influence, but it did not dissipate the trust in secular materialism and the great confidence of many in the prospect of scientific solutions to social and economic problems.

A Christian philosophy of education is quite different. It begins with a theistic philosophy of life, acknowledging the reality of a supernatural power and the revelation of a personal God as disclosed in the Scriptures. Christian higher education, according to Professor Earle Cairns, "may be defined as that process of the nurture of the individual through the creative teaching of our Hebrew-Christian and Greco-Roman heritage so that, knowing Christ as Savior, he may grow into an integrated whole, the free man of God, measured by the stature of Christ and fitted for every good work for the glory of God and the good of man."[21] A Christian philosophy of education of course acknowledges that there is a large body of valid data about humankind and the world based on observation and experience and recorded in the humanities, social sciences, and natural sciences.

That reservoir of experience constitutes the cultural heritage of western civilization, available to Christians and others alike, which Christians will want to appropriate, evaluate in the light of God's revelation and authority, and apply to the needs of their lives. Christians do not quarrel with others about the verifiable data of human experience, but they often differ about the source, meaning, and application of those data. "The frame of reference for all evaluation in the Christian college comes from the Scripture as God's special revelation. . . ." wrote Dr. Cornelius Jaarsma, professor of philosophy and education. "Our entire liberal arts curriculum belongs in this framework. All classroom teaching should be oriented toward this end."[22]

Returning to the campus from their retreat at Winona Lake in 1946, the faculty prepared to meet a student body of 1,524, with the normal ratio of half men and half women nearly restored after the imbalance of the war years. Housed in the gymnasium, while the new men's dormitories on College Avenue were being completed, were eighty-seven veterans, their long rows of double-deck beds reminiscent of service accommodations.[23] To teach this largest student body in Wheaton's history, there were 107 faculty members. Teacher-pupil ratio continued to improve, from seventeen to one in 1940 to fifteen to one in 1946, an evidence of the administration's desire to comply with the North Central Assocation's standard of teacher-pupil ratio of fourteen to one.

For at least a decade after the war one of the most crucial concerns at Wheaton was admissions. Many faculty members agreed that the most unenviable position on campus was that of director of admissions, held by Dr. Albert S. Nichols. He had the difficult task of determining who should be admitted and who, for want of accommodations, had to be denied admission—and sometimes these were children of loyal friends and alumni. In an effort to be objective, Dr. Nichols devised a point system which took into consideration a student's academic achievement, Christian testimony as revealed in an autobiographical statement, special abilities, and recommendations. Although these instruments for determining admissions served their purpose in a time of crisis, and were a genuine effort to be fair, the plan was never altogether satisfactory. *Record* editor Bill Standridge had his opinions about admissions and wrote editorially: "It is the responsibility of the college to accept no more students than can be adequately, thoroughly, and fully prepared for the life of highest possible service to Christ. And no one has a right to request or accept a place at Wheaton if they are not wholly committed to Christ and the advancement of his church."[24]

The typical Wheaton student in those days, according to a portrait prepared by the public relations department, "calls Illinois home, is a Baptist, reads the *Moody Monthly* in his home, chose Wheaton because of the influence of other students, and looks toward the mission field for post-college work."[25] In 1947, students planning to go to the mission fields of the world numbered 342; 254 were expecting to teach; and 202 looked forward to the ministry. Nearly all students came to Wheaton College with strong Christian convictions and the motivation to achieve.

The fall of 1946 marked the beginning of a long relationship between Wheaton and West Suburban Hospital in nearby Oak Park. Affiliation of the hospital with the College had been advanced in the summer of 1945 by Dr. Oscar Hawkinson, chairman of the training school committee at West Suburban.[26] Dr. Edman's vision of such a program for the College came after Esther Salzman, a graduate of Wheaton in 1929 and assistant to Ada Rury, director of the college infirmary, left to become director of a nurses' training program at a hospital in Kinkwa, China. There Esther learned the language, taught the nurses, and kept the hospital together in the long trek westward to escape Mao Tse-Tung's communist forces during the war.[27]

Dr. Russell Mixter, chairman of the biology department, was chosen as program coordinator of the Wheaton College-West Suburban program.

Other faculty members joined him in teaching courses at the hospital. Student nurses admitted to the program, by a joint committee from the College and the hospital, spent three and a half years at the hospital to acquire their R.N. and an additional year and a half at the college to secure a B.S. degree in Nursing Education. The program opened with 60 students, rose to 178 by 1949, and remained at approximately that figure for many years.[28] Student nurses were, from time to time, brought by bus to the campus for concerts and social events; and the nurses' chorus participated in the annual baccalaureate service.

Campus Life

A new monthly campus magazine released its first issue in October 1946, under the editorship of Ruth Lindal, with Homer Dowdy as assistant editor, and David Norbeck as business manager. *Kodon* featured short stories, general articles, personality sketches, photographs, and cartoons. The name *Kodon,* meaning "bell" in Greek, was chosen because the tower bell was "the most significant part of campus lore, a symbol of Christian scholarship as it fulfills its purposes with a clear, true message, remaining undisturbed by storms, living above circumstances." The magazine announced its debut with a public entertainment, featuring Freddy Giles, '47, the campus comic known and loved by everyone during his student days, in his "first post-Navy appearance."[29]

The *Wheaton Record* staff members, fulfilling their weekly publication responsibilities were pleased with the "All American" honors for excellence granted the paper twice in 1946 under the editorship of Bill Standridge, and again in 1947 under Paul Allen as editor, marking the fifth time the award had been received. "All American" honors were first won by the paper in 1940 under Jeanne Cooke, and in 1945 with editor Elizabeth Fletcher.

The *Tower* staff, headed by editor Helmuth Bekowies and business manager Prescott Williams, were busy preparing the 1947 annual, which the class dedicated with affection and respect to Katherine B. Tiffany, professor of English. In the spring of 1946 the editor had announced that the *Tower* would no longer sponsor the Artist Series, which had made a fine contribution to campus life, but had lost about $450 annually for six years. On Thanksgiving night in 1946, the Student Council brought to Pierce Chapel the Trapp Family Singers—not so well known then as they were to become after *The Sound of Music*—in a concert of carols, madrigals, and folk songs. The Baroness von Trapp introduced the songs and presented her seven daughters and one son, who were seated around a small table set with two lighted candles. For students and faculty, who had only the one day for a holiday, the concert was unforgettable.

Speech and writing activities usually aroused good student response, partly because they provided training and experience closely allied with professional aspirations and partly from the sheer joy of creative effort. The

Cook Oratorical Contest, a popular fall event made possible by a gift from Jonathan Cook, grandson of Jonathan Blanchard, attracted six contestants in November 1946. First awards of twenty-five dollars to Kari Torjesen, who had come to Wheaton from Norway, and to Brooks Sanders. Other students prepared for speech recitals, sought places on the debate squads, and used their speaking gifts for leadership roles in the literary societies and Christian organizations.

Campus Radio

The idea of a campus radio station was suggested by alumni secretary Ted Benson in 1946. With technical advice from physics professor Paul Martin and a student committee of Ray Morgan, Carolyn Young, Dave Sunden, Ed McCully, Bill Thompson, Len Rogers, and Clarence Bass, the station went on the air in 1947. Broadcasting over local telephone wires from the top floor of Blanchard Hall with the call letters WHON, the station was strictly a campus activity.

In 1948 WHON joined the Intercollegiate Broadcasting System and was able to change its designation to WETN, call letters that came close to the spelling of Wheaton. Within three years the station was broadcasting twenty-three hours a week: daily chapel, church services, news, home and away football and basketball games, music by student groups, and "Radio Workshop," produced by the speech department.

The station was succeeding splendidly in fulfilling its objectives of training and service. Many of the students who volunteered their time and enthusiasm to WETN did so because they were interested in careers in Christian radio or because they wanted a better understanding of how radio could be used in Christian service.

WETN moved from its first cramped quarters in Blanchard Hall to the east end of Pierce Chapel, where it remained until 1958. Expansion of programming and the acquisition of improved equipment made still another move to more adequate studios imperative. A substantial gift by the Class of 1958 made possible the construction of a new broadcasting location on the lower level of Breyer Hall. Unfortunately, the station was still limited to campus coverage, leading some students to call it "the weak squeak." A breakthrough came, however, in 1962 when the Federal Communications Commission granted Wheaton a license to operate a 10-watt FM educational station at 88.1 megacycles. The broadcast radius was expanded to two miles. With Frazer Browning as station manager, the new facility began service with a chapel broadcast on February 27. In 1968 the College employed its first professional manager when Dr. Stuart Johnson, '67, became a member of the speech communications faculty.

Another major step forward came in 1979 when WETN was authorized to increase its power to 250 watts, enlarging its broadcast radius to six miles. Station Manager Johnson announced that WETN would endeavor to em-

phasize programs not generally available in other nearby stations. He
planned to schedule contemporary Christian music and, with Conservatory
assistance, offer more classical music, which he felt was little heard on
nearby stations. The station, now operating 24 hours a day every day, is
valued as an interesting service to campus life.

In the President's Absence

Under the aggressive leadership of President Carl F. H. Henry, '38, the
Wheaton Alumni Association initiated in 1946-47 the worthy project of
bringing to campus recognized evangelical scholars who would discuss subjects bearing directly on the Christian world and life view. The Jonathan
Blanchard Lecture Series was announced, with the prospect of three to five
lectures, philosophic in nature, to be presented annually.[30] The first lecturer
was Dr. Martyn Lloyd-Jones, minister of London's Westminster Chapel and
president of the British Inter-Varsity Christian Fellowship, who spoke during the summer session in August 1947.[31] Prior to the lecture series the
Alumni organization had instituted an annual faculty study grant, shared in
1945-46 by Dr. Russell Mixter and Dr. S. Richey Kamm, who undertook
special studies in science and political science. The grant, which paid the recipient's salary and $250 travel expenses, was awarded in February 1947 to
President V. Raymond Edman to complete an in-progress study in the history of missions from New Testament times to the age of William Carey.
Called *The Light in Dark Ages*, he had been at work on the book for ten
years.[32] Trustee approval of the president's time of absence came at their
February 1947 meeting, prior to the public announcement. At the same
trustee meeting chemistry professor and assistant to the president in academic affairs, Dr. Roger Voskuyl, was named acting president and dean of
the faculty.[33]

President Edman began his leave following the three-day faculty fall conference at Winona Lake, Indiana, where the theme was "The Spiritually Effective Faculty." There the faculty again gave clear evidence of their
dedication, eagerly seeking to know and do God's will. Dr. Edman reminded his colleagues, that "for the young hearts who come to us for life's
preparation, we are to be people of prayer, of persuasion, of passion."

Acting President Voskuyl in his address to the faculty, after announcing
that he could not and would not try to fill Dr. Edman's shoes, set forth a
comprehensive administrative plan for the management of the academic life
of the College. The academic affairs committee, which had done splendid
work in its 1944-45 study and recommendations, was renamed the educational policies committee and was given enlarged responsibility as a policy-
making body. Its policies, after approval by the faculty, were to be executed
by the administration and the divisional and departmental chairmen, a
practice that was followed for a number of years.[34]

The third annual North Central Association Workshop report was given to the conference by Dr. Earle E. Cairns, who had represented the College at the University of Chicago at a workshop during the summer of 1947. Wheaton had sent Dr. Voskuyl to the University of Minnesota in 1945 as its first representative to the North Central Workshop, which was designed to encourage improvement in the preparation of public school teachers in liberal arts colleges. Dr. Cairns observed that "Wheaton is not lagging in practice or policy as compared with other schools."[35] He reported that Professor Barton, of the University of Chicago, one of the workshop leaders, "stated that he honors Wheaton because Wheaton knows what it is trying to do and proceeds to do it with the best modern methods possible as applied to its particular philosophy."[36]

Small-group discussions at the faculty retreat proved to be the intellectual tune-up the faculty needed as they prepared to meet their students again in the fall. Relaxation was provided by the college football team, practicing at Bethany Camp, when they hosted the faculty at a "T-shirt Tea" and offered a humorous program. The following afternoon the faculty reciprocated with a variety program in charge of Wyeth Willard.[37]

After a distinguished and heroic career as a Marine chaplain in the South Pacific during World War II, W. Wyeth Willard had been invited to speak at the mid-winter evangelistic service in February 1946. Impressive in appearance, affable, filled with yarns about his war-time experiences, he impressed the students and President Edman, who recommended him to the trustees for appointment as assistant to the president, with responsibilities to speak in chapel from time to time, travel and speak for the College, and counsel students.

Shortly after the fall term began, with a maximum enrollment and ten new faculty members adjusting to their responsibilities, a young Swiss, Hans Bürki, who had come to the United States to study Christian education, was made a graduate teaching fellow and was assigned courses in German. Bürki, recommended by C. Stacey Woods of Inter-Varsity Christian Fellowship,[38] was attractive in appearance and engaging in manner, with just enough of a foreign accent to make him sound persuasive and authoritative. He shortly began to hold Bible study classes which attracted a large student following. One evening in October, after having been on the campus a little over a month, he was invited to speak to Pi Gamma Mu, the social science honor society, on a Christian philosophy of education.

Although the meeting drew a large gathering of students, no faculty members were present to hear Bürki suggest that Wheaton appeared to be moving toward secularization in much the same way that Oxford, Cambridge, and European schools had become non-Christian. Those who loved the Lord, he declared, should lay down all pride and pray for revival. Students should "leave all extra-curricular activities" and "battle for lost classmates." The College, said the speaker, had "replaced the Word of God with world-and-life view systems" which are a mixture of Christianity and humanism.[39] In the stir of controversy that followed his talk Bürki wrote to the editor of the *Record*, which had given extensive first-page coverage to the event, to say that his intentions had been misunderstood and that he had really been speaking about colleges and education in general rather than of Wheaton in particular. Dean Roger Voskuyl called the *Record* editor to his office to point out to him "the possible damage such an article could cause throughout the country," referring to the manner in which the student paper had reported the Bürki address. The editor "admitted that he had not reported the article fairly," thus supporting Bürki's contention.[40]

The views of a young stranger, zealous for the Lord in his own way, though uninformed about the history of Wheaton College and American higher education, might have been of limited and local consequence had not President L. E. Maxwell of the Prairie Bible Institute, Three Hills, Alberta, Canada, and editor of the Institute's rather widely distributed paper, the *Prairie Overcomer*, taken notice. The *Overcomer*, in its December 1947 issue carried as news the substance of Bürki's talk to Pi Gamma Mu as evidence that Wheaton College was deteriorating spiritually and was in need of prayer. Friends of Dr. Edman in New England brought the article to his attention, and he wrote to President Maxwell, a friend, from Boston on January 21, 1948. He declared that "this attack on the work of God at Wheaton has been a source of very deep grief to me.... It is a matter of very great regret that you should feel called upon to broadcast the opinion of an immature student without making any inquiry at the College."

Other problems arose during Dr. Edman's leave of absence. One of these involved the status of Dr. C. Gregg Singer, chairman of the faculty in June 1945, who had signed the doctrinal statement of the College but suggested a reservation when he crossed out the word "premillennial" in the seventh article. Why the College had accepted his application with this reservation, Dr. Singer himself could not say.[41] Some time afterward Dr. Edman requested a conference with Dr. Singer in which he asked him if he were a postmillennialist. "Absolutely not" was the reply. Did he believe in the bodily return of the Lord Jesus Christ? The response was "Absolutely" and that the return would be "cataclysmic."[42] Dr. Edman appeared to be satisfied with the answers, and no more was heard of the matter until late fall of 1947, when Dr. Singer was asked to prepare a statement clarifying his millennial views. In April 1948, he declared that after a careful study of several reformed theologians he felt he could harmonize the premillennial view with covenant theology, and, in consequence, was ready to accept Article 7 of the college doctrinal statement, in which the premillennial view of Christ's return is set forth.[43]

In the spring of 1948 while the president was on leave in Boston, several instructors began to feel that acting President Voskuyl had given evidence of administrative skill and might be a more effective leader. Dr. Voskuyl had no knowledge of such thinking among his colleagues. But clearly the College could not continue to serve its students effectively, nor appeal with confidence to its constituency from a position of weakness—a divided house. In

June Dr. Edman, at the urging of the Executive Committee of the Board of Trustees and of Board President Herman Fischer, suggested to Dr. Singer that he might find a larger usefulness at another institution and urged him to consider seriously such a prospect. He submitted his resignation on July 13 after being assured that he had not been dismissed and after trustee action assured him of his salary for as long as a year.

During the spring of 1948, when criticism of the Edman administration was mounting, gossip often ran its loose and irresponsible course. Whisperers failed to search for supporting evidence, rumor was too readily accepted. But when campus troubles subsided and a calmer perspective prevailed, most people were willing to acknowledge that Dr. Edman might have been indiscreet in some circumstances, but nothing more.

In August 1949, a year after his departure from Wheaton to teach at Salem College in North Carolina, Dr. Singer wrote a gracious letter of apology to President Edman for "any conduct which wrongfully hurt you or gave a wrong impression of you."[44] He acknowledged that he might have been misinformed about some matters and felt that the president had also been misinformed about him. Dr. Edman responded in kindly terms and gladly accepted the apology. Several years later Dr. Singer returned to speak at Wheaton, with the president's approval, at a conference held in Pierce Chapel.

In April 1948 Chaplain Willard, the president's assistant and his loyal defender, had gone to Boston to apprise him of campus unrest, and urged him to return to make clarifications where he could. Willard arranged for a group of students to string up a banner across the front of the Chapel for the president's arrival with the words: "Welcome Home, President Edman." David Howard, president-elect of the student council, was asked to arrange an appropriate chapel service at which Dr. Edman would speak. Arriving early for the service, Howard told the students—who knew nothing of the simmering dissatisfaction—that it would be a heart-warming experience for Dr. Edman if they would rise and cheer when he entered Pierce Chapel, which they did, even before Dave Madeira's words of welcome. Elisabeth Howard, David's sister, presented Mrs. Edman with a lovely bouquet of flowers. Dr. Roger Voskuyl, as evidence of student esteem for his role as acting president, was given a Bible, after which Dr. Edman offered his chapel message.

Dr. Edman was present for commencement 1948, but then returned to Boston with the expectation of remaining for the summer to complete his work. On July 5 Herman Fischer wrote the president a long letter surveying some of the vexatious problems the College faced, among them the urgency of a clear delineation of the lines of responsibility between himself and Dr. Voskuyl. The letter urged Dr. Edman to plan to be in Wheaton for as much of the summer as possible.

When student leader David Howard returned to campus in early June for the summer term, he learned that students were incensed over what they believed to be Dr. Singer's "dismissal," and they were looking to him for action. After talking with Dr. Singer, the dean of students, and others, Howard sought the advice of Dean Charles Brooks, who urged him to return to Philadelphia—at Dr. Brooks's expense— for a consultation with his father, Trustee Philip E. Howard. The elder Howard noted that in offering counsel he faced a dual responsibility, that of father and trustee of the College. Philip Howard resolved his difficulty by calling for a special meeting of the Board of Trustees in August, a legitimate request since, under the by-laws of the college, any trustee was allowed to request a meeting when he felt urgency required it.[45] Chairman Fischer supported the president with an attorney's skill, separating fact from rumor, prejudicial assertion from supportable judgment.

When the issue was put to a vote, a majority of the trustees gave President Edman a strong degree of support and urged him to exercise his authority with firmness and confidence. For Dr. Edman, the action seemed to be not only a vindication but also a divine mandate to press on. Shortly after the Board had met, Chairman Fischer assembled the faculty for an evening meeting at which he made it clear that Dr. Singer had not been dismissed and no charges had been presented.

At one of the early chapel services, as the fall term began, President Edman faced the student body and said: "If I have offended anyone this summer, I am deeply sorry." With the August action of the Board of Trustees, a Student Council resolution of confidence, and his public statement to the students, a turning point was reached in the career of V. Raymond Edman. Though other problems were yet to be resolved, he now knew he was facing a rising rather than a setting sun.

Revival at Wheaton

The second semester evangelistic services in 1950, preceded by earnest prayer, began in Alumni Gymnasium on Sunday evening, February 5, with local evangelical churches cooperating. For the week-long series of services Pastor Edwin Johnson, a North Park graduate then serving the First Mission Covenant Church of Seattle, was the speaker. He urged his hearers to clear their lives of known sins so that the grace of God might be manifest in them. Tuesday was announced as a day of prayer on which classes would be suspended so that students could assemble in small groups. Accordingly students met at scheduled times throughout the day from seven in the morning until eleven at night.

The Wednesday evening service gave no promise, as it began, of becoming an extraordinary occasion. On the platform, besides President Edman and Pastor Johnson, were George Beverly Shea, soloist; Bud Schaeffer, song leader, senior class president, and one of Wheaton's basketball greats; Bill Wareham, pianist; and the Stam twins, Betty and Marion, who were to play a trumpet duet. Earlier in the day one of the student rebels had come to Dr.

Edman's office to tell him that he had had a change of heart, wished to amend his ways, and requested a few minutes in the evening meeting to tell of his transforming experience with Christ. The meeting began with a hymn, followed by the chorus "Send a Great Revival in My Soul."

Then Dr. Edman responded to the request for a few minutes of testimony. Later he recalled that he had "mentally set aside the time from 7:10 to 7:20 for testimony. At 7:20 it seemed that the last testimony had been given; but another student arose, and then a half dozen, then twenty-five or more, to wait tearfully in their places for an opportunity to tell of God's dealings with them."[46] Just as Dr. Edman was about to pray, another boy asked for prayer for himself and the opportunity to speak. Glancing at the clock, the president said: "All right, Gene, you are the last one."[47] But before the student had finished speaking, others were rising in all parts of the chapel; and it seemed as if a quiet sense of solemnity, guided by the Holy Spirit, was descending on all who were present. There was no shouting, no crying aloud, nothing unseemly. No lurid confessions stirred the group. Mostly students told of taking God for granted, of feeling superior to other Christians, of pride, dishonesty, gossiping, unfaithfulness to the college code of conduct, unfairly criticizing the faculty and administration, and resisting the known will of God for their lives.

For more than forty hours there were always students or faculty in the prayer room. In the main auditorium, testimonies, now limited to five minutes each, continued until midnight, with many students still standing. Dr. Edman then told those who still wished to speak—there were more than a hundred—to come forward and seat themselves in the choir loft behind the platform. So the meeting went, through the night, all day Thursday, when classes were cancelled. Thursday night, and Friday morning. At nine P.M. Thursday, twenty-six hours after the meeting, began, Pastor Johnson had his first opportunity to speak. He offered a brief message on Psalm 1. At one point a note was passed up to Dr. Edman carrying word that Billy Graham, then in Atlanta, had heard the news of the revival and that night would be having a special prayer meeting for Wheaton. One student—who had been particularly critical of the president in 1948, and was later to earn a Ph. D.—sent up a note which said: "I've done you an injustice, I must confess tonight. If time runs short, please include me."[48]

The Chicago press, quick to learn of the extraordinary event, dispatched reporters to the scene in the early hours of Thursday morning. A University of Chicago student, hearing of the revival by radio, phoned the *Chicago Tribune* to ask if a reporter could give him a ride to Wheaton. Arriving at three A.M., he stayed on long enough to realize his need, and sought help in finding Christ as Savior. The wire services carried the story of the revival across the nation, and news magazines like *Time, Life,* and *Newsweek* gave coverage through pictures and text.

The United Press story, used by the *New York Times* and *Detroit Free Press,* was widely picked up as good copy:

The marathon college revival meeting gained new fervor today as students and faculty members headed into their 28th hour of spontaneous confession and prayer. The crowd in the college chapel dwindled near dawn to 90 husky youths and sweater-wearing co-eds, 40 of whom were still waiting on the dais to give their public confessions of sin. But as the sun rose, students came directly from breakfast to the meeting to resume their singing and praying in praise of the Lord.

College authorities were concerned that the press might sensationalize the revival and exploit the student testimonies; but on the whole, the newspaper stories were fair, objective, and even commendatory. At nine A.M. Friday, February 10, Dr. Edman, fearing that curiosity seekers might begin to move onto the campus, brought the meeting to a close. Far from home, the debate team and the chapel choir also felt the moving of God's Spirit in their midst, the debate team in Florida and the chapel choir near Louisville, en route from Florida.[49]

For many—students, faculty, administration—the revival seemed like a cleansing; wounds were healed, fractured relationships amended. Loving concern to know and do God's will was everywhere evident. When asked by the *Record* to sum up the fruits of the 1949-50 school year, Dr. Edman said: "The past year has been unusual and outstanding: the gift from Texas, beginning of the Memorial Center, gift of the library, and above all, revival, all in one year."[50] Later, asked by *Kodon* to cite the happiest time of his life, he wrote: "What happiness can surpass that of seeing young hearts conquered by the Savior and their becoming more than conquerors through him."[51] From the revival year class of 1950, 100 members, more than a quarter of the class, found their way to the mission field.

CHAPTER 12

Mid-century: Spiritual Outreach, Intellectual Growth

Wheaton College entered the second half of the twentieth century and, like the country at large, moved through its first decade with optimism as well as with some apprehension. Continuing post-war prosperity initiated vast investments in public and private education at all levels and gave promise at Wheaton of further expansion. It seemed certain that by 1960, the end of the first hundred years of the College, the centenary plan would be completed. In his 1950 report to the Board of Trustees, President Edman reminded them of the steady enlargement of the student body, faculty, annual budget, and assets of the College.[1] Enrollment had reached 1,727.

At the same time, the cold war following World War II created a national uneasiness and general support for a strong defense policy; and an intense anti-communist sentiment gave rise to intemperate figures like Senator Joseph McCarthy. The Korean War, 1950-1953, a United Nations effort to prevent that country's being overwhelmed by communism, was fought largely with American money and troops, a small number of whom were Wheatonites. In 1951 a larger number of men than women were admitted to the College on the assumption that some of them would be drafted for service in the Far East. The 1957 launching by the Russians of Sputnik, the first outer space missile, orbiting the earth at 18,000 miles an hour—an alien missile, wrote Hannah Arendt, "dwelling among heavenly bodies as though it had been admitted tentatively to their sublime company"[2]—was a wound to national pride and a strong inducement for educational institutions to intensify their work in science, mathematics, and technology. Racial tensions were an embarrassment to many Americans committed to justice, equality, and compassion. All of these events interested students and were reflected in the life of the campus.

Reserve Officers Training Corps

The cold war environment was a strong persuasion for a number of colleges, including Wheaton, to request the government to establish Reserve Officers Training Corps on their campuses. Trustee Philip Howard, following his attendance at a meeting of the Military Affairs Committee of Colleges in Washington in 1950, recommended the introduction of ROTC at Wheaton, the first unit of which was activated on June 20, 1952.[3]

There was no significant objection to the institution of compulsory ROTC for Wheaton freshmen and sophomore men in September 1952, nor to Registrar Enock Dyrness's statement that no exemptions would be made "except for conscientious or physical reasons."[4]

With Lieutenant Colonel George D. Callaway as commander of the campus unit, 300 cadets constituted the first classes in military science and used lower North Hall as their place of instruction. On the days their classes met, or they were assigned to drill, students wore full military uniforms. An advanced program of courses in military science, fully elective, during the junior and senior years, led to a cadet's being commissioned at commencement a Second Lieutenant in the United States Army Reserves. The first class of officers was commissioned in 1955. A high of twenty-eight military graduates was reached in 1965, followed by a slow tapering off to a low of seven in 1978. With the introduction of full military scholarships for students who would enter the army in active service after their commissioning, the number began to rise again, with fifteen officers graduated in 1980.[5] Jody Bradshaw, commissioned a Second Lieutenant in 1979 and named a Distinguished Military Graduate, was the first woman to be commissioned by the Wheaton unit. When the local military trainees numbered as many as 400 in the 1950s and early 1960s, they were a very visible element on campus.

From 1952 to 1969 ROTC continued as a requirement for all freshmen and sophomore men, although always a few students and faculty members were philosophically opposed to the program as alien to the spirit of a Christian liberal arts college. Presidents Edman and Armerding, however, both of whom had served in the military, always gave strong support to the program, believing that it was a contribution to the stability and security of American life. To the alumni Dr. Edman wrote, when the unit was established: "Christian young men should have opportunity for officer training at a Christian college and, when needed, should serve their country as leaders rather than enlisted men. There is a call today for a Joshua, a Gideon, a David, as well as for an Elijah and a Paul. ROTC at Wheaton is the answer."[6]

Some hostility toward ROTC was to be expected in the tempestuous late sixties. In *The Crucible*, a supplement to the *Record* of March 28, 1969, student Del Morrisette wrote that ROTC was both "irrelevant and unChristian" at a Christian liberal arts college; but in the same issue William Southcombe, another student, claimed that "very few people feel that ROTC should be eliminated from Wheaton." A few students demonstrated peacefully before Edman Chapel as the ROTC unit marched in for its annual military chapel service. On April 24, 1969, the *Record* carried a front page story to the effect that thirty sophomore and freshmen men planned to boycott the annual May review at McCully Field as a measure of protest against the compulsory requirement. The requirement was then under review by the educational policies committee, and the boycott was presumed to depend on the decision of that committee. The committee's recommendation of reducing the requirement from two years to one year, won the support of both the Faculty Senate and the Board of Trustees. In June 1975, the Student Government 14-0 vote in favor of a wholly voluntary ROTC, was sparked less by political or philosophical considerations than by a steady erosion of student interest in the military. In the fall of 1975 ROTC, at the suggestion of the unit commanders, was offered on a voluntary basis to both men and women.

By the 1980s ROTC enrollment began to rise substantially, especially when the Wheaton unit was joined by recruits from area colleges. In 1983 there were 183 cadets enrolled in the program, twenty of whom would be commissioned second lieutenants at the end of the year. In the junior-senior group there were four women. From time to time graduates of the Wheaton program, career army men, have returned to serve as instructors in the unit. In 1983 Colonel William F. Ladd, '61, became the first alumnus to head the Wheaton College department of military science.

Board of Trustees

Members of the Board of Trustees, charged with maintaining the financial stability of the College, the safeguarding of Wheaton's Christian heritage, and the ongoing of an academically strong institution, numbered twenty in 1950, as authorized by the charter. In accepting the responsibility of trusteeship, these men gave substantial portions of their time and often of their resources. Elected for a ten-year term, members represented a broad regional and professional base: Herman A. Fischer, Wheaton, attorney; William McCarrell, Cicero, Illinois, Henry A. Ironside, Chicago, E. Joseph Evans, Boston, David Otis Fuller, Grand Rapids, Michigan, ministers; Lewis L. McShane, Springfield, Massachusetts, Philip E. Howard, Philadelphia, Robert C. Van Kampen, Wheaton, publishers; Gedor Aldeen, Rockford, Illinois, George

Traber, Perry, New York, manufacturers; Thomas Crofts, Wheaton, educator; Robert E. Nicholas, River Forest, Illinois, Taylor Ferguson, Wheaton, Hugo Wurdack, St. Louis, investment brokers; Thorstein Burtness, Oak Park, Illinois, Edgar Dival, Wheaton, executives; Allan Emery, Boston, merchant; Foster Oury, Chicago, contractor; Dr. P. Kenneth Gieser, Wheaton, physician; and V. Raymond Edman, college president. In 1953 the election to the Board of Dr. Stanley Olson, '34, dean of the Medical School of Baylor University and two-term alumni representative to the trustees, brought valuable academic insights to the administration of the College. Dr. Olson was granted an LL.D degree at the June 1953 commencement.

All teaching faculty were approved by the trustees, the president, the dean of the College, and the chairman of the department in which the appointment was to be made. Dr. John Fadenrecht, professor of education, was named acting dean of the College, following the resignation of Dr. Roger Voskuyl in 1950 to become president of Westmont College. The following year, Fadenrecht, a quiet, patient, man became dean of the College, a responsibility he held until 1965. When Dr. C. C. Brooks left his post as dean of students in 1952 to take a similar position at Westmont College, Arthur Volle, '38, was named by the trustees to succeed him.[7]

Concern for faculty financial needs was evident in trustee discussion, but salary advancements during the Edman administration were modest. Wheaton instructors did not feel that they were well compensated; faculty salaries compared poorly with quality institutions of comparable size. There were many expressions of gratitude by the faculty when the Alumni Association announced in February 1952 its intention to contribute $3,000 a month to faculty salaries. Said Dr. S. Richey Kamm: "The rising costs of living have made it exceedingly difficult for our present faculty and staff to meet their family budgets." Charles B. Weaver, '24, National Alumni Fund Chairman, was well aware of the need and was happy to labor in the faculty's interest. President Edman often suggested to the faculty that teaching at Wheaton was like missionary commitment, a "glad service unto the Lord," and many instructors saw their calling at Wheaton in just that way.

The low salary scale was a consequence of conservative fiscal policies and the trustees' reluctance to raise tuition enough to allow for an attractive schedule of compensation. There were fears that rising fees would price many worthy students out of a Wheaton education. Though the appropriations for faculty welfare were meager by current standards, a modest life insurance policy was provided for faculty and staff as well as a small, institutionally managed pension program. In 1951 the College became part of the Social Security System, which had been instituted by the government in 1935 and in which membership was voluntary until 1954.[8]

Wheaton's First Venture Abroad

By the 1970s Wheaton had an extensive summer study-travel program in the Holy Land, England, France, Germany, Holland, and the Far East, giving students the opportunity to live, study, and travel in countries whose culture was of special interest to them. In 1980, 290 students participated in these programs.[9] The first venture abroad, however, antedating the others by a good many years, was suggested in 1951 by Trustee Philip Howard. He proposed a grant of $1,000 from the *Sunday-School Times*, of which he was publisher, to initiate archaeological excavations in the Holy Land at Dothan, directed by Dr. Joseph Free of Wheaton College.[10]

Archaeology had been introduced at Wheaton in 1936 by Professor Free, who had been trained at Princeton and the Oriental Institute in Chicago, and was listed in the catalog as Bible Archaeology, under the Bible Department. Archaeology has long been considered an important aid to biblical studies, enabling students to study the Bible in its historical setting; a major in the subject was first offered in 1940. Professor Free began field work in the Holy Land at Dothan in the spring of 1953, assisted by his wife Ruby, who accompanied him on all his excavations, as well as by English Professor and Mrs. Clyde Kilby, who served as photographers and recorders. For several years, thirty to forty students and six instructors made an annual spring pilgrimage beginning with the Bible Lands Cruise and ending at Dothan.

Dothan, located sixty miles north of Jerusalem, the area where Joseph's brothers watered their flocks and where Joseph was sold into slavery to Midianite merchants, proved to be a rich repository of ancient artifacts. Brought to the surface, brushed, polished, and painstakingly reconstructed by the Frees, and their helpers, were lamps, vases, tools, weapons, and pieces of jewelry, ranging in date from 3000 B.C. to A.D. 200. In the spring of 1957 the houses, walls, and narrow streets of the days of Elisha, 850 B.C., were painstakingly uncovered.[11] Under Professor Free's energetic leadership, the excavations continued until 1964. That program of Near Eastern Studies, distinctive among the offerings of liberal arts colleges, brought Wheaton considerable acclaim in academic circles.

Dr. Free was founder of the Near East School of Archaeology in Jerusalem, used as a center for the Dothan excavations. He also founded the Near East Archaeological Society, and initiated in 1956 the first Archaeology Conference at Wheaton. The twenty-fifth annual conference was held in November 1980.[12] An extensive collection of Tell Dothan artifacts, on loan from Ruby Free Gieser, is displayed in Blanchard Hall.

Touching the World for Christ

"F.M.F. Tonight" the sign over the women's gymnasium read. For more than two decades on Wednesday nights, the Foreign Missions Fellowship, missionary arm of Inter-Varsity Christian Fellowship, met on Wednesday nights to fulfill its purpose "to help every student find his place in the Lord's program of world evangelization."[13] Meetings in Pierce Chapel were preceded by twenty prayer groups gathered to pray for specific missionary needs around the world. The group maintained a tract table, had its own publication, "Horizons," sent deputation teams to other colleges, and supervised a large world map in lower chapel with the legends "Lift Up Your Eyes" and "Look on the Field." In 1952 F.M.F. organized on campus the first Missionary Emphasis Week, with Dr. Oswald Smith, of Toronto, Canada, as the speaker. During the Christmas vacation many students journeyed to the University of Illinois at Urbana for the great triennial missionary conference, when nationals and missionaries from every continent presented the urgent needs of their people for a Christian witness.

On the honor roll outside the president's office are the names of 636 missionaries from the classes graduated during the 1950s. They went to every country open to missions as evangelists, teachers, linguists, doctors, nurses, dentists, technicians, and missions administrators. From the class of 1950—many of whose members served in World War II and the Korean War and saw at first hand the need for Christ in distant lands—one hundred students, more than a quarter of the class, found their way to the mission field.

Among F.M.F. members were Jim Elliot, '49; his wife, Elisabeth Howard Elliot, '48; Ed McCully, '49; and Nate Saint, '50. In an Ecuadorian jungle Jim, Ed, and Nate carefully planned and executed "Operation Auca," intended to bring the message of Christ to a fierce Ecuadorian jungle tribe of Indians. On January 3, 1956, the three men—with their associates, Pete Fleming and Roger Youderian—landed in a plane piloted by Saint on a narrow strip of sand near Auca territory. All of the men were in excellent physical condition (Jim Elliot had been a soccer player and CCIW champion wrestler at Wheaton, and Ed McCully a member of the football and track teams). They built a tree house, established two-way radio contact with their wives, and made a brief contact with three curious Aucas. On January 8, when the wives at Shell Mera lost radio contact with their husbands, a rescue party of Ecuadorian soldiers, American soldiers, and Quichua Indians was organized. Saint's plane was spotted but there was no sign of life. News of the men's disappearance and the subsequent word that all five had died at the hands of Auca spearmen shocked the world. Details of the tragedy were carried by newspapers throughout the country for several days, and tributes were given to the courage of the five young martyrs. *Life* magazine sent its noted photographer, Cornell Capa to cover the tragedy which he called "the most remarkable missionary story of the century." In *Through Gates of Splendor* Elisabeth Elliot told with grace and moving simplicity the story of her husband and his four friends. This book, the first of many by this gifted author, sold over a half million copies in English and was translated into nine languages.

As a memorial to the young men the two men's dormitories on College Avenue were named Elliot Hall and Saint Hall. The athletic field at College Avenue and Chase Street was renamed McCully Field in the fall of 1956, when a concrete stand with a 4,500-seating capacity was added to the field. For the surviving young families the Five Missionary Martyrs Fund was established, with Dr. V. Raymond Edman, Dr. Clyde Taylor, and General Wil-

The Gospel Heralds, 1953. L. to r.: Orley Herron, Carl Farley, Warner Dickson, David Burnham, James Andrews, piano.

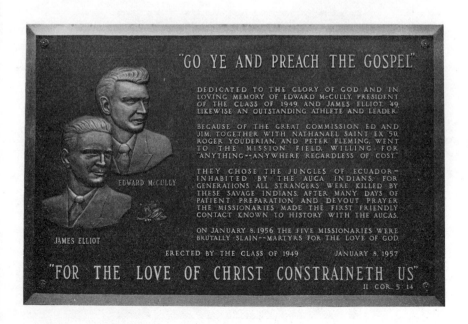

Memorial plaque honoring missionary martyrs in foyer of Edman Chapel.

Wheaton students gather children for Sunday school work in Chicago.

At football games, rain or shine, Chaplain Welsh was always on the sidelines with the team.

liam K. Harrison as trustees. On Founders' Day, 1957, a large brass memorial plaque honoring the young martyrs was unveiled in the lobby of Edman Chapel, a gift of the class of 1949, of which Ed McCully had been president.

Wheaton students found other opportunities to witness to their faith. Scott Vining, '48, began a ministry to Chicago's West Madison Street "Skid Row" where derelicts from many parts of the land, in poverty and shattered health, sought escape from reality in beggary and alcohol, their daily agony their only common measure of humanity.

To bring a word of hope in the name of Christ to these drifters, and to help them get in touch with loved ones as the first step of recovery, Wheaton men left Williston Hall by bus at 8:30 on Sunday morning. Working in pairs they struck up conversations with men at street corners, slouched in doorways, huddled around small fires in rusted oil drums. Street meetings drew interested listeners, some to scoff, some to give thoughtful consideration to the proclamation that Christ loved them. Not uncommon was the experience of Dave Burnham and Orley Herron, roommates and football teammates, who encountered a Princeton Ph.D. threatening to commit suicide after nineteen years of aimlessness and failure. He was dissuaded from his intention and led to a saving knowledge of Christ.

While the men were leaving for a day of service on skid row, another group of students, usually numbering about 300, were assembling to pray about the Colored Sunday School work on Chicago's poverty-ridden South Side. After devotions, the group left for the city by car, bus, and the Aurora and Elgin electric railway, fondly called the "Roarin' Elgin." Students traveled in groups of two or three through tenements and apartments, asking for permission to take the children to Sunday School in the afternoon, and returning after lunch to pick them up.[14] Students witnessed to the parents and left Christian literature, planned parties for the youngsters, and occasionally brought a small group to the campus for a Saturday game.

The Colored Sunday School work—so designated before the substitution of "black" for "colored"—continued well into the 1960s, but ceased for a time with the eruption of racial violence in Chicago. Begun by Francis Breisch, '49, and Floyd Potts, '49, in a storefront on Blue Island Avenue on the South Side, the cessation of the work was viewed with a sense of loss by the children's parents and black church sponsors.

Other students started hospital visitation. At Cook County Hospital in Chicago, one of the largest in the world, they prayed and read the Bible to the ill and lonely. Some journeyed weekly to Elgin State Hospital to bring comfort to the mentally disturbed residents. Forty students participated in the ten Young Life clubs in the Chicago area; others were interested in Child Evangelism, Youth For Christ, Hi-C, Pioneer Girls, and Boys' Brigade.

Such student outreach efforts were supervised by the Christian Service Council—successor to the Student Christian Council—organized in 1944 and supervised by Marjorie Glover, '31. In 1956 the Council filled over

1,000 engagements by gospel teams and student service agencies, representing nearly half the student body.

Undergirding Christian Council and student efforts to touch the world for Christ, the fall and mid-winter evangelistic services were a major force in encouraging students' spiritual commitment and preparing them for living the Christian life. Among the well-known evangelicals who came for the weeks of special services during the decade following the revival of 1950 were Dr. Harold Ockenga, Dr. A. W. Tozer, Dr. Paul Rees, Dr. Walter Wilson, and Dr. Northcote Deck.

The Chaplain: A Friend on Call

In the summer of 1948 Board Chairman Herman A. Fischer wrote to Dr. Edman, then in Boston, that "a chaplain is a luxury we cannot afford."[15] Nevertheless, by the mid-1950s the need for a chaplain became apparent, and through the next three decades many new student services were added to the college program.

Wheaton's first chaplain was Evan Welsh, '27, debater and varsity football player in his undergraduate days. He served as pastor of College Church for thirteen years and returned in 1955 to his alma mater from a large Presbyterian church in Detroit. At the June commencement of that year he was awarded a Doctor of Divinity degree. Arriving on campus, he was told by Dean Fadenrecht to create the office of chaplain and to write his own job description. From the beginning, his great strength was his continual accessibility to students, who saw in him an understanding, humble, and warm-hearted friend, a wise counselor, one who listened and loved anyway, a man of earnest Christian commitment. His crew cut, colorful sports jackets, and energetic pace about campus were familiar to everyone.

Chaplain Welsh often spoke in chapel, represented the College in speaking engagements, encouraged the Foreign Missions Fellowship and student prayer groups, comforted the ill in the infirmary, where he made daily calls, visited with Alumni clubs in various parts of the country. For many years he and his wife, Olena Mae, '41, maintained a Friday night open house at their home for all who wished to come for snacks, fellowship, and prayer. For foreign students as well, the Welsh home was a haven of friendliness and understanding. Following his retirement in 1970 he was made alumni chaplain, a position he held until his death.

Students who were lonely or discouraged could always turn to the chaplain for comfort. One night a returning student who had gone to Chicago for the evening had stayed overlong and found herself alone and frightened in the city, the last train and bus for Wheaton having left. Though she called Chaplain Welsh at 1:30 A.M., he told her to remain where she was and unhesitatingly drove into the city to find her—returning her to campus at four A.M.[16]

When Chaplain Welsh died in December 1981, a thousand friends and admirers gathered in Edman Chapel on a clear, cold Sunday afternoon to honor the memory of this small figure, so long among them on the campus, constantly hurrying on errands of love and mercy. He always had time to pause for a friendly chat and a sincere word of encouragement. His life radiated the life of Jesus Christ to his many friends and to the young people he served in Christ's name.

In 1970 James M. Hutchens came to the chaplaincy following his service in Viet Nam, where he was the first chaplain wounded. For his valor in combat, *Time* magazine called him one of the "clerical heroes" of the war.[17] Hutchens had served in the army, 1955-56, at Fort Campbell, Kentucky, and was there converted. Resolving to prepare for the chaplaincy, he was graduated from Wheaton in 1960, where he played three years of Crusader football.

For his service in Viet Nam, Hutchens was awarded the Bronze Star and the Purple Heart. Of his experiences in the Asiatic war he wrote movingly in *Beyond Combat* (Moody Press, 1968). During his two years at Wheaton, Chaplain Jim followed the pattern of service established by his predecessor and endeared himself to many students. He and his wife Pat left Wheaton to devote themselves to Jewish missions.

H. LeRoy Patterson became chaplain in 1972 after a seventeen-year pastorate in Park Ridge, Illinois. Following his graduation from Altoona (Pennsylvania) High School, Pat had won an athletic scholarship to play football at Pennsylvania State University; but during the summer had read J. Wesley Ingles's novel about Wheaton, *Silver Trumpet*, which influenced him to come to Wheaton College. He spent three and a half years at Wheaton, starring in football and track, and then, having decided to enter the ministry, completed his undergraduate degree at Gordon College and entered Gordon Divinity School.

To his ministry among students Chaplain Patterson brought compassionate understanding and strong devotion to the spiritual and intellectual goals of the College. His chapel talks, practical, earnest, always touched with a sense of humor, were popular with students and faculty alike. With a larger administrative role than his predecessors, Chaplain Patterson planned and supervised chapel services, giving them a continuity which a faculty committee had not previously achieved. He was enthusiastic about small chapels, meeting once a week for a limited time, where students were offered a number of topics as alternatives to the main morning chapel. The idea of small chapels was not new, as any reader of the 1910 catalog would discover. There it is noted that on Monday students met in "small groups, each being under the supervision of a member of the faculty." The chapels provided an opportunity for the "cultivation of a more intimate acquaintance between teachers and students, and for the discussion of personal religion, habits of dress, etiquette, and various other subjects in a freer and more confidential way."

Chaplain Patterson's office also planned the special services and the annual Staley Lectures. His chatty, anecdotal column of student advice, "Ex Cathedra," published at the request of *Record* editors, ran from 1973 to 1975. His books, *Now That You've Said "I Believe"* and *Good Morning, Lord: Devotions for Athletes,* were much appreciated by students.

Chaplain Patterson's successor in the fall of 1983 was Dr. Victor R. Gordon, who came to Wheaton from Sioux Falls College, South Dakota, where he served as chaplain for five years. A graduate of Stanford University, he earned a Ph.D. at Fuller Seminary. "Chaplain Vic" has been warmly received on campus and has promptly involved himself in student life. "My purpose in coming to Wheaton," he told a group of parents, "is to give myself as servant and pastor in every way I can to help your sons and daughters become the men and women they are called to be."

Early Graham Crusades

Since Billy Graham is Wheaton's best known graduate, it is appropriate to note here how he came to prominence in this era. There was an extraordinary response to the early Billy Graham Crusades. Dr. Edman regularly reported the results in chapel, and they were noted in the secular and religious press as well. Many students were stirred to give their lives to preaching and evangelistic service at this time when people seemed unusually receptive to the gospel and its promise of a new and better way of life.

In September 1949, Billy Graham, '43, began the Los Angeles campaign, which was to bring him to national attention. With his assistants, Grady Wilson, '43, as associate evangelist, Cliff Barrows as director of music, and George Beverly Shea as soloist, Graham began his nightly preaching in a huge tent—soon to be known as the "Canvas Cathedral"—which accommodated 6,000 people. William Randolph Hearst, an admirer of the work of Youth For Christ and publisher of the *Los Angeles Herald-Examiner,* sent word to his staff, "Puff Graham," which meant, give him prominent headlines and full photographic and news coverage.[18] Lengthy coverage of the crusade carried in the Hearst chain of newspapers was picked up by the Associated Press and dispatched throughout the country.

Perhaps the most astonishing event in Graham's early career was an Act of Congress—sponsored by a group of both Democratic and Republican lawmakers—authorizing a gathering on the capitol steps. Speaker of the House Sam Rayburn, who made the final decision approving the rally, said: "This country needs a revival, and I believe Billy Graham is bringing it to us."[19] The Washington meeting, held on February 3, 1952, a clear crisp day, drew a large crowd. Campaigns in New York's Madison Square Garden and many of the great cities of the world were yet to come.

Shortly afterward, the evangelist came to the campus for a broadcast from Pierce Chapel of the "Hour of Decision," radio ministry of the Graham Association then aired on more than 200 stations of the ABC network. Following the program, broadcast later by transcription, Billy spoke to the students of his alma mater about the great need for missionaries in Japan after the devastation of the war. "Not even the Apostles heard the pleading for the Gospel from foreign lands as we hear it today," he said.[20] It was the first opportunity for Wheaton students to hear Billy Graham, to observe how his commanding presence, his skillful control of voice and gesture, and his fervent dedication to the Lord's service could move large audiences to make life-transforming decisions. In November 1956, at a special convocation, a Litt. D. degree was conferred on Graham, with Dean John H. Fadenrecht reading the citation, President Edman presenting the degree, and Ruth Bell Graham, '43, placing the academic hood on her husband's shoulders. Graham spoke to the college community on the crises in Hungary and Egypt, then centers of world attention.[21]

During the Edman administration numerous academic conferences and lecture series were initiated, part of the effort to keep students well informed about contemporary events and the flow of ideas. Conferences were held during this time in business, philosophy, writing, science, and art and music.

Business Conference

The vision of Professor S. Richey Kamm led to the organization of the first Business Conference, held in the fall of 1948, under the sponsorship of the division of social sciences, with Professor Kamm as director. He felt strongly the need for preparing students to bear a Christian witness in all areas of life: the arts, sciences, professions, business, and government. It was a necessary emphasis. Many young people came to Wheaton believing in a clear demarcation between sacred callings, such as the ministry and missionary service, and the secular. Professor Kamm did much to bridge that gap in understanding. With his encouragement many able students entered business and government service, persuaded that they could exercise a firm Christian witness wherever they established their lives.

The theme for the first Business Conference was "The Christian in Business" and a representative group of businessmen from the Chicago area met with students to discuss issues related to the subject. The second conference, under the leadership of Professor Richard Williamson, addressed itself to "The Christian in Industrial Management," with guest speakers Morris Townsend, a New York investment counselor, and Maurice C. Smith, president of the Bristol Manufacturing Corporation and a trustee of the College. In 1955 the conference became a dinner meeting called Business Forum, with William Geidt, '42, director of advertising for Inland Steel Corporation, as speaker. Later, course work in business administration and secretarial science was phased out in order to concentrate on economics.

Philosophy Conference

For many years philosophy was under the supervision of the Bible department, then known as the department of Bible and philosophy. The work in philosophy was generally taught by men whose principal concern was not philosophy but biblical studies, apologetics, or other disciplines. Professor Gordon Clark, a published scholar and rigorous Calvinist, who taught at Wheaton from 1936 to 1943, brought new depth and effectiveness to the teaching of philosophy. Theologians like Carl F. H. Henry, '38, Edward Carnell, '41, and Paul Jewett, '41, were trained under him. During the Buswell era Clark and the president, also a strong Calvinist, worked well together.

Dr. Edman and Professor Clark, however, did not agree theologically; and early in the 1940s Dr. Edman announced that there would be no philosophy major the following year. Dr. Clark was distressed, a rupture was created, and he left Wheaton. In the mid-1940s philosophy was taught in succession by Dr. Cornelius Jaarsma, Edmund Tratebas, '44, and Dr. John Luchies, no one of whom gave the subject full time or had philosophy as the central core of his training. Professor Arthur Holmes, '50, who had completed an M.A. in theology at Wheaton and later was to take his Ph.D. at Northwestern University, had a strong interest in philosophy, and was appointed director of philosophy in 1957. The move was an indication that philosophy was growing to include the whole spectrum of this ancient discipline, though the subject was still kept under the protective custody of the Bible department.[22] With the approval of President Armerding, however, the philosophy department became autonomous in 1967, representing a victory in Professor Holmes's effort to have its competence and reliability acknowledged.

The first Philosophy Conference, initiated by Professor Kenneth Kennard, '48, was sponsored jointly with the Bible department and was held in November 1954 to honor the 1,600th anniversery of the birth of St. Augustine. Originally intended to provide educational enrichment and dialogue with other evangelicals in philosophy, it increasingly provided a forum for exploring philosophical issues of concern to Christians in that field and attracted others besides evangelicals.

In 1955 the conference took note of the widespread interest in the work and influence of Soren Kierkegaard. Guests included Dr. John Fisher, '47, of Temple University; Dr. Warren Young, Northern Baptist Seminary; Dr. Edward J. Carnell, '41, of Fuller Seminary; and Dr. J. Oliver Buswell, who spoke in chapel on "Kierkegaard and Religious Experience." It was Dr. Buswell's first appearance at Wheaton since his departure from the campus in 1940.

Among the eminent scholars who have spoken at the Philosophy Conferences were Professors Eliseo Vivas, Northwestern University; Kenneth Sayre, Notre Dame University; John Wild, Harvard University; Paul Holmer, Yale Divinity School; William Frankena, University of Michigan; Ninian Smart, University of Lancaster, England; Paul Ricoeur, the Sorbonne; and Alan Donagan, University of Chicago.

The conference, which attracts students and teachers from across the country, has developed high respect in the philosophic profession. Out of it various cooperative endeavors have developed, an informal network of Christian professors and ongoing dialogue.

Christian Writers' Conference

In 1956 Dr. Clyde S. Kilby, chairman of the English department, concerned about what he believed to be the poor quality of evangelical writing, began to plan a Christian Writers' Conference. In *Wheaton Alumni* in July 1961 he stated the conviction that had prompted him to initiate the conference: "The problem of Christian writing is not so much that of making it Christian as making it structurally and intellectually sound."

The first conference was held in June 1956 in conjunction with the college Inter-Session, a two-week summer term. Among the speakers were Professor Chad Walsh, Beloit College; Dr. Frank Gaebelein, Stony Brook School; and Frederic Babcock, book editor of the *Chicago Tribune*. Margaret Mortenson Landon, '25, returned to Wheaton for the 1959 conference. By then well known for her novels, *Anna and the King of Siam* and *Never Dies the Dream*, she spoke from experience on "The Discipline of Writing."

By 1971 the Conference was offering an equal emphasis in writing and literature and became known as the Conference on Writing and Literature. Among the many writers who shared their insights and knowledge of writing techniques were Grace Irwin, Canadian novelist, Joe Bayly, '41, J. Wesley Ingles, '26, and Elisabeth Elliot, '48, whose theme was "Writing as Personal Discovery." Professor Calvin Linton, dean of arts and sciences at George Washington University, amused and stimulated his hearers with his "How to Write Without Saying Anything." One of the best-known writers to have spoken at the conferences is Madeleine L'Engle, author of award-winning books for both adults and children. Affable and perceptive, she draws large student audiences and has often returned to the campus.

From the mid-1970s onward, as the holdings of the Wade Collection increased (see chapter 16), and as the writers represented in that collection grew in popular appeal, the conference often gave attention to them. The 1979 conference was devoted to the Inklings, a group of Oxford writers, with particular emphasis on C. S. Lewis and J. R. R. Tolkien. It drew together a half dozen scholars, among them Humphrey Carpenter, a British writer and biographer of Tolkien; Thomas Howard, Gordon College; and George Sayer, of Malvern College, England.

The Dorothy Sayers Festival in the spring of 1978 was organized by Professor Beatrice Batson, chairman of the English department, and Professor Barbara Reynolds, Nottingham, England, lecturer in Italian at Cambridge for twenty-two years and visiting professor of English at Wheaton for the year. The conference was an acknowledgment of the growing interest in the work of Dorothy Sayers in Christian apologetics, drama, and translation. When Dorothy Sayers died, leaving her superb translation of the *Divine Comedy* unfinished, Professor Reynolds completed the work.

Joining Professor Reynolds for the occasion in lectures and a symposium were Kay Baxter, a distinguished writer on religious drama and former director of the Religious Drama Society of Great Britain, and James Brabazon, Cambridge graduate and BBC television writer and actor. Together they presented a sensitive appreciation of Dorothy Sayers's work. An unusual contribution to the festival was a concert in honor of Lord Peter Wimsey, debonair detective in Sayers's novels, directed by Wheaton conservatory professor William Phemister. A student presentation of Sayers's drama, *The Zeal of Thy House*, performed in St. John's Lutheran church and directed by Professor James Young, was among the contributions to a memorable occasion.

Others who came to the College for English department conferences were Peter Hawkins, Yale University; Walter Ong, St. Louis University; Donald Marshall, University of Iowa; and John Knott, University of Michigan. For the 1983 conference the theme was "The Moral Imagination" and featured C. A. Patrides, University of Michigan; Sister Maura Eichner, College of Notre Dame of Maryland; Bruce Lockerbie, Stony Brook School; and Walford Davies, University College of Wales and Kilby Professor of English at Wheaton for the fall of 1983. Summer Writing Seminars brought to the campus Madeleine L'Engle, Gary Youree, and Larry Woiwode.

The intention of all these conferences was to inform, motivate, and inspire young writers through hearing and mingling with successful writers and editors. From the beginning, Dr. Kilby, his colleagues, and Dr. Melvin Lorentzen, his close associate in planning and directing many of the conferences, saw the annual gatherings as a service to all evangelical students interested in writing and their instructors. At times young people and faculty representatives came from twenty-five to thirty colleges and observers from fifteen to twenty publishing organizations. Although there is no way of measuring the consequences of these conferences, the sponsors have felt that they have had a significant impact on the whole range of Christian writing and literary tastes during the past quarter century.

Fine Arts Symposium

A Fine Arts Symposium, with the theme "The Fine Arts in a Christian College Environment," was held in November 1959. Instructors in the Conservatory and the art department felt they had an important mission in helping students to appreciate the value of great music and art in their lives. Realizing that young people cannot cherish what they do not know and experience, the departments of music and art hoped to enlarge the students' range of understanding in two vital areas of the liberal arts program.

Among the guest lecturers were Dr. Henry Bruinsma, director of the school of music at Ohio State University, and Professor Robert Kilgore, director of the College of Fine Arts at Illinois Wesleyan University, who drew attention to "Modern Art in the Liberal Arts Setting." A lecture-demonstration by Russian-born composer Alexander Tcherepnin of DePaul University centered on "Trends in Contemporary Music." At an evening banquet LaVahn Maesch, director of the Conservatory at Lawrence College, spoke on "Art, Entertainment, and Education."

Other art forms were treated when Joseph Coleman spoke on "The Philosophy of Architecture for the Christian Church"; Phil Austin, Chicago free-lance artist, addressed his student audience on "Composition and Communication in Water Colors"; and Jean Sandberg Gerstung, '51, talked about "Figure Sketching and Portrait Painting."

Science Symposium

At a science symposium in January 1960, a *Time* reporter, having heard that approximately one quarter of the Wheaton student body was majoring in one of the sciences, asked why science was so strong at Wheaton.[23] He might have been told that Wheaton had a strong science division because it had a dedicated faculty, adequate equipment, and intense motivation of both teachers and students. Then too, the trustees and the administration had been supportive of the science division. They shared the convictions and goals of the instructors that a need always exists for scientists who are Christian to bring their unique point of view into research, teaching, and the professions that draw on the insights of science.

Faculty members of the science division met each Tuesday at noon for a bag lunch seminar to discuss new developments in their disciplines as well as other problems: creation, evolution, the nature of human beings and the universe. Since those issues are closely related to theological and philosophical convictions, they are continually matters of intense concern at Wheaton. On the subject of evolution Dr. Russell Mixter, professor of biology, came to be regarded as a faculty spokesman, partly as a result of the publication in 1950 of his research titled *Creation and Evolution*, done under an alumni grant. The monograph was issued by the American Scientific Affiliation, founded in 1941 as "a group of scientific men devoting themselves to the task of reviewing, preparing, and distributing information on the authenticity, historicity, and scientific aspects of the Holy Scriptures in order that the faith of many in Jesus Christ may be firmly established."[24]

To mark the 100th anniversary of the appearance of Charles Darwin's *Origin of Species* in 1859, hundreds of commendatory and explanatory books, monographs, and articles were published around the world. Anticipating that international celebration, the American Scientific Affiliation commissioned a volume of studies, published in 1959, and edited by Russell L. Mixter, which appeared under the title, *Evolution and Christian Thought Today*. Interest in the subjects of these papers, together with their high quality, led members of the Wheaton science division to invite some of the writers to participate in a science symposium in February 1961 on "Origins and Christian Thought." That event stirred up trouble for the College that rippled through the community, alumni ranks, and Wheaton constituency in many parts of the land.

Throughout Friday and Saturday, February 16 and 17, speakers focused their scholarly insights on origins. Dr. Walter Hearn, of Iowa State University, discussed the "Origin of Life"; Dr. Frank Cassel, '38, of North Dakota State College, presented a paper on the "Origin of Species"; and James O. Buswell III, '48, then studying at Columbia University, spoke on the "Origin of Man." On Saturday a panel, moderated by Dr. Stanley Parmerter, chairman of the division of science, discussed "Origins and Christian Thought Today."[25]

Nothing extraordinary was likely to have happened in consequence of the weekend gathering had not several local residents heard ideas expressed that they thought suspect. Pastor Harold Warren, of the First Baptist Church, hearing what he presumed to be expressions of evolutionary thought, spread the word that Wheaton was countenancing evolution and theistic evolution. He did not take into account that a liberal arts institution of any merit needs to accept a reasonably free play of ideas, and that it does not by that exercise of freedom necessarily embrace all that is said. Two very conservative religious news journals conveyed the word that Wheaton and its science faculty seemed to find theistic evolution acceptable. President Edman began to receive letters from alumni and friends of the College, some of them expressing indignation at what the writers believed to be departures from the faith, some of them requesting clarification of what had actually been said.

To counter the charges that were being lodged against the College, some of them by well-intentioned friends, President Edman gave much time and exhibited extraordinary patience. All who wrote were sent (1) a copy of the College's doctrinal platform, with its clear statement about the divine origin of man and the universe as special acts of creation, (2) Edman's own statement in the May 1961 *Bulletin* under the title "The Discipline of Defamation," and (3) a copy of "Christianity and Science at Wheaton." The latter, an eleven-page statement prepared jointly earlier by committees of the faculty, trustees, and administration, was intended to assure inquirers that Wheaton science teachers were both orthodox in theology and competent in science. A second draft of this statement appeared in the May 1962 *Bulletin*. Both the Bible and science divisions were asked to give assurances that no instructor held theistic evolutionary views or was teaching that theistic evolution was an acceptable way to harmonize Scripture and science.

In a letter to the president, signed by Bible professors Kenneth S. Kantzer and Samuel J. Schultz, the men declared that "we do not know a single person in the Biblical Education Division who would hold to either of these viewpoints." For the science division Professor Russell Mixter gave similar assurances. Those responses substantiated President Edman's confidence in his faculty and whenever questions were raised—usually the consequence of ill-founded rumor or distorted statements out of context—about the orthodoxy of Wheaton's science and Bible departments on the nature of creation, he staunchly defended them.

A major consequence of the controversy aroused by the science symposium was the presentation to the Board of Trustees on October 13, 1961, of the following resolution, proposed by Trustee David Otis Fuller:

Realizing our great need of safeguarding Wheaton College from the inroads of error and apostasy, I move that this statement—"They are convinced creationists who believe in an historical Adam and an historical Eve, the parents of the human race, who were created by God and not biologically descended from lower forms of life..." be incorporated in our statement of faith which every trustee, faculty member and full-time staff member signs in good faith every year.

Animated discussion occurred among the trustees and in faculty committees before that proposal, somewhat refined, was finally incorporated in the 1964 catalog as a footnote in the doctrinal statement. The footnote, or addendum, reads:

Wheaton College is committed to the Biblical teaching that man was created by a direct act of God and not from previously existing forms of life; and that all men are descended from the historical Adam and Eve, first parents of the entire human race.

Anyone who asked why a matter of such high consequence to the philosophy of Wheaton College should have been given footnote status—and there were those who did, including some faculty who were never happy with the additional statement—would have been given a reasonable answer. The College had received bequests for its endowment fund, and others were promised, on the assurance that Wheaton would never change its doctrinal statement. To alter the statement in any way would have subjected the institution to possible legal challenge. Further, the trustees believed that any alteration of the doctrinal statement would set a precedent that could make later changes, perhaps less worthy ones, more readily achievable.

In 1978 the addendum—for purposes of clarification—was moved from footnote status into the main statement of article four of the platform, with slight modification and enclosed in parenthesis. The new statement, which does not alter the article, reads:

(By this statement we affirm our belief that man was created by a direct act of God in His image, not from previously existing creatures, and that all of mankind sinned in Adam and Eve, the historical parents of the entire human race.)

Tiffany Lecture Series

To honor the memory of Orrin E. Tiffany, professor of American and world history from 1929 to 1945, the Tiffany Lecture Series was established, largely through the efforts of Professor Tiffany's wife, Katherine B. Tiffany, who was a professor of English, along with the Alumni Association and members of the history department. The first of the Tiffany lectures, in February 1953, brought to the campus Kenneth Landon, '24, then the officer in charge of the Thai and Malayan Affairs Section of the State Department. Landon and his wife Margaret had served for eleven years as missionaries in Siam and could speak from experience on "The Importance of Southeast Asia in International Affairs," at a time when there was much concern about China's intentions in the Far East.

The Tiffany Lecture Series has brought other distinguished lecturers to the campus, among them in 1956 Dr. Quincy Wright, professor of international law at the University of Chicago, and in 1960, the centennial year, the young governor of Oregon, Mark Hatfield. Robert Ekvall, '20, long-time missionary in Tibet, presented a lecture in 1962 on "China in Asia; Asian Crisis." For the eighteenth Tiffany Lecture, in 1971, Dr. Leonard Binder, professor of political science at the Universiy of Chicago, reflecting a strong current interest in the Middle East, lectured on "Israel in Contemporary International Relations."

In 1973 Mrs. Tiffany informed June Weitting, then college librarian, that she was working on a history of the Tiffany Lecture Series, which she wanted to turn over to the College when it was completed. "K.B.," as her friends called her, was a woman of astonishing energy, who navigated the streets of Wheaton until she was past ninety in an ancient car, sans power brakes or power steering. She renewed her driver's license at age ninety-three. In her report she noted that the lecture fund stood at about $30,000, most of which she had contributed. "If anyone is interested in knowing the source of the contributions by the largest giver," she wrote, "he may be told that most of the amount was earned by editing other people's manuscripts, editing three doctoral theses, manipulating a few small securities, proof reading, and making patterns for brass plaques."[26]

Other efforts to broaden students' intellectual and cultural awareness lay behind such activities as the annual History Lectures, sponsored by the history department and its chairman, Dr. Earle E. Cairns, and the lecturers provided by the Student Union-sponsored Campus Forum, later to become the Lyceum Lecture Series.

The History Lecture invited distinguished historians from the area to speak on subjects of current interest which would enliven students' understanding of history as one of the foundational disciplines of a liberal arts education. Louis Gottschalk, of the University of Chicago, initiated this series in 1952 when he spoke on "Revolutions in the 18th, 19th, and 20th Centuries: A Comparative Study." In 1954 Dr. Paul Knaplund, a native of Norway and chairman of the history department at the University of Wisconsin, read a paper on "The Missionary Factor in British Imperial History." Dr. Timothy Smith, of the University of Minnesota and a Nazarene minister, offered a summary of his then unpublished book, "Educational Focus in American History." The series of lectures continues to make a significant annual contribution to the intellectual life of the campus.

Campus Forum brought to Wheaton a diversified group of speakers under the direction of Roger Kvam, '54, and other student leaders who followed him. An early forum visitor was Gordon Keith Chalmers, president of Kenyon College, who declared that American education had become "geared to the present, to the logical, to the problems of current culture." Such devotion to the relevant, the timely, was the consequence, Chalmers felt, of "forty years of emphasis on rationalism, which left too little room for the imagination."[27] Other Forum speakers included Sidney Harris, *Chicago Daily News* columnist, whose talk was on "How to Read a Newspaper"; Illinois Senator Paul Douglas speaking on "Ethics in Government"; and Bennett Cerf, publisher, humorist, columnist, and editor whose topic was "American Humor."

After Cerf's talk Frederic Babcock, book editor of the *Chicago Tribune*, who had arranged for the New Yorker's visit to the campus, wrote in his column, "Among the Authors": "He came out to Wheaton this fall, talked for an hour without notes, about books and the effect of TV on books, and about the future of America and its literature. He was witty and informative. The youngsters were with him from the start. Some of the oldsters sat on their hands and dared him to entertain them, but long before the end they were joining in the applause." Shortly after his return to New York, Cerf wrote Babcock a letter, part of which was quoted in the latter's column. Said Cerf: "Those Wheaton College boys were a revelation to me. After my lecture five of them drove me back to Chicago, and I became so intrigued in talking with them that I sat up with them until 1:30 a.m. at a ham and egg joint on State Street, arguing about such unlikely subjects—for me, anyhow—as morality, temperance, and posterity."[28] The anecdote was pleasing to readers friendly to Wheaton who had grown weary of the media's tendency to emphasize Wheaton's prohibitions rather than its normal responses to life and the times.

The Student Union, most active of student service groups on the campus in the 1950s and 1960s, administered in 1961 a budget of $40,000 for social, informative, and inspirational programs like the Lyceum Series, Faculty Firesides, coffee hours, international cafes, Washington Banquets, films, and the Artist Series—programs broad enough in their scope to touch nearly every student.[29] The Lyceum, which succeeded the Campus Forum in the early 1960s, undertook to present a more regular series of programs than the Forum had. Sponsored in part by the Union and in part by subscription tickets, the Lyceum, with Professor Edwin Hollatz as faculty sponsor along with a committee of students, presented such speakers as Henry Kissinger, William F. Buckley, Jr., Lowell Thomas, Jr., Meredith Wilson, Harry Golden, Howard K. Smith, and Charles Taft.

Faculty Firesides and Book-of-the-Semester

Faculty Firesides, in the 1950s, were planned to bring students and faculty together to discuss current issues in an informal setting. On a typical evening in November 1955, President Edman and Spanish professor Louis Rasera hosted students in the Edman home for conversation on "Catholicism and Fundamentalism." At Dean Arthur Volle's home the dean and Dr. Richey Kamm discussed "Social Aspects of the Gospel." Dr. Clyde Kilby and Professor Russell Platz led a conversation on the "Christian Attitude Toward Popular Music" at the Platz home, and Professor Frank Houser offered guidance on "Christian Courtship." At another Fireside, Professors Kenneth Kantzer and Raymond Ludwigson spoke on "Neo-orthodoxy: Can We Accept It?" while Professors Howard Claassen and George Bate speculated about a subject that was to become much larger, "The Night I Slept with Atomic Energy."[30]

Another effort to enliven the campus intellectually was the Book-of-the-Semester series, begun in 1962, sponsored by the Scholastic Honor Society, working with a faculty reading committee. Dr. Beatrice Batson and Professor Robert Warburton gave enthusiastic leadership to this adventure of the mind. The program called for the selection of one book, which it was hoped all students and faculty would read, and come thoroughly to understand through a series of public lectures—sometimes by the author himself—forums, dormitory and class discussions throughout the semester, and a chapel convocation. The first book was Bernard Iddings Bell's *Crowd Culture*, a severe judgment of the low estate of American popular culture.

Perhaps the most notable of the contemporary scholars who came to speak about one of their works was Arnold Toynbee, author of *A Study of History*, whose *Civilization on Trial* was the Book-of-the-Semester in the spring of 1963. He came to Wheaton from a guest lectureship at Grinnell College, at the urging of Professor Donald Boardman, who became acquainted with him while the two were on a teaching assignment in Pakistan.[31] Extensive effort was made to prepare students for Toynbee's coming, but his convocation lecture was a disappointment to many; he could not be heard well and he failed to address himself to his major historical theses.

For a consideration of Albert Camus's *The Plague*, the fall 1963 Book-of-the-Semester, Germaine Bree, a Camus authority from the University of Wisconsin, was engaged to speak on November 22, 1963. It was the day of the assassination of President Kennedy, but Professor Bree arrived and delivered her lecture to a small group. She explained that she was already in flight when the tragic news from Dallas came; otherwise she would not have spoken. Like many other fine things the Book-of-the-Semester program wore thin in time and vanished, but it had been a noteworthy contribution to academic life at Wheaton.

Some of the class discussions generated through engagement with the ideas advanced in these books were no doubt similar to those described in *Christ the Tiger* by Thomas Howard, '57. Published ten years after Howard's graduation from Wheaton, the book is in part an account of the author's intellectual and spiritual pilgrimage through college and beyond. At one point he writes of his experiences in a class in aesthetics he elected in his last semester:

We began, in this class, to read Benedetto Croce, Jose Ortega y Gasset, Roger Fry, Herbert Read, Bernard Bosanquet, and I. A. Richards, and we shouted at each other and tore our hair and tried to define beauty and truth and goodness and wrote great splashy papers and looked at paintings and listened to Mozart and wondered if we would ever be able to pull ourselves together. . . . But I felt that once again a door had been blown open and that I could never again insist that there was nothing on the far side.[32]

In the mid-50s and 1960s there were emerging trends peculiar to Wheaton and of a non-political nature. Numerous evidences of serious intellectual interests were developing in most areas of thought affecting evangelical Christianity. There seemed to be in classroom, in discussion, in print, in the spirit of the times, a keen awakening to academic excellence, intellectual curiosity, scholarly confidence in the contributions evangelicals at Wheaton could make within the larger society. A growing vision was developing of the expanding place conservative Christians were willing to take in that society.

Centennial Gymnasium

Board of Trustees in the Centennial year. First row, l. to r.: Foster Oury, William McCarrell, President Edman, Robert Nicholas, Herman A. Fischer, P. Kenneth Gieser, Thorstein Burtness. Second row: Robert Keating, alumni, Taylor Ferguson, Howard Fischer, alumni, Maurice Smith, George Traber, George Bennett, Charles Weaver, Robert Van Kampen.

CHAPTER 13

A Century
of Progress

THROUGH HIS LAST TWENTY YEARS OF SERVICE TO
Wheaton College, President Edman was an indefatigable traveler, logging
well over a million miles in numerous missions to all the continents. From
the two-week trip to visit missionary schools in Central America in March
1946, to his attendance at the Billy Graham Crusade in West Berlin in 1966,
he visited at least twenty-five countries. Mrs. Edman and Dr. E. Joseph
Evans were his frequent companions. In May 1947 he and Evans conducted
missionary school surveys in Ethiopia at the request of Emperor Haile Selassie, who granted the Wheaton president an audience to which Edman made
reference in the last address of his life.[1]

Dr. Edman was a prolific writer. From his books it is possible to chart the
inner and outward movement of his life with considerable detail. In the
twenty-one years between 1947 and 1968, his output included twenty-one titles, from the first slender pamphlet, *Swords and Plowshares*, to *Look Unto
the Hills*, published posthumously in 1968. In addition to the books there
were articles, editorials, magazine columns, monthly communications—often of substantial length—for the *Bulletin of Wheaton College*, and hundreds of letters to people who wrote to him for advice, or in response to
something he had written.

Most of his writing was devotional in nature and drew its substance from

Scripture, his knowledge of history and political science, his own experiences, and his encounters with students and faculty at Wheaton College. His style was simple, lucid, warm, frequently aphoristic. From his pen came such thoughts as "It's always too soon to quit"; "Keep chin up and knees down"; "Not somehow, but triumphantly"; and "Never doubt in the dark what God has told you in the light." Alternately mystical and literal in his approach to Scripture, at heart he was a sentimentalist, like a good Swede, and a romantic; but in his sincerity, was always ready to speak the truth in love. He loved to speak of the "college family," suggesting a closeness that bound the whole campus community together in a relationship of caring.

Swords and Plowshares appeared in 1947, when the havoc of World War II was fresh in everyone's memory. Its opening words were: "Never has the prospect of peace seemed more remote than at this time, and with the coming of the atomic bomb it is indeed a time when men's hearts are failing them for fear."[2] The brief work traces peace efforts from early European times to the creation of the United Nations and suggests why they have failed, concluding that "real peace will never come to this world until the Prince of Peace returns in power and glory."[3]

Among his best-known devotional works were *The Disciplines of Life* (1948), *The Delights of Life* (1954), *Sweeter than Honey* (1956), and *Not Somehow—but Triumphantly* (1965). The first of these was a series of twenty-one chapel talks, each examining a discipline beginning with the letter *D*: duty, discipleship, danger, darkness, disability. *The Delights of Life*, twenty-eight pieces prepared during an illness, was a companion piece and continued the alliterative use of *D*, elaborating the theme that happiness arises not from things but from inner resources.

Three works were of a different sort. *The Light in Dark Ages* (1949) is a history of missions from apostolic times to the end of the eighteenth century, with extensive notes and bibliography. It is dedicated to the Edmans' four sons: Charles, Roland, David, and Norman. *Finney Lives On* (1951), published a year after the 1950 Wheaton revival, traces the life and development of the evangelistic methods of that nineteenth-century revivalist. *They Found the Secret (1960)*, one of his most popular works, highlights well-known Christians, earlier and modern, who confronted and overcame adversity. The idea for the book came from Robert Walker, editor of *Christian Life*, who first published the pieces as magazine articles.[4] Mrs. Rowena Carr, Dr. Edman's secretary, transcribed and prepared this and several other works for the press.[5]

Many of his chapel talks, sermons, and baccalaureate and commencement addresses were published in evangelical magazines or appeared in the *Bulletin of Wheaton College*. Of these the most widely read was his baccalaureate address to the class of 1949, entitled *Karl Marx. . . or Jesus Christ*, of which more than a half million copies were printed and distributed.[6] The work was translated into German, Spanish, Greek, Japanese, and several other languages, and was also offered in braille.

Wheaton Centennial

As early as February 1956 President Edman suggested to the trustees that they appoint a committee to work with faculty and administrators in planning activities for the academic year 1959-60, marking the 100th anniversary of the founding of Wheaton College.[7] In 1958 Richard Gerig, '49, joined David Roberts in the public relations department with the responsibility of planning and coordinating Centennial programs.

The purpose of the celebration was "to give praise, to express gratitude, to glorify God for his blessing and faithfulness," as well as to "reaffirm founding principles of Christian commitment, to call upon God for continued guidance and wisdom in charting the course of our future academic program and physical growth."[8] The theme for the year, "Dedication in Education" was prepared by David Roberts, and Dr. Edman recommended Psalm 100 as psalm for the year, with its affirmation: "For the Lord is good; his mercy is everlasting; and his truth endureth to all generations." A Centennial Hymn was written, with words by Robert Zondervan, '59, and music by Jack Goode of the music faculty. In the public announcement of the Centennial, President Edman set the tone for the events to begin in September:

> By the inductive method of scientific research the Christian educator studies the works of God; largely by deductive methods he learns the will of God from the Word; and it is by the receptivity of simple faith that he accepts the Worthy One as his own. Such has been the educational philosophy and program of Wheaton during the century now drawing to a close, and to which wholeheartedly and unreservedly we dedicate ourselves in the new century, as our Lord tarries.[9]

For the Centennial expansion program two projects were chosen: a new chapel-auditorium, to accommodate audiences too large for Pierce Chapel or Alumni Gymnasium, where many concerts were held; and a new gymnasium to meet the needs of a growing student body. It was hoped that the latter, the trustees' special project, would be ready by September 1959. Ground was broken for the Centennial Gymnasium—to be built at a projected cost of $400,000 by J. Emil Anderson and Son—on November 2, 1958, following the alumni Homecoming Sunday worship service. No longer would Wheaton's outstanding basketball teams of the 1950s have to play in cramped quarters. The new gymnasium, of brick to harmonize with other campus architecture, seated 3,400. At completion, fully equipped, the building cost $524,000.[10]

"This is it," Dr. Edman wrote to the alumni in June 1959, after examining plans for the new chapel-auditorium prepared by the Anderson firm.[11] Ground-breaking for the building had been delayed for nearly a year after preliminary plans and specifications by two builders were rejected. The Anderson design pleased everyone; and the promise to complete the building with organ, furnishings, seating, equipment,and parking lot for $1,450,000 was within the range the trustees thought manageable.[12] The final cost was to be $1,525,000.

The Alumni Association took the lead in the drive for funds, pledging to raise $500,000. On hand the trustees had $250,000, enough to justify the act of faith implicit in the ground-breaking at the June commencement.

The first scheduled event of the anniversary year was the Billy Graham Crusade, September 27 to October 4, combined with the fall evangelistic services. For the first crusade meeting 18,000 people gathered on Sunday afternoon on the field north of the new gymnasium, where Fischer Hall and the Wheaton Christian Grammar School now stand. For the week of services the attendance was 101,000, with 2,800 responding to the invitation to commit their lives to Christ.[13] The $30,000 budget for the crusade was fully met, and $6,000 in additional contributions was turned over to the "Hour of Decision."[14]

Throughout the year seven academic symposia were held, bringing distinguished scholars and lecturers to the campus in archaeology, theology and philosophy, language and literature, fine arts, science, education and psychology, and social sciences. The Illinois State Historical Society held its sixtieth annual meeting at Wheaton College in the centennial year, October 9-11. One of the Society's meetings was a Blanchard memorial program, at which Trustee Charles B. Weaver, a grandson of Jonathan Blanchard, presided, Dr. Clyde Kilby was the speaker, and Dr. Earle Cairns officially opened the collection of Blanchard materials.

For the Centennial Homecoming the student-faculty committee chose the theme, "A Century of Praise," used effectively in the building decorations and the class floats displayed at the football game. To the Homecoming building decoration each year students gave long hours of preparation, often beginning weeks in advance, and carefully guarding their productions from general view until they were ready to be displayed the night before Homecoming. Later generations of students would find it difficult to imagine the effort that went into those elaborate, often beautifully crafted exhibits.

On October 18, 1960, following the traditional Sunday morning alumni worship service in Pierce Chapel, President Edman led the congregation across the street to the site of the new chapel for the cornerstone-laying and dedication. He noted that the occasion marked the end of an era; the Homecoming gathering in Pierce was to be the last of its kind. The cornerstone, larger than most, bears the college seal and Ephesians 2:20"... Jesus Christ Himself being the chief cornerstone." In the sealed copper box placed inside the cornerstone are materials from the office of the president, the alumni office, the centennial office, and such memorabilia as a college catalog, copies of the *Record*, the *Wheaton Daily Journal*, and items from the Graham Crusade.[15]

A week before Homecoming, students supported the student council's decision to enforce the dress-up code for Friday night in the dining hall and the

Groundbreaking for Centennial Gymnasium, November 1958. President Edman at the microphone, Coach Harvey Chrouser turns over a spadeful of earth. Second row, l. to r.: Coaches Leroy Pfund, George Olson, Willis Gale, Trustees Robert Nicholas and Robert Van Kampen, Chaplain Welsh.

Billy Graham Crusade, September 27–October 4, 1959, south of present location of Fischer Hall.

Coach Gil Dodds times his runners. L. to r.: Tom Wright, Kikuo "Cookie" Moriya, and Taylor McKenzie.

Edman Chapel

Stupe, requiring "jacket and tie for men, dress shoes and stockings for women," during a year in which there would be many visitors on campus. Candlelight and floral centerpieces created an atmosphere for gracious dining that later generations of students abandoned as too formal.[16]

Focal point of the Centennial year was the celebration of Charter Days, January 9 and 10, the first of which marked the actual 100th birthday of Wheaton College. For the occasion, a cold, crisp day, the faculty appeared in academic attire, together with representatives of forty-six other colleges and universities and thirteen learned societies. Dr. Harold John Ockenga, acting president of Fuller Seminary, presented an address titled "For Christ and His Kingdom." He emphasized "the fearless pursuit of truth," which should "be the mark of a Christian college or university above all other institutions."[17] With President Edman presiding, honorary Doctor of Divinity degrees were conferred upon Harold John Ockenga and John Walvoord, '31, president of Dallas Theological Seminary; and upon John Brobeck, '36, University of Pennsylvania School of Medicine, the Doctor of Laws degree.

At the Centennial banquet in the evening, attended by over 900 trustees, alumni, faculty, and staff in Centennial Gymnasium, awards were presented and veteran alumni honored. A challenge from Charles Blanchard Weaver, '24, reminded everyone of their "goodly and Godly heritage" as Wheatonites. President and Mrs. Edman cut into a seventy-five-pound, four-foot-high, four-tiered centennial cake, with a minature "Tower" on its top, prepared and presented by Marvin Carney, a local baker. On behalf of the Secretary of State of Illinois, David Roberts gave President Edman his 1960 orange and blue license plates, marked 1860 000 in honor of the centennial year. Climax of the evening was an address by former president James Oliver Buswell, Jr. To Dr. Buswell's delighted surprise President Edman announced before the singing of the "Alma Mater," that the Graduate School building had been renamed Buswell Hall and that a new sign had been placed on the building during the banquet.[18]

Eleven months after ground-breaking, on May 16, 1960, the new chapel-auditorium was first used for the regular morning chapel service, with President Edman presiding. Present were all graduate and undergraduate students, faculty and staff, several trustees, and many friends of the College. Everyone was astonished with the size and beauty of the building, broad rather than deep, with its seating capacity of 2,400. (The president had told the architect that he wanted the students as near to him as possible.) The deep French blue upholstering and carpeted aisles, light blue walls, and blue cathedral glass windows, create a restful atmosphere. From the ceiling eight colonial chandeliers with multiple lights enhance the beauty of the auditorium. A twelve-foot extension, a gift of the class of 1935, can be raised to platform level to accommodate major symphony orchestras.

The east wing of the building, financed largely by a grant from the S. S. Kresge Foundation, accommodates an additional 300 in a lounge, the Heritage Room, a classroom (later named the Kresge Room), and Wurdack

Baccalaureate service, Edman Chapel, June 1960.

Founders Day, January 9, 1960. L. to r.: President Edman, Dr. John Brobeck, Dr. James Oliver Buswell, Jr., Dr. John Walvoord, Dr. Harold John Ockenga, speaker for the occasion.

Chapel, honoring Trustee Hugo Wurdack. Towering above the building is the lighted spire with its four-faced clock, a gift of the class of 1962, and a Schulmerich carillon system given by Harold Anderson. The spire was the highest structure in DuPage county at the time, visible for miles around. Installation of the Schantz organ, the gift of Mr. and Mrs. A. Harold Anderson and Mr. and Mrs. Paul Brandel, with its sixty-five ranks of pipes and four-manual console, was completed during the summer. The three organ chambers above the platform contain 3,781 pipes. Dedication of the instrument took place at the October Homecoming, with Conservatory organists Jack Goode and Gladys Christensen performing.[19] Involved in planning for the chapel were Edward Cording, director of the Conservatory, and Harold Faulkner, business manager, who served the College from 1945 to 1973 as advisor on many campus projects. Essential to all these operations was Howard White, '41, controller for the College, who began his service in 1946.

The first public event in the new auditorium was the performance of "The Abundant Century," a dramatic portrayal of ideas and faiths in conflict, written and directed by Jack Odell, a professional writer, with the assistance of Professor Edwin Hollatz and co-chairmen for the festival, Edward Cording and Professor Clarence Nystrom. In the pageant President Edman and Dr. J. Oliver Buswell, Jr., representing themselves, were shown in the battle for people's minds against false prophets. Representing Jonathan Blanchard and Charles A. Blanchard were John Huffman, '62, and Joe Nystrom, '61. Nearly a hundred costumed students participated in the colorful performances.

At a meeting of the Board of Trustees on June 10, 1960, two days before the baccalaureate service, Robert Nicholas made the following proposal: "Because of his devotion to the Lord Jesus Christ and his inspiration and spiritual leadership of the students and the whole college family and because of our love and affection for him, the trustees of Wheaton College hereby name the new chapel building Edman Chapel." The honoree was deeply moved and pleased. "Measuring the Measureless" was Dr. Edman's first baccalaureate address given in the auditorium, before a capacity audience of "brave sons and daughters true" along with their parents and friends from the community.

The Centennial year closed with commencement services in Centennial gymnasium, where nearly 5,000 people gathered for the exercises. For several years prior to this occasion the ceremonies had been held on the campus mall. Preceding the academic processional from the tower to the gymnasium, the Edman Chapel carillon was played and the tower bell tolled briefly. Mark O. Hatfield, then governor of Oregon, presented the commencement address "Whither Status Quo!" which examined several major governmental agencies and urged a larger vision of their usefulness. Hatfield was granted an honorary degree, together with Wheatonites Franklin S. Dyrness, Malcolm Forsberg, and William J. Jones. By the time the exercises were over a rain shower had cleared and the sun shone on the academic pro-

Professor Edmund Wright at the Schantz organ.

Centennial Commencement in Centennial Gymnasium, June 1960.

cession to the tower, while the graduates greeted parents and friends.[20] The gift of the graduating class, financed and constructed by members of the class, was the Centennial Fountain, located in the center of the quadrangle, with its display of lights and water.

Throughout the Centennial year a number of faculty publications appeared. Professor Clyde Kilby's *Minority of One*—a sensitive and thorough biography of Jonathan Blanchard, was written under an Alumni Association grant. Issued during the Founder's Day celebration in January, *The Word For This Century*, a collection of eight essays based on the Wheaton College statement of faith, reaffirms its evangelical commitment, relating it to the needs of the time. Edited by Dr. Merrill C. Tenney, dean of the graduate school, the book was written by Wheaton graduates, teachers, and administrators, as the contribution of the Graduate School to the Centennial. From the pen of Professor Samuel Schultz, chairman of the Bible department, came *The Old Testament Speaks*, a widely used text (now in its third edition) that offers an overview of Old Testament history. *Saints and Society*, by Earle E. Cairns, chairman of the department of history, is a study of the evangelical revivals and social reforms of the nineteenth century. *Evolution and Christian Thought Today*, a symposum of thirteen Christian scientists and theologians, has been described in chapter 12. Two of Dr. Edman's many books also appeared in that special year, *He Leadeth Me* and *They Found the Secret*.

For President Edman the year was a gratifying one, but it was also a time of testing and anguish. In June 1959 he suffered a detached retina. Eight weeks of recuperation were necessary before he was able to go to his cabin at Honey Rock near the end of the summer. The development of cataracts during the fall dimmed his vision; but, as he said to a *Record* reporter, "Although my eyes have been affected, I'm still able to see through the students."[21] The cataracts were removed from both eyes in February 1960 and healing seemed to be progressing satisfactorily, when on March 14 a new retina detachment occurred, and another in the left eye in April. Advisors suggested that he go at once to the Massachusetts Eye and Ear Infirmary in Boston, where new techniques had been developed to deal with retina detachments. Accompanied by his son Roland, he traveled to Boston and was successfully operated on by Dr. Charles L. Schepens. Slow recuperation followed at the home of the Reverend E. Joseph Evans, his old friend and counselor.

Difficult as the year was, President Edman joined the entire college family in acknowledging the Centennial as a celebration of God's providential guidance in preserving Wheaton College through a century of growth and service. It was a time also to remember the pioneers from New England—strongly influenced by Puritanism and the evangelical movements of Charles G. Finney—who brought to the Illinois prairies the idea of a liberal arts education undergirded by a theistic vision of life which confessed the sovereignty of God and founded its intellectual development on Hebrew-Christian sources.

Sophomore tree planting, May 1961. President V. Raymond Edman joins the class at the tree planting. Class advisor Dr. Edward Hakes watches with class officers. L. to r.: Beverly Fritch, secretary; Jane Paddon, vice president; Daniel Horner, treasurer; Thomas Getman, president.

Dean Corrine Smith, '37, receives the Distinguished Service Award to Alma Mater from Howard Fischer, '38, member of the Alumni Board of Directors, 1957.

On Parent's Day in the fall of 1961, President Edman presided at the dedication of the new women's dormitory, known as Smith Hall. Built on the old site of President Charles Blanchard's home, Smith Hall honors Mrs. Corrine Smith, who joined the faculty in 1929 and served as dean of women from 1937 to 1961.

Wheaton College Women's Club

From the time when Mary Blanchard assembled a group of women to scrub and clean the rooms of Illinois Institute, through the days of commencement luncheons when trustee wives brought picnic baskets of food, and on to the present, the women of the College have contributed their energies and talents to campus life. The lounge in the east wing of Edman Chapel, known as the Heritage Room, was beautifully furnished by the Women's Club, which raised the money and supervised the project. Here portraits of Mary Bent Blanchard and Miriam Armerding, procured and presented by the Club, are displayed, together with portraits of the first five presidents.

Women faculty and faculty wives of the College and the Academy were organized by Mrs. James Oliver Buswell for fellowship and service to the College in 1929 and were known as the Faculty Women's Club. In 1954, when Mrs. Edman broadened the organization's membership to include women or wives serving in any capacity on the campus as well as trustee wives living in the area, the name was changed to the Wheaton College Women's Club. The honorary president of the club is the wife of the college president. Carolyn Rust, '43, during her presidency from 1956-58, initiated the idea of small interest groups in addition to the five or six general meetings during the year; these continue to be a source of friendships, service, and personal enrichment.

The Wheaton College Women's Club has helped to foster a sense of family in the college community, welcomed new faculty and staff, provided hospitality for students, and given money for special funds. Almost continually since 1936, Thursday morning prayer meetings have been held during the school year.

Academic Scene

Degrees were granted in thirty-three major fields to the centennial class. Majors with the highest numbers of graduates were education, literature, economics and business, geology, and history. Otto Walther was the lone graduate in Latin, a declining academic pursuit (the last Latin major was graduated in 1966). A decade later the general course in Latin, foundational to a liberal arts education in the Blanchards' day, had disappeared from the catalog.[22] Other majors offered in 1960 and soon phased out were secretarial science, home economics, general science, and botany. Zoology, for many years a popular major because it was recommended for pre-medical students, was combined with biology in 1967; biology and chemistry then became the preferred pre-medical majors.

For some time it had seemed to the trustees and some faculty members that there were too many majors for all departments to offer programs of breadth and depth. In 1955 the Board of Trustees had requested "reorganization of departments to eliminate, by consolidation, those that cannot be made into strong departments having, in addition to the chairman, a minimum of four faculty members."[23] At the same time enrollment was set at 400 in each of the four classes, with a maximum of 100 in the graduate division.

From the Educational Policies Committee there emerged a recommendation for the establishment of an Academic Council, composed of senior faculty members. The council was given a list of sixteen areas for investigation.[24] These matters drew the entire faculty into rigorous debate and resolute intention to preserve and strengthen quality education at Wheaton. Behind all of this endeavor was a sense of mission, a calling to provide a superior program for a choice group of young men and women.

A significant committee action was the listing of thirty-nine private colleges comparable to Wheaton in size, which would serve as a basis of study and comparison. Among the colleges were Amherst, Beloit, Carleton, De Pauw, Knox, Augustana, Lawrence, St. Olaf, Swarthmore, Valparaiso, and Wooster.[25]

The effort to combine departments reduced the number of offerings to twenty-seven by 1970, though the termination of a cherished field of concentration was never without anguish for both professors and students.

In the early 1960s one of the watchwords on many campuses was "excellence." Another was "values." What is their source? How are they communicated? Does a college education change student values? In an honors convocation address in 1963 Dr. Hudson T. Armerding, then professor of history, observed that the Christian student pursuing excellence must understand the limits of all human learning, must not break fellowship with those less gifted intellectually, must evaluate contemporary culture in the light of biblical values, and must always be conscious of the sovereignty of God. He cautioned against "intellectual pride or snobbishness" and "preoccupation with today's culture," which results in a "foreshortened perspective.[26] Nevertheless, the responsible pursuit of excellence was to be a worthy objective for the College.

For many years honors convocations in the fall and spring recognized students for outstanding academic performance. Once a formal occasion in which faculty appeared in caps and gowns, the convocations in recent years have shed these external evidences of academic formality. The convocation address by the president, a faculty member, or an invited guest commends the honorees for their diligence in achieving a standard of excellence, a tribute both to themselves and to the College. In the seventies other things besides the announcement of honors awards were included in the program:

alumni scholarship awards, department citations, athletic awards, faculty promotions and retirements, and announcement of the teacher-of-the-year selections.

Another of Wheaton's responses to this quest for excellence was the institution of an honors program in 1960, under the direction of Dr. Arthur Holmes, who approached his task with enthusiasm and high expectations. Speaking to a group of students, he expressed the hope that their zeal for the honors program might match his vision: "I pray that you may glimpse the vision of Christian scholarship, its contributions to man, its service to God, its undergirding of the Gospel, its transforming impact on the society, the values, and even the thought forms of our day."

Students of demonstrated academic superiority were invited to join the honors program and to submit an intellectual autobiography for committee evaluation. A few honors sections were offered in general education at the lower division level. Several upper division seminars encouraged interdisciplinary and independent study, providing students with a rigorous academic experience. They wrote papers, offered criticisms of each other's work, championed or rejected major theological, philosophical, social, and aesthetic theories, and learned how to defend their own values.[27] Some students wrote extraordinarily good papers, at times comparable to master's theses. At least one of them later grew into a book, Stephen Evans's *Despair: A Moment or a Way of Life*. A few discovered that they were not equipped for advanced research and should not make graduate study a goal.[28]

Dr. Holmes and Dr. Arthur Rupprecht shared responsibility for directing the decade-long program. It ended because many of the honors course features were incorporated into the regular curriculum, superior students gave their enthusiasm to social action in the decade of the sixties rather than to honors studies, and small group instruction and tutorials were expensive for the College.[29] But the pursuit of excellence as an academic ideal did not end.

As it did at Wheaton, in the early 1960s the subject of values became a concern on nearly every college campus in America, following the publication in 1957 of Philip Jacob's *Changing Values in College*. Jacob concluded after extensive research, that students' values change very little as a result of their college experience—the values they come with, they leave with. Confronted with that conclusion, Professor Edwin Hollatz spent the summer of 1960 at a University of Minnesota workshop sponsored by the North Central Association, working on a project entitled "An evaluation of the ways and means of implementing the educational philosophy of Wheaton College, with particular regard to the communication and reinforcement of values." In reporting on his study at the fall faculty workshop, Hollatz offered three suggestions: let the College (1) delineate more clearly the kind of students it expects to turn out, in the light of Wheaton's educational philosophy; (2) encourage a larger degree of student responsibility by offering them a fuller opportunity to participate in the operation of the College; and (3) improve the quality of teaching through intensive faculty commitment to the educational goals and values of the College and the initiation of creative learning practices in the classroom.[30]

Who Were Admitted to Wheaton?

For a good many years Wheaton required for admission a high school diploma, fifteen hours of prescribed high school credit, rank in the upper half of the student's class, commendable recommendations, and for a while the Otis IQ Test. But in 1957 the College had begun, a bit tardily, to require applicants to take the Scholastic Aptitude Test of the College Entrance Examination Board. The test was introduced for general use at the close of World War II but Wheaton was not convinced at the beginning that it provided the kind of profile the College wished to have of its entering students. Ultimately, however, it was recognized that small colleges aspiring to develop a quality program and eager to enroll applicants of superior capability were using the Scholastic Aptitude Test.

In 1960 Charles W. Schoenherr, '50, who had served as assistant dean of men and instructor in education, and was committed to a strong academic program, became director of admissions, following Dr. Albert Nichols. He was aware that for several years a number of students who could not qualify as entering freshmen at Wheaton enrolled at other institutions where their qualifications were acceptable, then transferred to Wheaton as sophomores or juniors on their grades only. Beginning in 1962 all transfer students were required to present SAT scores or their equivalent.

From among the applicants each year the committee on admissions selected "those who evidence a vital Christian experience, moral character, personal integrity, social concern, academic ability, and the desire to pursue a liberal arts education as defined in the aims and objectives of the college.[31] In evaluating those qualities, the admissions committee considered the applicant's academic record, autobiographical statement, which would make clear the writer's Christian convictions, College Entrance Examination Board scores and writing sample, recommendations from the high school principal, the pastor, and a business aquaintance, and participation in extracurricular activites. For the highly subjective letters of recommendation Schoenherr substituted a system of personal interviews for all candidates for admission.

The press for admission to Wheaton College was very strong through the fifties and sixties; but for lack of accommodations many qualified students, some of them children of alumni and loyal constituents of the College, could not be admitted. Sometimes the disappointed ones expressed their distress to the College and to Dr. Nichols, who had been making the final judgments as to who would be admitted. To minimize those pressures in the admissions office, Director Schoenherr established a faculty admissions committee, which, in consultation, selected the candidates for admission.

Outstanding athletic performance was recognized as a special ability, but a candidate for admission was given no more credit for that skill than a musician or debater was awarded for that talent. Preference was given to the children of alumni when they met all other qualifications.[32] Modest scholarship grants were made to incoming freshmen where need was clearly demonstrated. In 1964 such aid to freshmen totaled $70,000, a sum equal to the amount available to the entire student body a few years earlier.[33]

From 1960 to 1965 requests for information about Wheaton College—catalogs, applications blanks, general literature—averaged 8,400 a year. From among these in a typical year, 1963, somewhat over 1,450 made formal applications. Of these, 747 were sent acceptances, and 581 finally enrolled. For the year the total enrollment was 1,750. College Board Scholastic Aptitude Test scores showed that for the class entering Wheaton in 1964, slightly above 43 percent had verbal scores of 600 or above, and 43 percent had scores of 600 or over in mathematical aptitude. Such scores in both areas were regarded as very good.

Of the class entering Wheaton in 1964, an average year, 51 percent of the men and 84 percent of the women were at or above the 90th percentile of their high school graduating classes.[34] Those figures reveal Wheaton's selectivity in its choice of students; the College was enrolling an academically superior student body. In preparation for a comparative study among a specially selected group of colleges, known as the "Antioch Study," Wheaton gave a number of randomly selected freshmen the Comprehensive College Test, a general examination. On this test Wheaton freshmen placed well above the national norms in English, natural science, mathematics, humanities, and social science.[35]

When the academic performance of freshmen entering Wheaton came to be known generally, two problems arose. First, a number of students and their parents, who had once looked forward to a Wheaton education, felt little motivation to apply, since the prospects for admissions were limited. Second, some alumni and friends—and an occasional faculty member—wondered whether spiritual sensitivity and commitment were not being sacrificed to intellectual promise. To meet the first concern College spokespeople continually urged all who wished to come to Wheaton to go through the admissions procedure—their prospects for success might be better than they thought. To the second concern President Edman often gave assurances that there had been no diminution of devotion to the College's historic Christian commitment. The doctrinal statement and standards of conduct were unchanged, faculty and students engaged in Christian service as they always had, and instructors were still chosen for their Christian convictions as well as their academic competence.

Standards of Conduct

The members of the entering class in 1964, with their high Scholastic Aptitude Test scores, had signed an agreement, as part of their application for admission to Wheaton College, to adhere to its standards of conduct, which were re-emphasized in the college catalog and the student handbook. They would be required to sign this "pledge," as it was popularly known, each year of their residence at Wheaton. Students would clearly know that in "accepting the responsibilities of campus citizenship, which involves consideration and respect for the personal freedom and property rights of the local and academic community," they would refrain from the use of alcoholic beverages and tobacco, from gambling, from meetings of secret societies, and from attendance at theaters, including the movies. The standards applied equally to the administration, trustees, faculty, and staff.

From the early days of Jonathan Blanchard's presidency, there had been "rules," intended to guide students "in the successful improvement of their minds and hearts."[36] The rules served as well to help the faculty in their "aim to exercise a parental and moral supervision over the character and conduct of the students."[37]

At no time has the College claimed that the standards of conduct have the authority of Scripture. Rather, rules were established as a constructive effort to maintain an environment in which its purposes could be achieved. "Though the selection of the standards may appear to be arbitrary, Wheaton College has found that it must set its own standards in harmony with its own great underlying purpose,"[38] the 1950 catalog declared. Most students accepted the standards as an essential part of life at Wheaton College. Generally, the prohibitions denied them nothing they were accustomed to. If some one of the prohibitions annoyed a student, he was usually willing to accept a temporary abridgment of freedom. Some students accepted the restraints with reluctance, but honored their contractual obligation. A few resented the restraints from the moment of their arrival on campus. Occasionally students have been dismissed for violation of their signed agreement.

From time to time the statement of the standards of conduct in the annual catalog underwent changes, initiated by the trustees, or the president's council, or the spiritual life and standards committee of the faculty. From the beginning it was assumed that by coming to Wheaton, students acknowledged their willingness to accept the standards. But it was not until 1931 that the first catalog statement appeared requiring a student to sign an agreement to abide by the "standards of life." The agreement, it was announced in 1939, was to be "reaffirmed each year."[39] Those two changes represent the more strict approach to student affairs taken by Dr. Buswell in contrast with Dr. Charles Blanchard's somewhat relaxed administration.

The pledge became a year-round agreement in 1944, as the following statement from the catalog attests: "This agreement is considered a contract between the college and the student and is in effect whether a student is at home or in Wheaton.[40] Such an extension of control over student's cultural practices sometimes created problems; it put some students in conflict with their parents' life-style and the parents' authority in their own homes. Consequently, modification of the College's area of control was announced in 1961, when Wheatonites were told that agreeing to the standards of conduct "obligates the student to assume responsibility for honorable adherence to them while they are under the authority of the college."[41]

There were always students who felt that the statement of the standards of conduct did not supply an adequate apologetic to support the announced restrictions. The request for the formulation of a biblical basis for the code led to such a statement in 1952, a declaration twice as long as the statement of the year before. It asserts that "there is adequate Biblical basis for the idea of spiritual growth in the image of Christ (II Cor. 2:8)." Four Scriptural citations follow to make clear that this spiritual growth results in a "life consecrated unto God and separated from the world." Wheaton College must, therefore, provide "an environment conducive to the spiritual growth and development of young people who are not yet mature Christians."[42] Subsequently a statement of biblical principles governing personal conduct was substituted for quotations from Scripture.

The advent of television created a problem for the College in its effort to enforce a tenable standard of conduct. In their own homes or even the college lounge students could now see all kinds of movies if they chose to. Early efforts to supervise the choice of television programs on campus proved impractical and were abandoned. Consequently, the prohibition against movies was eliminated, as was the restriction against theater-going when student drama production was approved in the mid-sixties.

These modifications and accommodations were clear acknowledgment that the College had ceased to be an island of refuge from the heterodoxies of the world, as it once was thought to be. With increasing ease the secular mind, through the media, could bid for the allegiance of the campus community. Now responsibility was placed on students to confront alien values through exercising their own moral judgment. Consequently, a new kind of statement appeared in the 1968-69 catalog: "The college further expects its students to exercise Christian discretion and restraint in the choice of entertainment, including television, radio, movies, theater, and the various forms of literature."

Another modification in the pledge was made when the reference to "playing cards" was changed to "traditional playing cards," probably an acknowledgment that many students were playing Rook, with its own special cards—a harmless and challenging game, most people thought, so long as gambling was not involved. Dancing as an unacceptable practice was changed in the 1968-69 catalog to read "social dancing" because folk dancing was recognized as an appropriate cultural form for use in some classes and on certain occasions.

In 1974 a new effort was made to set forth the standards of conduct in postive terms, suggesting that though the College had chosen its own pattern of acceptable social practices, it did so in the light of biblical principles and believed that the standards were conducive to the development of

Christian character and behavior. To meet the objection that the long-familiar list of prohibitions in the catalog left unstated other forms of conduct and disposition clearly denounced by biblical precept, a more inclusive statement was added. It cites as morally wrong within the Wheaton College community "specific acts such as drunkness, stealing, the use of slanderous or profane language, all forms of dishonesty, including cheating, occult practices and sexual sins such as premarital sex, adultery, and homosexual behavior."[43] Condemned also are attitudes of greed, jealousy, pride, lust, bitterness, needless anger, an unforgiving spirit, and harmful discrimination and prejudice based on race, sex, or socio-economic status.

The rise of new kinds of moral and health perils in the seventies made it necessary to add, for the first time, in the catalog a prohibition against the use of "non-medical narcotic or hallucinogenic drugs including marijuana."[44] The seventy-six-line statement on the standards in the 1975-76 catalog contrasts interestingly with the eight-line statement in the 1930-31 catalog, where there was no effort to surround the standards with a moral, biblical context. A simpler, less exhausive "Statement of Responsibilities of Membership in the Academic Community of Wheaton College" was prepared by a faculty-student committee under the direction Dr. Arthur Holmes, chairman of the philosophy department, and approved by the Board of Trustees in January 1975.

Early in President Armerding's administration the College initiated the policy of requiring the student to sign a statement of commitment to the standards of the College at the time of admission. The practice of an annual signing continues with little student objection to the procedure. Most students found the 1975 statement of responsibility acceptable.

For many years student opinion, both favorable and unfavorable, about the pledge found its way into *Record* editorials and letters to the editor. Attendance at the theater and movies was usually the principal center of contention. Some students felt that imposed standards of conduct inhibited independence of thought and action at a time in their intellectual development when independent thinking was being encouraged. Some always declared that they wanted to think through the standards for themselves and voluntarily accept the rules. Unquestionably, well-reasoned student comment encouraged the administration to initiate change from time to time.

On one of his visits to Wheaton Billy Graham was asked to comment on the pledge. *Record* reporter Anna Ruth Olsen summarized his response. "Then, as now, there were mixed feelings among the students about the keeping of the pledge." However, Dr. Graham said he kept it, and as far as he knew, so did most of the others. In giving his reasons for favoring the pledge, he referred to it as a "discipline."[45]

Wheaton's statement of commitment to institutional standards of conduct is one of several elements that have made its educational program distinctive. In the 1960s, when many people were asking whether small colleges could survive, some educators declared that institutional survival depended on the development of a unique educational program. Writing in the Spring 1961 *University College Quarterly* of Michigan State University on "What Makes A Good College?", Manning Pattillo observed that "the imaginative development of a distinctive educational idea, a distinctive teaching method, a distinctive location, a distinctive constituency—these are the means of building strength in a college." He then cited several small colleges with such distinctives—among them Dartmouth, Swarthmore, Antioch, Berea, and "Wheaton with its emphasis on biblically-oriented education."

Music for All

For more than a decade, with enrollment expanding rapidly, President Edman, Edward A. Cording, director of the Conservatory, and members of the music faculty were acutely aware of the need for a new music building. Limited quarters in Pierce Chapel were no longer adequate for a quality music program.

Funds for the McAlister Conservatory of Music, ground-breaking for which came on April 8, 1962, were received principally from two sources.[46] The larger contribution came through the efforts of Logan Fulrath, a New York attorney, whose daughters Grace and Irene were then enrolled at Wheaton. Fulrath, his legal associates, and Guaranty Trust Company of New York were executors of the estate of Amelie McAlister Upshur, which had as its intention grants to schools and colleges in memory of Mrs. Upshur's father, William H. McAlister. Fulrath encouraged the overseers of the estate to make a sizable gift if the building would bear the McAlister name. In the entryway of the music building is a brass plaque with the words: McAlister Conservatory of Music / Erected 1962 / To the Glory of God Through the Ministry of Music.

A Georgian building was planned—in accordance with an earlier resolution of the Board of Trustees that this was to be the prevailing style of the campus—and was erected by J. Emil Anderson and Son. A second substantial contribution to the construction cost of $600,000 with furnishings, was made by Charles B. Phillips of Aurora, Illinois. Contacted first in March 1949 by W. Wyeth Willard, President Edman's assistant, Phillips had expressed the wish that just once someone would bring him a gift rather than ask for one. When Willard visited him November 1950, he presented him with a gift—a bunch of bananas. The elderly man remarked that this was the first time anyone had given him something since John D. Rockefeller gave him a dime years earlier. He further commented: "Don't be surprised if I do something for Wheaton College." Some time later he purchased a $300,000 annuity, and then in 1962 canceled $93,000 of the annuity contract in order to transfer the funds to the Conservatory of Music Building Fund.[47]

Dedication ceremonies for McAlister Conservatory took place on June 6, 1963. The year in which McAlister opened, there were 105 students ma-

Professor William Nordin conducts the Men's Glee Club, 1955.

McAlister Conservatory of Music.

joring in music and 900 students studying music in some form.[48] Fifteen full-time and five part-time instructors made up the teaching staff.

Talented students who wished to commit the time to it were assured a memorable experience when they joined one of the musical organizations. In the summer following the dedication of McAlister, the Men's Glee Club made its first European tour, visiting twelve countries. Director of the men's group was Clayton Halvorsen, who had come to Wheaton from Moody Bible Institute in 1957, and had assumed the leadership of the Glee Club upon the retirement of Professor William Nordin. A highlight of the year for the Men's Glee Club was the commencement concert, always before a crowded house and performed with creative finesse.[49] The Women's Glee Club, directed for many years by Mignon Bollman Mackenzie, had two trips, one at the semester break and one at spring vacation. Women who were accepted for the club, and who practiced five hours a week and stayed with the group three or four years, would be likely to sing in each of the major areas of the country.

The Concert Choir usually had forty to fifty men and women. It began in 1963 with director Rex Hicks, who had studied with Robert Shaw. The choir was scheduled in 1964 for a two-week spring tour in the Southwest, principally in Texas. Wheaton's Band, under "Prof" Russell Platz, its long-time director, initiated a busy year with the annual band camp at Williams Bay, Wisconsin. The Homecoming concert would be the first of a series in the Chicago area, followed in the spring by a concert tour to some section of the country. One year, in an extraordinary effort, the sixty-five-piece band went by train to California.

All music groups are goodwill representatives of Wheaton College and have as a central part of their purpose a witness for Jesus Christ. A consistently high quality of musicianship, its own unique witness, characterizes each of these groups.

One of the distinguished services of the Conservatory to campus life and the community at large has been the presentation of the Artist Series of concerts. From their inception in 1954—when concerts were held in Alumni Gymnasium—the series was managed by Professor Alton Cronk, who came to Wheaton from Houghton College in 1950.[50] Though he retired from teaching in 1976, he continued to oversee the Artist Series until 1983, his discriminating taste and skillful management making the concerts at Wheaton among the best of their kind in the Midwest. Many of the great artists of the time have performed at the College, including Marian Anderson, Roberta Peters, Artur Rubinstein, Rudolf Serkin, Isaac Stern, Yehudi Menuhin, and Van Cliburn.

Directors of the Conservatory of Music in the modern era have been: Robert L. Schofield 1928-34; Peter Stam, Jr. 1934-48; Edward A. Cording 1948-70; and Harold M. Best since 1970. Through their leadership Wheaton has developed a superior program of music education, leading to the Bachelor of Music degree, with majors in performance or composition, and the Bachelor of Music Education. As a department of the College the

Conservatory also offers a program leading to the Bachelor of Arts degree.

Dr. Robert L. Schofield (1928-34), a warm-hearted, genial person and fine organist, was devoted to his students. During the Depression he often paid for the meals of some of them until they could secure funds to care for themselves.[51] To strengthen the music department, he worked energetically in limited space, at a time when Pierce Chapel also housed the art and speech departments. Under the direction of Peter Stam, the Conservatory, in spite of the Depression, added instructors, many new courses, and quality equipment. Through his efforts the Conservatory secured accreditation in 1937 by the National Association of Schools of Music, an organization in which Stam served as treasurer for many years. Among the memorable teachers of the Stam era were Dr. Frank Van Dusen, nationally known organist, and Lillian Powers, a piano teacher of rare ability.

Edward A. Cording, who succeeded Dr. Stam as director of the Conservatory, had majored in music at Wheaton, and three years after his graduation in 1933 became Wheaton's first director of public relations, a position he held until 1943. He served the Conservatory with distinction and a deep sense of Christian mission through the years of the music department's largest growth. Cording was responsible for establishing a fine music library and introducing a plan for auditioning students before admission to the Conservatory. He also appointed music department area chairmen in 1967.

Reginald Gerig, '42, a pianist who joined the faculty in 1952 after training at the Juilliard School of Music, was in charge of piano studies. An alumni study grant enabled him to complete *Famous Pianists and Their Technique* (1974), a widely used text. Russell Platz became director of wind instrument instruction and music education. After coming to Wheaton in 1950, he taught the whole range of wind instruments with skill and dedication. He also created and directed fine concert bands. To direct the work in organ, Gladys Christensen, '49, was chosen. Following graduate work at Northwestern, she returned to Wheaton as a faculty member in 1954. To oversee theory instruction Ellen Thompson, a graduate of Houghton College and Columbia University, was selected. She was for a time also director of the Women's Glee Club. Alton Cronk, who completed graduate work at New York University, became director of studies in the history and literature of music. Rex Hicks, who came to Wheaton from Pasadena Nazarene College in 1963, supervised the study in church music and directed the concert choir until 1981.

Long service to the College and excellent musicianship brought great respect to Mignon Bollman Mackenzie and H. William Nordin. Mrs. Mackenzie was a fine soloist, teacher of voice, and director of the Women's Glee Club. Resourceful and imaginative, respected by her professional peers, dedicated to the ideals of the College, "Mrs. Mac" served Wheaton for thirty-nine years (1928-1967). Professor Nordin, impressive in appearance, graceful in his conducting, taught voice and directed the Men's Glee Club from 1931 to the time of his retirement in 1958. His oratorio work with the College and community chorus was especially significant; he developed the chorus from a small struggling group to a membership of 300.[52]

Others who taught in the Conservatory during the Edman era included Dr. Lester Groom, organ, who was characterized by Director Cording as "one of Wheaton's great teachers of music" (1946-50); Jack Goode, who succeeded Dr. Groom after his death and remained at Wheaton until 1967; Maurice Dobbins, a fine violinist and director of the Chapel Choir and symphony orchestra (1946-52); and Rolf Espeseth (1957-62). Often described as "a musician's musician," Espeseth composed the musical score for the Centennial Festival, "Abundant Century."

The Golden Era of Athletics

During the Edman era Wheaton had its longest period of sustained success in athletics, a time in which many of the college teams achieved extraordinary records.

What factors contributed to Wheaton's athletic accomplishments? A sound philosophy of intercollegiate athletics was foundational. In addition, strong administrative and trustee support was a continuous encouragement to coaches and participants. Further, an unusual number of promising young athletes came to the campus after World War II, and, under skilled and dedicated coaching, developed into superb competitors. Quite a few found their way to Wheaton because they became Christians during their military service and at the conclusion of the war sought a Christian college.

The philosophy of athletics developed during this era stated that "because a liberal arts curriculum is concerned with the development of the whole person, extracurricular activities become an integral part of the students' education." Athletic competition allows the student to engage in a struggle that brings self-discovery, that reveals latent leadership capability.[53] Athletic directors during this era were Edward A. Coray (1926-1951) and Harvey C. Chrouser (1951-1977). They and the entire corps of coaches encouraged team members to believe that, in their unique way, they performed to the glory of God and for the advancement of "Christ and His Kingdom." During this time Wheaton competed in intercollegiate football, basketball, baseball, soccer, cross-country, wrestling, indoor and outdoor track, tennis, and golf, bringing out about 225 men to complete the teams. Membership in the College Conference of Illinois, which changed from time to time, brought Wheaton into regular competition with North Central, long its principal athletic rival, Illinois Wesleyan, Lake Forest, Augustana, Carthage, Millikin, and Elmhurst.

During the 1950s Wheaton, the largest school in the conference, dominated its competitors, particularly in football, basketball, and track, so that at the urging of CCI officials, the College agreed to transfer to another stronger conference, or to play an independent schedule. The independent schedule, however, failed to generate the high degree of enthusiasm that CCI competition had; so Wheaton was happy for the invitation to return in 1965 to the expanded College Conference of Illinois and Wisconsin. Student and community support for the football team was strong, week after week, in sunshine or rain and mud. Year after year teams were encouraged by "Prexy" Edman on the bench with the teams, together with the reassuring figure of Dr. Clarence Wyngarden to render medical aid to the injured.

Wheaton football teams, under the coaching of Harvey Chrouser between 1947 and 1961, won a total of nine CCI Championships. Seven of these were consecutive championships between 1953 and 1959. In 1957 the team was rated fourth in the nation among small colleges and seventh in 1958. In 1958 and 1961 Wheaton football teams were undefeated. Between 1946 and 1963 the Crusaders compiled the extraordinary record of 119 victories, 21 losses, and 7 ties. The 1958 team, with a string of nine consecutive victories, achieved the best record of all the Wheaton teams. Among small colleges it led the nation in total offense, had twelve players cited for all-conference honors, and rolled up some stunning scores. Lake Forest was defeated 48-0, Augustana 67-12, and Elmhurst 90-6.

In 1961 newly appointed head coach Jack Swartz, '52, a fine end in his student days, had the rare privilege of directing an undefeated team in his first season of coaching. A 20-7 victory over a strong North Central team brought the Little Brass Bell back to Wheaton after a year's lodging at the Naperville college.

Probably the two most widely acclaimed of Wheaton's football players have been Charles Schoenherr, '50 and David Burnham, '56. Both were all-state high school athletes before they came to Wheaton. Schoenherr arrived on campus from Racine, Wisconsin, in the fall of 1946 and established himself at once as a hard running back. In 1947 his 115 points made him the leading scorer in the nation. Perhaps his most unusual performance came in the 1949 Lake Forest game, won by Wheaton 34-19, when he scored all five of his team's touchdowns. In his senior year Schoenherr gained 937 yards in 142 carries, a performance that ranked him thirteenth in the nation in rushing, won him all-conference honors, and little All-American acclaim. Schoenherr later became president of Sterling College, Sterling, Kansas.

Davd Burnham, son of an Akron, Ohio, pastor, and now a trustee of the College, came to Wheaton after having received offers of athletic scholarships from forty-five other institutions. A high-stepping back the opposition always found hard to bring down, he gained 2,780 yards in three seasons for the Crusaders, 1,448 in the 1953 season for an average of ten yards a carry. For three years his performances won for Dave All-Conference and little All-American honors, and selection as quarterback on the 1953 little All-American team.[54] Drafted by the Washington Redskins for a professional career, Burnham instead joined his father as an assistant in his home church in Akron.

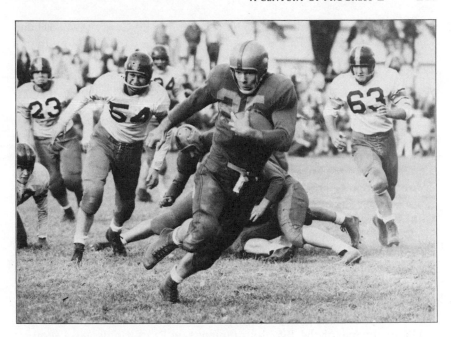

Dick Camp, '58, now chaplain at the U.S. Military Academy, West Point, New York, carries the ball for Wheaton.

Crusader football team after its last game of an undefeated season in 1961. At left, Coach Donald Church; right, Coach Jack Swartz.

246 WHEATON COLLEGE: A HERITAGE REMEMBERED

Basketball teams, under the skilled coaching of Ed Coray (1943-51) and Lee Pfund (1951-75), had extraordinary successes, particularly in the 1950s, when the teams were playing in Alumni Gymnasium. Between 1947 and 1960 Wheaton had fourteen consecutive winning seasons and won all six of its CCI conference championships. In those days of high success, students packed out the gym.

Between 1947 and 1960 Crusader teams turned in 252 victories against 76 losses. Perhaps the most remarkable records were compiled during the years between 1956 and 1959. The 1955-56 team won 28 and lost 4, winning 24 games straight, a record good enough to get them a bid to compete in the National Association of Intercollegiate Athletics tournament in Kansas City, where they placed fourth among the small colleges of the nation. The following year, 1956-57, the season record was 23-1, which brought to Wheaton the CCI title and a bid to participate in the small college national championship tournament, organized by the newly formed National Collegiate Athletic Association. In regional playoffs Lee Pfund's men defeated Duluth 84-75 and Beloit 77-75 to win the right to participate in the finals at Evansville, Indiana. In the quarter finals Wheaton defeated South Dakota 90-80 and Los Angeles State 71-53.

The final game of the 1957 tournament saw Wheaton defeat a scrappy Kentucky Wesleyan team 89-65 for the national championship. The Wheaton starters were forwards Bob Whitehead and Mel Peterson, center Dick Kamm, and guards Don Anderson and Bill Gerig. Valuable substitutes were Roy Roe and Stan Chamberlain. When the team returned to Wheaton on Saturday afternoon, they were greeted in Alumni Gym by 1,000 cheering fans.

The next year, 1957-58, the team, with a 27-3 record, went again to the NCAA finals, this time finishing fourth. An incredible record of 56 consecutive conference victories, and four CCI championships, over a period of four seasons was completed by the 1958-59 team. These achievements were the effort of a balanced and skillful team, but Mel Peterson must be cited as one of the most extraordinary performers in the history of Wheaton basketball. An all-state high school player in Michigan, he passed over many college and university offers to come to Wheaton, where he made the varsity in his freshman year. In the NCAA championship game he was chosen most valuable player. For two years he was named by the United Press and the Associated Press to the small college All-American first team. By the end of his career, he was third among small college all-time high scorers.

During Coach Ed Coray's last eight years, all winning seasons, with one conference championship, a number of outstanding players were developed: Bud Schaeffer, Dick Gross, Marv Johnson, Bob Wilson, Ralph Christensen, and Norm Pott. Both Schaeffer and Johnson were named to the all-conference team for four years. For colorful performance, accuracy of shooting, and spectacular floor play from his guard position, Bud Schaeffer was an unforgettable figure on the court. Johnson stands second in the all-time individual scoring records, averaging twenty points a game, and led the team in scoring in 1948-49. All three of Coach Pfund's sons— John, '65, Kerry, '71, Randy, '74—have played on Wheaton teams and all have been in the top twenty high scorers.

Wheaton won wide acclaim for its track teams, especially during the years that Gil Dodds served as coach, 1945-1959. Known to sports writers throughout the country as the "Flying Parson" while he was holder of the world indoor mile record and was winning races on every major indoor track in America, Gil never lost a race in four years of competition.[55] In 1943 he was given the Sullivan Award as the "athlete who has contributed the most to further the cause of sportsmanship" for that year. He came to Wheaton to study in the Graduate School in 1945 and served as a student coach, under Carl DeVries, for two years before becoming a full-time coach in the athletic department. His presence drew many Christian track- men to Wheaton. A strict disciplinarian and master strategist, Dodds coached cross-country, indoor track, and spring track with extraordinary success. Under his guidance spring track teams, well-balanced in field and running events, won twelve out of thirteen conference championships.

In cross-country the Doddsmen brought to Wheaton nine straight state championships between 1945 and 1953, and twice finished first in the small college division of the nationals. In 1956 the team won the state championship and was undefeated. When the NCAA championship meet was held in Wheaton, Wheaton placed fifth among twenty-seven teams.

Among Gil Dodds's runners was Taylor McKenzie, '54, a Navajo Indian from New Mexico, who was later to become Dr. McKenzie, the first Indian physician among his own people. Perhaps no runner won more acclaim for Wheaton than Kikuo ("Cookie") Moriya, a Japanese whom Dodds met in 1950 in the Far East while traveling around the world for the Pocket Tes- tament League, a Bible distribution society. Subsequently Moriya became a Christian and entered Wheaton as a sophomore in 1952 at the age of twenty-seven. In two and a half years at the College, the 5-foot 6-inch, 135-pound runner won forty-six races. In 1954 he was the two-mile NCAA champion, the "outstanding athlete" of the Midwest Relays in 1954, Cen- tral Collegiate cross-country champion in 1954, Michigan AAU mile champion in 1955, Central AAU mile and two-mile champion in 1954 and 1955, and CCI mile record holder. At his graduation in 1955, he was the mile and two-mile record holder at Wheaton.[56]

Immediately after World War II, interest in soccer was limited in the Midwest. The 1949 *Tower* editor wrote, perhaps with some exaggeration: "For the last ten years Wheaton has been responsible for keeping alive the international game of soccer in the Midwest." Bob Baptista, '48, who had been coaching at Roberts Wesleyan, took over the team in 1951, a respon- sibility he continued until 1967. During Baptista's seventeen years as coach, his teams had only one losing season. His best team record was in 1966, when the Crusaders were undefeated 11-0-3, a good enough record to give them a tie for the Midwest conference crown and the championship in the NCAA Mid-East Regionals, played at Ohio Wesleyan University, where Wheaton defeated Wooster 1-0, and Lake Forest 3-0.[57] Many of Wheaton's soccermen have won individual honors as All-American players, all-conference selections, and honorable mentions in both categories.

Returning to campus in 1946, after service in the Navy as an athletic officer, George Olson began his career as wrestling coach at Wheaton. Wrestling, like other sports during the golden era of athletics, was successful, and drew strong competitors to the College. From 1946-47 to 1964-65 Wheaton wrestling teams scored 138 victories against 63 losses and 4 ties. During these nineteen years the teams had only three losing seasons. The best records were compiled by the 1956-57 and 1957-58 teams, each with eleven victories and one defeat. Both also won the CCI tournament, as did the 1958-59 team.

Lee Pfund, '49, had an exceptionally long career as baseball coach, piloting Crusader teams from 1946 to 1975. He has observed that baseball is the only major sport not limited by time. "You have to get the opposition out; the clock will not bail you out." Those who play baseball for Wheaton, and in most small colleges, do so for the love of the game. They never know the wildly cheering crowds common to football and basketball. Coach Pfund was elated to win the CCI title in 1951, the third year of his coaching. The team finished second a number of times but did not win the championship again.

Tennis coaches during the Edman era were Ed Coray, 1946-50; Frank Bellinger, 1951-60; and Jack Swartz, beginning in 1961. Wheaton won its first CCI tennis championship in 1952 and again in 1953, in the latter year with victories in nine dual meets against one loss. Among the key players in those successes were Ken Carter, Tom Leafstrand, Dave Burnham, Bob Popp, Dick Bergland, Jim Means, and Reinhard Buss. Leafstrand compiled a 22-2 three-year record, based to some extent on his ability to shift the racquet from hand to hand so that every ball was played forehand. The 1957 championship team, with an 8-2 record, had as key men Bob McCall, Buddy McCalla, John Kay, Bill Kelly, and Bill Gerig. In 1962 Dennis Bennema played through an undefeated season and won All-American honors in the national playoffs. That year, when the team was not competing in the CCI, they compiled a 12-2 record.[58]

Ice hockey began informally in 1957-58 and had a second start the winter of 1962-63, when Bob Curtis organized a team which played on a rink behind the stands of McCully field. In its second season the team posted a 5-6 record playing area college teams. By 1965 the team was playing in a four-team college league and seemed to be nearing varsity status.

Gymnastics, first encouraged by Coach Bill Gale, graduated from a half-time entertainment at basketball games to a varsity sport in 1956, under Coach Bud Williams. The Orange and Blue gained its first victory against Central Michigan with a team built around Don Eilers, Kim Lashlee, Paul Falcone, and Dave Thillen.

NCAA Division III national champions, 1956–57. Front row, l. to r.: Bob Whitehead, Don Anderson, Mike Easterling, Don Voss, Bill Gerig. Back row: Coach Lee Pfund, Dick Kamm, Stan Chamberlain, Roy Roe, Mel Peterson, John Dobbert, Bruce Ellingson.

Spring Festival, 1959.

Golfers played their rounds under the direction of Coach Gale without the benefit of applauding crowds. They played with creditable success against such schools as Northern Illinois University, Lake Forest, North Central, the University of Chicago, and Augustana.

Women's Athletics

Women's athletics for many years was under the direction of Ruth Leedy, '32. Through much of the Edman era, intercollegiate athletics for women was limited to tennis, a sport in which they established a splendid record. Women who wanted athletic activity had the opportunity to participate in a varied program set up and supervised by the Women's Recreation Association: hikes, game nights, tennis, softball, basketball, volleyball, bowling, ice skating, and skiing. WRA regularly planned sports appropriate to the seasons. Sport Days, held both at Wheaton and on other campuses, brought the women into competition with other school teams in basketball, volleyball, field hockey, and other activities. On those occasions Wheaton teams were always strong competitors.

Women's tennis teams, coached by LaVern Bjorklund, compiled a superb record from 1955-1960 against such competition as North Central, Northern Illinois, the University of Chicago, and North Park College. In the early 1960s the women were offering strong teams in field hockey and basketball, beginning intercollegiate play in both. Women's athletics was growing steadily and many of the women and some coaches were eager for increased scheduling of intercollegiate contests.

Intramurals

Rounding out the college athletic activity was a full intramural program for men and women. Run by the students themselves, these contests—between classes, residence halls, or literary societies—generated much enthusiasm and sometimes intense rivalry. Often many more students than those who competed on intercollegiate teams found recreational opportunities in this way.

One of the very successful campus activities of the time was the Spring Festival, initiated in 1944, and offered biannually thereafter, by the women's physical education department under the direction of its chairman, Ruth Leedy. LaVern Bjorklund inherited the Festival when she became department chairman in 1958. From a small beginning the Festival grew steadily in magnitude and beauty, requiring of directors and performers many hours in planning, practice, and performance.

Varied activities absorbed the attention of audiences who consistently filled the gymnasium for one afternoon and two evening performances. Music, men's gymnastics, marching groups, rope jumping, living statues, and other novelty acts made up the program. Costuming for the marching groups was usually striking, sometimes elaborate. With the introduction of the quarter system as the seventies began, however, students no longer had the time to give to this impressive project, and it expired.

CHAPTER 14

The Final
Edman Years

URING THE LATER YEARS OF THE EDMAN ERA THE TRUST-
ees, administration, faculty, and student body continued to be aware of the
need for Wheaton to keep pace with the times, make accommodation to innovations in higher education, deepen and enrich the academic and spiritual
life of the campus, and provide adequate physical facilities. At the same
time, in a widely troubled era, there was continuing resolution to maintain
Wheaton's distinctives.

New tendencies in college teaching asserted themselves rather strongly in
the activistic sixties. Audiovisual centers urged instructors to make use of
new media techniques. Some teachers saw these technologies in education as
a threat to their security. In response to complaints of poor teaching, administrators were urging the use of innovative methods to vitalize the presentation of material. Colloquiums and seminars often replaced lectures.
Students sometimes worked together with the professor in determining the
materials to be used and the goals to be achieved in a course. Many alternatives to conventional pedagogy were forced by students disenchanted with
what they characterized as antiquated methods. All of these trends influenced academic life at Wheaton.

The Board of Trustees was acutely conscious of the need for a new men's
dormitory, science building, and library. They were also eager to encourage

quality instruction, to work for faculty salary improvement, and to initiate long-range planning. All such components of a total vision for Wheaton and its future were readily conceived, but far less readily financed. In a typical college year, 1962-63, the budget was $4,296,600.[1] The money came from tuition (the largest portion), endowment, gifts, and grants (from individuals, corporate sources, alumni), and from the sale of annuity contracts. The highest single cost item in the annual operating budget always is personnel: salaries and benefits for faculty and staff.

The establishment of a number of national, non-government programs after World War II had helped Wheaton to meet its budgetary commitments. Recognizing the new demands that were being made on colleges and universities to train a vast student population, such corporate leaders as Frank W. Abrams of Standard Oil and Irving S. Olds of U.S. Steel urged the industrial community to give regularly to higher education, particularly to non-tax-supported institutions. Many gifts were in the form of scholarships and unrestricted institutional grants. In December 1955 the Ford Foundation announced a $206,000,000 grant to the nation's private, accredited colleges and universities, such donations to be placed in the institutions' endowment fund for at least ten years to be used for faculty salaries only. The Ford decision was in recognition of the fact that after the removal of price controls following World War II a rapidly rising cost of living had left college and university teachers financially strained. Wheaton's share of the Ford allocation was $382,000.

Some student tuition came to Wheaton through long-term, low-interest loans made to students under the National Defense Education Act of 1958. Since this money was paid directly to the students, the Board of Trustees felt that accepting these funds did not conflict with its determination to reject federal funds for education. The refusal to accept government aid appeared at first to have been a consensus agreement rather than a written declaration. In 1964 Dr. Edman told the Board, during a discussion of federal assistance, that there was no firm policy, nor was it felt any was needed then,[2] though the rejection of federal aid seems to have become unwritten policy.

In 1961-62 the average faculty salary within each rank was: professor $7,347, associate professor $6,400, assistant professor $5,759, instructor $5,029.[3] The low salary level was readily recognized by the trustees and administration, judged by North Central Association and other agency standards; and the range between veteran faculty members and newcomers was too narrow. Among the groups interested in improved faculty salary standards, none was more active than the Alumni Association. Alumni giving, under Executive Secretary Edward Coray, had increased from $43,000 in 1951 to $200,000 by 1959; and there were plans to augment that sum substantially. Asked by questionnaire what programs of the College they had a strong desire to support, 74 percent of the alumni named faculty salary support as their first choice, 18 percent said student aid, and only 8 percent favored gifts for construction.[4] In 1952, therefore, the Alumni Association contributed $36,000 as a starter for faculty salaries, and proposed to give $540,000 during the five years following.[5] It was a strong show of affection by the "old grads" for their esteemed mentors.

The GI Bill of Rights, a noble instrument of gratitude, officially known as the Serviceman's Readjustment Act of 1944, providing educational benefit for veterans of World War II and the Korean War, assisted more than two generations of students in completing their college education. Non-veterans and women students were also in need of assistance as the cost of a college education rose; increasing numbers of lower-middle class and lower-income students likewise were desiring to enter the groves of academe. Wheaton's commitment to student aid was to grow year by year, following a national trend. In 1960 some $60,000 was allotted for this purpose, and $150,000 was added the following year, made possible by a rise in tuition, which increased Wheaton's educational budget by $275,000. In 1961, endowed scholarships provided $16,000 in student aid, general financial assistance provided $60,000, revolving loans $19,000, contributions from The Century Club and faculty educational rebates $24,000, and National Defense Loans $103,000—a total of $222,000.[6] Generous as those early efforts seemed, Dr. Edman reported to the Board of Trustees in January 1964 that student financial aid then available to Wheaton students was "about one-half that recommended by the College Scholarship Service." On the same occasion he noted that, in spite of the Alumni Association's splendid effort, faculty salaries were still below the national average.[7]

Trustee interest in encouraging the faculty to strive for excellence in teaching was evident with the establishment of the Teacher-of-the-Year Award at commencement 1960. The first recipient of the award, carrying a gift of $500, was Angeline Brandt, professor of mathematics. The Teacher-of-the-Year is chosen by peer nomination with final selection made by an anonymous faculty committee. Two awards were made in 1961: to Kenneth Kantzer, professor of Bible, as senior teacher, and to Walter Kaiser, instructor in Bible, as junior teacher.

For continuing study toward an advanced degree, or for study and teaching abroad, the Board of Trustees has always been generous in its policy of granting leaves of absence. Responding to this policy, faculty were alert to opportunities for intellectual enrichment and for enlarging their competence in their disciplines. Detailing some of these adventures in learning and teaching will suggest the range of faculty interests. When neo-orthodoxy had become a strong theological force and was regarded by many evangelicals as a perilous influence, Kenneth Kantzer went to the University of Göttingen for eight months to study its origins, and from there to the University of Basel for five months' study with Karl Barth. One trustee, who later withdrew his objection, was apprehensive about the undertaking, but otherwise there was no opposition to Kantzer's desire to study the movement at its source. In 1959-60 Donald Boardman, professor of geology, went to the University of Peshawar in Pakistan under a Southeast Asia Treaty Organization grant to teach geology and establish the University's department of geology.

The Fulbright Act, passed by the Congress in 1946, made available, from the sale of World War II surpluses to countries overseas, funds to finance an exchange study-teaching program between the United States and many countries throughout the world. Frank Green, professor of chemistry, was the first Wheaton recipient of a Fulbright teaching grant: he was appointed to teach chemistry at the University of Cairo and at Ibrahim University in Egypt during the year 1952-53. A Fulbright assignment took S. Richey Kamm to the University of Dacca in Pakistan in 1959-60 to teach political science and the first courses at the university in American history. Other Fulbright teachers were Paul Bechtel, American literature at Istanbul University in Turkey, 1968-69; Donald Boardman, geology, for a second visit to Peshawar University, Pakistan; and Neal Brace, chemistry, at the University in Wuppertal, Germany, in 1978. Peter Veltman received a study grant for work in Dutch language and literature at the University of Amsterdam in 1949-50. Under a direct contract with the government, Robert Stone went in 1959 to Kabul, Afghanistan, for two years, to teach linguistics. Joseph Spradley went to Haigazian College in Beirut to teach physics, with the expectation of remaining for three years.

Of great value to the Wheaton academic community were generous study grants initiated by the Danforth Foundation of St. Louis in 1955 to college instructors well advanced in their Ph.D. programs, with reasonable expectation of completing them through this grant. Among Danforth recipients were Arthur Holmes, Peter Veltman, Arthur Volle, Robert Warburton, Thomas Askew, and James Murk. Other sources of support for faculty research were the National Science Foundation, the Atomic Energy Commission, and the American Council of Learned Societies. Physicist Howard Claassen was awarded the Guggenheim Fellowship for research in Israel.

In 1962 Claassen gained international attention in science for his successful bonding of xenon and fluorine to form xenon tetrafluoride, a chemical reaction previously thought unachievable. Undertaken with two assistants, an experiment that had failed hundreds of times before, he succeeded on the first attempt at Argonne National Laboratory. In consequence of Claassen's experiments, textbooks had to be changed, referring no longer to inert gases but only to noble gases. In 1963 the Chicago Junior Association of Commerce named Claassen the Chicagoan of the Year in Science. The same year James Kraakevik, who had served as a consultant to the U.S. Naval Research Laboratory in Washington, D.C., was selected to participate in an international conference on atmosphere and space in Switzerland.

The National Science Foundation one summer sent a group of twenty secondary school teachers to Wheaton's Black Hills Science Station, providing each a stipend, travel and tuition costs, and underwriting Wheaton staff salaries. Numerous other grants from the National Science Foundation provided study and research opportunities for Wheaton scientists. The

Foundation contributed half of $12,000 expended in 1963 for the purchase of a physiograph, a number of light microscopes, and reference works for the biology library—the entire enterprise under the supervision of biologist Ray Brand. The Atomic Energy Commission provided opportunities for study and teaching in nuclear research and atomic energy for a number of Wheaton's science teachers, among them Paul Wright and Frank Green. Harold Fiess did post-doctoral work as a research associate in chemistry for ten summers at Northwestern University. Bernard Nelson had a long association in research with the G. D. Searle Company.

In the early post-war years few grants were available in the social sciences and humanities, in comparison with the physical and natural sciences. Nevertheless, Wheaton professors in the humanities and social sciences took advantage of opportunities for professional growth by summer study, travel, research for writing, attendance at conferences, and service in professional organizations. In an early effort to encourage teachers in the humanities, Congress established in 1965 the National Endowment for the Humanities, from which Professors Mark Noll, of the history department, and Roger Lundin, of the English department, have had grants for summer study at the Univerisity of Iowa and Northwestern University.

Alumni grants for study and writing, instituted in 1956, provided time for faculty to work toward advanced degrees and engage in research. Grants between 1956 and 1965 went to Professors Samuel Schultz, Bible; Merrill Tenney, Bible; Clarence Hale, Greek; Berkeley Mickelsen, Bible; Thomas Kay, history; Gerald Hawthorne, Greek; and Edwin Hollatz, speech.

In 1961 the faculty took a significant step toward achieving a closer relationship with the trustees; it requested, and received, permission to organize the first Faculty Welfare Committee—later the Personnel Committee.[8] Members of the committee, who were Edward Hakes, Cyril Luckman, and Paul Bechtel, secured agreement from the trustees that they would issue annual teacher contracts, would adopt the TIAA retirement program in place of the very inadequate institutionally managed system, and substantially increase life insurance and health benefits for faculty and staff. The committee's effort to initiate a program of sabbatical leaves failed, the trustees feeling at that time that alumni study grants were an adequate substitute.

Academic Departments

For many alumni who have been inspired by great teaching, the institution is the faculty. The Wheaton faculty and administration were cognizant of new developments in various fields of knowledge and encouraged innovation in teaching, at the same time being mindful that innovation must be accountable. It cannot be casually wandering through beguiling academic pathways, the sort of waywardness that seemed to have captured a number of campuses in the sixties in their extreme quests for newness.

In 1961 student requests for the introduction of Russian language courses were voiced, won administration support, and the courses were first offered in 1963. The delay was in large measure owing to difficulty in finding a suitable teacher at a time when teachers of Russian were in great demand. Alice Naumoff, a colorful and controversial Jewish Christian from New York, initiated the work. But Russian never achieved the student support that had seemed likely. Within a few years interest in that language had waned to the point that the program was terminated.

When Russian was introduced, it became the sixth language to be offered by the department of foreign language under the chairmanship of Clarence B. Hale. Wheaton continued to offer a major in Greek, one of the very few colleges of its size that did so. Post-war emphasis on science and technology also evoked renewed interest in language. Use of the language laboratory effectively supplemented classroom work. A general education requirement of two years of foreign language made it necessary to offer courses in Latin, Greek, French, German, and Spanish. Language clubs, classroom instruction, and laboratory supervision kept members of the department busy.

The English department, directed by Professor Clyde S. Kilby, had the largest number of majors in 1964. To meet the student's general education requirement in literature, the department usually recommended Western World Literature, believing that it provided a broad introduction to the humanities and strengthened the student's commitment to the liberal arts philosophy of education. Students in upper-division courses, from Medieval and Renaissance times to the twentieth century, were challenged with new ideas and issues. Writers like T. S. Eliot, Hemingway, Faulkner, Camus, Beckett, Brecht, and C. S. Lewis were discussed intensively. Freshmen writing received much attention because it is difficult to teach effectively and its results are not easily and immediately measurable. The innovative use of a writing sample as part of the admissions procedure helped faculty to discover students of superior writing capability, as well as those with need for instruction.

One of the earliest of the International Study Programs was Wheaton-in-England, sponsored by the literature department and first directed by Professor Joe McClatchey in 1975. Other directors have included Professors Leland Ryken, Erwin Rudolph, and Rolland Hein. After visiting literary shrines in England and Ireland, the group settles in at St. Anne's College, Oxford, for three and a half weeks of study and lectures by Wheaton and Oxford professors. Journeys to sites associated with Keats, Byron, Wordsworth, the Brontës, Joyce, Yeats, and many others give the student a memorable literary experience.

Wheaton has had a strong emphasis on speech training and speech-related activities, requiring all students to have basic instruction in this discipline. Chairman Clarence Nystrom, with Professors Edwin Hollatz and Eleanor Paulson, provided a general speech course for all students and a variety of advanced courses, with limited work in speech correction for students wishing to major in the field. Radio station WETN-FM, staffed and managed en-

1971 Teachers-of-the-Year. Dr. Robert Webber, junior teacher, left; *Dr. Morris Inch, senior teacher,* right.

Professor Beatrice Batson explains a passage in literature.

tirely by students under the sponsorship of the speech department, provided training in radio performance for a number of students. Public performance of drama had not yet been approved at Wheaton, but the speech staff was confident that drama would soon take its place with music and art as one of the campus forms of creative expression. The department was located in Plumb studios, a college-owned frame residence on Irving street.

In six years psychology advanced from one of the smallest to one of the largest departments at Wheaton.[9] In 1958 the department, with eleven majors, operating as a subdivision of the education department, had one full-time professor and three part-time instructors. By 1964 there were ninety majors taught by three professors and three part-time instructors. One-third of the students were going on to graduate school and two or three senior majors were being elected to the Scholastic Honor Society annually. Department status was granted to psychology in 1962 with Dr. Onas Scandrette as chairman. The department, seeking to develop a Christian perspective on the psychological nature of human beings, found that its strongest challenge came from behaviorist and evolutionary theories.

The science division continued to evidence the vigor it had been encouraged to develop during the presidencies of Charles Blanchard and J. Oliver Buswell, Jr. Both men believed that the foundations of Christian faith were being undermined by modern scientific theory, and that scientists who are Christian needed thorough training. In the four science departments—biology, chemistry, geology, and physics/mathematics—twenty-one professors held Ph.D. degrees, one-third the total for the College. The biology department, with Professor Russell Mixter as chairman, supervised a full program in inadequate laboratory quarters in the west end of Blanchard Hall. In spite of limitations in space and equipment, a broad offering of twenty-seven courses prepared a steady flow of students for careers in science and medicine.

The physics and mathematics department, also operating in seventy-five-year-old quarters in the west end of Blanchard, was likewise restricted by inadequate facilities. The physics and mathematics staff, directed by Professor James Kraakevik, offered courses that met the general education requirement, prepared teachers, and readied students for graduate study. Aided by grants from the Atomic Energy Commission, the department was able to establish a radioisotopes laboratory and a 512-channel analyzer. The College also had a small program in atmospheric physics supported by the Navy. In 1963 Wheaton secured an IBM 1620 computer; its academic use was committed to the physics department, which began to offer courses in programming each semester. Student enrollment in the courses of this department doubled in the decade 1951-1961, further evidence of response to the new technological age.

After moving into the new Breyer Chemistry Building in 1955, the chemistry department had space to offer a much more adequate program. The department had over fifty chemistry majors who had earned Ph.D. degrees from leading graduate schools by 1945, and it was approved by the American Chemical Society in 1949. Separate laboratories for general, organic, analytical, physical, instrumental, and advanced organic work were a luxury to professors who had once labored in west Blanchard Hall. Argonne National Laboratory near Chicago provided facilities for further research.

Occupying quarters on the third floor of Breyer Hall was the geology department, with Professors Donald Boardman and Douglas Block offering a diversity of courses. Wheaton was then one of the few evangelical colleges offering a degree in geology. Some students chose to meet their general education requirement in science by electing the general course in that field, their interest aroused by what geology has to say about the age of the earth, based on rock formations. They saw geology, in part, as an apologetic tool to support their theological convictions.

Summer field courses, required of majors but open to others, were offered annually at the Wheaton College Science Station in the beautiful, rugged Black Hills of western South Dakota. Facilities at the station include an education building, laboratory, library, dining hall, outdoor swimming pool, cabin dormitories for student men and women, faculty cabins, and a guest cabin. During World War II campus officials were once reminded that the Black Hills Station was a thousand miles from Wheaton, that tires and gas were scarce, and perhaps the station should be closed for the duration of the war. When Carl. F. H. Henry, who had visited the Black Hills and had been impressed by the experience, heard of this prospect, he sent the trustees a telegram: "Beer trucks are still rolling in Los Angeles. Don't close the station."[10] The station remained open. Professor Boardman, who for many years was director of the Black Hills facility, made major contributions to its growth.

The education department prepared nearly a third of the student body for teaching in public and private institutions. In 1965 Wheaton received 12,000 requests for teachers, a somewhat exceptional year; but there has always been a large demand for Wheaton-trained teachers. Department Chairman Peter Veltman and Division Chairman Willard Jackman supervised the student teaching program in which twenty-eight area public schools provided the teaching laboratory experience. A distinguished achievement award from the American Association of Colleges for Teacher Education in 1965 cited Wheaton for its "Program of Excellence." Students completing the Wheaton teacher training program were eligible to teach in thirty states, an arrangement made possible by Wheaton's being accredited by the National Council of Accreditation of Teacher Education.[11] Because of a growing awareness of the value of outdoor education, student teaching hours at Honey Rock Camp in cooperation with the physical education department were introduced in 1964.

In economics and business administration, a department led by Chairman Arne Howard, a student could complete a major by selecting thirty hours of course work. In the sixties business administration was gradually phased out and efforts were concentrated on economics. Among the offerings, in addition to elementary principles, were courses in the history of economic thought, American economic theory, labor economics, money and banking, and business law. To enrich the experience of its students, the department provided guest lecturers, participation in intercollegiate learning programs, and competition with nine other colleges in a business games activity.

In his centennial statement on "The Bible in Wheaton's Liberal Arts Program," President Edman observed that "the Bible has always been basic in the persuasion and program of Wheaton College, both curricular and extracurricular." He noted further that "the religious perspective is helpful in achieving a significant intellectual unity and deepened moral sense."[12] Since all students were required at this time to take sixteen hours of Bible, the Bible department met the largest number of students and had the largest departmental faculty, with ten members, under the chairmanship of Professor Kenneth Kantzer. Besides students who were meeting their general education requirement in Bible, were those majoring in the field who planned to enter seminary to prepare for the Christian ministry, pursue graduate study, serve on the mission field, or enter other types of Christian teaching and service.

Twenty-two course offerings provided a range of opportunities for students after they had taken the required courses in Old Testament, New Testament, doctrine, and apologetics. The last two had replaced the traditional senior courses in ethics and theism and were intended to help students evaluate new theological trends like the neo-orthodoxy of Barth and Brunner and the demythologizing of Bultmann. The department's role as a unifying center of the college program required that it meet from time to time with representatives of other disciplines to discuss concerns of mutual interest and contemporary issues.

Christian education offered courses to prepare students as directors of Christian education, teachers of Bible in public and private schools, leaders in child and youth organizations, religious journalists, pastors' assistants, and missionaries. Students majoring in this field had many opportunities to engage in internship experience in local churches and youth groups, and to do supervised summer field work at Honey Rock Camp.

The department of history and political science offered work foundational to the acquisition of a broad liberal arts perspective on the world. Some students majoring in history and political science became interested in a semester of study at another institution or spent the junior year abroad.

Professor Earle Cairns, chairman of the history department, had published three books and Professor S. Richey Kamm, who directed the work in political science, received a grant in 1963 from the class of 1936 to do research on "The American Heritage and the Communist Challenge." As a result of his study, he prepared a bibliography, a syllabus for teachers, and set up a summer institute for teachers.

Sociology and anthropology supplemented each other's efforts. Sociology offered courses in social theory and practical work, and the Chicago area provided an extraordinary laboratory for understanding human problems. Graduates found positions in mental health, child and family service, community organization, Christian service agencies, law, and teaching. Anthropology gave students multicultural and crosscultural insights not otherwise provided in the curriculum.

In fine arts the general education requirement was two hours in either art or music, an arrangement, the director of the art department commented, which left "half of the student body without any appreciative acquaintance with one of these fields." Students met their requirement in art by registering in a survey program that emphasized art principles applied to everyday life, based on functional and aesthetic qualities.[13] The department offered student majors work in studio and outdoor painting, sculpture, basic design, interior design, art history, and the teaching of art. Field trips to the Art Institute of Chicago and to notable architectural sites broadened their art experience. Professor Karl Steele was director of the department.

Professional courses in the physical education department prepared students for certification as teachers in elementary and secondary schools, in camping and recreation, and in youth organizations. All students were required to take a course in physical education meeting twice a week during the first six semesters of their enrollment and one course in health education. The intercollegiate athletic program was administered by the chairman of the physical education department. Director of physical education for men was Harvey Chrouser and for women LaVern Bjorklund.

Honey Rock

The physical education department members—together with other faculty personnel—have also supervised an immensely successful enterprise, the Honey Rock Camp in northern Wisconsin, near the town of Three Lakes, 350 miles north of Chicago. Though many persons have contributed their resources, time, and skills to the development of Honey Rock, Harvey Chrouser was the tireless, driving force behind its growth. From the beginning his vision was for the development of a group learning program in a wilderness setting.

In 1951 he proposed to President Edman that the College move from sponsoring a local summer day camp, known as Wecoldac, to an outdoor laboratory to instruct physical eduction majors in leadership. Tom Buis and Dr. Gus Hemwall, of the first Honey Rock Fellowship, leased the camping site and facilities to the College and underwrote the initial financing. The trustees and registrar Enock Dyrness endorsed the curriculum, and President Edman suggested an advisory board of businessmen and interested friends. In 1951 there were 161 two-week campers under the supervision of college personnel and students: by 1966 there were 725.

Facilities were completed for housing and feeding campers, for crafts, waterfront activities, classroom instruction, medical needs, guest housing and a rustic chapel. The Virginia Dyrness Memorial Chapel, dedicated in 1955, was a gift of Dr. and Mrs. Enock Dyrness, together with family members and friends, in memory of their daughter, who had been killed in an automobile accident on her way to the camp.

Besides the summer youth camping sessions, and the Vanguard programs, various academic departments have developed programs, offered for college credit at what came to be known as Honey Rock Wilderness Learning Center. Vanguard, a late summer program, now known as High Road, elected mostly by incoming freshmen men and women, is an experience in wilderness living and stress situations in a Christian context. Coach Bud Williams was associated with the Vanguard program for seventeen years. The annual leadership school, outdoor education school, wilderness learning seminars, internship programs, and the winter leadership schools are held at the Wilderness Center. These activities, together with weekend retreats by college groups, winter camping by groups from many parts of the Midwest, and others, have made Honey Rock Camp operational the year round. The camp is unequaled among college programs for wilderness education, and Chrouser and his staff have helped many colleges and universities begin such a program.[14] By 1980 Honey Rock Camp owned 600 acres, valued, with its facilities, at $2,000,000.

Over 2,600 students and campers have enjoyed Honey Rock. Roger Sandberg, '75, became director of the camp in 1979.

In August faculty and staff families who wish to may spend a week at Honey Rock Family Camp at moderate cost. Usually about 180 Wheaton "family members," often including the president and his family, enjoy a time of fellowship and relaxation together.

North Central Association Review

Since its accreditation by the North Central Association, Wheaton College, like other institutions, has been subject to a regular ten-year review. In the committee's 1964 report the examiners noted as elements of strength: a clear concept of the institution's purpose; the academic quality of the student body; administrative stability; financial stability; excellent record-keeping; good counseling, with few discipline problems; student involvement; faculty publications; new facilities; and off-campus stations such as Honey Rock Camp and the Black Hills Science Station.

Accreditation was reaffirmed, though the committee noted areas needing improvement, among them student housing, at a time when 62 percent of the men and 17 percent of the women were living in off-campus houses. The report called attention to the crowded condition of the library, with limited seating areas for study.

With the median salary for all faculty ranks at $6,875, improvement in this area was called one of the most pressing needs. The absence of a sabbatical program was noted, and attention was called to the fact that slightly over half the faculty were Wheaton graduates, too high a proportion. The committee questioned the faculty's independence, citing the Faculty Handbook's request that teachers submit book manuscripts to the office of the dean prior to publication and that they clear with the educational policies committee before affiliation with non-campus organizations other than professional associations. Both of those requirements were subsequently eliminated.

Finally, classes were judged too small, a costly operation; long-range planning needed to be more specific; and a 1964 catalog statement to the effect that Wheaton is "conservative in its religious, political and economic views" seemed to the committee to endanger free and open discussion in the classroom. The report was, all in all, however, welcomed by the trustees, administration, and faculty as an encouragement and institutional guide for years to come.

Campus Scene

About 500 new students came to the campus each year in the early sixties and soon had a sense of belonging as they were greeted and tested through a four-day orientation program. "Prexy" Edman welcomed them and the director of admissions, Charles Schoenherr, conducted the placement test and familiarized them with campus layout. One of the get-acquainted evenings was devoted to a "Why Wheaton?" program, a time of devotion and praise, followed by a student response to the roll call of states. Several of them told their new classmates why they had chosen Wheaton. Soon they would develop a sense of class identity, elect officers, be introduced to their faculty class sponsors, engage in rivalry with the sophomores, and continue as a unit throughout their four years at Wheaton. Class organization was an important, unifying force in campus life.

Registration in Alumni Gym brought new students to the major business of adjusting schedules, after which they were ready to make arrangements for housing, food service, and activities tickets. The unavoidable last station was for paying bills.

Tension in the Early Sixties

College students in the sixties found themselves part of an angry, bombastic, and violent decade. President John F. Kennedy and his brother Robert, the attorney general, were assassinated, the country was drawn into a distant and exasperating war in Viet Nam, racial tensions arose and intensified, anger stalked the ghettos, and portions of major cities smoldered in ashes. Some of the nation's great universities briefly became captives of radical activism. President Johnson's promise of the "Great Society"—largely destroyed by the cost and consequences of the Viet Nam War—was a rallying cry that inspired students, but in the end left many of them cynical and disillusioned. Although touched by the stresses of the times, violent confrontations did not arise on the Wheaton campus. External cultural transformations were evident locally as elsewhere. Long hair and a new informality of attire were general. Folk music was emerging, even in church worship services.

A Bible Forum organized an evening discussion on "Civil Disobedience," with faculty members Samuel Schultz, Earle Cairns, and Kenneth Kennard participating, together with two black guests, the Reverend Herbert Oliver, '47, and Chicago attorney George Leighton. The group made clear that civil disobedience was not historically centered in the integration issue; but at the time segregation was largely responsible for sporadic outbreaks of civil disobedience.[15] A small group of students organized Inner-City Christian Action to work for improved race relationships in Chicago. They invited to campus Chuck Stone, editor of the *Chicago Defender,* then the only black daily newspaper in the city. Subsequent to his coming, Stone wrote editorially in the *Defender:* "Some students struggling through the barriers of Southern backgrounds or Northern racially conservative tradition were nonetheless seeking independent answers within the Christian gospel. Whatever Christ died for, these wonderful kids at Wheaton are trying to find out."[16]

A spectrum of well-known speakers was brought to campus to help students understand the complexity of their time, including Henry Kissinger, William F. Buckley, Howard K. Smith, Edward Teller, Alistair Cooke, Bill Moyers, and Charles P. Taft. An active Young Republican group helped to sponsor visits to the Wheaton community of Richard Nixon and Barry Goldwater.

Though the administration of Wheaton College has been conservative in conviction, in matters of politics and economics it has not denied the right of expression to those of liberal persuasion. The Clapham Society was organized in 1961 as a forum for the presentation of liberalism in economics and politics. Named after a group of nineteenth-century English evangelicals who fought for reform, the Wheaton Clapham Society required candidates for membership to present their ideas before their peers, who would assess their liberal quality. In 1962 officers of the group were Stan Richard, Norm Wetterau, Julie Cavett, and Ron Watson.[17]

Student Activities

Student publications are a sensitive area on most college campuses. Administrative restraint on what may be printed usually brings wounded pride and cries of censorship; but publication without restraint may encourage irresponsibility. At Wheaton the publications board—its members drawn from students, faculty, administration—had general oversight of the *Record, Kodon,* and *Tower,* essentially to keep these student efforts accurate, responsible, fiscally sound, and in good taste. Nevertheless, editors of student publications, particularly the *Record* and *Kodon*, did not spare from criticism the College, student institutions, and the evangelical response to the arts.

Kodon editor Wesley Craven knew that the fall 1962 issue of the magazine would be controversial. In "A Warning from the Editor" he wrote: "It is the conviction in this office, that, in the arts the Fundamentalist Christian world, and more specifically Wheaton, is sadly short of its potential, and far behind its contemporaries. Therefore the copy of this magazine will remain (as long as the present staff remains), free and limited only by the criteria and the boundaries of artistry."[18] After the winter issue, similarly contentious in tone, the Board of Trustees suspended the publication for the remainder of the year. An examination of the contents of those two issues suggests that they represent youthful zeal and an impatience with others who did not share their enthusiasm for the arts, rather than any show of vulgarity or offensiveness of language. In the fall of 1963 *Kodon* resumed publication.

An independent twelve-page publication, issued by a group of students under the title of *Brave Son*, made its appearance in the spring of 1962, with the approval of college authorities and the publications board, on the understanding that it was a trial effort and would not go off campus. Thoughtful and well written, the articles were, like those in the controversial issues of *Kodon*, quite critical of the College and of contemporary Christian culture. The pamphlet, without a secure financial base, struggled bravely through three issues and expired. *Critique*, another independent student publication, issued in Glen Ellyn by John Hommes and Philip McIlnay in March 1963, without college approval, lasted only briefly.

Out of these controversies a new supervisory plan for student publications was developed under which student editors were elected by a student publications board and approved by the college committee on student publications, a committee appointed by the president. It was agreed by all that there would not be administrative censorship, but advisors would read all copy, and editors would be responsible for what was published. Wheaton editors who attended student publications conferences frequently returned telling of how surprised other student editors were at the freedom enjoyed by Wheaton writers and editors.[19]

A frequent center of criticism by the *Record* was the college food service, which had always been managed by Wheaton College. Though the critical charges were often exaggerated, the inadequate dining facilities aroused a fair complaint. But the opening of a new two-story, air-conditioned dining hall, with 300 additional seats, in the fall of 1964, helped to allay criticism. When James McKellin, '34, food service director for twenty years, accepted a similar position at the University of Illinois Medical Center in Chicago, Wheaton employed an outside caterer. From that time onward all food service has been contracted by the Board of Trustees with an outside agency. Since 1966 Saga Corporation has been the caterer.

Once during the sixties a furor arose when a bearded student was told by his physical education instructor that he would have to shave or forfeit his credit, since beards "do not represent what Wheaton is trying to do."[20] Students and faculty alike rallied to the young man's support. Demonstrations were held at the PE and ROTC departments; speeches were made in the dining hall; a poster read: "Lincoln Would Not Be Welcome Here." Following extended deliberation, the educational policies committee rescinded its earlier prohibition against beards—then a symbol of rebellion—in the graduation line. At this meeting one administrator member of the committee, who defended the prohibition with tenacity, seemed unaware that on the wall behind him in the committee room was a large portrait of Jonathan Blanchard with a handsome white beard.

The class of 1964 for the senior sneak boarded the NorthWestern in Wheaton to spend a beautiful May weekend at Silver Cliff Ranch in Colorado. As the westward bound train pulled into Mendota, Illinois, for a brief stop, startled seniors saw through their train windows a group of juniors exhibiting the senior bench. Quickly senior men swarmed off the train, overwhelmed the small contingent of daring juniors, and took the bench aboard. President Edman, traveling with the seniors as their guest, explained with good humor to the bewildered passengers what was happening. Possession of the 700-pound slab of concrete known as the "senior bench" had long been a focal point of upperclass rivalry. Bench protocol was simple: the possessors were required to show it three times a year (allowing the opposition an opportunity to seize it), and the senior class was required to pass it on to its sister sophomore class if it held the bench at the end of the year.

Fine Arts Festival

After several weeks of promotion with colorful campus signs, a Creative Arts Festival was held in March 1962 under the general chairmanship of Judi Chaffee and sponsored by *Kodon*. Student writing in poetry, short story, essay, and the one-act play were judged by a panel which included Pulitzer Prize-winning poet Gwendolyn Brooks and Sidney J. Harris, nationally syndicated columnist.[21] First prize awards went to Wesley Craven in the short story, Harry Strachan for an essay, Gerald Schneider for poetry, and Linda Franks for a one-act play. Winning entries were published in the spring *Kodon*, distributed to students during the festival. The three-day program included films, a coffee hour where the winning poets read their work, dinners, and panel discussions with the guest artists and faculty.

The second festival, in the spring of 1963, enlarged its appeal to the campus by adding competition in painting, photography, and music. First place music award for his "Fugue No. 2" went to John Nelson, '63, now conductor of the Indianapolis Symphony Orchestra. The Festivals stimulated student creative effort, provided opportunities for hopeful enthusiasts to meet professional artists, and encouraged the campus community at large to discover that the arts could be both entertaining and significant.

Atlantic Creative Writing Contests

For eighteen years, from 1958 to 1975, Wheaton regularly sent entries in poetry, short story, and the essay to the *Atlantic* Creative Writing Contest. Sponsored by the *Atlantic* magazine, the contest drew entries from many schools, principally from private liberal arts colleges. Many of the papers submitted by Wheaton students were personal essays—reflective, analytical, or narrative—prepared for writing course assignments. Some had been written for literature courses and refined in advanced creative writing classes. Most of the entries were prepared and submitted under the direction of Professor Helen deVette, with assistance from Professor Melvin Lorentzen.

The top five papers in each category were published by the *Atlantic* and distributed to participating schools. After the first place papers, the next fifteen were given "Honorable Mention," and the next twenty were named "Merit" papers. Wheaton had at least one work published in sixteen of the eighteen years it participated in the contest. On four occasions three works were published in a single year. In 1960 Wheaton had six of the Twenty award winners; in 1961 it had eight of twenty. In the short story division Jeanne Murray won first place in 1965 for "The Nameless Year," Mary Lynn MacDonald in 1969 for "Not As It Has Been," and Thomas Hagen in 1970 for "The Alms of Fortune." Besides her winning short story in 1965, Jeanne Murray also submitted a first-place poem, "Elegy on Michael's Final Going," the first time any contestant had won two first awards. For her achievement Jeanne, and her instructor Mrs. deVette, were given a summer school scholarship at the Breadloaf School of English in Middlebury, Vermont. Dean Ebner was the first first-place winner for his essay, "Longinus, Sublimity, and *Paradise Lost*" in 1958. In all, Wheaton submitted nearly 100 award entries. For many writing students, until the contests ended in 1975, the coming of spring meant eager waiting for the announcement of the *Atlantic* writing awards.

Wheaton became well known for its writing achievements through the wide distribution of the yearly *Atlantic* booklets. Each spring the *Atlantic* listed the names of all the winners in one issue of the magazine. Participation in these annual contests were both an incentive and a proving ground for Wheaton's talented young writers.

Perry Mastodon

Excitement spread rapidly on October 16, 1963, when a workman on a project to deepen an artificial lake on the property of Federal Judge Joseph Sam Perry in nearby Glen Ellyn, discovered a large mysterious bone. Perry's request for assistance in helping to identify the bone brought Professors Cyril Luckman of the biology department and Douglas Block of the geology department to the scene, where they made a tentative judgment that the

Professor David Bruce and students at the Wheaton College Science Station in the Black Hills of South Dakota.

Dedication of the Perry Mastadon location, Science Hall, January 1975. L. to r.: Richard Rush, designer; Dr. Douglas Block, President Armerding, Judge Sam Perry, Dr. Gerald Haddock.

bone was that of a mastodon. Further probing through the next five days by Block and a group of students headed by geology major Jon Stoen confirmed the earlier judgment.

Judge Perry gave permission to Dr. Donald Boardman, chairman of the geology department, to continue the excavation and supervise the reconstruction of the mastodon. Hundreds of people lined the banks of the lake, which had been drained, to watch the search for additional bones. The skull, two tusks, large leg bones, vertebrae, and ribs were encased in plaster of Paris, to prevent disintegration, and taken to Breyer laboratory to dry out. Chicago's Field Museum, which has the only other mastodon exhibit in Illinois, offered counsel and assistance. Carbon dating subsequently indicated that the mastodon had died about 11,000 years ago.

Richard Rush of Glen Ellyn, who had been trained at the Art Institute of Chicago, expressed interest in preparing an appropriate display of the mastodon. His Chicago studios had planned museum displays in many parts of the world. When the college science building was being designed in the late 1960s, Rush and architect Joseph Herstowski, of the J. Emil Anderson and Son company, planned a suitable display area as an integral part of the building. To acquire ideas for an authentic and artistic display, Dr. Boardman, supported by an Alumni grant, visited nearly every mastodon exhibit in North America and Europe.

To meet the cost of the project, ultimately $100,000, the college sponsors sought and received generous support from the community and foundations. A major contribution, secured through the efforts of David Roberts, director of public relations, was made by the Edwin F. Deicke Foundation of Wheaton. The mastodon display is housed in the Edwin F. Deicke Exhibit Hall, part of the science building. The mastodon is mounted on a turntable, set in soil among rocks and hedges from the Perry property, in a circular room thirty feet in diameter with floor-to-ceiling curved windows twenty feet high. As the turntable rotates, one side of the animal reveals a simulated hide, while the other is open to reveal the bone structure, which was reconstructed in fiberglass. The push of a button from inside or outside the building activates the turntable and a tape recording which narrates the story of the "Perry Mastodon." The restored skeleton is nine feet tall, sixteen feet long; the animal is estimated to have weighed about six tons.

The exhibit, one of the best of its kind in the world, was dedicated as part of the Founder's Day Program, "Science and Christian Responsibility," on January 18, 1975, more than ten years after the discovery. Present for the occasion were Judge Perry, Richard Rush, President Hudson T. Armerding, Mr. and Mrs. Edwin F. Deike, Dr. Douglas Block, and Dr. Gerald Haddock of the geology department. Hundreds of public and private school children and their teachers visit the mastodon exhibit each year.

One day, late in November 1975, the campus was astonished and amused to hear the mastodon speak for himself. An ingenious and somewhat daring student, later discovered to be Larry Shackley, had created his own tape in the studios of WETN, and substituted it for the official recording. The narrator explains that when the giant creature emerged from its ice cube it was shot by Judge Perry with anesthetizing bullets and taken to Wheaton College. There a life support system was attached, keeping the behemoth alive ever since. The mastodon, the tape continued, has been taught to talk, sing, perform elementary dance steps, and use a three-by-five litter box. Daily it consumes forty gallons of milk, 200 pounds of steak, and 7,000 chocolate chip cookies. It is attended by twenty trained workers. The tape concluded with lively music from "Baby Elephant Walk."

Administrative Changes

At its December 1962 meeting the Board of Trustees heard and approved the report of its long-range planning committee, under the chairmanship of Charles Weaver, calling for a reorganization of the administrative structure of the College. The recommendation asked for the creation of the office of provost, under which were to be consolidated the offices of dean of the College, registrar, admissions, and student personnel. Reporting directly to the president would be the provost, dean of the graduate school, director of public relations, and business manager. It was believed that this rearrangement of administrative responsibility would achieve a more efficient exercise of authority, particularly in academic affairs. For the new office of provost, Dr. Hudson T. Armerding, '41, was chosen, with instruction to begin his new duties on February 1, 1963. Since 1961 he had been serving as professor of history at Wheaton, and prior to that had been dean of Gordon College nine years and acting president of Gordon for a year and a half.

The provost was to "plan the long range academic program of the college," to serve as chairman of the academic council and the educational policies committee, "to nominate to the president suitable teaching and academic administration."[22] He was also to relieve the president of routine details so that Dr. Edman could give more time to public relations. Trustees at the same time made it clear that Dr. John H. Fadenrecht would continue as dean of the College and that Dr. Richard Gross, then acting dean of students, would become dean of students, a role he fulfilled with singular success at a time of transition and student unrest. Working closely with Dean Gross was Dean of Women Jean Kline, who brought fine sensitivity to her responsibilities. Dr. Arthur Volle, who had been serving as dean of students, became the College's vocational counselor, a position he held until his retirement in 1980.

The provost worked with faculty committees and department heads in reexamination of the general studies requirements at a time when science, philosophy, and social sciences were being strongly emphasized in higher education generally. Long-range planning obligated Dr. Armerding to evaluate the usefulness of teaching machines and closed circuit television. The latter was widely acclaimed as a promising way of using the gifted teacher more effectively and of reducing instructional costs by having large general courses taught by a single instructor before a televison camera. Though much study was given to this kind of educational program, Wheaton at this point did not enter into it to any significant degree, beyond the use of tapes, records, and classroom films.

Provost Armerding was hardly established in his office and familiar with his responsibilites when a new call to service was laid before him. At a meeting of the Executive Committee of the Board of Trustees on July 9, 1964, Dr. Edman requested that he "be relieved of his administrative responsibilities in order to serve more effectively in a larger field, his title to be Chancellor of Wheaton College."[23] The committee approved the recommendation and agreed to submit it to the full Board of Trustees when they met in September. Pending that meeting, the personnel committee of the Board was authorized to begin discussions of an appropriate candidate to succeed President Edman. Prior to the September meeting, Board Chairman Herman A. Fischer wrote to his colleagues commending President Edman's request. He cited the fact that during the Edman administration the student body had grown by one-half, the faculty had been greatly enlarged, and the college plant had "increased several times over both in magnitude and in adaptation to college needs."[24] There were now new pressing needs—completion of a new dining hall, a men's dormitory, a science building, and an addition to the library, Fischer pointed out. "We believe," he concluded, "that Dr. Edman's enlarged mission will contribute materially to the solution of many such problems."

The personnel committee of the Board of Trustees submitted its recommendation to the Executive Committee on August 6, 1964, that President Edman's request to be named chancellor be approved. It also unanimously recommended the naming of Dr. Hudson T. Armerding as president of the College, along with a careful delineation of his duties and responsibilities. Other candidates besides Dr. Armerding were considered; but there was no search committee, and no public request for nominations was issued. At its September meeting the full Board of Trustees approved the Executive Committee recommendations and set January 8, 1965, Founder's Day, the 105th anniversary of the College, for the joint inaugural ceremony for Dr. Edman and Dr. Armerding, at which time Dr. Edman would be completing twenty-five years as president of the College. Dr. Edman was enthusiastic about his new assignment and wrote his sons to that effect.

The joint inauguration ceremonies brought to Wheaton as guests delegates from 120 colleges and representatives from fourteen learned societies. Nearly 4,000 invitations had been sent out, the entire student body of 1,800 included among them. The mid-morning service began with the invocation by Dr. James Oliver Buswell, Jr., Wheaton's third president. Greetings from the North Central Association were brought by its president, Dr. Clyde Vroman. Representing the Board of Trustees was Norris R. Aldeen, Rockford businessman. Following an anthem based on Psalm 100, sung by the

Concert Choir, Chaplain Welsh read the Psalm, which had been the scripture for the centennial year. Dean John H. Fadenrecht spoke for the faculty, Ted Ryan, student council president, pledged the support of the student body. The ceremony of investiture for both men was conducted by Herman A. Fischer, chairman of the Board of Trustees. Dr. Carl Armerding, father of the new president and professor of Bible emeritus, offered the prayer of commitment, while Dr. Edman presented the charge to his younger associate and former student.

In concluding his inaugural address, titled "Entrusted with a Vision," Wheaton's new president declared: "I record again my dedication to Jesus Christ as Saviour, Lord, and Master of my life, and I accept the commission to serve 'For Christ and His Kingdom.' " Dr. E. Joseph Evans pronounced the benediction.

Into His Presence

In his new role as chancellor Dr. Edman was assigned an office on the second floor of McAlister Conservatory with Mrs. Rowena Carr as secretary. Without delay he began to schedule trips in various parts of the country to represent the College. At the annual faculty, staff, trustee dinner in January 1966 he was awarded a thirty-five year service pin by Dr. Armerding, who commended him for his long and distinguished service to the work of the Lord at Wheaton College as teacher and administrator.

In May Dr. Edman set out as tour leader of a group visiting the Holy Land under the sponsorship of the Billy Graham Evangelistic Association. A member of the Board of Directors of the Graham Association, he had served as chairman of the team committee for many years. In Beirut, though he was overweary from his travels, he visited an alumni group. During the night when he suffered chest and arm pains, he was conscious of the onset of a heart attack. In the morning he consulted LaVand Syverson, '54, then associate director of the American University Hospital, who urged him to enter the hospital at once. After four days there and several days as the guest of the Syversons, he began his flight home in easy stages by plane.[25]

In November and December Dr. Edman suffered a second and third heart attack, the latter confining him at Delnor Hospital, in St. Charles, from December 23 to mid-January. For everyone who came to see him he had a cheery greeting, a favorite verse of Scripture, often a word of prayer. In January 1967 he was granted a six-months spring and summer leave of absence for convalescence. He was pleased, and the campus community was inspired, when he was able to appear on the platform for the 1967 commencement. A month earlier he had reached his sixty-seventh birthday.

On September 22, 1967, he was scheduled to speak in chapel—his first public address in ten months—having gotten permission from his physician, Dr. Clarence Wyngarden. On that morning, wearing his class of '68 jacket, he joined the early morning prayer group before going to his second floor office, to which he was regularly carried by seniors Stanley Shank and Paul Rowell. His chapel message, "In the Presence of the King," began with his recollection of a visit with Emperor Haile Selassie of Ethiopia in 1947 and an account of how carefully he prepared, according to protocol, for the occasion. He then noted for his hearers how much more important it was to be ready to enter into the presence of the King of kings. Moments later, while speaking, he collapsed and died. His last words were: "Over these years I have learned the immense value of that deep, inner silence as David, the king, sat in God's presence to hear from Him."

Certain that his days were numbered, he had left detailed instructions with Dr. Armerding for his funeral. There would be no "viewing," and he had requested a private burial service with only the family in attendance. He asked to have the closed casket placed in the vestibule of Edman Chapel two hours before the service. Favorite hymns and Scripture passages were noted, and he requested that tributes should be brief and should honor the Lord rather than himself. At the service on Sunday afternoon, September 24, a flag-draped casket, after resting in the foyer for two hours, was brought to the front of the chapel as the memorial began. Dr. E. Joseph Evans, of Boston, Dr. Edman's long-time friend and counselor, offered the invocation. Dr. Merrill C. Tenney, dean of the Graduate School, read Psalm 24. Billy Graham used Ecclesiastes 3:1-8 as the basis for his reflections on the life and work of his friend and spiritual mentor. "He was born in God's time," said the evangelist, "and he influenced two generations of young people. . . . He touched more lives personally than any man I ever knew."[26] The "Hallelujah Chorus" was sung by a 250-voice choir of students. Brief tributes were offered by Coach Harvey Chrouser, speaking for Honey Rock Camp, Colonel Meadows for the ROTC, Dan Reigle for the student body, Dr. Paul Wright for the faculty, and President Armerding for the administration. Dr. Edman's life text, Nahum 1:7, in his own handwriting, was reproduced on the back of the memorial service program.

Dr. Edman's death had been widely announced by press and radio, and a large crowd assembled to honor his memory on that Sunday afternoon. Edman Chapel was filled and many others heard the service in Pierce Chapel. Dr. Armerding and Chaplain Evan Welsh conducted the private graveside service on Monday morning at the Wheaton Cemetery. Two favorite hymns, "Trust and Obey" and "Beneath the Cross of Jesus," were sung, three volleys were fired by the Conquer Rifles of the Wheaton College ROTC, and a muted "Taps" drifted across the quiet cemetery.

When Dr. Edman completed his service as president in 1965, Wheaton College had experienced twenty-five years of remarkable growth. The college faculty numbered 125 full-time and 20 part-time or visiting teachers. There were 1,700 students enrolled and 100 in the Graduate School, compared with 1,100 students on campus in 1940. The total assets of the College were in excess of $30 million compared with $6 million in 1940; the endowment had grown to $7,500,000 from $660,000 in the president's inaugural year; the operating budget was $4,500,000 compared with $730,000 in 1940.

At the memorial service, Billy Graham had said that Dr. Edman was "a mystic in the finest sense of the term. Part of his life was always in heaven and part on earth." President Edman in all earnestness had sought to be a responsible citizen of both realms. During the late years of his administration, he recognized the warning signals heralding a revolution against authority and tradition, against the kind of world that had been dear to him, and he cried alarm. At times his benign temperament was unsuitable for the burdens of administration. Realization of the complexity of the times, of his advancing years, and of the multiplying difficulties of administration led him to ask for release from the presidency and the new assignment as chancellor.

He was a romantic idealist who always expected high quality performance from his associates; in the nature of things some of them occasionally disappointed him. Faced with others' failures, he remained unfailingly kind, reluctant to force a confrontation, hopeful that, through the efforts of other administrators and in the providence of time, things would work out. Though there were occasions when strong academic leadership was lacking, he gave vigorous support to programs developed through faculty planning when he believed them to be wise. He worked in an era when administrative authority was less generally exercised through a shared judgment of the president and faculty committees.

He was always a congenial friend of students, who were astonished by his gift for remembering names. He had a humorous story, a pungent epithet, a skillfully turned pun, for every occasion. His thoughtfulness of others, part of his nature, had its roots in the spirit of the Scriptures. Intellectual posturing or false pride in his accomplishments had no part in his makeup. He made careful use of time, rising at five A.M., sometimes as early as four A.M., to begin the day with Bible reading and prayer with "friend wife." By six A.M. he was ready to join a group of faculty, staff, and students for morning prayer. Of the College's and his own resources he was always a frugal steward. Whatever his limitations may have been, he embodied a cluster of virtues that endeared him to thousands of students and friends of the College around the world.

A bronze bust of Dr. Edman, a gift of the class of 1968, was unveiled on baccalaureate Sunday, June 9, 1968. The work of Helen and Holger Jensen, '21, of Santa Monica, California, the bust is located in the foyer of Edman Memorial Chapel.

Dr. Clarence B. Wyngarden, College physician 1939–1976, and nurse Jerayne Barnes, 1964.

PRESIDENT HUDSON T. ARMERDING, 1965-1982

CHAPTER 15

Hudson T. Armerding, A Man for His Times

W HEN HUDSON TAYLOR ARMERDING BECAME PRESIDENT
of Wheaton College in January 1965, he knew he would need for his task all
the resources that his heritage, training, experience, and personal dedication
to Christian higher education had established within him. He was born on
June 21, 1918, in Albuquerque, New Mexico, where his father, Carl, was engaged in an itinerant Bible-teaching ministry among the Plymouth Brethren.
A severe case of malaria had forced Carl to give up mission service in Honduras and return to the United States. While on a preaching journey to
Manitoba, Canada, he met his future wife, Eva May, daughter of a Scottish
mother and English father, whom he married in 1917.

Five children were born, one dying in infancy. Hudson was the oldest, followed by Evangeline Louise, Helen Winifred, and Geraldine May. Though
the elder Armerding had not completed high school, he enrolled, with the
encouragement of his wife, at the University of New Mexico, where he completed his degree with honors and was elected to Phi Kappa Phi. Young
Hudson early developed a love for scouting and camping through his father's absorption in those activities. He also had an early appreciation of
American Indians, many of whom he met through his father's summer conference ministry. At the age of eight Hudson contracted pneumonia, which
led to complications requiring an operation to preserve his life.

"My conversion," he writes, "resulted from the reading of a Sunday School paper. In this paper was the story of a young man who went to a gospel meeting and filled out a decision card. The paper had a facsimile of the card. I cut it out, completed it, and pinned it to the curtain by my bed. Then I told Mother that if Satan came that night, he would realize that I was a Christian."

In the fall of 1935 the Armerding family sailed for New Zealand, where Carl had established an itinerant ministry among the Brethren Assemblies and where a well-to-do contractor had promised to provide passage money and a home in Wellington. During his first year in New Zealand, Hudson was employed on a sheep and cattle ranch; the work was hard and the pay meager. In that year of decision he determined that "it was in the will of the Lord for me to come back to the United States to attend college here."[1] From his earnings with a British automobile firm, he was able to provide his own passage money. His father sold a small piece of property in Albuquerque to help meet his son's expenses during his first semester at Wheaton College in the fall of 1937. An aunt and uncle in Oak Park, Illinois, provided a home for him during his first year, obligating him to commute to Wheaton.

As a freshman he successfully auditioned for the Men's Glee Club, in which he continued for four years. He was greatly attracted by the teaching of Dr. Edman and resolved to major in history, though earlier he had thought he would concentrate in Bible. In his junior year he roomed in a co-operative house on Lincoln street known as "The Friars," where he was able to earn half the $45 a semester rent by cleaning the house. During his junior year he became a student assistant to Dr. Edman, grading examinations and keeping records, a relationship maintained even after Dr. Edman became president (since the new president continued to teach one class).

Through all of his years at Wheaton, Hudson was a member of the Aristonian Literary Society and served as its president during his senior year. From the training he received in his Friday night "lit"—public speaking, debate, extempore speaking, parliamentary procedure—came much of the speaking skill he evidenced as an administrator. In his senior year he was elected class treasurer and business manager of the Men's Glee Club. Elected to Pi Gamma Mu, social science honorary society, he graduated with honors with the class of 1941. On Dr. Edman's recommendation, and with the promise of a generous scholarship and stipend, he entered Clark University, Worcester, Massachusetts. Thinking seriously of entering the diplomatic corps, he was especially interested in that university's new program in international studies. He was able to begin his graduate work because his draft board in Oak Park had classified him 4-D, ministerial student, since he was traveling and speaking at religious meetings with the Wheaton Quintet. When the attack on Pearl Harbor occurred he endeavored to volunteer for the Navy when a recruiting team came to his campus. Told that he was underweight and lacked two courses in mathematics to qualify him for the Navy program, he set out to meet both deficiencies. On the day before he received his M.A. degree in 1942, he was sworn into the Navy. On the same occasion a young man he had known at Herbert Hoover High School, Ted Williams, baseball star with the Boston Red Sox, was also sworn in.

After training at Notre Dame University and Columbia University, he was commissioned on December 2, 1942, and ordered to report to the *U.S.S. Wichita*, a heavy cruiser, in Norfolk, Virginia, then being readied to join the Pacific Fleet. In all, his ship was involved in eleven naval engagements. In his free time he conducted a Bible class for some of the sailors.

On his first leave from the *Wichita* in September 1943, Hudson visited his parents, who had moved from New Zealand to Canada and then to Wheaton in 1943. While at home, he met Miriam Bailey, '42, who had returned to campus to teach at the Conservatory. On his second leave in December 1944, before his return to sea for the final year of the war, Hudson and Miriam were married at the Armerding home. During the time of separation the young couple felt called to missionary service with students in China. With that in mind, at the end of the war Hudson enrolled in a doctoral program with a concentration in Asian history and institutions at the University of Chicago. He was awarded his Ph.D. degree in 1948.

Shortly after his return to Wheaton, he had accepted a part-time position in the social science division of the College, teaching on Monday, Wednesday, and Friday and attending the University on Tuesday, Thursday, and Saturday. Since unsettled conditions in China now blocked their desire to serve as missionaries there, the Armerdings accepted a call in 1948 to Gordon College, where Hudson was to head the history department for a year. In 1952 he was asked to become acting dean of Gordon College, and subsequently dean, a position he held until 1959. From 1951 to 1954 Dean Armerding served as pastor of Trinity Baptist Church of Brockton, the town in which the family was then living. Here he was ordained to the Christian ministry.

In the spring of 1959, Dr. T. Leonard Lewis, president of Gordon College, died from a heart attack. Dr. Armerding served as acting president of Gordon from the spring of 1959 until September 1960, when the new president, Dr. James Forrester, was installed. When Dr. Edman came for the inauguration of the new president of Gordon, he invited his one-time student assistant to return to Wheaton College to teach in the history department.

During his first year of teaching, Dr. Armerding was given several special academic projects by President Edman. In the fall of 1962, Charles Weaver, representing the Board of Trustees, invited Dr. Armerding to accept the newly created office of provost of the College. His initial disposition was to decline, having known something of the problems and stresses of administrative work. But Trustee Weaver was firm, telling Dr. Armerding that he should do his duty rather than be guided by personal desires.[2] He began his work as provost with the second semester of the 1962-63 year.

In the summer of 1964, a member of the Board of Trustees asked Dr. Armerding if he was fully in accord with Wheaton's statement of faith and standards of conduct. With some surprise he answered he was; otherwise he would not be teaching at Wheaton.[3] Later he discovered that the Executive Committee of the Board of Trustees had nominated him to succeed Dr. Edman as president.

Trustees of the College at the time of President Armerding's inauguration in January 1965 were Robert E. Nicholas, financial consultant, Oak Park, Illinois; E. Joseph Evans, Bible teacher, Boston; Thorstein Burtness, railroad executive, Wheaton; P. Kenneth Gieser, physician, Wheaton; Taylor Ferguson, financial consultant, Chicago; Foster Oury, contractor, Chicago; David Otis Fuller, pastor, Grand Rapids; Billy Graham, evangelist, Montreat, N.C.; V. Raymond Edman, chancellor; Robert Van Kampen, publisher, Wheaton; Allan Emery, merchant, Boston; George Bennett, investment counselor, Boston; Stanley Olson, educator, Houston; Norris Aldeen, manufacturer, Rockford; William McCarrell, pastor, Cicero, Illinois; Charles Blanchard Weaver, banker, Chicago; Herman A. Fischer, attorney, Wheaton; George Traber, manufacturer, Perry, N.Y.; Maurice C. Smith, manufacturer, Bristol, R.I.

This group of men had committed themselves to oversee the life and resources of an institution which then had a student body of 1,799 undergraduates and 104 graduate students, a faculty of 135 in the undergraduate division, and a plant valued at $10,500,000. Student expenses, fixed by the trustees, were in President Armerding's first year, $2,100 for two semesters, covering tuition, room, board, and books. Of the actual cost of maintaining the student at Wheaton the individual then paid 80 percent.

In his inaugural address President Armerding said: "To the educational world we pledge our continued commitment to rigorous scholarship and academic excellence. We welcome the opportunity to measure up to the exacting standards which membership in the academic community demands." To the evangelical world he pledged "continuing fidelity to the historic truths of our Christian faith and the practice of that faith in our particular area of service." He noted that the student's education was inextricably related to international crises and domestic social ferment and that the institution itself would not be free from those tensions. Speaking to the members of the campus community he said: "I pledge my continuing efforts to make this a vibrant, creative association where mutual concern and helpfulness and commitment to common educational and spiritual ideals will enable us all better to glorify the God whom we seek to serve."

President Armerding Begins His Service

Though he came to his office in a time of national unrest, President Armerding's words expressed optimism about the future of Wheaton College and of Christian higher education. Organizational and academic changes were instituted gradually. To assist him in administrative matters, the new president chose two veteran faculty members: Dr. Peter Veltman to serve as dean of the College and Dr. Robert Baptista as dean of the faculty. Dr. Velt-man, who had joined the faculty in 1948 and was at the time of his appointment chairman of the education department, was to have responsible to him the registrar, dean of the Graduate School, admissions officer, dean of students, and dean of the faculty. He was, in effect, assuming the obligations formerly carried by Dr. Armerding as provost. Dr. Baptista, a member of the physical education department and soccer coach, who had returned to his alma mater in 1951, was responsible to Dr. Veltman and was charged with the administration of faculty affairs and educational policies. Their appointments began July 1, 1966.[4] Dr. Veltman replaced Dean John Fadenrecht, who had expressed the desire to return to the classroom.

A major concern for President Armerding, at the outset of his administration, was to assure Christian friends, parents, and alumni that Wheaton College was what it had historically been—and by public statement professed still to be—an evangelical Christian institution. Some people, in a continuing backlash from the 1961 science symposium, still raised questions about Wheaton's anchorage in historic Christian orthodoxy. Pastors sometimes complained that students returned to the local church acknowledging uncertainty about their faith. Some students were unsettled by the mood of the times: rising anger over Viet Nam, discord at a number of the great universities, racial tensions, impatience with many evidences of perceived injustice. A few of these had come to Wheaton only in compliance with their parents' wishes. To eliminate that kind of coercion, President Armerding advised admissions officers to admit only students who declared themselves to be Christians and who wanted to enroll at Wheaton.

The decision to admit only applicants who were professing Christians had a significant consequence. The twice annual week of special services during chapel and early evening, scheduled at the beginning of each semester and often known during the Edman era as evangelistic services, underwent a change of emphasis. The services were no longer centered on leading students to confess Christ as Savior, though it was always possible that some students, believing they were Christians when they entered Wheaton, would later discover they were not and were in need of a conversion experience.

During the Armerding administration these chapel weeks were times of teaching, inspiration, self-examination, and dedication of life and talents to Christ's service. They were known as "Spiritual Emphasis Week" or the "Week of Special Services." Whatever the name, these days of worship were for bringing life's centralities into focus, of re-examining priorities so that Christ might have the preeminence in young lives.

Of concern to President Armerding was the fact that a few faculty members, in their commitment to academic excellence and intellectual integrity, felt it imperative to raise difficult theological questions in class—questions sometimes incapable of altogether satisfactory resolution. That teaching technique demanded strenuous mental exercise by teacher and student. The president thought that this method was not always used effectively, sometimes leaving students unsure about old certitudes.[5] Often what was perceived as "narrow fundamentalism" was subjected to searching judgment, but out of the analysis the reconstruction was sometimes incomplete, the president felt. Aware of those tendencies in some classrooms, one Board member questioned whether all faculty members at that time really did affirm the doctrinal statement without reservation. President Armerding did not doubt the institutional loyalty of his faculty, but to satisfy the inquirer he and Dr. Fadenrecht interviewed faculty members one after another, all of whom declared that the statement of faith expressed their own convictions clearly. Nevertheless, the president resolved to institute, through appropriate procedures, a more perceptive and comprehensive review of faculty candidates before their appointment and a more thorough review for promotion and tenure.[6] Dr. Armerding had no intention of redirecting the College into a different mold "but only to reaffirm that we were what we claimed to be."

Meeting the Challenge of Change

Early in the Armerding administration the Board of Trustees appointed a long-range planning committee to chart Wheaton's course for five to ten years into the future. The committee's initial task was to establish the mission of the College and then to describe the essential needs in fulfilling that mission. The work included clarifying academic goals, suggesting curriculum development and faculty size, identifying building requirements, estimating budget obligations, proposing a new calendar, and other necessary details.

Members of the committee were President Armerding, Chancellor Edman, Trustees Taylor Ferguson, Robert Van Kampen, and P. Kenneth Gieser; administration representatives Peter Veltman, Harold Faulkner, David Roberts, and William Pollard; faculty members Earle Cairns, John Fadenrecht, and Arthur Holmes; alumnus Joseph Weeks; and students Ric Craig, student council president, and David Livingstone, representing the junior class. The inclusion of students on a strategic committee was in response to requests made not only at Wheaton but on college campuses generally for student participation in the formulation of policy. Students were soon to be included on other faculty committees, where they made valuable contributions, and were granted the right to have representatives at faculty senate meetings as observers.

For many years much of the academic life at the College and student activities of the campus were subject to policies established by the faculty, meeting at four P.M. every Tuesday afternoon. Preceded by a half-hour for tea and informal conversation, the meetings were regarded by most instructors as a stimulating time. For a handful of old-timers the Tuesday assembly was nearly a sacred gathering with which nothing, however consequential, should interfere.

The work of the faculty was carried on through major committees: educational policies and curriculum, faculty personnel, student affairs, spiritual life and standards, and numerous subcommittees. All of these committees were important, but the spiritual life and standards committee was crucial to preserving the vital spiritual tone of the campus. Recommendations and committee reports were presented to the faculty of 135 as a whole, who debated them lengthily and with intensity before calling for a vote to accept or reject. In theory the procedure was in the best tradition of academic freedom, but it had disadvantages, often generating excessive and time-consuming debate. Then too, young instructors freshly arrived on campus, with a limited knowledge of Wheaton, had the same voting authority as senior professors, long familiar with the history and values of the College.

To establish what at the time seemed to be a more efficient deliberative body to deal with increasingly tense issues, the Board of Trustees gave approval in June 1966 to the recommendation of President Armerding, the academic council, and the faculty for the establishment of the Wheaton College Faculty Senate.[7] Members of the senate were the president of the College, six administrative officers, six divisional chairmen, and eighteen faculty members elected by the faculty for three-year terms. President Armerding served as chairman of the senate and Professor Arthur Holmes was elected vice-chairman, with Professor Earle Cairns serving as secretary. Monthly reports of the senate's work were given to the full faculty.

For one thing, the senate would observe and evaluate the operation of the four-course system, instituted in the fall of 1965, whereby a student was limited in a term to four four-hour courses. The intention of this curriculum reform was to reduce the number of courses a student could take during the year, thus encouraging greater concentration of effort and more comprehensive control of subject matter. The change was also intended to curb the proliferation of courses, particularly two-hour courses, once numerous enough to allow students to elect as many as six or seven in a semester, resulting in great fragmentation of effort.

The four-course plan continued until 1970, when, after extensive faculty study and planning under Dean Veltman's direction, the quarter system was introduced. At the time the faculty and administration believed it to be a more flexible academic program, which would also make better use of the college facilities. The plan provided for three eleven-week quarters and one ten-week summer quarter. All students were required to take one summer quarter for which they were released from one regular quarter for study, work, travel, or other experiences of academic value related to their major field of interest. Required of all students was one integrative course which would draw together the substance of the chosen discipline. Wednesday, when most classes were not scheduled to meet, was set aside as a campus day—without the chapel requirement—for committee meetings, lectures, campus events, and individual study. Students called the day "Glorious Wednesday." Hoping that all the promises made for the new program would be fulfilled, the campus community entered into the quarter system with enthusiasm.

Commencement processional, 1966. President Armerding stands at rear with Dr. John Brobeck, commencement speaker.

Westgate. Home of Presidents Buswell, Edman, and Armerding. Now the Alumni Association office.

Minority Education

Another faculty concern in the mid- and late-sixties was that Wheaton was often faulted by student groups, some faculty, and external observers for not having a larger number of black and other American minority students on campus. Further criticism arose over Wheaton's failure to appoint more than one black faculty member in those crucial days, though the administration made a genuine effort to find others. It was a time of intense search by colleges and universities throughout the country for black instructors when there were not enough to go around—and when black college presidents pleaded with educational administrators not to draw away their faculties.

Because there were few minority students on campus, some people charged Wheaton with being discriminatory, a judgment the College persistently denied. Wheaton always declared that, in the tradition of Jonathon Blanchard, its doors were open to all students who could meet the entrance requirements and the financial obligations—and that all students were equally entitled to financial assistance.

To make clear that the College was not discriminatory, or racist, as some alleged, President Armerding addressed the student body on the subject in chapel. He affirmed his conviction that "the Bible teaches the value and integrity of the human personality" and that God has created all people in his own image—of whatever race or culture. "We are firmly persuaded that equality of opportunity should be given to all" and that "where segregation in education is based simply on race this definitely should be eliminated." Further, he said, "we have no discrimination in the admission process as far as race is concerned. Instead, we admit students on the basis of their qualifications."[8] The Wheaton application form did not ask for information about race and did not ask for a photograph until after a student had been accepted for admission and had agreed to matriculate.

When a group of students requested the right to organize a campus chapter of the NAACP, permission was granted in the spring of 1965 by the Board of Trustees, after the Board had been assured by their own inquiries that the national organization had no subversive ties. The local chapter agreed to accept supervision by the student affairs committee rather than the national NAACP. Howard Hess and Mickey Palmer, students who had pushed for the establishment of the local group, spearheaded the drive for members among students, drawing about thirty members into the chapter. The organization, however, with Dr. Lamberta Voget serving as faculty advisor, never generated large interest and eventually disbanded.[9]

To show their concern for minority students—a sensitivity evidenced by many Wheaton students—seniors Randy Baker and Bob Vischer went to Selma, Alabama, in March 1965 to join Martin Luther King, Jr., and 2,500 others in a planned march from Selma to the state capital at Montgomery to urge the governor to support the rights of blacks granted to them under the constitution. Some marchers were roughed up, including the Wheaton students; others fled when they were turned back by the state police.[10]

Concerned that Wheaton was not doing what it should, nor as much as many other colleges were doing about minority education, Dean Phillip Hook and Dean Veltman received approval in 1968 for a pilot program to recruit a small number of disadvantaged blacks and Puerto Ricans, students with a Christian commitment and potential for college work, from inner city New York and Chicago. The hope was that through tutoring and counseling these newcomers could succeed at the college level, as well as modify some of their hostility toward the white community. But the culture shock was too severe and these special students reacted negatively, their prejudices seeming to harden. Professor Ozzie Edwards, a black sociologist and 1958 graduate of the College, was hired to help bridge the gap for these students. After one year Edwards left Wheaton to join the faculty at the University of Michigan, and subsequently the faculty of Harvard University. Although the program failed at first, in part for want of adequate time for proper planning, it was an initial and valiant effort to do something where nothing was being done before.

In 1969 Dean Hook resigned, citing "administrative fatigue" as his reason. He was succeeded by Dr. Henry Nelson, who brought to Wheaton a fine background of experience as dean of students at Taylor University and Trinity College. Under his direction, and with additional staff members trained for the compensatory education program, the effort to help minority students began to show steady improvement. Dr. Armerding made it clear that he wished the program to recognize the needs of all American minority groups. He was pleased to note for the trustees in 1969 the presence of two Asian faculty members, Professor Narl Hung in chemistry and Professor David Tamashiro in philosophy. In the same year Major James Sanger, the first of several black officers in the Wheaton ROTC program, was appointed by the Army to serve at Wheaton.[11]

At a human rights seminar in April 1981, held at the Graham Center, moderator Richard Linyard, a trustee, expressed the hope that funds would be provided to "promote a racially and culturally diverse campus community." He was aware of earlier efforts to achieve that goal. In 1978 Nadine Smith, '74, herself a minority student in her undergraduate days, was named assistant to the dean of students for minority affairs. Her post was created to make available to minority students a full-time advisor, who would also counsel and encourage potential minority applicants for admission. Adjustment had been difficult, Miss Smith understood, for most minority students in shifting from an urban environment to Wheaton's suburban academia.

Joyce E. Suber succeeded Nadine Smith in 1980 as director of minority student development. Later she was named director of multi-cultural student development. To Dean Henry Nelson she presented a carefully organized report on the status of minority students on the Wheaton campus, together with recommendations for improvement of their position. At the time there were in the undergraduate program 73 minority students: 15 black Americans, 36 Asian Americans, 5 American Indians, 17 Latino Americans. These students represented less than 4 percent of the total enrollment.

Not all multi-cultural students respond to the special services provided for them, but most of those who need it are grateful for assistance in learning to make essential academic and cultural adjustments. The most active multi-cultural group in 1980, predominantly black, was S.O.U.L.—Student Organization for Urban Leadership. To give the organization a broader vision of service the name was changed in 1983 to B.R.I.D.G.E.—Building Relationships in Discipleship, Grace and Experience. In 1984 multi-cultural students were 4 percent of the student body, the largest number of these being Asian Americans. The College hopes to raise the number of multi-cultural students on campus to 12 percent by the late eighties.

President's Annual Report

In his Annual Report to the Board of Trustees October 1966, covering his first full year as president, President Armerding told of his efforts to improve communications among the administration, faculty, and student body. Continuing and enlarging on the practice he had begun as provost, the president met with student leaders twice a month, had lunch in the North Party Room with any who wished to come for informal dialogue, went occasionally to the dormitories in the evening for chats and prayer, used student assemblies for heart-to-heart talks about the state of the campus, and met with faculty by departments for lunch in the Colonial Room of the Student Center.

The report noted that the freshman class admitted in 1965 was highly selective academically: 10 percent had been valedictorians, 65 percent were in the highest tenth of their class, and only 3 percent were below the upper third. During 1965-66 an additional effort had been made to refine the admission procedure through personal interviews with all applicants. Thirty-five interview committees were set up in various parts of the country, many of them composed of alumni, in an effort to discover whether prospective students had a commitment and lifestyle compatible with Wheaton's values.

The greatest enrollment gains during the year, the report further revealed, had been noted in the divisions of education, Bible, fine arts, and science. In the course of a five-year period, 1960-65, gains were registered in literature, history, philosophy, German, sociology, psychology, music, and physical education. Business and economics suffered a sharp decline, the result, evidently, of economic conditions and widespread distrust within the American academic community of the business establishment. At the 1966 commencement the largest number of degrees were awarded to students in literature, followed by biology, education, history, psychology, mathematics, and sociology.

Thirty-one students participated in the 1966 Summer Missionary Project.

Largely financed by students, faculty, and staff, the SMPers have done volunteer service in Asia, Africa, Europe, and South America—nineteen countries in all, in cooperation with twenty-one mission boards. The purpose of these annual summer ventures in short-term missionary service, initiated in 1958, is to render assistance on mission fields where it is needed, in the love of Christ, and to give students the experience of missionary work firsthand. Wheaton set the pattern for all other schools in this innovative student-based and directed activity. Through it students have found their life calling. During the year over a thousand students, representing some thirty campus organizations, participated in Christian service activities in the Chicago area under the supervision of Christian Service Council director William Lindberg, '62.

In 1966 the College moved from the practice of charging tuition in terms of hours scheduled by a student to a uniform comprehensive fee for everyone carrying between twelve and eighteen hours. The system, then coming to be widely used, allowed able students to choose an additional elective without added cost. The first comprehensive fee was fixed at $660; board was $230 and rooms ranged from $125 to $180 a semester. For the year the total cost—including fees, books, and incidentals—was approximately $2,400. For faculty and staff families with children of college age there was the welcome news of a full rebate of tuition fees, or, for the first time, faculty and staff children might choose to have their Wheaton tuition applied to the tuition costs at any one of eleven other Christian colleges of similar evangelical persuasion.

Many students and their families could not have met this financial obligation had it not been for the student aid program, which in 1966 amounted to $490,000. Funds came from the following sources: national defense loans, $205,665; college loans $31,879; scholarships $20,000; financial assistance $224,549; and special funds $7,907. National defense loans and college loans were returnable; all other grants were not. A percentage of all tuition fees is contributed annually to the fund known as "financial aid" to create that resource.

In his report the president further observed that students were taking advantage of the personal and vocational counseling services offered by Dr. Volle. During the 1965-66 year 900 students visited his office, half of them with vocational concerns. Other students came for counseling about emotional problems, forty of whom were referred to off-campus therapists for diagnostic evaluation and continuing treatment. They were temporary casualities of the tumultuous times. Dr. Armerding assured the Board that "emotional disturbance continues to be a significant though not serious problem in our college population."[12]

During the year, inquiries about Wheaton had declined from over 8,000 to 6,655, though the number of students who completed the application procedures for admission was still far in excess of the number who could be admitted. Nevertheless, the number of completed applications declined by

12 percent, representing a national trend. Many young people, men in particular, were asking themselves whether a college education was worth the effort and expense, especially if it were to end with a summons to Viet Nam. The decline in inquiries, President Armerding thought, was further attributable to the fact that there were fewer eighteen-year-olds, that state institutions had greatly enlarged their accommodations, and that there was uncertainty among some families about reported unsettled conditions on the Wheaton campus.

President's Retreat

To encourage a frank exchange of views at a time when communication was crucial, Dr. Armerding, together with Dean Baptista, initiated the President's Retreat. The first one was held in May 1967 at the Fellowship Deaconry, Elburn, Illinois, with thirty-eight guests in attendance, representing the trustees, administration, faculty, alumni, and student body. From the opening dinner session on Friday night to the concluding summary on Saturday afternoon, varied opinions about daily life, achievements, disappointments, values, and goals of Wheaton were fully expressed. No restraint was imposed; honest dialogue was encouraged.

Dr. Arthur Holmes, professor of philosophy, in the keynote address, spoke of his dream for Wheaton College as a "liberal arts college . . . dedicated to unceasing intellectual inquiry by faculty and students, to the pursuit of truth and beauty and goodness wherever these may be found, to the appreciation of our own cultural heritage and that of others, to the development of the whole person to the glory of God. . . . The dream is not of a loose conjecture of faith and learning, but of a creative integration, one in which faith guides and inspires understanding and gives meaning to human knowledge and experience, one which is devoted to the lucid articulation of Christian perspectives and their interrelation in a coherent world and life view."

Evangelicalism had a rich heritage both of Reformed theology's emphasis on the sovereignty of God over all life and thought, Dr. Holmes continued, and of the Pietist's emphasis on the personal spiritual life. American fundamentalism has tended, however, "to focus on pietism at the expense of the Reformer's cultural mandate."[13] In consequence many evangelicals did not fully understand and appreciate the role of Christian liberal education. Professor Holmes warned his hearers of "narrowing the definition of evangelicalism by taking dogmatic positions on doctrinal matters which other evangelicals, past and present, safely leave open, or by . . . isolating themselves from the mainline of religious life and thought."[14]

At the 1969 retreat attention was given to the crisis of faith being vividly expressed by some theologians and educators. Artists and writers were thrusting rapier-like judgments against ancient certitudes and strongholds of belief. Amid these whirlwinds of doubt some Wheaton students were spiritually shaken, or found their faith wavering. Some had become social activists, but were indifferent to their Christian heritage. It was suggested that those may have come to Wheaton uncommitted or "with a borrowed faith." Chaplain Welsh commented: "They were good honest kids—victims of the temper of the time. We lost some literally and some temporarily." The need for faculty love and understanding was imperative. An effective integration of faith and learning needed to be demonstrated. A compassionate presentation of the gospel in all its fullness was called for. But the majority of students, it was agreed, remained firmly committed to Christ.[15]

For the 1970 retreat thirty-nine invited guests met at Cedar Lake, Indiana. In the President's Perspective, Dr. Armerding observed that a Christian college is a community of volunteers, not draftees; that Wheaton is not primarily a vehicle for rehabilitation or evangelism. He re-emphasized what was to be a familiar imperative of his administration, that academic disciplines must be integrated with the text and meaning of the Scriptures if education is to be authentically Christian. A matter of considerable concern was the steady growth of public higher education while the enrollment in many private colleges was declining. Nevertheless, the president felt that Wheaton was "poised on the threshold of the most significant period of its history."[16]

Dr. Armerding's declaration of confidence in Wheaton's future came at a time when private colleges were faced with sharply escalating costs. Many responsible observers of the educational scene were again asking: "Can the private college survive?"

The annual retreat proved to be a valuable time of sharing insights, clarifying values and goals, transmitting the authentic information necessary to dissipate misunderstanding, exchanging criticisms in love, and strengthening the sense of community among those entrusted with the mission of Wheaton College to serve "For Christ and His Kingdom." These presidential retreats continued through the Armerding administration.

Antioch Study

In 1965 the Carnegie Corporation had agreed to fund a two-year study of the future of colleges in America. One of the colleges selected for examination was Wheaton. Director of the project was Morris Keeton, professor of philosophy and religion at Antioch College, whose academic association led to the project's being known as "the Antioch Study." Named as associate director was Conrad Hilberry, professor of English at Kalamazoo College, who had participated in the North Central review of Wheaton in 1963. Dean Veltman was designated to assist the study team in whatever ways might be needed.

Keeton and Hilberry, in the preface to their study, state that their thinking about the project was influenced by statements made by Dean William C. DeVane of Yale College in 1964. "There are prophets abroad in the land today," he said, "who foresee the early demise of the liberal arts tradition in higher education in America, and the consequent end, or at least the drastic revision, of the college which has been the home of that tradition . . . hat is most needed now . . . is for some of our most eminent universities and strongest colleges . . . to set up models of what the college ought to be and how it must function if it is to justify its position in the total plan of the country's educational establishment."[17]

When they came to enlist some of the "strongest colleges," said Keeton and Hilberry, they wanted to present models of "how a college can be what it ought to be."[18] The twelve colleges selected for the study were chosen for their diversity of purposes and tradition, and for their academic strength. The College of St. Thomas (Minnesota), Earlham, and Wheaton represented "Catholic, Quaker, and conservative Protestant religious positions."

The authors of the Antioch Study in their published work, *Struggle, and Promise: A Future for Colleges*, open the first chapter, which profiles Wheaton College and Berea College, with a bold statement. "The typical liberal arts private college of the mid-twentieth century is obsolete. Its sovereign isolation, its protected students, the one-track careers of its faculty, its restricted curriculums and teaching and its tepid purposes make it unsuited to the needs of the decade ahead. To have a bright future, private colleges must struggle to surmount these defects in a context of significantly altered purposes." In the troubled spirit of the mid-sixties, when many former certainties about the means and ends of liberal education were being brought under severe judgment, the criticisms seemed justified.

The profiles of the colleges in the study are essentially descriptive rather than prescriptive. To identify the distinctive qualities of each of the institutions was the central purpose of the writers. The sketch of Wheaton, written by Conrad Hilberry, is objective, fair, appreciative, even to the delineation of its financial structure. The author notes that fund-raisers from other colleges were sometimes incredulous when they learned that Wheaton had eleven men in the field living in eleven sections of the country, traveling 500,000 miles a year, and keeping in touch with the constituency. Often they would ask Director of Public Relations David Roberts how he could afford to send men out to farms and come back with a ten-dollar bill. "Yes, but what if they came back with the farm?" was Roberts's reply.[19] The first of the field men was W. E. Elliot, who in 1935 took over the assignment of what President Edman called "friend-raising."

After sketching the essential tone and qualities of the Wheaton campus, the writer raised the kind of inquiry that Wheatonites have often had to contend with: "Faculty from more liberal colleges are tempted to conclude, on hearing of Wheaton's religious position, that no education can occur there. What self-respecting college teacher would permit an institution to tell him that he must not drink or smoke or go to the movies? Worse yet, who would submit to signing a doctrinal loyalty oath each year? Questions like this reflect a kind of reverse provincialism, an unquestioned assumption that no one who accepts arbitrary limitation on his behavior or who publicly subscribes to a religious platform can be well-educated and intellectually alive. Wheaton's restrictions on behavior and belief do create strains, but there can be little question of Wheaton's academic respectability and vigor."[20]

After examining the high scholastic aptitude test scores freshmen bring to Wheaton and the scores of seniors on the Graduate Record Examination—"significantly higher than seniors in widely representative comparison groups"—Hilberry suggests that "the impression these statistics convey is of an abler-than-average student body, competently trained, going on to successful graduate work or jobs, often in fields that incorporate an element of Christian service."[21]

One faculty member, who had taught elsewhere, is quoted as having said, "Sometimes things get rough around here. Then you say, 'oh, but those great kids! It's worth staying.' "[22] The faculty in general are commended for their loyalty to the College, their training, and their classroom effectiveness, but objection was raised to the "inbreeding," with more than half the teaching staff then being Wheaton graduates. Hilberry felt that the "Wheaton faculty members are best-known outside the Evangelical world for their work in science and literature, citing Professor Howard Claassen's work in physics and Professor Clyde Kilby's contributions to the study and appreciation of C. S. Lewis.[23] Considerable attention is given in the study to the addendum to the doctrinal statement, and the difference of opinion it aroused, as an example of tensions that arise on campus from time to time, and were sometimes, in the mid-sixties, acute.

The unrest of that era led Hilberry to write in his concluding paragraph: "The vision of Wheaton that moves the more liberal students and faculty is not the vision that sustains the Trustees. What looks like liberal education from one angle looks like apostasy from another. It is thus hard to see how Wheaton, in the next years, can remain placid—unless the students grow silent, the faculty stop reading, and the Trustees lose interest in doctrine. But while the contest goes on—and partly because it goes on—students will continue to come to Wheaton from Evangelical homes and receive excellent training in chemistry, music, psychology, biology, and whatever."[24]

Participation in the Antioch Study was a gratifying experience for the administration and faculty alike. From the published study came a clear identification of strengths on which to continue to build. Equally valuable were insights that would lead to a broadening of Wheaton's vision of its mission as a Christian liberal arts institution.

CHAPTER 16

New Programs,
New Buildings

I N THE LATE SIXTIES AND EARLY SEVENTIES A COLLEGE PRESI-
dency was one of the most hazardous jobs in America. The tensions were
often severe enough to break the will and destroy the vision of the most resolute. Average tenure in office was under five years. Lost beyond recovery,
it seemed, was quiet decorum on campus, the code of courtesy, any sense of
concern about proper attire that characterized the fifties.

Instead, there was continuing protest—in part an outcome of the "free
speech movement" on the campus of the University of California at Berkley
in 1964—over the Viet Nam War and President Johnson's determination to
press on in spite of severe American losses; over the extension of minority
rights; and over the emergence of a counter-culture which rejected many of
the norms of the fifties. To the rigors of academic life the counter-culture's
frequent response was to drop out, suggesting that a college degree was
worth neither the time nor the money required. It wished to take no responsibility for modern society's directions. Many found congenial media in the
arts through which to express their discontent. Disheveled attire worn on
campus and to class—sometimes even to church—was a convenient means
of announcing that the old accommodations to an affluent society were no
longer acceptable. The rise of the new morality, undergirded by "situation
ethics," was a value system that challenged Wheaton students to defend
their commitment to absolutes.

Wheaton's membership in the National Student Association became a concern in 1967 when that organization gave evidence of becoming radically politicized. Largely controlled by students from eastern urban campuses, the association began to make numerous demands for student power. "All regulations of a non-academic nature," NSA declared in a resolution made at its 1967 congress, "which apply solely to students should be determined only by students." The Wheaton administration, faculty, and many students found NSA's pronouncements unacceptable; but the administration did not wish to terminate unilaterally Wheaton's membership in the organization.

Dean of Students Phillip Hook suggested, in consultation with student government president Dan Reigle and the faculty, that a campus referendum be held on a proposal to withdraw from NSA. Withdrawal was approved by 71 percent of the student body, terminating Wheaton's six-year membership. More congenial to Wheaton students was the College's affiliation with the American Association of Evangelical Students. The AAES, representing twenty-four evangelical campuses and about 15,000 students, had as its 1967 president Wheaton senior Paul McGuinnes.

Continuing evidence of student concern at Wheaton about national affairs came in October 1969, with a unanimous student government recommendation urging students to reflect on the war and its consequences during a national Viet Nam War moratorium. The moratorium was suggested by the New Student Mobilization for the Viet Nam War, organized by 500 student body presidents and encouraged by Senator Mark Hatfield.[1] Sympathy on campus for such activities led some people to wonder if Wheaton was becoming "radical."

Later the same month thirty Wheaton students demonstrated peacefully against the Viet Nam War in front of the Draft Board Office at the Wheaton Post Office. They notified college officials of their intention and were asked to assemble off campus for their march down town so that the event might not seem to be college sponsored. At the meeting site Wheaton students joined others from North Central College, College of DuPage, Bethany Seminary, and Maryknoll Seminary. The group sang "We Shall Overcome" and were addressed by a representative from Maryknoll.[2]

Wheaton's participation in the Peace Corps program was another evidence of constructive interests among students during the years of unrest. The Corps, set up by an act of Congress in 1961, was intended to provide trained men and women for service in foreign countries, usually Third World nations, where their skills were needed and where they went by invitation of the host country. Their mission on the two-year assignment was also to promote understanding of the United States. In 1965, a typical year, four Wheaton students went out on the program: Elizabeth Ramm, Mary Ann Seume, Roger Miller, and Craig Noll.[3] In the summer of the same year the annual Student Missionary Project sent twenty volunteers to fields of service from Alaska to Latin America to India. There, through teaching, construction, nursing, and other ministries, they presented the gospel of Jesus Christ.

Academic achievement did not suffer among the majority of students during those unsettled times. Seven Woodrow Wilson Fellowships were awarded to Wheaton students between 1962 and 1966. Financed by the Ford Foundation, the fellowships were intended to train potential college teachers at a time when an acute shortage was developing. It was expected that the grant would lead to the completion of a Ph.D. program. Many evaluating agencies during those years judged the academic quality of an institution, in part, by the number of Woodrow Wilson grants it had received. The first Wheaton winner was Merold Westphal in philosophy in 1962. Other winners during the four years were Kenneth Shipps, philosophy; Dan Kuhn, literature; Debbie Hess, French; David Jeffrey, literature; Paul Souder, physics; and Stephanie Bartlett, literature. In 1966, when Wheaton had two winners, grants had been made in only 380 of the nation's 2,200 eligible schools.[4]

The winds of discontent and change touched the Wheaton campus in varying degrees of intensity. Though the shock waves were far less disturbing than on many other campuses, they were severe enough to trouble President Armerding and his advisors deeply. At his press conference a few students regularly demanded immediate changes in the organization and values of the College to meet their vision of a new order of freedom. The president listened with patience, then offered an even-tempered explanation, usually supported by Scripture, as to why things came to be as they were.

One day in chapel Dr. Armerding called to the platform a student whose attire and lifestyle gave him the outward appearance of a campus rebel. The president embraced the young man, telling him he appreciated him as a person and a brother in Christ. Earlier in the day President Armerding had heard this student in a prayer meeting pray earnestly for the College and its leader. The students responded with a five-minute standing ovation.

Throughout that disquieting era, Dr. Armerding was encouraged in part by an historian's awareness that most cultural disruptions moderate or pass away in time. Most of all, he was strengthened by an unfaltering confidence in the provision of God for Wheaton's continuing mission as a Christian liberal arts college faithful to its heritage.

Student activities and campus events continued in familiar patterns during this period. Some campus organizations experienced diminished membership and declining enthusiasm when numbers of students turned to political activities as more worthy of their efforts than activities that had, it seemed, little significance beyond the college community.

The *Tower*, edited by the junior class, could no longer secure enough staff members and had to appeal for assistance from the other classes. Nevertheless, the all-campus *Tower* staff of 1967 maintained the excellent standards of their predecessors who had achieved fifteen All-American ratings. *Tower* had a budget of $30,000 for that year. In his dedication statement honoring Dean Richard Gross, '53 editor Leif Torjesen wrote: "Here at Wheaton we live under the same confusion and tensions which mark our society as a whole, although we have largely translated them into the language of men in their relation to God. It is the personal and personally devastating ambiguity which perhaps more than anything else frustrates those who would live with direction and simplicity."[5] Dean Gross, Torjesen went on to suggest, had helped students move through those ambiguities to stable ground.

The *Record* won its share of honors, receiving All-American semester ratings in 1967-68. Commended for its editorial leadership on campus, the paper was kept lively by columnists and prodding letters to the editor. Its reporting of campus events was thorough and energetic, rendering a dependable history of the times. In its columns were articulate judgments on higher education, Viet Nam, poverty, segregation and inner city problems. *Kodon*, with its more limited readership of students interested in the arts, reflected in its poetry, stories, and drawings the experimental forms of the day. Content such as abstract art, impressionism, surrealism, and the absurd, puzzled many readers; but the editors persisted in their efforts to make modern art forms meaningful to their generation.

Drama Comes Alive

A notable cultural advancement was achieved when the first regular drama, Shakespeare's *Macbeth*, was performed by a student group under the direction of Professor Edwin Hollatz, in Edman Chapel, March 21-25, 1966, as part of the Creative Arts Festival. The performance was made possible when an ad hoc committee, appointed by President Armerding, recommended lifting the long-standing ban on staging plays, though it did not recommend the establishment of a drama department or a major in drama. Drama was to be under the direction of the department of speech communication.

President Edman had reaffirmed in 1955 what had been the "historic position of the college" in prohibiting the production of "printed drama." He wished to encourage the writing and production of "locally inspired presentations of spiritual, historical, and cultural values."[6] Throughout the Edman administration, and for many years before, there had been numerous skits, performances, pageants, and similar kinds of presentations at Homecoming, commencement, historic occasions, and class activities, but they were never known or advertised as dramas. Students were often amused at the euphemisms employed to render acceptable some of those performances that were little different from drama.

Among the plays produced by Barbara Nicholich, '57, first director of drama at Wheaton (1967-69), were Molière's *Tartuffe* and Anouilh's *Antigone*. From 1969 to 1972 Ken Blackwell served as director and offered to appreciative audiences Euripides' *Medea*, Shakespeare's *Othello*, and Kaufman and Hart's *You Can't Take It With You*. In the fall of 1972 Dr. James Young, with a wide background of experience, came to Wheaton as visiting professor of speech and director of drama, on leave from the University of Massachusetts. For the fall play he chose and directed Arthur Miller's *The Crucible*. Subsequently he was asked to accept a permanent faculty appointment, beginning in the fall of 1973. He agreed to do so only if a place other than Edman Chapel could be found for a performance area. The Chapel, he felt, was much too large for the effective presentation of drama, had too spacious a platform, and lacked the essential dressing rooms. Through the efforts of Professor Hollatz and Dean Nelson space was made available in the lower level of Fischer Hall for the speech department and for Nystrom Theater, named in honor of Professor Clarence Nystrom, who had taught speech at Wheaton from 1935 to 1967 and was department chairman for many years. The play chosen for the dedication of the theater was *Look Homeward, Angel*, Kitti Frings's adaptation of the Thomas Wolfe novel. For the event Dr. Nystrom came from California.

Among the plays produced under Dr. Young's direction were Samuel Beckett's *Waiting for Godot*; Bertolt Brecht's *The Caucasian Chalk Circle*, Shakespeare's *Midsummer Night's Dream*, with contemporary innovations; and T. S. Eliot's *Murder in the Cathedral*, given in Glen Ellyn at St. Barnabas Episcopal Church. Innovations in the drama program have included the formation of drama workout groups that function throughout the year, experimentation in the relationship between the actors and audience during the play, and some effort to explore the theological implications of modern drama. In a decade and a half of drama at Wheaton a high standard of excellence has been established by Dr. Young; students have responded to his skilled leadership with enthusiasm. Some plays have been directed by Michael Stauffer. A support group from the Wheaton College Women's Club has given assistance with costumes and props. The first of the full-length musicals, usually performed in the spring, was *Brigadoon*, given in May 1968.

In the fall of 1968 Francis Schaeffer made one of his several visits to Wheaton for a week of special services. Founder and director of L'Abri Fellowship, a study and workshop center in the Swiss Alps, Schaeffer made a strong impression on students. His intense, no-nonsense manner of delivery, his knowledge of student concerns, his ability to analyze modern art, music, and literature and to bring them under the judgment of biblical truth, all were a fresh and vital experience for the campus. His knowledge of the intellectual world was wide. He championed mainstream values in new ways. To many students, Schaeffer seemed to personify the integration of faith and learning. Later President Armerding was to tell the trustees that Schaeffer had had a calming influence on the campus that lasted throughout the year. Others whose visits had impact on the lives of Wheaton students in the sixties were Dr. Harold Ockenga, Dr. Robert Munger, Dr. Edmund Clowney, Ray Ortland, Ray Stedman, David Burnham, and Tom Skinner. Student responses following one of Ray Ortland's evening meetings lasted through the night.

Christopher Fry's The Lady's Not for Burning *given in Nystrom Arena Theater, March 1977. L. to r.: Brian Hanlon, J. Randall Petersen, Mary Jane Williams, Barbara Carter.*

Faith and Learning Seminar in session with Professor Holmes, July 1975.

Summer Seminar on Faith and Learning

President Armerding's continuing concern that the Wheaton faculty should in their teaching stress the unity of all knowledge in God's design led to the institution of the Summer Seminar in the Integration of Faith and Learning in 1969. Reading some of the writing of Professors Gordon Clark, Cornelius Jaarsma, Dr. Frank Gaebelein, and others had given the president a perspective he hoped his own faculty could achieve.

With the assistance of Roy M. Horsey, a Chicago businessman, who offered to underwrite the program, President Armerding invited Dr. Gaebelein, highly respected as an educator, editor, and Christian leader, to be director of the first seminar. Dr. Gaebelein was asked to develop its format, the objective being to relate Christian convictions and values to the various academic disciplines.

Participants in the seminar, open to faculty members at large, read widely, listened to stimulating lectures by the leader and guest consultants, participated in rigorous group discussions involving the broad range of liberal studies, interpreted their own disciplines and chatted informally over lunch and coffee in the North Party Room. As a culminating experience each participant wrote a paper. Subjects discussed included the biblical doctrine of creation in contrast to other world views, problems in historic and contemporary theology, the influence of the arts on modern thought, and the effect of science and technology on contemporary life. For the best paper, in the judgment of the leader, a $500 prize was awarded.

Members of the first seminar, intended to represent a wide range of disciplines were Professors Carol Kraft, German; William Henning, French; Leland Ryken, literature; Ralph Alexander, Old Testament and archaeology; Alfred Hoerth, archaeology; Miriam Hunter, art; Alvin Moser, sociology; Eleanor Paulson, speech; and Joseph Bean, physical education. Winner of the essay prize at the end of the first summer was Leland Ryken for a paper titled "A Christian Approach to Literature." Many of the papers found publication and some were enlarged into books.

Dr. Gaebelein served as director of the seminar for four summers, 1969-1973. For the summer of 1974 Dr. Vernon Grounds, president of Conservative Baptist Theological Seminary, Denver, Colorado, was guest director. In 1975 Professor Arthur Holmes, chairman of the Wheaton philosophy department, assumed the leadership and has continued in that role. Faculty participants have commended the seminar and acknowledged their appreciation for a learning experience that has brought new dimensions to their teaching.

Buildings Rise

Fischer Hall. The last of the buildings authorized by the trustees during the Edman era, and the first completed during President Armerding's administration, was the Herman A. Fischer Residence Hall. In March 1964 the campus planning committee recommended that the building be located on the north end of what had been known as Graham Field. After sketches submitted by the builder, J. Emil Anderson and Son, were approved, groundbreaking was held at Homecoming, Sunday, November 1, 1964.

By February 1966, the building was completed—at a cost of $2,600,000, including furnishings and landscaping—and men students from Saint and Elliot Halls moved into their new college home. When the building opened it seemed astonishingly attractive, its lounges almost sumptuous compared with any of the other student accommodations on campus. A few students, conscious of the sacrifices being made by American troops in Viet Nam, and of a rising counter-culture hostile to "the establishment," resented the opulent image the dorm seemed to them to convey.

When the trustees came to name the building, they wished to honor their chairman, Herman A. Fischer, Jr., for his long service to Wheaton. Fischer agreed to the use of his name only if it was understood that the building was also a memorial to his father, Herman A. Fischer, Sr., long-time professor of mathematics and treasurer of the College.

After Dr. Henry Nelson became dean of students in 1969, he suggested that Fischer Hall become a residence for freshmen men and women in equal numbers. Some of the trustees resisted the plan, though the majority gave approval after examining the proposal thoroughly, and after being assured by Dean Nelson and his associates that every safeguard would be taken to prevent improper behavior in such a living arrangement. When the Freshmen Residence Hall Program was initiated in the fall of 1970, men were housed in one wing of the building and women in the other. They shared in common only the lounges.

Dean Nelson received nearly a hundred letters—some of them irate—expressing fear that in initiating the Freshmen Residence Hall Program, Wheaton was embarking on the practice of unrestricted inter-room visitation that was then becoming common in other schools. Many letters and telephone calls from the dean's office were necessary to calm alarmed friends and reassure them that the carefully arranged program would not encourage inappropriate relationships. The plan worked well and soon won general approval.

Traber Hall. The opening of Fischer Hall in 1966 considerably reduced the critical need for student housing. But, in the opinion of the trustees and the administration, too many students were still living in private homes off campus. With the goal of housing at least 85 percent of the student body in campus-owned facilities, the trustees authorized the construction of a new dormitory to house 234 students. The builder would again be J. Emil Anderson and Son; financing would come from the investment of annuity surpluses not otherwise encumbered. Begun in April 1969, and designed to be connected with Smith Hall, the new building was intended as a residence for women. The seven-floor structure, with six residence levels, was the tallest building in Wheaton at its completion.

With the resolution to make Fischer Hall a men and women's residence, the administration decided to extend the new Residence Hall Program to Smith Hall and to the new dorm, which was at first called the Tower. Smith would remain a women's residence and the Tower, planned for women, would be a men's residence. Seven hundred students, faculty, and friends attended an open house at the Tower in September 1970. At the 1972 Homecoming the building was named Traber Hall in honor of George M. Traber, Jr., a trustee of the College from 1942 to 1968.

Students returning in the fall of 1970 to the women's residences and Fischer Hall found themselves the beneficiaries of considerably relaxed and simpler dormitory rules. All women and freshmen men had automatic permission to be out of their dormitories on week nights until one o'clock and on Friday and Saturday nights until two o'clock. Women wishing to leave campus overnight simply filled out a slip indicating where they were going and with whom, and placed it on the main desk of their dormitory. The policy left women considerably more freedom than before and more nearly equalized their privileges with those of men. The plan was intended to give more responsibility to the student. "We don't care less than we did," said assistant dean Bill Lindberg, "we just wanted to show students the respect we think they deserve."[7] Violators of the rules were required to report to a Student Peer Board, made up of resident assistants and students elected to the Board.

Science Hall. Funds from the $7,000,000 Wheaton Advancement Program, initiated by the trustees in 1967, were expected to provide for a new science hall and a new library. Half the money was to be added to the college endowment and half was designated for the two buildings. The program, strongly supported by the alumni, did not meet its goal in 1969 as planned, but ultimately accomplished it through estate bequests.

The science hall was chosen as the first of the two buildings to be constructed because it had been for some time at the top of the list of building priorities prepared by the Campus Planning Committee. Connected to the Breyer Chemistry Building, it would complete the construction plans for the science program at Wheaton. Further, it would allow the biology and physics departments to move out of their antiquated quarters in Blanchard Hall. In addition, more of the gifts to the Advancement Program were designated for a science building than for a library.

Ground was broken for the science building during the 1969 commencement weekend, with president Armerding, Dr. Raymond Brand, chairman of the division of science, and builder A. Harold Anderson participating in the ceremony.[8] The building was underway by May 1970, with the cost projected at $2,000,000. For economic reasons, and because the building might at some time in the future be expanded, the Georgian style of other campus buildings was set aside. The first two floors house the mathematics and physics departments, the third and fourth levels the biological sciences. Facilities include fifteen instructional laboratories, fifteen student and faculty laboratories, six classrooms, a 225-seat lecture hall, faculty offices, a seminar room, display area, greenhouse, roof-top observatory with multiple telescopes, and lounge. Final cost of the building was $2,600,000, with the largest single contribution being a $400,000 gift made anonymously by a Chicagoan.

Completed ahead of schedule, the building was put into use during the 1971 spring quarter. Dedication cermonies were held on October 9, with Dr. Roger Voskuyl, executive director of the Council for Advancement of Small Colleges, and former Wheaton dean of the College and professor of chemistry, giving the address. He declared that the mission of science at a Christian college is "to inform, to sharpen the intellect, to understand the world and its people, to alleviate suffering, to advance the fulfilling life, to push back the frontiers of knowledge, for the glory of God and the betterment of his people."[9]

Library. Authorization for the construction of the new library at an estimated cost of $2,400,000, came from the Board of Trustees in the spring of 1974. Permission to proceed with the building had been delayed for some time because funds were being received slowly and because, in consequence, the plans had to be redrawn several times in a more affordable design. The plans finally adopted, however, called for a modular structure which made possible expansion to the north, should that become necessary at some future time. Land for that purpose is being preserved. The cost included remodeling and refurnishing the Nicholas Library, to which the new building would be connected. Ground-breaking ceremonies took place at the June commencement.

Need for a new library had been recognized for some time, the Nicholas Library having been built in 1951 for a student body of 1,500, with shelving for 147,000 books. By 1974 there were 1,925 students and the book collection had grown to 165,000 volumes.

The new Library-Learning Resource Center was planned to accommodate 500 users at any one time and to be adequate for a book collection of 225,000 volumes. Housed in the Nicholas Wing are the music library and listening posts, the education library, the Marion E. Wade Collection, the V. Raymond Edman Collection, and the College archives and rare books.

Dedication ceremonies were held in Edman chapel at Homecoming on October 18, 1975 when President Armerding spoke on "Christian Nurture." Much of the early planning of the building had been done by former librarian Robert Golter in consultation with architect Joseph Herstowski. Students were pleased with the new library's wood furnishings, spacious lounge and lobby, additional carrels, and special study rooms. Faculty members were grateful for new research offices. Especially delighted was Library Director Paul Snezek, who had come to Wheaton in 1970 as assistant to the director and was advanced to the directorship in 1977.

In 1980 the Board of Trustees authorized naming the library the Buswell Memorial Library, in honor of Wheaton's third president, J. Oliver Buswell, Jr. Present at the naming ceremony on October 18 were Dr. Buswell's four

Arrival of the Charles Williams papers, now a part of the Marion E. Wade Collection.
L. to r.: Librarian Paul Snezek, Ruth Cording, Professor Beatrice Batson, Barbara
McClatchey, Professor Clyde S. Kilby, Martha Kilby, Miriam Armerding, Betty Goddard.

Buswell Memorial Library.

children: Jane Foxwell, Ruth Noe, Dr. James O. Buswell III, and Dr. John Buswell. Remarks were made by Director Snezek, Dr. Clyde Kilby, curator of the Wade Collection; and Dr. James O. Buswell III, professor of anthropology at Wheaton for fourteen years and later dean of graduate studies, William Carey International University. Dr. James Buswell noted his father's love of books and the great diversity of subject matter in his personal library. He recalled, too, the former president's devotion to the classics, citing his practice in his early years at Wheaton of presenting his charge to the senior class in Latin, which he had written and memorized.[10] The bronze plaque in the lobby of the library characterizes President Buswell as a "theologian, author, scholar, and exponent of Christian higher education."

When the new library became Buswell Memorial Library, the Graduate School building, Buswell Hall, was renamed Schell Hall, honoring Dean Edward R. Schell, who directed the affairs of Wheaton Academy for many years when its classes met in that building.

Special Library Collections

The Archives. When the new library was completed in 1974, sufficient space became available to house the college archives and a number of special collections.

The archives of the College, located on the upper floor of the Nicholas wing of the library, were first kept in a small, wholly inadequate room in the basement of that building. As early as the 1940s Professor S. Richey Kamm had expressed concern lest materials associated with the Blanchards and the history of Wheaton should slip away, irrecoverably lost. At the time, no one was designated to discover, organize, and preserve those records. Professor Clyde S. Kilby, in writing *A Minority of One*, a biography of Jonathan Blanchard, used in his research many primary documents which he carefully indexed in the book. This volume helped the college community, and many other readers, to recognize what a rich treasury of records and artifacts associated with the history of Wheaton College lay in scattered locations. A historical project committee, directed in turn by Dr. Kamm and Dr. Earle E. Cairns, made numerous suggestions for organizing the college archives. Miss Julia Blanchard, after her retirement as librarian, had been designated college archivist; regrettably, it was more of an honorary title than a working assignment since she was then aged, rather infirm, and unable to serve actively.

When the Centennial celebration of 1959-60 ended, Richard Gerig, chariman to the Centennial committee, brought all of the material assembled for the year's activities to the library. It was a substantial beginning effort to collect the archives of the College. In 1962 librarian Robert Golter asked Ruth Cording, '33, to serve as part-time archivist, organizing and cataloging materials then held, and to search actively for other resources associated with Wheaton's history. In her eight years as archivist, Mrs. Cording gave dedicated and wise direction to the building of a fine collection of documents. In 1976 Roger Phillips became archivist, and under his efficient direction the book holdings doubled and the collection of papers quadrupled. He was assisted by Bill Favata, who succeeded him, and by Betty Terry.

The archives include the papers and correspondence of five Wheaton presidents, official records and minutes of the Board of Trustees, faculty meeting minutes, complete files of all college publications such as the *Bulletin of Wheaton College* (which includes the catalog), the *Wheaton Alumni*, *Faculty Bulletin*, *Tower*, *Record*, *Kodon*, and minutes and reports of faculty committees. Additonally, there are news clippings dating back to the thirties, an extensive file of photographs, the papers and class notes of several professors of the past, along with publications and manuscripts of faculty members. Over a hundred cassette tapes record the voices of alumni recounting their experiences as Wheaton students.

Rare books number some 3,000, the most valuable of which is probably Martin Luther's study of the Psalms, written in Latin and published in 1519. The owner of the volume, Sigismund, was enrolled at Wittenberg in 1520 and wrote extensive marginal notes, as clear today as when they were penned. Two large pulpit Bibles—one published in Holland in 1713 and one in Germany in 1739—are fascinating volumes to examine. A massive, nine-volume Greek thesaurus of over 18,000 pages, published in Paris in 1865, is an awesome witness to the prodigious scholarship of an earlier age, and an antiquarian's delight to handle.

The William S. Akin Collection. The most diversified of the special collections under the supervision of the library, in its range of subjects and historical eras represented, is the William S. Akin collection. It numbers over 4,000 volumes, with many first editions, masterpieces of fine bookmaking.

An energetic man, Bill Akin liked to tell friends how, as a ten-year-old at his first confession before an Episcopal priest, he was sent to read Samuel Johnson's *Devotions and Prayers* as penance. Intrigued by the little volume, he resolved someday to own a first edition of it. That initial spark of interest became a lifelong passion for collecting first editions and rare books. As a salesman who traveled widely he learned where the best bookshops were, how to discover and purchase rare books, and how to enjoy the companionship of many of the best authors.

William S. Akin's friendship with Wheaton College began in 1950 when, as librarian of the Union League Club in Chicago, he read W. Wyeth Willard's history of Wheaton College, *Fire on the Prairie*. In an enthusiastic review of the book he said: "Read *Fire on the Prairie* and you have the solution to the world situation." President Edman's brother Elner, also a member of the Union League, brought the review to the attention of his brother, who arranged to meet Akin. A close friendship developed, which lasted through the remainder of Dr. Edman's life. On his frequent trips to the campus Akin would usually bring with him several choice volumes. Often he had astonishing stories about how the books, some of which he had preserved for years, had come into his possession. Sometimes he would invite librarian Paul Snezek to bring his station wagon over to the Akin apartment in Evanston for a consignment of books.

Among his many books three unique collections reveal Akin's special interests. A Charles Dickens collection numbers over 200 volumes by and about the author, some of them first editions, many of them published in the nineteenth century. Over 150 different editions of *Pilgrim's Progress*, a few of them dating from the early eighteenth century, represent another of his enthusiasms. This collection is an especially good example of the collector's delight in illustrated books and fine binding. Another grouping of volumes includes some eighty books by and about Daniel Defoe and Christopher Columbus. There are works by the Brontë sisters, Sir Walter Scott, Cervantes, and Herman Melville. Several rare volumes of the works of Samuel Johnson represent Akin's continued devotion to that great eighteenth century English author. The Akin Collection is a superb example of the discriminating tastes of a bibliophile extraordinaire.

The Madeleine L'Engle Collection. Madeleine L'Engle first came to Wheaton College in 1972, at the invitation of Professor Melvin Lorentzen, for the 17th annual Writers' Conference. Doug Olsen and Helen deVette of the English Department had strongly urged that this outstanding writer of children's books be introduced to Wheaton audiences. L'Engle's lectures— insightful, genial, witty, charming, personal—won a warm response from students and faculty. Thereafter she visited Wheaton a number of times, speaking again at the Writer's Conference in 1976 and delivering the commencement address in 1977.

In 1963 Madeleine L'Engle won acclaim for *A Wrinkle in Time*, which was selected for the Newbery Award, the most prestigious honor for a children's book. In 1981 her *Ring of Endless Light* was a Newbery Honor book. The breadth of her talent includes the writing of distinguished works for adults as well as for children. Among her outstanding adult titles are *A Circle of Quiet, The Summer of the Great Grandmother, The Irrational Season,* and *Walking on Water.* She has won numerous other awards for her more than thirty books.

Professor Clyde S. Kilby approached Madeleine L'Engle in 1975, suggesting that she deposit her papers and manuscripts at Wheaton College, an invitation she accepted. After approval in January 1976 by the Board of Trustees of the plans for a special collection, she began donating her materials, often bringing some of them with her on her trips to Wheaton. The L'Engle Collection is comprised of the author's books and manuscripts, galley proofs, reviews, artwork and photography, and many personal letters. Some of these are letters and drawings from admiring children. Watercolors, chalk drawings, and oil paintings by the author include scenes around Crosswicks, the country home in Connecticut which Madeleine and her husband, Hugh Franklin, an actor, often share with their three married children and their families. The Franklins reside in New York where Madeleine is writer-in-residence and librarian at the Cathedral of St. John the Divine. At the May 1984 commencement Madeleine L'Engle was awarded an honorary doctor of literature degree.

The Blanchard Libraries. The Blanchard Libraries reflect the interests and activities of the first two presidents of Wheaton College. Donated in 1962 by Julia Blanchard, daughter of Charles Blanchard, and John F. Blanchard, Jr., one of the great-grandchildren of Jonathan, it includes over 350 volumes, not a large collection for two college presidents. But it is quite likely that many of the books owned by Jonathan and Charles did not find their way into this collection. The publication dates of these books span the whole of the nineteenth century. The earliest work is dated 1797. Most of the books belonging to Jonathan Blanchard have to do with slavery, Masonary, law, the constitution, and theology. Charles's books reveal his interests in the classics, education, expression, history, literature, philosophy, theology, and collections of sermons.

One of the books is titled *Select British Eloquence: of the Past Two Centuries.* The flyleaf carries the name of Jonathan Blanchard and under it the inscription: "C. A. Blanchard, from his father, August 20, 1877." The collection is an excellent resource for students of the life and times of nineteenth-century America.

The Alumni-Faculty Fine Arts Collection. The Alumni-Faculty Fine arts Collection consists of scholarly and artistic works of Wheaton alumni and past and present faculty members. It brings together about 400 authors, thirty of whom are still actively teaching. Included in the collection is the manuscript of Kenneth Taylor's *Living Bible,* which has sold over 25,000,000 copies.

Funded by the Alumni Association, the collection was initiated in 1976 for the purpose of preserving the creative productivity of the alumni and faculty of the College. Over 1,300 volumes are included in this special grouping.

The Marion E. Wade Collection. One of the major academic and scholarly events in the history of Wheaton College was the establishment of the Marion E. Wade Collection. It is an assemblage of books, manuscripts, reviews, letters, and other materials related to seven British authors: C. S. Lewis, J. R. R. Tolkien, Charles Williams, Dorothry L. Sayers, G. K. Chesterton, George MacDonald, and Owen Barfield. Though the collection is housed in the library building, it is a separate unit and is largely supported by income from the Marion E. Wade Memorial Fund and gifts of friends.

The Wade Collection was initiated, and grew to its present distinction, primarily through the tireless efforts of Clyde S. Kilby, professor of English and, for a number of years before his retirement in July 1981, curator of the collection. He says that when C. S. Lewis's *The Case for Christianty* fell into his hands in 1943, he "read it right though feeling almost from the first sentence that something profound had touched my mind and heart." In July 1953, he visited Lewis in his rooms at Magdalen College, Oxford, a meeting out of which grew an exchange of letters and a friendship.

In 1961 Professor Kilby began teaching a C. S. Lewis seminar one evening

308   □ WHEATON COLLEGE: A HERITAGE REMEMBERED

a week at his home. A similar seminar on J. R. R. Tolkien followed in 1964. In a two-week Inter-Session course beginning in 1962, he chose to introduce students to Lewis, Tolkien, Charles Williams, and George MacDonald. On a trip to England in 1964 he visited the Kilns, the Lewis home outside Oxford, and met Lewis's brother, Major Warren Lewis, a professional soldier and author of books on French history. Through that friendship, Wheaton College received many C. S. Lewis manuscripts and letters, as well as a substantial number belonging to Major Lewis himself. The Major was also immensely helpful in providing Professor Kilby with the names of a large number of Lewis's correspondents from whom in due course letters and other valuable items were received. When Owen Barfield, C. S. Lewis's solicitor and long-time friend, came to Wheaton to lecture on Lewis at the annual Writers' Conference in 1964, another helpful link with the British author was established.

It was out of his growing interest and its contagion among students that Professor Kilby, with the eager cooperation of librarian Robert Golter, began seriously in 1965 to build the collection. It began with whatever volumes were already in the college library, together with fifteen Lewis letters and a small gift of $500. Books and letters were placed inside a very small "cage" and users were locked in; when they finished they had to shake the door in order to bring the librarian to unlock it. To make the letters available to researchers, Mrs. Ruth Cording and a student assistant began the process of cataloging items. A vast encouragement came when the Class of 1966 contributed its class gift of $2,688.

Glenn Sadler, a Wheaton graduate studying in Scotland in 1965, agreed to help in the quest for Lewis books, manuscripts, and letters. To him Professor Kilby wrote: "All through this whole matter for nearly a year I have felt the hand of the Lord as never before in any particular event in my life." He felt clearly it was God's "intention to give us the collection at Wheaton College." Such acknowledgments of divine blessing were expressed many times as new and valuable accessions were made to the Wade collection.

Later in 1966 Professor Kilby wrote to Mrs. Mary Willis Shelburne, of Washington, D.C.—whose name he had gotten from Major Lewis—inviting her to contribute to the collection 145 letters she had received from C. S. Lewis between 1950 and 1963. She readily assented to the request. Afterward, learning that Mrs. Shelburne was aged and in financial need, Professor Kilby arranged to have her receive the royalties from the publication of the letters, issued anonymously under the title *Letters to an American Lady*. In 1967 Dom Bede Griffiths, a monk in south India, sent to the collection the forty-two letters he had received from Lewis between 1932 and 1963, the year of Lewis's death. Father Peter Milward sent fifteen letters from Tokyo.

Possibly the most valuable single collection of letters to come to Wheaton were 223 from Lewis to his lifelong friend Arthur Greeves. The letters had been given by Greeves shortly before his death to Major Lewis, who in turn gave them to Professor Kilby.

Lewis was known to have destroyed many of his manuscripts, yet the collection was able to acquire two from Mrs. Joan Bennett, a sixteenth-century specialist at Cambridge University: *An Experiment in Criticism*, an important Lewis work, and *Dr. Donne and Love Poetry in the Seventeenth Century*. Through letters of appeal, friendships, and his ten visits to England between 1964 and 1980, Professor Kilby has been the guiding spirit in the growth of the collection, though he readily acknowledges that gifts and helpful encouragement have come from many "friends of the collection." Valuable additions also came through an arrangement between Wheaton College and the Bodleian Library at Oxford by which each agreed to exchange with the other xeroxed copies of its Lewis manuscript holdings. In 1967 Owen Barfield acknowledged that Wheaton "already had enough materials to force a British scholar to come there."

Professor Kilby and librarian Golter promptly agreed that the collection should be centered around the "Oxford Christians," particularly Lewis, Tolkien, and Williams. Chesterton and Sayers also seemed appropriate. George MacDonald was chosen for his intrinsic merit and his acknowledged influence on Lewis, and Owen Barfield for his long friendship and debates with Lewis. Together these authors produced more than 400 books: expository and critical works, novels, plays, and children's stories, as well as innumerable articles and periodical reviews.

In 1972 the collection was moved to larger quarters in the Charles Albert Blanchard Memorial Room on the first floor of the west end of Blanchard Hall. The following year Professor Kilby was officially made curator. Early in 1976, the collection, having again outgrown its quarters, was established in the Nicholas wing of the new library in an attractive room arranged and decorated under the guidance of Mary Wade Rigler, daughter of Lillian and Marion Wade. In the new location Marjorie Mead was to serve as assistant to the curator.

Professor Kilby's visit to Oxford in 1966 to assist J. R. R. Tolkien in the completion of the *Silmarillion* established a friendship between the two that was to be helpful in procuring some of Tolkien's material for the collection. The development of the George MacDonald library has involved a long and tedious search for all his editions. Over 400 volumes by and about this prolific nineteenth-century author are now owned by the College. One current bibliographer suggests that the MacDonald collection is more complete than that held at either Harvard or Yale. Books by and about Lewis, numbering over 1,000, together with the letters and manuscripts, support the general acknowledgment that Wheaton's Lewis collection is the most comprehensive in the world. Similar distinction may be claimed for the Sayers, Williams, and Barfield collections. With over 2,000 volumes, manuscripts, and letters the Chesterton collection likewise is one of the best of its kind.

By 1982 the collection numbered over 6,000 books. Other prized holdings include four pieces of furniture from the Kilns. In addition to Lewis's desk and chair is the handsome, handcarved wardrobe which was part of the inspiration for *The Lion, the Witch and the Wardrobe*.

What began as the C. S. Lewis Collection in 1965 was renamed the Marion

E. Wade collection in 1974 in honor of the founder and president of Service-Master Industries, Inc., who, with his wife made substantial gifts to the collection, was a friend of Wheaton College, and a devoted reader of C. S. Lewis. After his death the Marion E. Wade Memorial Fund was established by Wade's ServiceMaster associates. Dr. Lyle Dorsett, formerly professor of history at the University of Denver, became curator of the collection in 1982.

Closely associated with the Wade Collection is the Anglo-American Literary Review *Seven*, edited by Barbara Reynolds, British scholar, along with Beatrice Batson and Clyde Kilby. Printed in England, published by Wheaton College, the review is devoted to studies of the seven authors represented in the Wade Collection. Fourteen advisors, two for each author in the collection, one American and one English, constitute the editorial panel. The launching of *Seven* with the first issue in the spring of 1980 was celebrated with a dinner at the Authors Club in London. Among those present for the ceremony were U.S. Ambassador Kingman Brewster, Owen Barfield, and Professors Reynolds and Batson.

The Frederick Buechner Collection. The most recent materials to be added to the special collections are the papers of Frederick Buechner, a gift of the author in 1982. Buechner first won acclaim with the publication of *A Long Day's Dying* in 1950, when he was twenty-four and an instructor in English at Lawrenceville School. Since then he has written twenty books. His works include *The Return of Ansel Gibbs, Peculiar Treasures: A Biblical Who's Who, Wishful Thinking,* and *Lion Country,* in which appears his best-known character, Leo Bebb. For *Godric* (1980) he was nominated for a Pulitzer Prize. He has received awards from the American Academy and from the Institute of Arts and Letters.

Buechner has given the William Beldon Nobel Lecture at Harvard, the Lyman Beecher Lecture at Yale, and the Smyth Lecture at Columbia. In *The Sacred Journey* he began a gracefully written, often witty, portrait of himself which he continued in *Now and Then.* Born in New York City in 1926, he was graduated from Princeton in 1948, attended Union Theological Seminary, and was ordained a Presbyterian minister in 1958. He lives and writes in Vermont. "I want to say," he once wrote, "God is afoot in the world, and we encounter Him in all sorts of curious ways." In his inventive fiction Buechner has sought to delineate some of those curious ways.

The Buechner Collection includes manuscripts, correspondence, sermons, scrapbooks, foreign language editions of his books, a CBS film production of a novel, sermon notes, revisons of his work, class notes from Princeton and Union Seminary, and dissertations about his work.

CHAPTER 17

Assessments, Visitors, Outreach

In THE EARLY SEVENTIES A NEW ATMOSPHERE OF MODERATE tranquility settled upon many campuses. Although there was still lingering distress over Viet Nam, the waves of student protest seemed to have passed their zenith. A student writer in the 1971 *Tower* observed: "Students want time for America to rest; most people are sick of violence. The majority of students couldn't care less about the old war cries." Some of the angry mood on campuses was defused when the Nixon administration adopted a draft lottery, which meant that more than half the male students would not be called for service. The sound and fury of youthful discontent was subsiding.

To the 1971 *Tower* editor, President Armerding, speaking of his administration, expressed gratification for his "best year so far," and referred to the "positive student acceptance" he had felt for his administration. The editor conceded that students were no longer interested in trying to dislodge Blanchard Hall from its moorings. They now realized that "the struggle for change at Wheaton is a process, not a demolition derby."[1]

When students talked about change they wanted a larger role in campus community government; they wanted opportunities for a freer interaction with contemporary culture: art, music, literature, drama, public affairs. Like generations of Wheaton students before them, they asked for better facilities, a stronger faculty, and a less rigid curriculum that would allow for a wider range of electives. High on the list of priorities was a desire for a more diversified and mature social life on campus. They would appeal for these goals through their publications and student organizations. They also wanted their academic life to be more "relevant"—to use a popular word of the time—to their future vocational and professional needs. The appeal for greater relevance was heard on campuses everywhere, some of it in reaction against the traditional liberal arts program. Colleges like Wheaton were forced to make rigorous defenses of their academic practices and goals.

In the 1970s students became absorbed in national issues such as government control of education, the conquest of space, nuclear power and the threat of nuclear war, the preservation of a clean environment, conservation of energy, war and peace, abortion, the spread of secular humanism, women's rights. Local concerns providing grist for discussion included: the value of a liberal arts education in a technological society, the Christian's role in government, the survival of private higher education, accountability, the nature of Christian ministries, education for minorities, and campus governance.

Uncertainty continued about the long-term survival of private higher education. President Armerding again expressed the fear that private education as it was then known might not exist in another ten years. "It will prevail," he observed, "only if the American public believes that the distinctiveness is worthwhile." The president told the faculty and administrators at the fall retreat that Wheaton's distinctive is that it "provides an illustration of a community that functions on the basis of biblical principles of authority and responsibility."[2] There are many other Wheaton distinctives, but the president's words were reminders of the foundational imperative.

Christian College Consortium

Disenchanted with their times and with American culture in general, many young people in the early seventies were choosing not to go to college. Others were electing to go to public institutions, where costs were lower and lifestyles were freer. Applications for admission to Wheaton dropped from slightly over 2,000 in 1961, the all-time high, to 1,211 in 1971. But an adequately prepared number of applicants still met the enrollment goals the College had set when other institutions were having difficulty filling their dormitories and some were being forced to close. When Wheaton's own trend of declining numbers of applications reached its lowest figure in 1971, the College realized that more energetic recruitment efforts were imperative. It was then that Paul Sutcliffe was appointed as admissions counselor and the first full-time recruiter. The next year applications for admission once more began to rise.

Realizing the need to strengthen their programs and to confront the difficult issues of their time with shared wisdom, a group of ten evangelical colleges formed the Christian College Consortium in July 1971. Founding members were Bethel, Eastern Mennonite, Houghton, Gordon, Greenville, Malone, Seattle Pacfic, Taylor, Westmont, and Wheaton. The group chose Dr. David L. McKenna, president of Seattle Pacific College, as the first chairman of its executive committee. Later Eastern Mennonite College withdrew and four other colleges were added: Asbury, George Fox, Messiah, and Trinity.

Commenting on the initiation of the Consortium President Armerding observed: "In a day of increasing competition from public education the Consortium will not only make the various constituencies more aware of the member colleges, but will also encourage the schools to sharpen their distinctiveness as private institutions."[3] It was the distinctiveness of these colleges—quality education that is Christian—which would keep them alive in an increasingly competitive market. The schools planned to exchange information on admissions policies, costs, academic performance, and procedures for integrating faith and learning. The weaker institutions hoped to gain strength and insights from the stronger ones. At consortium schools the cost of an education was consistently highest at Westmont, second highest at Gordon, and third at Wheaton—all three in very high cost-of-living areas. Admissions figures from the various institutions indicated that Wheaton was admitting 60 percent of its applicants while others were admitting 80 to 90 percent.

Among consortium-sponsored activities were a student-faculty exchange program, an American studies program, and the summer faith and learning seminar at Wheaton, which the consortium did not originate but agreed to support. The American studies plan enabled students to observe our political system at work in the nation's capital. Faculty and students, under the exchange program, were able to spend a semester or a year at another of the consortium schools. The faith and learning seminar, originally offered each summer, is now given biennially, alternating with an advanced seminar.

In the beginning some consortium enthusiasts dreamed of founding a Christian university in the heartland of America, but the academic and financial problems were insurmountable.

In the March 1972 issue of *Universitas*, the consortium's bulletin, edited by Professor Melvin Lorentzen of Wheaton College, Dr. McKenna wrote: "There are more colleges than the evangelical community can support. Therefore, these colleges must fish for friends, funds and freshmen in the same small pool. . . . by and large, evangelical Christian colleges have had to begin fishing in the larger public pool in order to meet the resource demands for educational growth, quality, and now survival." At the end of the decade it was possible to see that some of the alarms that drew the group together had not been realized. Nevertheless, the organization continues to have useful functions.

In 1976 the Christian College Coalition, an outgrowth of the consortium, was organized with Dr. J. Richard Chase, president of Biola University, as its first chairman. The coalition, intended to bring together a much larger group of Christian colleges than the consortium, in 1981 numbered sixty-three members from the east to the west coast. Wheaton holds membership in both organizations.

Confidence in the Survival of the Christian College

Vice President for Academic Affairs Robert Baptista did not concur with the gloomy forecasts heard in the seventies of the decline and fall of the private colleges. The College would outlast the doomsayers, he was confident, "if the Wheaton faculty continues to carry a disciplining role in which academic excellence is combined with a lifestyle that exemplifies Christian love, integrity, and concern." Essential, too, Baptista believed, was the need for Wheaton to resist the dual pressures of secularization and isolation.[4]

Dr. Baptista spoke often of the centrality of the faculty in preserving and strengthening Wheaton's distinctives. He was fond of noting that in an earlier day a college faculty was known as a community of scholars, and was expected to be little more. Although good teaching is always the fundamental skill, the modern Wheaton professor is expected also to serve on working committees, to be a counselor and guide to students, to be a role model of Christian maturity, and to engage in research within his or her field.

Dr. Baptista urged faculty members to assess their interests and abilities and select the areas in which they feel they can make the greatest contribution to the College.[5] Some instructors chose to develop their counseling skills, some concentrated on writing, others worked on developing innovative teaching methods, or scholarly research. In the year prior to his departure from Wheaton in 1973 to become president of Sterling College, Dr. Baptista, together with the educational policies committee, recommended the reduction of academic divisions from six to four: Biblical studies, humanities, social studies, and physical and biological studies. That new alignment achieved a more traditional grouping of studies and effected a new academic efficiency.

Making the Bible department, together with archaeology and Christian education, a division within itself, is not traditional in liberal arts colleges; but the centrality of the Bible in the Wheaton academic design makes the arrangement logical. In 1970 a major in religion was added to those of biblical studies and archaeology, intended to prepare students for graduate work in seminary. "Our concern," said Professor Morris Inch, department chairman, "is to enable qualified men and women to enter the program of studies in higher educational institutions with a view to teaching later in similar institutions." The intention was also to give a broad pre-seminary training. Dr. Inch was not alarmed by a few people who thought that a major in religion rather than Bible might be somewhat less than evangelical.

An integrating core of biblical studies continued to be central in all students' general education program, with five courses required: Christ and

culture (centered on a Christian world and life view), Old Testament literature and interpretation, New Testament literature and interpretation, Christian thought, and an advanced elective. Like other sections of the College,
the Bible department kept alert to the changing needs of students and new
academic tendencies. Professors were ready to guide student discussions of
the charismatic movement, renewal programs in church and individual life,
ecumenicity, the Christian's social responsibility, the inerrancy of the Scriptures, and other concerns.

Grouped under humanities in the new alignment were the departments of
English, foreign languages, philosophy, art, music, and speech—guardians
of the life of the mind and the aesthetic sensibilities. These are the departments which keep alive the languages of Homer, Virgil, Cervantes, Pascal,
and Goethe; the literature of Shakespeare, Milton, and Wordsworth. They
introduce students to the great painters, ancient and modern; to Bach,
Beethoven, Chopin; to the noble thought structures of Plato and Aristotle.
In 1974 the foreign language department, as a service to the community and
the area, offered (by tapes and a tutor) instruction in some fifty languages
not ordinarily offered in college classes, among them Japanese, Swahili, and
Norwegian.

The science division was unchanged in its membership: chemistry, physics, biology, geology, mathematics. New developments in all the sciences
were a continual challenge. While the most arresting breakthroughs seemed
to be coming in biology, the science people at Wheaton realized that they
were working in interdependent disciplines and not competitive fields. Sub-
divisions in the traditional sciences were developing in bewildering diversity, but small colleges with limited resources and equipment could not
move fully into those enticing arenas. Nevertheless, they were able to appropriate the insights of the new fields. Wheaton scientists, as well as professors who worked in the humanities, aware of what seemed to be a
widening gulf between the sciences and the humanities, discussed amicably
what were said to be the acute perils of that dichotomy. They tried to become more understanding of each other's specializations—continuing in
friendly appreciation of areas of knowledge outside their own. Perhaps the
chasm had been declared to be wider than it actually was.

Social sciences brought together sociology, anthropology, psychology,
history and political science, economics, education, along with physical education and ROTC. Unprecedented growth in the social services, new developments in psychology, expansion in education at all levels, and
enlarging demand for economists provided attractive professional opportunities for graduates. Steady growth in the number of majors was experienced in all of these departments.

Dr. Robert Baptista's successor as vice president for academic affairs, rec-
ommended by a search committee headed by Dr. Arthur Volle, was Dr.
Donald Mitchell, dean of Montreat-Anderson College in North Carolina.
The new vice president was a native of New Zealand, where he received his

university and theological education and began his teaching career. Later he served as a teacher and administrator in Peru for eight years under the care of the Free Church of Scotland. He received his doctorate in church history from Princeton Seminary and taught history there.

Like his predecessor, Dr. Mitchell would be on the scene, in his six years of service, during some of the most challenging years of Wheaton's history. He found a cooperative and well-trained faculty of 146, including the graduate division. Among institutions at which this faculty had their graduate study were all of the Ivy League schools, all of the Big Ten institutions, Chicago, Johns Hopkins, the major California schools, and many others. Some faculty members had studied, traveled, or taught abroad. A number had received foundation grants or alumni awards to further their training. A few of them had joined the staff in Dr. Buswell's time, more than thirty years earlier; most of them were appointees of the Edman era; some were just beginning their academic careers.

Ten-Year North Central Review

Preparation for the ten-year accreditation review by the North Central Association of Colleges and Schools began in 1973 under the direction of Peter Veltman, dean of the College. He was assisted by Vice President Mitchell, other administrators, and numerous faculty members. By the end of the year all reports were completed and a 172-page document was dispatched to the association's central office in Chicago.

In April 1974 five educators from North Central Association institutions, comparable to Wheaton in size and academic programs, visited the campus for three days, observing the institution at work, interviewing administrators, faculty members, and students, and examining records. Early in August came word that the executive board of the Commission would recommend the continued accreditation of Wheaton for both its undergraduate and graduate programs. In April 1975, nearly two years after the accreditation preparations were begun, the North Central Association approved the recommendation of its executive board, assuring the College of accreditation for another ten years.

The report of the Commission sent to the College offered many commendatory judgments. It concluded that "Wheaton College is clearly a strong institution of quality." Cited as one source of strength was Wheaton's evangelical position: "The combination of constant vigilance against the erosion of evangelical faith and practice with intellectual stimulation is a major strength and distinctive mark of Wheaton." The College was praised as an institution of "unusual financial strength and vitality, where charges were moderate compared with other liberal arts colleges of quality." Administrators were described as "able, professional, knowledgeable, sensitive persons in whom the community had confidence."[6]

"Wheaton has a number of excellent faculty members," the report said further, "and more very good ones who offer good instruction and are deeply committed to the realization of the College's aims." "The graduate division seems to deserve its good reputation." "The Conservatory of Music is in a strong position." "Admissions are in a strong position because continuing selectivity for several years seems assured." Wheaton students were commended as "intelligent, interested, ready and able to talk about their education, their Christian commitment, their goals, themselves." Student services were declared to be outstanding. The dedication of the Alumni Association was impressive. Physical facilities were judged as "very good," except for urgent needs of the art department.[7]

The second part of the report asked a series of twenty-five questions which the observers felt should be answered by the College, not for the North Central Association, but for Wheaton itself. Among the questions were these: Given the financial stability of Wheaton, were the finances being "handled too cautiously"? Did the College have too large a budget for administration? Could the College "deal constructively with tensions and conflicts within the college community in a way consistent with its identity and convictions"? How does the doctrinal statement affect the recruitment and retention of faculty? Could Wheaton "afford not to have a sabbatical leave program"? Was the College aware that other institutions of comparable size and quality were "providing significantly more" computer facilities? In view of a depressed job market, was the College preparing too many teachers? Could Wheaton "increase the diversity of its student body without compromising its mission? Were women adequately represented within the administration and faculty of the College? Were the cultural achievements of minority groups in American life adequately presented? Was the College "allocating sufficient facilities and resources of the departments of art and drama" in view of the stated aims of the institution to enable the student "to appreciate beauty both in God's creation and in human literature and the arts"?[8]

Those were searching questions, providing an agenda for many of the departments of Wheaton for the remainder of the decade.

Title IX: Unrealized Fears

The enactment of Title IX of the Education Amendments Act in 1972 affected colleges and universities nationwide. President Armerding and the Board of Trustees, and their predecessors, had always been careful to avoid accepting federal grants for campus construction or subsidization of special research projects. The administration, however, saw no problem in Wheaton students accepting government loans for tuition, funds which the student borrowed from the National Direct Student Loan Fund and subsequently repaid to the fund.

But when Title IX was established, imposing standards on all educational institutions, public and private, there was some apprehension on campus that this regulation might lead to the imposition of federally supervised standards. Title IX declared that "no person on the basis of sex shall be excluded from participation in, be denied the benefits of, or be subjected to discrimination under any educational program or activity receiving federal financial assistance." The act, it was said, was not intended to institute practices inconsistent with the religious tenets of an educational institution. The regulations required an institution to complete a self-study before July 1976 and to modify programs and activities when that appeared appropriate.

President Armerding signed a letter of compliance in the fall of 1975, even though he and his advisors believed that some of the regulations went beyond the original act of enablement. In effect, Title IX required educational institutions to provide equal opportunities for men and women in every phase of an institution's program. What was quickly perceived by institutions throughout the country, small and large, as the area where inequality was most evident was in athletics: budgeted funds, playing fields, equipment, competitive teams. The new legislation was an encouragement to women's physical education at Wheaton and did strengthen some of the programs. New exercise equipment was purchased as a direct result. But a full program of competitive sports for women was well established before Title IX: tennis, volley ball, and field hockey in the fall; basketball, swimming, and gymnastics in the winter; softball and track and field hockey in the spring.

Another college program reevaluated under Title IX was the Reserve Officers Training Corps. Since no campus activity was to be discriminatory by reason of sex, the ROTC requirement would apply to women as well as men. Wheaton was hardly ready for such an adventure. Consequently, at the suggestion of Colonel Charles Wallis, then chairman of the department of military science, ROTC as a general requirement for men was dropped.[9] Thus Title IX accomplished what a faculty vote against required military science—an action rejected by the administration—failed to achieve. The faculty action was based on the long-felt conviction of a number of faculty members that compulsory military training on a Christian campus was inappropriate. The elimination of the ROTC requirement also defused the efforts of a group of students who for some time had carried on harassing tactics against compulsory military science. The fear initially expressed, that Title IX might force Wheaton into certain accommodations which in good conscience it could not make, has so far not been realized.

Another government edict which President Armerding had to accept, and which at the time seemed to be fraught with potential mischief, was the Family Educational Rights and Privacy Act of 1974. The legislation gave college students the right of access to their files and records, with the privilege of challenging their accuracy. Failure of institutions to comply subjected them to possible withholding of National Direct Student Loans and Supplementary Educational Opportunity Grants.[10] The act was initiated to allow students to contest statements in their confidential records that might be damaging to them in their present or future life or career.

Dean Henry Nelson announced that Wheaton would comply with the act and invited students to come to his office to discuss their records with counselors. He was prepared for a flood of requests for the right to examine confidential files, but to his astonishment very few students wished to see their records.[11] Thus far the Privacy Act has not affected the Wheaton program adversely, nor has it been an embarassment to anyone in the personnel services.

Demands for Accountability

Heard everywhere during the early Mitchell years was a new catchword, *accountability*. Businesses, churches, philanthropic organizations, colleges and universities—all began to scrutinize their operational practices with a new sense of responsibility toward those whom they served. At the 1973 meeting of the Association of American Colleges the theme was: "Autonomy, Authority, and Accountability." By 1974 nearly half of the states had passed legislation requiring accountability in education.

To the faculty at its 1975 fall workshop President Armerding said: "Higher education in general, and Wheaton in particular, is obliged to take into account a new emphasis in the field of education, that of accountability." Besides excellence in classroom performances, the president declared, accountability at Wheaton meant mature Christian discipling of students by their instructors. Teachers were to be exemplifications of "a full life that is the product of meaningful communion with the Lord and faithful obedience to his commandments under all circumstances."[12] Accountability meant, further, seeking the best interests of one's colleagues rather than self-enhancement. The college is also accountable to the society in which it lives, meeting its needs while at the same time declaring the values by which it lives. Finally, said President Armerding: "We must realize that God holds us accountable".

The appeal for accountability was not intended to deny the right to hold and express, within Wheaton's structure of values, divergent opinions, a privilege cherished and guarded by nearly everyone in academic life. Periodically the administration issued assurances, sometimes at faculty urging, of the College's allegiance to academic freedom and its resolution to preserve that right for the faculty. Without the right to pursue truth fearlessly in all of its ramifications, scholars are in bondage and their conclusions are often suspect.

Nor was the call for accountability intended to stifle intellectual curiosity or to restrain creative effort. Instructors were urged to be creative in their course design and teaching methods. Students sought to fashion creative worship services or creative campus activities. The effort to nurture and exercise the creative energies of students was immensely fruitful. They learned that creativity, pursued with integrity, can bring new vitality to every sphere of life.

An early opportunity to exercise financial accountability came in 1973 when Wheaton learned that it was to be one of the beneficiaries, together with Messiah College of Grantham, Pennsylvania, of a trust established by Leonard S. Fry, of Mercersburg, Pennsylvania. Fry was the owner and chief executive officer of the PBS Coal Companies in western Pennsylvania, Maryland, and West Virginia.

Fry had become interested in Wheaton College through his association with Frank Weller, College field representative in Pennsylvania. The friendship had begun when Weller served as Fry's pastor in Mercersburg and continued after Weller commenced his association with Wheaton. When Fry's coal holdings became exceptionally productive, Weller urged him to create a trust fund—though he made no suggestion about including Wheaton College—so that his resources would be used according to his wishes.

At the time he established his trust, Leonard Fry had not visited Wheaton nor had he met anyone associated with the College except Weller. He had seen Billy Graham on television and admired his achievements. Shortly after completing his plans for the ultimate disposition of his resources, Fry suggested to Weller that they and their wives drive out to Wheaton, which they did in June 1973. They met Dr. Armerding and other college officials, stayed as guests in Fischer Hall, made a tour of the campus, and were pleased with their experience.

Within less than a year after his visit to the campus Leonard Fry died of cancer at the age of fifty-seven. Complications arose from several provisions of his will, resulting in extended litigation before a settlement was agreed on in the court in Chambersburg, Pennsylvania, in August 1977. College Attorney and Vice President for Financial Affairs William Pollard made many trips to Pennsylvania to represent the college interests. Finally, Wheton and Messiah agreed to an arrangement by which each would receive trust assets worth $12.2 million as its share of the estate, the largest bequest either institution had ever received. For Wheaton the sum was nearly equal to its entire endowment fund.[13]

The Provident National Bank of Philadelphia became the trustee of Wheaton's share of the estate and will hold the principal for sixteen years. At the expiration of that time the principal will be released from the trust to be used at the discretion of the College trustees. Interest from the trust is being applied to meeting current budgetary needs. When investment yields, in the late seventies and early eighties, exceeded 10 percent, income from the Fry estate was well above $1 million a year. Students, hearing about the bequest, thought the tuition costs might be reduced, or at least restrained. But they were cautioned not to expect too much since the cost of all goods and services used by the College was rising steadily.

One of the outcomes of the concern for accountability was the reestablishment by Dr. Mitchell in 1975 of the Office of Institutional Research and Planning. Chosen to head the office was Richard Kriegbaum, who completed a Ph.D. at the State University of New York at Buffalo, and who, while there had worked on a cost analysis of services for the Christian College Consortium. Dr. Kriegbaum's office was a center for institutional research, planning, and evaluation of academic performance. This kind of on-campus service had been initiated in 1969 when Dr. Benjamin Sprunger was named director of learning resources. That appointment was intended to consolidate learning and data resources into a unified program. But institutional research had languished after Dr. Sprunger's departure to become president of Bluffton College in 1971.

An early effort of the Office of Institutional Research to improve faculty teaching performance and emphasize accountability was the initiation of a new teacher evaluation program known as the Purdue Cafeteria System. Both students and administration felt that the classroom effectiveness of some teachers could be improved. Under the Purdue plan the teacher chooses 35 evaluative statements out of a list of 200 by which he or she would like students to judge the quality of his or her teaching. Faculty members were urged to have students evaluate at least one of their courses each quarter and all of their courses at least once every three years. Some faculty members liked the system and thought it told them what they wanted to know about student perception of their course presentation. Others believed that the program was ineffectual and resisted its use; student evaluations often cancel one another out. The Purdue System was replaced in 1982 by an on-campus constructed evaluation instrument which proved to be superior.[15]

Distinguished Visitors

The annual Staley Distinguished Christian Scholar Lectures are supported by a fund set up in 1969 by Dr. and Mrs. Thomas F. Staley of Rye, New York. A stockbroker and Christian layman, Staley decided that one of the great needs of the day was to help strengthen small Christian colleges. Thus he established the lectureship that bears his name, designed to provide scholarly, evangelical speakers for religious emphasis programs in small Christian colleges.

Wheaton chose its Staley lecturers to represent a broad range of academic disciplines. They talked of the crises of western culture, the diminishment of the Christian frame of reference in contemporary America, the rise of secular humanism, the urgency of recovering Christian ethical norms. The first of these lecturers, in 1971, was Addison Leitch, professor of Old Testament studies at Gordon-Conwell Theological Seminary. The second was one of Wheaton's own distinguished graduates, Carl F. H. Henry, '38, then coming generally to be known as the dean of evangelical scholars in theology. Sometimes his extraordinary vocabulary puzzled students, but he was always challenging and exhilarating. He was then associated with Eastern Baptist Theological Seminary and was a former editor of *Christianity Today*. Other Staley lecturers included historian Stanford Reid of the University of Guelph, in Canada, in 1974, and scientist David Willis of Oregon State University in 1975. Literature professor Calvin Linton, George Washington University, spoke in 1977. Nicholas Wolterstorff, professor of philosophy at Calvin College, came in 1978.

Excited conversation was heard everywhere on campus on Wednesday afternoon, October 11, 1972, when Senator George McGovern, Democratic nominee for president of the United States, spoke in Edman Chapel. To prevent the occasion from being seen as a political rally, attendance was limited to students, faculty, staff, and a few invited guests. In an effort to avoid any show of partisanship, an announcement was made by the College that President Nixon had also been invited to speak at Wheaton, an opportunity he was unable to accept, though he sent a Republican representative. Though Senator McGovern's political views were shared by only a minority of students, he was given an attentive hearing as he spoke of his own Christian background. His talk was clearly Christian in tone as he related the message of the New Testament to political and social obligations.

"Some Christians believe we are condemned to live with man's inhumanity to man," said the Senator from South Dakota,"—with poverty, war, and injustice—and that we cannot end these evils because they are inevitable. But I have not found that view in the Bible. Changed men can change society, and the words of Scripture clearly assign to us the ministry and mission of change."[16] Challenging ideas were set before the students with conviction, with charitable fairness, with no evidence of hollow political clichés.

Few campus events have aroused as much intensity of student feeling as the coming of Senator Mark Hatfield—who had visited Wheaton on other occasions—to speak in chapel on February 15, 1974. President Armerding had a strong conviction that programs of a purely political nature should not replace a regularly scheduled worship service in Edman Chapel. Consequently, several days before Senator Hatfield's appearance, the president had announced that he had not been invited to speak in Edman Chapel; the meeting would be scheduled as a convocation in Pierce Chapel.

President Armerding's action was also, in part, prompted by Senator Hatfield's frequently expressed disapproval of American involvement in Viet Nam both before and during the war. The president was distressed also by Senator Hatfield's apparent support of the "Post Americans," a group of students at Trinity Evangelical Theological Seminary, some of whose attitudes Dr. Armerding characterized as "anti-war, anti-capitalist, anti-American."[17]

As Senator Hatfield, an honorary alumnus of Wheaton College, walked across the platform of Pierce Chapel, he was given a standing ovation. After a few opening remarks, and some witty small talk, he submitted himself for forty-five minutes to a wide range of student questions, reiterating his opposition to America's involvement in Viet Nam. Asked about Watergate, which had not yet come to its conclusion, the Senator from Oregon expressed reluctance to judge President Nixon until all the evidence was in. The student-faculty audience responded with warm applause to most of what was said. The *Record* editor summed up the full-page coverage of the event with the headline: "He Came; He Spoke; and We Were Conquered."[18]

President Ford Visits Wheaton

A notable moment in the history of Wheaton College occurred on March 12, 1976, when President Gerald R. Ford became the first President to visit the campus. He was brought to the College through the efforts of student government, which presented a petition to the White House bearing 1,721 names. On the day of the President's appearance some students began lining up in the chill air at 4:30 A.M., I.D. cards in hand, to assure themselves of a good seat. Once inside Edman Chapel, students settled themselves comfortably for the long wait. At 9:00 the Concert Band and the Men's Glee Club began a musical program. At 9:50, with the announcement, "Ladies and Gentlemen: The President of the United States," Gerald Ford commenced his walk down the blue-carpeted center aisle of Edman Chapel, escorted by Dr. Armerding, while the Concert Band, hardly audible above the unrestrained applause of the audience, played "Hail to the Chief."

Platform guests included Illinois senator Charles Percy, local congressman John Erlenborn, and Wheaton mayor Ralph Barger. Student government vice president Doug Beers offered the invocation, the Men's Glee Club sang "A Mighty Fortress is Our God," and Dr. Armerding spoke words of greeting: "We are a Christian community...and as such we pray for you daily, Mr. President."[19] Todd Gray, president of student government, introduced the President, who spoke for twelve minutes and answered eight questions.

Voicing strong support for private higher education and for volunteer private support of such institutions, President Ford said: "Wheaton College is a fine example of privately supported institutions that have made America great." In the question period he touched upon domestic and foreign affairs: relations with Rhodesia and China, social security, the C.I.A., Watergate. The President concluded by saying that the questions reflected a high quality of students and faculty. The following morning the *Chicago Tribune* said: "There was no sign of hostility as the students put the president under a 20-minute barrage of tough, incisive questions that shamed the professional reporters who question him daily."[20]

Following the questioning, students presented to their guest a plaque and an orange and blue Wheaton blanket inscribed with the president's name. They reminded him that by turning the blanket upside down the W at the center would become an M, representing Mr. Ford's Alma Mater, the University of Michigan.

A little more than a month later, Charles Colson made the first of several appearances at Wheaton College. Student government, working with Milton Richards, '69, of the Fellowship House ministry in Washington, was responsible for bringing Colson to the campus. The memory of his indictment and conviction for his part in the Watergate break-in was still fresh. For his participation in the illegal action he was found guilty of obstruction

President Gerald R. Ford visits Wheaton, March 12, 1976. L. to r.: Trustee Gunther Knoedler, Betty Knoedler, Professor Gerald Hawthorne, Professor Arthur Holmes, President Ford, Dr. Hudson T. Armerding.

Republican candidate Ronald Reagan arrives at Edman Chapel, October 1980.

of justice and served seven months in a federal prison. In his best-selling autobiography, *Born Again*, Colson had told of his transformation from an offender before the law to a man made new through the grace of God. His testimony was being widely heard and warmly welcomed in evangelical circles.

Colson told a near-capacity Edman convocation audience on April 28, 1976, that "I didn't change my life, God did." He urged students to become participants in the political processes in order to change the world for good. Students listened with extraordinary attention as they observed what God could do in the life of a man frequently referred to in the press as one of the toughest of the Watergate offenders.

Colson left the campus with a "Try God" button in his lapel and under his arm a C. S. Lewis anthology given him by Professor Clyde Kilby, who had edited the work. The volume was particularly appropriate since Colson acknowledged in *Born Again* that reading C. S. Lewis had had a significant part in his conversion to Christ and the transformation of his values.

In October 1980 Republican presidential candidate Ronald Reagan came to Wheaton College at the invitation of the campus Republicans. Edman Chapel was filled early in the afternoon by students and area residents eager to see and hear the former California governor. State and county political figures, including Governor James Thompson, filled the platform and spoke at some length when Reagan failed to appear at the scheduled time. A busy day of campaigning, which had begun in Youngstown, Ohio, delayed his arrival by one hour.

Candidate Reagan's address centered not on war or the proliferation of nuclear arms but on education. He praised Wheaton as a school with a mission. Reagan promised, if elected, to form a task force to analyze federal educational programs. He expressed support for tuition tax credits for parents sending children to non-public schools. At the conclusion of his address Reagan laughed heartily when he was presented with a stuffed mascot-sized replica of Perry Mastodon by Brad Bright, president of the campus Republicans. Obligated to hurry off to his next campaign stop, the visitor had no opportunity to tour the campus or chat informally with groups of students.

Human Needs and Global Resources Program

Reports of widespread famine in Asia, Africa, and South America were heard frequently by Americans in the mid-seventies. Daily the media reported droughts and crop failures.

Distressed about world hunger, in which half a billion people perpetually face starvation, Wheaton Professors Howard Claassen and Bee-Lan Wang in 1974 organized an ad hoc committee of faculty and students to design a Third World study/service program. Together with colleagues from many disciplines, they proposed the curriculum and fashioned the program's name, HNGR—Human Needs and Global Resources. A three-year trial program was approved by the College in 1976 and Dr. Wayne G. Bragg, '53 (G '57), a history and anthropology major at Wheaton, with a Ph.D. from the University of Texas and field experience in Latin America, was appointed director. He came to the College from his position as coordinator of technical and professional services at the Institute of Latin American Studies in Austin, Texas. Following the trial period, during which funds were received from grants and private sources, the program was established as a regular part of the curriculum under the social science division. In 1980, following an outside review, its financing became part of the college budget.

The aims of HNGR were to raise awareness on campus about world conditions; to involve students in programs designed to help other people and learn from them, particularly in the Third World; to provide cross-cultural educational experience for those who participate; and to help educational systems to adapt continually to the needs of global society. "Students are examining whether the standard way of using their future professions—making money and being successful—is really the only way,"[21] Professor Bragg said on one occasion.

To study Third World problems at first hand, the first four HNGR interns went overseas in 1977. In 1978 there were thirteen and in 1979 twenty. Most of the interns—who committed themselves for five to twelve months of service—have been from the social and physical sciences, a few from the humanities. Through the program students are thrust into the center of world concerns.

In 1979 Dr. Bragg developed the student government "Labor for Your Neighbor" project, which provided housing for victims of hurricane David in the Dominican Republic. Under the same project student voluteers went to work in refugee camps in Thailand. To build further on some of those efforts Professor Bragg prepared a three-year proposal for Jarabacoa, Dominican Republic. There a local committee and the Evangelical Association for Development helped in building a cannery, operating a school, directing a medical clinic, beginning a church, instituting a nutritional program, and assisting small businesses.

As students from a variety of majors became interns with HNGR, faculty members from various departments became interested in the internship programs and helped to plan them. Others revised courses or created new ones. Literature major Ken Grafham worked in Lahore, Pakistan, during the summer and fall of 1981. He drew up a production-cost analysis on handcrafted rugs, traveling from village to village outside the city. "By the end of six months," he said, "I really understood how a Christian living in a Muslim country feels."[22] Ken lived with a Pakistani pastor in a *busti*, a Christian neighborhood of some fifty families, surrounded by similar Muslim communities. "It's been the best thing about my college experience," he declared. "The program captures what Wheaton intended to give—a liberal arts education. It forces you to adjust, to act, to learn in a new situation and apply what you've learned in books."[23]

CHAPTER 18

The Graduate
School and the
Billy Graham Center

THE FIRST GRADUATE COURSES AT WHEATON COLLEGE WERE
announced in the 1936 *Summer School Bulletin* and the catalog number of
the *Bulletin of Wheaton College.* The program was principally intended for
teachers seeking a Master of Arts degree in liberal arts subjects, which was
then being urged by the North Central Association as a requirement for certification. The summer announcement stated additionally that "work leading to a Master of Arts in Christian Education will also be offered."[1]
Graduate courses in the liberal arts were soon phased out, however, at the
suggestion of the North Central Association. The accrediting agency contended that the College at that time lacked an adequate library and a faculty
prepared to offer graduate level study in so many fields.

The Wheaton College Graduate School had its beginning in 1937 when a
generous gift from the estate of John Dickey, Jr., a Philadelphia attorney,
was designated for the purpose of establishing and maintaining a "theological seminary training course at Wheaton College."[2] The bequest, given in
part to honor Dickey's father, was made on condition that the program be
initiated within six months.

The Board of Trustees acknowledged the gift with the following resolution: "In view of the bequest of the late John Dickey, Jr., of Philadelphia,
Pennsylvania, the Trustees of Wheaton College, Wheaton, Illinois, hereby
establish within the Theological Department of the college the John Dickey

Memorial Theological Training Course."[3] It also authorized the preparation of course work to meet the stipulations of the will.

Progress in the development of an advanced study program in theology, about which President Buswell had long been enthusiastic, was hampered by the fact that funds from the Dickey residuary estate did not become fully available until the 1960s, when the last designated heir died. (The bequest, together with accumulated interest, amounted to $337,000.) Nevertheless, the College decided to press on with the enlargement of its graduate offerings, then limited to a master's degree in Christian education. Supported by the tuition fees of a rather small group of students—plus moderate help from the general college budget—the graduate program was forced to operate frugally, sharing undergraduate faculty, classrooms, library, the resources of the college radio station WETN, the instructional media center, and recreational facilities. Things brightened considerably, however, when in 1945 the graduate program moved into its own building—soon to be named Buswell Hall in honor of Wheaton's third president—at the northeast corner of Franklin and Irving streets, vacated when Wheaton Academy moved to Prince Crossing in West Chicago.

The 1938 college catalog made the first general announcement of the John Dickey, Jr., Memorial Theological Seminary Training Course, directed by Dr. Henry Thiessen, chairman of the Bible department. Under the new program students could pursue a Bachelor of Theology degree or a Master of Arts in Theology. Eighteen courses were offered for students in quest of the new degrees. That year the first five students were enrolled in a two-year course leading to the M.A. in Theology.[4]

By 1946 the Bachelor of Theology course had become a three-year program leading to a bachelor of Divinity degree. The B.D. degree program was subsequently discontinued for want of enough students to justify the cost. Thirty-six courses were now offered in that division. There were thirty-nine full-time and twenty part-time students enrolled in graduate work, an encouraging growth from the handful of students listed in 1937.

Dr. Thiessen had come to Wheaton in 1935 from the Evangelical Theological College, later to become Dallas Theological Seminary. There he had been professor of New Testament and Greek. Nebraska-born, he had studied at Northwestern University, Northern Baptist Seminary, and Southern Baptist Seminary. He was author of *Introduction to the New Testament* and *Introductory Lectures in Systematic Theology*. Attracted by the climate of California for health reasons and the new work at Westmont College, he left Wheaton to teach there in 1946.

Successor to Dr. Thiessen was New England-born Merrill C. Tenney, educated at Gordon College and Harvard, who came to Wheaton from Gordon in 1943, where he had been professor of New Testament and New Testament Greek. Under his exceptionally able leadership the Master of Arts degree was expanded to include majors in Old Testament, New Testament, theology, church history, missions, and Christian education.

Dr. Tenney was a thorough scholar and genial administrator, who governed the Graduate School with a minimum exercise of authority. As dean he guided the school through a period of growth and rising academic prestige. His effective teaching, friendly counsel, and ready wit made him a popular teacher. An effective speaker, he was widely in demand throughout the country for Bible conferences, special occasions, and preaching services. A prolific writer, he was author of ten books and editor of four, including the five-volume *Zondervan Pictorial Encyclopedia of the Bible*, with the assistance of Dr. Steven Barabas. Of his many books, probably the best-known is *John: The Gospel of Belief*.

Dr. Tenney retired as dean of the Graduate School in 1971, but he continued as part-time teacher of his favorite courses until 1981. In his last administrative year 142 students were enrolled in five fields: pastoral studies, theological studies, historical studies, missions communications, and Christian education. The total number of courses offered, some of them given in two- and three-year sequences, was 127. The biblical studies major under Dr. Tenney's direction, and the Christian education major under the leadership of Drs. Mary and Lois LeBar, developed the scholarly reputation of the Graduate School. To mark his seventieth birthday in 1974 twenty-eight of Dr. Tenney's former students honored him with a *Festschrift, Current Issues in Biblical and Patristic Interpretations*, edited by Dr. Gerald Hawthorne, professor of Greek in the undergraduate college.

Graduate School Growth

A graduate degree program in communications, believed to be the first of its kind in a school of theology, was established in the Wheaton College Graduate School in 1968. Credited with providing the initial inspiration for the program were Dr. H. Wilbert Norton, '36, professor of missions and evangelism in the Graduate School, and James Johnson, executive secretary of Evangelical Literature Overseas, who became an instructor in the program. Advanced work in communications at Wheaton was intended for graduates of Christian colleges, students from other cultures, staff members of Christian organizations, and others desiring professional development.[5] Beginning with two graduates in 1970, the program achieved wide recognition and has attracted students from all parts of the world. The communications department combines behavioral science, theology, research, and practical techniques in the communication of biblical truth to the modern world in its diverse cultural settings. Internships give students radio and television experience in Chicago and some opportunities abroad, including summer study programs with executives of the British Broadcasting Company and Evangelical Broadcasters in The Netherlands, a program largely arranged by Myrna Grant.

An announcement by the Board of Trustees in the fall of 1973 that the work in communications would henceforth be known as the Billy Graham Graduate Program in Communications generated a good bit of publicity for

At the inauguration ceremonies for Dr. H. Wilbert Norton (left) as dean of the Graduate School. Retiring Dean Merrill C. Tenney (center) and President Armerding.

Honorary degree recipients at 1975 commencement: Trustees Richard Linyard and Ruth Graham. Center, *President Armerding.*

the Graduate School. Graham considered the action of the Board "a great personal honor." Dr. James Engel, who came to Wheaton in 1972 from Ohio State University, was made director of the program. However, when the Graham Center opened in 1980, the Graduate School, to avoid confusion, decided to stop using the designation "Billy Graham Graduate Program of Communications."

Succeeding Dr. Tenney as dean of the Graduate School was Dr. H. Wilbert Norton. After his graduation from Wheaton, he had secured degrees from Columbia Bible College and Northern Baptist Seminary, and served in the Congo from 1940 to 1949. He was president of Trinity College in Deerfield, Illinois, from 1957 to 1964, before coming to his alma mater in 1965. Almost at once, after becoming dean, Dr. Norton assisted in the effort to establish a relationship between Wheaton College and Daystar: International Institute of Christian Communication in Nairobi, Kenya, conceived to prepare academically qualified men and women to communicate effectively the message of Jesus Christ to the people of Africa and Asia.

In 1971 Wheaton agreed to give four hours of graduate credit and three years later, eight hours, for student internship at Daystar. By 1977 Wheaton agreed—with a Wheaton representative in residence each year—to grant an M.A. degree at Daystar, chiefly for the benefit of African students, pastors, and missionaries. Through the efforts of Dr. Peter Veltman, dean of the College, the program was included in Wheaton's accreditation by the North Central Association in 1979. The first graduate, in 1979, with a Wheaton M.A. earned at Daystar, was Emmanuel Twesigye, a Ugandan. He entered Vanderbilt University in the fall of that year to study for a Ph.D. degree.

In 1975 the Graduate School established a program at HCJB, Quito, Ecuador, through which personnel of that missionary radio station could earn an M.A. degree through extension work. Dr. Armerding thought that this program, and others like it in other areas, "could have world-wide implications."[6] Resident Wheaton faculty members held short-term courses for the staff who qualified throughout the stated period of the program. The Quito study plan went through only one cycle of four summers, ending when those who entered the study program completed it.

When the Graduate School marked its fortieth anniversary in 1977, two hundred of its more than 1,400 alumni had earned doctorates at leading universities. Many alumni were serving as presidents and deans of colleges and seminaries throughout the world. Others held positions on the faculties of those and similar institutions.[7]

During his years of service as dean, Dr. Norton saw both programs and student body grow, the program in psychological studies being introduced in his last year. At his retirement in 1980, there were 305 full-time students and 34 special students, many of them from abroad. Friends and colleagues of Dr. Norton remember his friendly manner, ready humor, devotion to the College, and steady allegiance to the Kingdom of God.

Coming to Wheaton from Bethel Seminary to succeed Dr. Norton as dean of the Graduate School in 1980 was Dr. Ronald Youngblood. He had a brief tenure of one year and was followed by Dr. James Plueddemann, who was named acting dean.

With the opening of the Graham Center in 1980, spacious quarters on the second floor became available to the Graduate School. It was a splendid improvement over the limited quarters on Franklin Street, its home for thirty-four years. Other departments in the Graduate School, besides communications, are educational ministries, theological studies, and psychological studies.

The Graduate School, from its beginning, has operated under the same Board of Trustees and administration as the undergraduate division of Wheaton College. The Tyndale Foundation graciously provided funding for the first five years until the graduate program came under the college budget. Faculty and students subscribe to the same doctrinal statement and standards of conduct as the rest of the campus. Since Wheaton College is interdenominational, the Graduate School, with a faculty representing several denominations, endeavors to present fairly the theology and practices of all Christian groups loyal to the revealed Word of God.

In 1980, after eight years of increasing enrollment, there were 315 students from 160 colleges and universities, 28 countries, and 29 denominations. Approximately 2,100 alumni are active as pastors, teachers, administrators, missionaries, psychologists, editors, broadcasters, and executives.[8] Because the Graduate School is accredited by the North Central Association of Secondary Schools and Colleges, students may apply to enter doctoral programs at major universities.

In 1977, at the suggestion of Vice President Donald Mitchell, and with the approval of the administration and Board of Trustees, the use of the designation "John Dickey, Jr., Memorial School of Theology" was terminated. The action was prompted by the awareness that confusion with the graduate program often arose from the fact that the undergraduate Bible department was designated in the catalog as "The Orlinda Childs Pierce Memorial School of Theology." The latter was named for the wife of a benefactor who wished to honor the memory of his wife, the same benefactor whose gift to the College in 1935 resulted in naming the then chapel building "The Orlinda Childs Pierce Memorial Chapel." Students graduating with a major in Bible or Christian education between 1938 and 1972 were given a certificate indicating that they were graduates of the Orlinda Childs Pierce Memorial School of Theology. In 1977 the simple designation "Wheaton College Graduate School" became official.

Late in 1983 a new arrangement for uniting graduate and undergraduate programs was developed. The graduate programs in biblical studies, educational ministries, counseling psychology, and communications were integrated with undergraduate biblical studies, Christian education, psychology, and communications. With this new alignment, the expectation is that more students who want graduate training in these four fields will remain at Wheaton for their master's degree. Further, the change will allow for the use of a single faculty and bring the graduate program more into line with university practice. From 1984 onward the M.A. Degree will be granted by Wheaton College rather than the Graduate School.

The Billy Graham Center

In January 1969 the Board of Trustees of Wheaton College unanimously adopted a resolution "that the Billy Graham Evangelistic Association be asked to consider making Wheaton College the repository for the Association records."[9] Later that same year Trustee Robert Van Kampen reported to the Board that Billy Graham was "willing to assist the college financially to enable it to become the repository for his papers and other materials...provided the College will agree to establish a chair of Evangelism with sufficient additions to the endowment to underwrite its costs."[10] The Board voted to send word to Trustee Graham of the willingness of the College to enter into such an agreement.

A few days later President Armerding initiated correspondence with Billy Graham expressing his pleasure with the Board action. "I am most gratified," he wrote on October 15, 1969, "for your interest in having your collection here at Wheaton and certainly concur in the thought that there should be a chair of Evangelism here at your alma mater." Three days later Graham wrote President Armerding from his home in Montreat, N.C., that it would "take at least a year to make a decision,"[11] whether or not to move his papers to Wheaton. If the materials were to come to Wheaton, he thought, "the old library would be the proper place to house them." Wheaton was at the time planning a new library.

To advance the prospect of the Graham collection being brought to Wheaton, President Armerding authorized the learning resources committee, of which Dr. Benjamin Sprunger was chairman, to prepare a study which would show how a new building housing the Graham collection would fit into the Wheaton academic program.

The study, awesomely called "Complex for the Study of Media: 20th and 21st Century Evangelism," was completed in May 1970. It proposed the development of a Fine Arts and Communications Complex for the Study of Evangelism, to be located in the block where Edman Chapel and the library stand. The vision of the planners was for the old library to become a center for art, music, drama, and literature. At the corner of Jefferson and Irving streets, facing east, the new library would be built. West of the library, and to the rear of Edman Chapel, the Graham Center would rise. The study, of course, was advanced in the early stages of negotiations, well before the Billy Graham Evangelistic Association's choice of a location.

Other cities—including Minneapolis and Charlotte, North Carolina, Graham's home city—vied with Wheaton for the privilege of having the Center located there. Advances were made also by the University of North Carolina, Baylor University, and Cornell University.

In January 1973 President Armerding sent to Billy Graham at his home in Montreat, North Carolina, a copy of the resolution adopted unanimously by the Wheaton College Board of Trustees inviting Graham to locate his archives and library on the campus. Bound with the president's letter and the resolution were letters from business, cultural, educational, and political leaders commending the College's strategic geographical location, the proximity of many colleges, seminaries, universities, mission boards, church-related associations, and cultural centers. Sent along also was a slide-tape presentation to make vivid all that the letters promised. Those persuasions, together with Graham's warm attachment to his alma mater, strongly influenced the Billy Graham Evangelistic Association in its decision to accept the invitation of Wheaton College.

The proposed Center was to be administered during the early planning and development stages by a joint committee consisting of five members from the Wheaton College Board of Trustees and five members of the Graham Board, with Allan Emery as chairman. Trustees P. Kenneth Gieser and Allan Emery were members of both boards and served as liaison between the two groups. In 1975 Articles of Incorporation and By-Laws of the Billy Graham Center were filed, and the Board of Directors of the Billy Graham Center elected, with representation from both the College and BGEA. Dr. Gieser was elected chairman of the board and remained in that capacity until the building was completed and officially given to the College at the time of its dedication.

Public announcement by the Billy Graham Evangelistic Association to locate the Center in Wheaton was made at Homecoming on October 11, 1974. Dr. Donald Hoke, '41, director of the International Congress on World Evangelization, held at Lausanne, Switzerland, in 1974, began work as project coordinator in December 1974, with authorization to draw up the proposed budget, supervise development of the museum and library which would house the Graham materials, and work with the architect in integrating design and educational functions. The building would also house the Graduate School and a proposed new International Institute of Evangelism.

Billy Graham became aware, by the spring of 1977, that there was some uneasiness in the community, and among a minority of the faculty, about so large a structure as the Center being built on the campus. The faculty concern was that the Billy Graham Center would overshadow the undergraduate program. They also felt that future donations might be directed to the Center's programs rather than to the undergraduate division of the College.

To ease Billy Graham's concerns, Vice President Donald Mitchell was sent to Montreat for an extended conversation with Billy on April 23, 1977.[12] The two agreed to send Leighton Ford, '52, Graham's associate, to the campus to explain the planned program to the campus community in a morning chapel. They further agreed to present the plans for the Center to the faculty in a multimedia exhibit, and to assure them that programs of the Center would be fully financed by the Graham Association. The conference between the two men resulted in significant clarifications and did much to allay uneasiness. In May 1977 President Armerding wrote to Allan Emery, declaring that it was a "heart-warming experience for me to hear you tell us at the Board meeting that the Graham Center will be coming to us 'free and clear' and will be ours to administer."[13]

A few days prior to the ground–breaking President Armerding observed that the Center would "allow Wheaton to participate in ministries on a world-wide scale." Graham Center Board Chairman Gieser noted at the same time that the Center would not overshadow the College. "It is wholly owned and controlled by the College," he explained. "Billy wants it that way. He wants it to be an on-going ministry, not a monument."[14]

During the early discussions of the planners, it seemed desirable to add to the library and archives of Billy Graham other elements to be housed in the Center. Why not install the Graduate School in the building? Why not include a dramatic representation of great episodes of Christian history, emphasizing the achievement of eminent spiritual leaders, including Billy Graham? Special programs of study in missions and preaching could have a proper place. Before long it became evident that the suggested location for the Center, to the rear of Edman Chapel, would be inadequate for the size building necessary to accommodate the enlarging concept of the Graham Center. Other sites were considered, and the Board finally agreed on the south side of Seminary Avenue as an appropriate location. The College agreed to clear the land and relocate the institutional service center, then in the middle of the block. But it was soon discovered that the ground was not firm enough for the planned five-story, 192,000-square-foot center.

To prepare an adequate foundation, more than 1,000 telephone-pole-sized pilings were driven deep into the ground and capped with concrete. The operation produced a great thumping clangor, shattering the academic quietude for several months. Cost of the unplanned operation, borne by the Graham Association, was $212,000. The cost of the building, furnishings, and maintenance endowment promised by the Billy Graham Evangelistic Association was first fixed at $21 million. A nationwide fund drive to raise that sum had been announced early in 1976, together with a statement that no construction would begin until $18 million had been pledged, $10 million for the building and $8 million for the maintenance endowment. Subsequently the total figure was reduced to $15.5 million. Even that was far above what the planners had originally supposed would be necessary; a sharp inflationary surge in the mid-seventies had escalated prices. The cost of relocating the service center, $785,000, to the east of the soccer field and behind Saint and Elliot Halls, was principally accepted by the Graham Association. The service center was named Chase Service Center in 1980, honoring Harold A. Chase, who served the College for thirty-four years as chemistry instructor, plant engineer, and superintendent of buildings and grounds.

During the planning for the Center, Billy Graham expressed the wish that his name not appear on the building until after his death. He thought "Wheaton Center for Missions and Evangelism" would be an appropriate name. Subsequently, however, he was persuaded that since funds had been widely solicited for the Billy Graham Center, and since any change of name might suggest a division within the ranks, the retention of the original name was desirable.

Groundbreaking for the Graham Center came on September 28, 1977. Dr. Graham, President Armerding, Board Chairman Delbert Nelson, and builder A. Harold Anderson each turned over a spadeful of earth as a symbolic indication that the building was underway. Among the honored guests were Mrs. W. F. Graham, Billy's mother, who turned over a bit of earth with the aid of her smiling son, and Billy's wife, Ruth. In his remarks for the occasion Dr. Graham again emphasized: "Our desire is not to build anything which could be interpreted as a monument; our desire is solely to glorify God."

Six months after the ground–breaking, and after examining the preliminary designs for the museum, a significant part of the Center, Billy Graham again expressed the fear that it might too greatly glorify him. At a meeting at the O'Hare Hilton Inn, Chicago, April 24, 1978, Graham declared that he wanted the museum to be "something students would respect. . . . It must be dignified and not have a so-called 'Disneyland' character." Present at the meeting besides Graham and President Armerding, were Wheaton Trustees Delburt Nelson, Allan Emery, Kenneth Hansen, Kenneth Gieser, and Graham representatives T. W. Wilson and Cliff Barrows.[15]

Prior to that meeting, executive director of the Billy Graham Center, Dr. Donald Hoke, had resigned his position, and Dr. David Johnston, vice president for finance, was named acting director. The following year Dr. William A. Shoemaker, '52, who had served for seven years as vice president for research at the Council for the Advancement of Small Colleges, Washington, D.C., became director of the Center. In 1980 Dr. Melvin E. Lorentzen, long-time member of the English department of the College, was appointed assistant director of the Center and, the following year, associate director.

Graham Center Completed

For the Billy Graham Center cornerstone-laying ceremony several hundred friends of Wheaton College and the Billy Graham Evangelistic Association gathered on the Saturday morning of Homecoming, October 13, 1979. Unseasonable cold and a driving wind forced brevity on all the participants. On the stone is a simple inscription:

Billy Graham Center
For Christ and His Kingdom
October 1979

Following the ceremony the gathering moved slowly up the hill toward

Blanchard Hall. There they could see the Center in perspective, noting that the exterior of the splendid building was nearly finished. Only the great white columns at the middle of the structure needed to be erected and the cupola raised. Days later many observers watched in awe as the cupola, in several sections, was raised to the roof by helicopter and finally attached.

In the fall of 1980 the handsome, modified colonial-style building—said to be the largest of its type in America—was ready. For the dedication ceremony some 4,000 people were seated in a special section for visitors or on the lawn across the street from the Center. It was a lovely fall day, with the leaves just beginning to turn amber and red. Bright sunlight framed the building against the sky as Dr. Graham spoke. "We hope and pray," he said, "that this Center will be a hub of inspiration, research, and training which will glorify Christ and serve every church and organization in preaching and teaching the Gospel to the world... This Center is being dedicated this day to the glory of God and the advancement of the Kingdom of Jesus Christ."

The principal address of the day was given by Dr. Charles Malik of Lebanon, former president of the United Nations General Assembly and the Security Council, who spoke on "The Two Tasks." An eloquent man, with a strong, resonant voice, he stirred his hearers with a vigorous plea for intellectual excellence in Christian higher education. "What could be more wonderful than for evangelicals to aim at achieving under God and according to God's own pace the two-fold miracle of evangelizing the great universities and intellectualizing the great evangelical movement? These two things are absolutely impossible; and yet at the same time because they are absolutely needed God can make them absolutely possible."[16] "What I crave to see," he added, "is an institution that will produce as many Nobel Prize winners as saints."[17]

A Saturday evening sacred concert, attended by 8,000 people, brought together Graham team song leader Cliff Barrows and soloists George Beverly Shea, Myrna White, and Ken Medema. Jeanette Clift George offered a dramatic portrayal of hymn writer Fanny Crosby, whose memorabilia are among the Center's archives collection. Filling the brightly lighted portico of the Center were a community chorus and orchestra directed by John Wilson, with Billy Graham team accompanists Tedd Smith and John Innes.

Dr. Graham's Sunday evening evangelistic message was on "The University of Life." Some 12,000 people braved a chill rain to hear the words of the man who had presented the claims of Christ to more people around the world than any other person in history. There were 300 responses to the invitation.

The Graham Center was now ready to fulfill the functions for which it had been conceived—all bearing witness to the Light. That witness is expressed through the museum on the first floor of the Center, the Graduate School on the second floor, the library on the third floor, and archives on the fourth floor. A number of special continuing education programs in evangelism, missions, and Christian ministries are directed from the admin-

Participants in the Graham Center dedication. L. to r.: Charles Malik, George Beverly Shea, Billy Graham, Alan Emery, trustee.

Dedication of the Billy Graham Center, September 13, 1980.

istrative offices on the fourth floor. The fifth floor remains temporarily unfinished.

In the east wing of the building is a small auditorium seating 500. It was named the Barrows Auditorium, honoring the director of music for the Billy Graham team since 1945, at a ceremony on the weekend of President J. Richard Chase's inauguration in September 1982. In the west wing of the Center is a matching structure, the interior of which was completed in 1983 through funds from a Kresage annuity contract. Described as the Campus Visitor's Center, it houses the advancement office, which includes development, planned giving, marketing/college relations, and admissions.

For the visitor to the Graham Center a walk through the museum is an impressive experience. At its center, the Rotunda of Witnesses announces the purpose of the exhibits: to celebrate the person and work of Jesus Christ. A series of nine hand-crafted sixteen-foot tapestries invites the beholder to reflect on the 2,000 years of Christian witness and experience. Among the nine figures portrayed on the tapestries, with quotations from their writings, are the Apostle Paul, St. Francis of Assisi, Luther, Pascal, and Wycliffe. Like all the quotations on the tapestries in the entrance hall, the words of Pascal are cause for reflection: "Not only do we know God through Jesus Christ; we only know ourselves through Jesus Christ."

Beyond the Rotunda in the general exhibit area are pictures, artifacts, and life-size figures of Christian leaders—with audio commentaries, together with impressively mounted quotations—all bringing alive the imperishable message of the gospel from the times of the early American heroes of the faith to the present varied ministries of the Graham Association. A small film theater reviews a Graham crusade. A section representing the blackness of the tomb and the radiance of the resurrection forms a stirring climax to the museum tour.

When Dr. Richard C. Halverson, '39, chaplain of the United States Senate, visited the museum, he said: "My first reaction was excitement—then joy—then awe—then tears—then ecstasy. It was as if I was being drawn to central, essential, primary issues."

Nearby a chapel with a central cross provides an opportunity for prayer, reflection, and thanksgiving. The white walls on the "Walk Through the Gospel" include inscriptions from the Bible. The museum ideas were developed by Museum Director James Stambaugh and a number of counselors. Builder of the museum was General Exhibits and Displays of Chicago.

Approximately 60,000 books, together with microfilm and other data sources, are housed in the Center library. In this collection the emphasis is on materials for research in evangelism, missions, and revival. An intensive effort was made by Richard Owen Roberts, first director of the library, to bring together distinguished works on missions and evangalism. His successor, Ferne Weimer, director of the library since 1976, has continued the effort to assemble a quality library.

The archives of the Graham Center are a special instructive resource for missionaries, pastors, leaders of Christian organizations, and researchers. Here are diaries, correspondence, official records, scrapbooks, photographs, films, tapes, and video cassettes, recording interdenominational Protestant evangelism and missions in America from Wesley to Graham, with distinctive strength in twentieth-century collections.

The Billy Graham materials, covering the range of his ministry, are the nucleus of this extraordinary resource, which exceeds 300 distinct collections. Also to be found in the archives are the records of Chicago businessman Herbert J. Taylor, one of those who helped to found Youth for Christ, the National Association of Evangelicals, Fuller Seminary, and other Christian agencies, through the Christian Workers Foundation. Here, too, are the papers of the Africa Inland Mission, Youth for Christ, Mission Aviation Fellowship, the China Inland Mission, and the papers and records of Billy Sunday.

In June 1984 Charles Colson, founder and president of Prison Fellowship, gave the papers of this organization to the Graham Center archives. Included in the gift were Colson's "presidential papers," which the College agreed to seal until after former President Nixon's death.

The collection, storage, and preservation of these documents is under the direction of Archives Director Robert Shuster, '73. The ultimate plan is to collect and organize information relating to all evangelical mission agencies for use by scholars and researchers.

From the beginning the vision of Billy Graham and the planners was that the Center would develop programs, periodic and ongoing, to help church leaders and church agencies in their task of evangelizing the world. Representative programs are the Institute for the Study of American Evangelicals, presently funded by a grant from the Lilly Endowment, and the Institute of Chinese Studies. The ISAE is under the direction of Professor Mark Noll, '68, of Wheaton, and Professor Nathan Hatch, '68, of Notre Dame University. It has already sponsored significant symposia and conferences.

With the training of international leadership for Christian service as one of its primary goals, the Center from its first year had a continual program of financial aid to international students accepted into Wheaton graduate programs and committed to return to full-time Christian service in their homelands. Originally funded from budget, in 1978 that ceased, and the first two scholarships were endowed—one named for the Armerdings and the other for the Hokes. The BGC scholarship program is now comprised of several distinct funds providing assistance to an ever-increasing number of graduate students—not only internationals, but also furloughing missionaries and pre-field missionary candidates.

"Through the programs that have been planned," Billy Graham said at the dedication of the building, "and others which will be developed in the future, this Center could be the keen cutting edge of a new thrust in Christian strategy and education in the fields of theology, Christian psychology, communications—all dedicated to the advancement of the Kingdom of

God." The chair of evangelism, referred to in the early overtures to Graham, waiting for adequate funding has yet to be established.

The governance of the Center since the dedication of the building in September 1980 has been under the direction of the Graham Center committee of the Board of Trustees of Wheaton College. When Dr. Shoemaker resigned in 1982 as director, Dr. David Johnston again accepted the interim role of senior administrative officer. In July 1984 Dr. James Kraakevik, who had been a member of the physics department for seventeen years and had missions administrative experience, became director of the Center.

Students question leaders of Christian Service Outreach's thirty-eight ministries before signing up.

Kevin Murphy makes new friends working in Indonesia with the Student Missionary Project, 1978.

CHAPTER 19

Students in
the Seventies

THE 1970S, A DECADE OF STRIKING CULTURAL CHANGES, posed severe challenges to Christian moral and ethical values. During the Christmas season of 1972 the United States pounded the North Vietnamese with the heaviest bombardment in history, an attack that hastened a national resolve to terminate the unpopular war. In the summer of the same year the Watergate break-in and subsequent cover-up efforts initiated a series of embarrassing revelations that were to result in the resignation of President Nixon in disgrace in 1974. A mid-decade recession was exacerbated by excessive inflation, and the Arab oil embargo sent U. S. companies scrambling to find domestic reserves, while buoyant entrepreneurs held their peace and announced a new age of solar power.

Astronomers were confident that black holes were a reality, not merely an airy cosmological theory. Gay liberationists boldly identified themselves, demanding political rights and social acceptance. Russian author Alexsandr Solzhenitsyn was exiled and took up American residence. Transcendental Meditation became popular. Women pressed for, and achieved, new rights on many fronts, but the ERA provoked a conservative backlash. In 1978 a nuclear accident at Three Mile Island, Pennsylvania, intensified the antinuclear movement. The stockpiling of nuclear weapons raised new moral imperatives. As the decade was ending, it approached the threshold of a revolution: the computerization of America.

That was the atmosphere of the 1970s—an ominous era, much of it fraught with peril. What was happening at home and abroad influenced significantly the lifestyle and attitudes of Wheaton College students—the books they read, the music they heard, the lectures and films they attended, the courses they elected, their classroom discussions, the careers they planned. They searched for the ways of wisdom in a Christian context and brought with them a cluster of values and convictions that gave anchorage to their lives. With them, too, came the shining radiance of youth, always hopeful, always confident that their energies could be used to usher in a better order.

How did these youth get to Wheaton? Where did they come from? What talents and what promise did they bring with them? Why had they come to Wheaton? Most of the new arrivals on campus in the seventies came, as they had for generations, through the influence of parents, pastors, alumni, or friends already at Wheaton. However, a much more vigorous recruiting program was now a strong factor in influencing many other students to make Wheaton their choice. In 1975, according to the carefully kept figures of Registrar George Cramer, who served the College from 1969 to 1978, and Associate Registrar Vivian Barnett, who came to campus in 1949, Wheaton sent representatives to twenty-five high school college nights, set up ten church college days on campus, and visited thirty-five selected high schools. They were also present at youth conferences, camps, and Sunday school conventions.[1] Publications describing the opportunities at Wheaton, friendly letters, phone calls, visits by alumni or field representatives, invitations to visit the campus—all were part of the effort to encourage promising students to select Wheaton. One-third of the class who came to Wheaton in 1976 did so as a result of recruitment efforts.

A young person arriving on campus from rural Arkansas or a mountain town in Montana would meet students from New England, the deep South, the Southwest, California, and many foreign countries. But from the moment of their arrival and signing in at the big tent in the center of the campus to begin their orientation, these newcomers were accepting membership in a community in which young people of diverse heritage and resources would be daily companions. Some students would be surprised to discover how many different kinds of evangelicals there are.

The geographical diversity of Wheaton students has often intrigued observers. Forty-five or more states are customarily represented in the student body, but the class of 1975, in its freshman year, was the first to have a representation from all fifty states.[2] States with the largest representations during the seventies, after Illinois, continued to be Pennsylvania, Michigan, New Jersey, New York, and Ohio. A high percentage of these students come from a constituency cultivated and built up by the College over the years.

Of the students who come to Wheaton, how many remain to graduate? The "retention rate," always regarded by colleges as a sign of institutional health, has been exceptional at Wheaton, well above the national average.

In 1970, part of the era of widespread campus unrest, the retention rate was 62 percent. The Wheaton record was established by the class of 1977, which at graduation had retained 74 percent of its original membership.[3] To evaluators of all kinds those figures witness eloquently to the fact that Wheaton was meeting student needs and expectations. They wanted to stay.

Commonly about 80 percent of an entering class at Wheaton are in the upper 20 percent of their graduating class. A number are valedictorians. In 1980 Wheaton enrolled thirty-five National Merit Scholarship winners, placing the college sixty-fourth among 699 colleges and universities with Merit Scholars in attendance. Wheaton was fourth among the twenty-nine Illinois colleges. There were fifty Merit Scholars the preceding year. Approximately half of those who graduate from Wheaton will continue their education in professional or graduate schools and seminaries. A number will strive for and be awarded the Ph.D. degree. In the number of its graduates who have completed a Ph.D. program Wheaton has a remarkable record. Between 1920 and 1980 a total of 1,047 alumni have pursued a doctorate to its completion.

Among 943 four-year, private undergraduate institutions Wheaton stands twelfth in this one measure of quality. At the head of the list in 1980 were Oberlin, Swarthmore, and Amherst colleges. Immediately following Wheaton are Williams, Manhattan, and Vassar colleges.[4] Among small colleges in Illinois whose graduates have completed the Ph.D. Wheaton ranks first. When all of the universities in Illinois are added to the list, Wheaton stands seventh.

Such achievements, helped to create judgments such as those in *Selective Guide to Colleges, 1982-83*, compiled by Edward B. Fiske, education editor of the *New York Times*. The book lists "26 of the best and most interesting four-year institutions in the country." Fiske notes that in spite of Wheaton's familiar list of prohibitions—which journalists can rarely resist listing— "Wheaton draws enough National Merit Scholars to put it on a par with the best colleges of its size." "Calvin College," the book declares, "ranks with Wheaton as the best academically of the country's evangelical colleges." Some students, after a week of hectic activity on campus, were a bit amused at the author's characterization of campus social life as "bleak."

Professional Preparation

In almost any year students arriving on campus with the intention of majoring in science are more interested in medicine than in any other profession. Between 1940 and 1980 nearly 900 Wheatonites, an average of twenty-two a year, entered medical or dental school.[5] Across the country and on the mission field around the world physicians who are Wheaton graduates are to be found, many of them in pioneering work.

In the early seventies the number of students seeking admission to medical school nationwide increased dramatically—40,000 applicants for about

14,000 openings. At the same time the number of Wheaton students gaining admission to medical school began briefly to decline. To help provide them with first-rate preparation in their quest for admission to medical school, Dr. Anthony Diekema, associate dean of the Univesity of Illinois College of Medicine, now president of Calvin College, was invited to campus in 1972 to make recommendations. Biology professor Cyril Luckman and chemistry professor Stanley Parmerter were leaders in the effort on campus to improve pre-medical preparation. Diekema's recommendations greatly strengthened the procedures by which students are prepared for the highly competitive national MCAT examination, necessary for admission to medical school. By the end of the decade about twenty-five students annually were being accepted for medical training. For the class of 1981 more than 90 percent of those who sought admission to graduate schools in the health professions for training in medicine, dentistry, nursing, medical technology, and other health care professions were admitted. In 1982 slightly above 92 percent of applicants were accepted.

Early in the 1980s the cooperative nurses' training program with West Suburban Hospital ended and a new plan was initiated. Wheaton entered into an arrangement with five schools of nursing by which a student may take three years of academic work on campus and additional training at one of the participating institutions. Under the arrangement, supervised by Professors Sara Miles and Albert Smith, a student may receive both an academic degree and an R.N. The cooperating schools of nursing are at Northwestern, Rochester, and Emory universities, Rush-Presbyterian-St. Luke's Hospital, and Goshen College.

Many students came to Wheaton in the seventies resolved to prepare for a career in Christian service, just as earlier generations of Wheatonites had. Some of them found their way overseas in the world mission of the church as evangelists, Christian educators, administrators, health service personnel, Bible translators. The honor roll outside the president's office—an impressive witness to Wheaton's contribution to world missions—lists 230 students, 73 of them graduate students, who went abroad between 1970 and 1980. Other students would remain in the homeland in pastorates, Christian education, youth work, campus ministries, health services, and in other labors for the cause of Christ and the service of the church.

Most of these Christian workers, as undergraduates, gained preparation through the outreach opportunities provided by the Christian Service Council. At the beginning of each year, usually after a chapel service, representatives of the more than thirty ministries assemble outside the Stupe ready to register students for a year of Christian service in an area of their special concern. These volunteers are from the student body at large, not only those who are committed to traditional careers of Christian service.

In early September 1982, over 800 students registered their readiness to serve in one of the Council's ministries. Dennis Massaro, '75, director of the Office of Christian Outreach since 1979, stated: "New ministries are beginning because of the great response, and our students are reaching out into numerous areas because they care. Caring fosters more caring."[6]

In 1976, when Lyle Schrag, '73, became director of the Christian Service Council—an office previously held by Bill Lindberg, '62, and Pat Milligan, G '75—the name of the office was changed to Office of Christian Outreach. The OCO became the umbrella for five campus ministries: Christian Service Council, Student Missionary Project, Youth Hostel Ministries, World Christian Fellowship, and Missions in Focus. Under the Christian Service Council's supervision students go to Chicago to tutor, minister at Cook County Jail, carry on a street witness, and work with such organizations as Young Life, Campus Life, and Navigators.

The history of missionary organizations on the campus goes back to the earliest days of the College. The Student Volunteer Band dated from before the turn of the century through the 1920s. In the 1930s a national student organization, Student Foreign Missions, was initiated, with the Wheaton branch known as Foreign Missions Fellowship. In the 1960s FMF became Student Mission Fellowship and briefly in 1975 the name William Carey Fellowship was adopted, before World Christian Fellowship came into use. This large group meets weekly to pray for missions around the world.

Youth Hostel Ministries and Student Missionary Project attract about twenty and thirty-five students each, annually. Budgets run from about $25,000 for Youth Hostel to about $40,000 for SMP. Through solicitation, concerts, and work projects students raise all the money themselves. Volunteers for these overseas assignments, whose expenses are paid from the fundraising budgets, attend cultural briefing sessions during the spring. Since the first SMP project in 1958, when twelve students went to Central America, over 600 Wheatonites have journeyed to eighty-five countries. Their assignments could range from testing for parasites to rebuilding damaged homes. For all of these ventures in the Lord's service the cooperation of many mission boards has been necessary.[7]

World Christian Fellowship sponsors Missions in Focus, held annually in the spring to explain missions opportunities, and brings to campus a veteran missionary as speaker for three days. Other missionaries and their families, as many as twenty or twenty-five, are also in attendance. Panel discussions, films, and conversations with missionaries provide clear impressions of mission life. Realistic assessment of some of the perils modern missionaries may face was suggested by a panel topic at Missions in Focus '82—"The Gospel at Gunpoint." Three missionaries spoke for ten minutes each on "Kidnapping and Abduction Policies," "Missionary Roles in Militaristic States," and "How to Penetrate Hostile Nations."[8]

During the 1970s the number of lawyers in America grew enormously. The proliferation of new laws, the growth of government social agencies, the activities of environmental groups, church-state conflicts, the ease with which private citizens could initiate litigation, all created need for legal services.

In the years immediately following World War II the law appeared to have little appeal for Wheaton students; they had not seen it as an opportunity for Christian service. But through counseling and faculty encouragement, as well as the helpfulness of Wheaton alumni already established in the legal profession, increasing numbers of students began to select law for their professional career.

Professor S. Richey Kamm, chairman of the political science department, was especially encouraging to prospective law students. A number of students were also encouraged to begin the study of law by Professor William Volkman, who taught business and economics from 1958 to 1964, and by college attorney and Vice President for Finance William Pollard, '60. Following Professor Kamm's death, the Kamm Memorial Symposium in Law and Society was established through the gifts of his family, colleagues, alumni, and friends. These annual symposiums—the first of which was held on May 1, "Law Day," and May 2, 1975—have helped students catch a vision of opportunities for service in the legal profession.

Pre-law students, like pre-medical students, were advised by a faculty committee, mostly on curriculum matters and preparation for the Law Students Aptitude Test. Professors Arne Howard and Mark Amstutz served as chairmen of the committee until the arrival of Carl Horn in 1979 as the college attorney. Horn took an earnest interest in the aspiring young attorneys on campus, organizing the Pre-law Society as a group for sharing mutual interests. When Horn left the College in 1982 for a position in the United States Justice Department, over 100 students were in the Pre-law Society.

Of Wheaton's academic departments whose graduates earn the Ph.D. degree, psychology is among the leaders. Through the direction of Professor Charles Henry, who came to Wheaton in 1971 following Professor Onas Scandrette as chairman of the department after the latter's retirement, the psychology department continued to grow in prestige and in the number of majors. In 1979-80 fifty-five freshmen declared their intention to major in psychology, most of whom centered their interest in clinical psychology. In 1979-80 six graduates completed Ph.D. degrees, placing Wheaton in that year tenth among colleges nationally in the total number of its graduates earning the advanced degree in psychology.[9]

The philosophy department, headed for many years by Professor Arthur Holmes, has long been held in high esteem by students, alumni, and the campus community. Other Christian colleges commonly look to Wheaton for leadership in this field. Twenty-five Wheatonites completed Ph.D. degrees in philosophy between 1960 and 1976. Some have established scholarly reputations as professors in other colleges and universities. Among these are John Fisher, '47, Temple University; Jasper Hopkins, '58, University of Minnesota; Stanley Anderson, '59, Bethel College, St. Paul; Stanley Obitts, '55, Westmont; Merold Westphal, '62, Hope College; Michael Detlefsen, '71, University of Minnesota at Duluth. Two have become college presidents: George Brushaber, '59, Bethel College, St. Paul; and William Hausman, '63, North Park College.

The literature department also numbers many Ph.D.s among its graduates. Since 1975 Professor Beatrice Batson, who was named Teacher of the year in 1962, has given strong leadership to this department and established high standards of scholarship. She has brought to campus distinguished lecturers, and with her colleagues has made the annual Writer's Conference an important contribution to campus intellectual life. She has inspired many students to cherish the values of the humanities and to give themselves to advanced study in literature. Since the Ph.D. in literature is usually a teaching degree, most of these graduates continue in academic life. Among these are Thomas Howard, '57, Gordon College; Robert Siegel, '61, University of Wisconsin at Milwaukee; Jeanne Murray Walker, '66, University of Delaware; David Jeffrey, '65, University of Ottawa, Canada; Edwin Craun, '67, Washington and Lee University; and Peter Hawkins, '67, Yale Divinity School.

In 1982 the departments of Bible, psychology, literature, and economics had the highest number of majors in the College. Economics grew steadily during the seventies to its position of strength at the end of the decade. In the late sixties economics lagged in student esteem on American campuses generally. When students became newly interested in income security, they grew more aware of the variables and complexities of economics. They discovered new opportunities in this field.

Professor James Halteman has seen his economics faculty grow from three to five members, has added diversity to department offerings, and has worked out an arrangement under which a student may concentrate on business or economics. Many of the students participated, with others majoring in political science and psychology, in the summer International Study Program, based in The Netherlands. Here in academic work and field travel in western Europe they have opportunities to meet academic, government, and business leaders. In 1983 the political science and economics departments, under the direction of Professors Mark Amstutz, Richard Rung, and James Halteman sponsored an international study group which traveled in western and eastern Europe, including an eight-day trip to Leningrad and Moscow. It was the first Wheaton trip into Soviet Russia. Students were able to talk with soldiers, several officials, and some private citizens in their homes. In these brief glimpses of Russian life, they sensed an environment of oppression. "It does us no good to ask, 'why?' because Soviet lifestyle will not change," one man said to student Richard Crotteau.

In 1980 the George F. Bennett Endowed Chair in Economics was established. The chair honors a leader in the Boston financial community, who among his many responsibilities and board memberships, served as treasurer of Harvard University for eight years. A devoted friend of Wheaton, George F. Bennett has been a member of the Board of Trustees since 1960. Under the terms of the endowment statement, the chair in economics is to be filled by an economist who supports and expounds the tenets of free enterprise and the integration of Christian faith and learning.

The idea of the academic chair had its origin in the fifteenth century, when a distinguished professor was granted a life sponsorship by his monarch or bishop. He was given an actual chair from which he taught while his students listened. In America the first endowed chairs were established at Harvard in the 18th century. The first holder of the George F. Bennett Endowed Chair in Economics is Professor Douglas Aide, who came to Wheaton from Ohio University in 1982.

All Wheaton students in these days, entering a variety of careers, were beneficiaries of a liberal arts education with its emphasis on both general education and specialization. At the close of World War II, a strong emphasis on specialization was restrained by appeals, such as the Harvard report, for preservation of the intellectual and spiritual heritage of the West that was falling victim of the free elective principle and too early specialization.

Like other institutions, Wheaton through faculty committees has periodically studied its program in general education and its general education requirements for graduation. As cultural changes modify the value and need for certain academic disciplines, for greater or lesser emphasis, modification in the general education requirements may be made, though there is never any desire merely to respond to contemporary values. In 1983 general education course work was required of all students: Bible, 14 hours; literature, 6 hours; philosophy, 4 hours; art, 2 hours; music, 2 hours; natural science, 8 hours; history, 6 hours; social science, 8 hours; physical education, 4 hours. Students must also demonstrate competence, either by examination or course work, in writing, speech, mathematics, foreign language, and ultimately computer science. International summer study programs will continue to be recommended as options, such as those that take students to East Asia, Europe, and South America. It is hoped that these experiences will cultivate active minds, a lifetime devotion to learning, breadth of understanding, and allegiance to elevated aesthetic and moral standards.

Art Department

Instruction in art was offered in the early years of the College as "drawing and painting." But it was not until 1936 that the art department was organized by DeWitt Jayne, '36. In 1947 one course in art or music appreciation became a part of the general education requirement. Subsequently, one course in art and one in music were to be a part of the student's experience, since it was felt that all students should be encouraged to enjoy great painting and music as an important element in their liberal education. Any effort to curtail or eliminate parts of these programs sends many students rushing to the ramparts to cry alarm, while others share their anguish in the columns of the *Record*.

The habitation of the art department has been rather like that of an itinerant painter, finding shelter wherever a host chooses to lodge him. For varying periods of time the department was housed in Pierce Chapel; Plumb Studio, a small house, demolished to make room for the Buswell Library;

the first floor west end of Blanchard Hall; and now Adams Hall, a sturdily built brick structure, completed in 1899 as the college gymnasium. Thoroughly renovated in 1982 to create attractive studios, exhibit space, and offices, the building seems to have provided a respectable and functional home for the art department. In a ceremony on January 27, 1983, the former women's gymnasium building was named Adams Hall in honor of John Quincy Adams, a local citizen and a chief benefactor when the gymnasium was erected.

For many years the art courses at Wheaton were taught by Professor DeWitt Jayne, Karl Steele, and Miriam Hunter, with occasional part-time assistants. For them, as for their later associates, all art was potentially a creative act of praise and celebration. At its best it is an offering from a talent given by God for his glory. Both Steele and Hunter were rather strongly committed to a representational philosophy of art, though Karl Steele, widely known for his chalk artistry, experimented with abstract metal sculpture and glass in a small shop he built in the basement of the west end of Blanchard Hall. With his artist's discernment, Professor Steele made many valuable contributions to campus planning.

Professor Alva Steffler, with principal interests in sculpture and graphic design, came to the chairmanship of the department in 1970. Feeling strongly a need for diversification, he encouraged students to work in modern forms. Professor Joel Sheesley, who shared Steffler's convictions, joined the art faculty in 1974 to teach painting, printmaking, and art survey. Steffler's ideas of what was appropriate for studio work and public exhibition sometimes brought him into disagreement with some of his associates, as well as with President Armerding. Consequently, a temporary adjustment of leadership was made and Professor Harold Best of the Conservatory and Professor William Henning, who was named Dean of Arts and Sciences in 1980, served in successive years as acting directors of the art department.

For a time the number of students majoring in art diminished. The college administration in the spring of 1982 seriously considered dropping the art major. The faculty, however, drafted a letter favoring the continuance of the major, students wrote letters to the president, and the editor of the *Record* protested the contemplated action.

Later that spring, the College interviewed and employed Dr. John Walford as chairman of the art department after bringing him to Wheaton from his home in England. The administration dropped plans for terminating the major and trustees authorized the renovation work that during the summer and early fall produced the present studios in Adams Hall. Professor Walford, an art historian trained at Cambridge and in The Netherlands, accepted his new responsibility with enthusiasm. His colleagues responded to his leadership. The arts, Walford has observed, "are parts of God's provision for our human well-being. The more these elements are absent from our lives, the more we are alienated from the fullness of life as provided by God."[10]

Professor Karl Steele with art student on front campus, 1975.

John Nelson, '63, left, conductor of the Indianapolis Symphony Orchestra and Professor Howard Whitaker, conductor of the Wheaton College Symphony Orchestra, receive Silver Baton Awards for Distinguished Contribution to the Arts from Illinois Bell Telephone Co., 1980. Second from left, representative of Illinois Bell; right, Conservatory Director Harold Best.

During the seventies Professor Steffler worked diligently to assemble a worthy collection of American art including oils, woodcuts, etchings, sculptures, lithographs, and watercolors. The oldest work is an oil portrait by Henry Inman dated 1845. A significant addition to Wheaton's holdings was the definitive collection of 700 superb etchings, drawings, and woodcuts by Allen Lewis, presented to the College by DeWitt Whistler Jayne, cousin of the artist and distant cousin of James McNeill Whistler. Displayed on the second floor of Buswell Library are most of the sixty original political cartoons given by two-time Pulitzer-Prize-winner Vaughan Shoemaker, drawn for the *Chicago Daily News* and the *Chicago American*. Another choice work is a signed copy of Ansel Adams's "Vertical Aspens, Northern New Mexico," hung in Buswell Memorial Library.

The art department is again drawing a good number of majors. In 1980 a dozen art majors, as part of the International Studies Program, studied art and architecture in Europe, visiting churches, castles, and museums. Two aspirations remain to be achieved: accreditation by the National Association of Schools of Art and the acquisition of a gallery to display the department's growing collection of American art.

Conservatory of Music

Professor Harold M. Best became dean of the Conservatory of Music in 1970. A Renaissance man in the breadth of his interests, he sees the Conservatory as a closely integrated part of the whole College program and Wheaton's philosophy of education. Often he speaks of excellence as a norm of stewardship and music as praise, an act of worship. "Our goal is to teach the discipline of music liberally, preparing students for a broad range of music careers," he observes. "In addition to developing an area of expertise, all students are equipped for a half-dozen different graduate programs when they complete their degree."[11]

When Dean Best came to Wheaton there were 120 students in the Conservatory. A decade later there were 185 preparing either for the Bachelor of Music degree, with concentration in performance, composition, or history of music, or for the Bachelor of Music Education, a teaching degree. Professor Best also heads the music department of the College, which grants a Bachelor of Arts degree in music.

The Conservatory's twenty-nine full-time and seven part-time instructors are highly prepared academicians and skilled performers. They have written books and monographs, have oratorio and orchestral experience, have given solo and group performances in many parts of the country, and have composed in a variety of genre. They participate actively in the Faculty Recital Series, offered for the campus and local community. Among many achievements by the faculty, Professor William Phemister has given numerous piano concerts in Southeast Asia and Africa. Supported by a grant from the Alumni Association, Professor Howard Whitaker composed an original work commissioned by the Indianapolis Symphony Orchestra. Professors Thompson and Chenoweth have written books on their disciplines. The Conservatory is accredited by the National Association of Schools of Music and the National Council for the Accreditation of Teacher Education.

A symphony orchestra and concert band are difficult to assemble. Skilled violinists, oboists, and bassoonists are not readily found, for they are commonly induced to enter institutions that can make substantial scholarship grants. When additional grants become available at Wheaton for promising young artists the instrumental organizations will benefit. Professor Best expects Conservatory enrollment to increase from 185 to 225, which would greatly strengthen the performing groups and enrich the total life of the community.

As they have for many years, each of the musical groups makes an annual tour of the major regions of the United States, a maturing experience, memories of which students cherish for a lifetime. In the 1960s the Men's Glee Club, under the direction of Professor Clayton Halvorsen, began a series of European tours during summer vacations, seven of them by 1982. On one of its ventures abroad the group sang in Limburg, West Germany, where they received the Folk Song Award in the Male Chorus Division of the International Choir Competition. At the International Choir Festival in The Hague in 1979 and 1983, the Glee Club received a unanimous first place from an international panel of judges. At the 1981 International Choir Festival, Director Halvorsen was acclaimed the outstanding conductor. In 1982 the Women's Chorale, under the direction of Mary Hopper, made its first journey abroad. Conservatory-sponsored music organizations and recitalists perform annually for over 35,000 individuals locally, throughout the United States, and abroad.

A unique addition to the Conservatory program in recent years has been the introduction of a degree program in ethnomusicology under the direction of Professor Vida Chenoweth, a pioneer in the field. She became a member of the faculty in 1979, after several years as a visiting instructor. Work with Wycliffe Bible Translators prepared her for work in New Guinea, where she and a colleague reduced to writing the language of a stone age people, the Usarufas, and in twelve years prepared a New Testament. She is a skilled analyst of non-western music systems, understanding and composing in them.

Faculty and Conservatory students have presented a high quality of music for chapel worship services, acquainting students with the great music of the church, along with the best contemporary Christian expressions of worship. The Artist Series has brought to Wheaton some of the world's finest orchestras and soloists.

The Conservatory, aware of contemporary trends in music, sees them as part of America's cultural history. For many years it felt uneasy about the unwritten campus ban on jazz, firmly held by Presidents Edman and Armerding, who regarded its origins and associations as inappropriate to a

Women's Chorale, 1981, directed by Professor Mary Ellen Hopper.

Combined choral groups and orchestra, under the direction of Professor Paul Wiens, perform Stravinsky's Symphony of Psalms, fall 1982.

Professor Vida Chenoweth assists Jean-Claude Namba of Cameroon in playing a call to worship on the "talking drum."

Concert Choir, 1984, directed by Professor Paul Wiens. Spring tour took them to New Jersey, Maryland, Pennsylvania, and Indiana.

Christian environment. Student appeals for non-dancing jazz performances on campus were in vain. The Executive Committee of the Board of Trustees, however, late in the Armerding administration, experienced rising pressure from students for a modification of the ban.[12] By the end of the decade presidential approval had been granted for the inclusion of the study of jazz in the music curriculum as an American art form. A year later WETN was broadcasting occasional jazz works, but within a clearly identified cultural context.

One of the appealing additions to the Conservatory offerings was the initiation of the Wheaton-in-Aspen summer program in Colorado, begun in 1980 under the direction of Professor Howard Whitaker. In this arresting mountain setting students study with Wheaton faculty and the Aspen Music School, encounter outstanding musicians, and hear live performances by superb musicians. Graduates of the Conservatory are to be found throughout the country as performers. John Nelson, '63, conductor of the Indianapolis Symphony Orchestra, is perhaps the best known. Two Wheaton trombonists, Eric Carlson, '82, and Douglas Yeo, '76, play side by side in the Baltimore Symphony. Many organists hold fine positions, among them David Sharp, '69, who is organist at Gordon McDonald's Grace Chapel in Lexington, Massachusetts. Eddie Thomas, '57, is a leader in black musical activities in concert, radio and television. Cheryl Woods, '72, and Sylvia McNair, '78, are heard in opera, oratorio, and concert nationally.

In the spring of 1978 the visitation committee of Dr. Eugene Bonelli and Dr. Robert Egan reaffirmed the accreditation of the Conservatory by the National Association of the Schools of Music. The observers noted in their report that they had witnessed "some examples of superb teaching which would be a credit to any institution in the nation."[13]

Clarifying the Vision

The union of a Christian philosophy and academic excellence is an ideal that every department at Wheaton aspires to achieve. In *The Idea of a Christian College* Professor Arthur Holmes writes: "Liberal education is an opportunity to become more fully a human person in the image of God, to see life whole rather than fragmented, to transcend the provincialism of our place in history, our geographic location, or our job."[14] A Christian college like Wheaton is continually having to redefine itself and its mission. To its students, its constituency, and to the academic community at large it must reiterate the quintessential nature of the truths it proclaims and pursues. To find and describe the compelling, sometimes mystic, points of juncture between temporal and eternal truth is part of Christian education. A Christian college like Wheaton goes on daily with energy, cultivating the life of the spirit while preparing the student for a worthy use of his or her days in society.

Each generation of Wheaton students must be shown that the statement of faith and the standards of conduct of the College are intended to provide a theological foundation and congenial environment in which an education that is Christian becomes possible. The standards of conduct have been altered in minor ways a number of times to make reasonable accommodation for cultural changes, but only rarely has the statement of faith been subject to reevaluation. Such a study, authorized by the Board of Trustees in response to requests for it, was made in December 1976. It brought together a distinguished committee of three alumni and one former faculty member: Dr. John Walvoord, '31, president of Dallas Theological Seminary; Dr. Edmund Clowney, '39, president of Westminster Theological Seminary; Dr. Carl F. H. Henry, '38, then minister-at-large of World Vision; and Dr. Kenneth Kantzer, dean of Trinity Evangelical Divinity School. The committee came to a clear consensus. In their judgment the statement should remain unaltered unless error is found in it. They cautioned that any major change could establish a precedent that might lead to other changes. At the same time, they recommended a preamble to the statement in the catalog, reiterating Wheaton's theological commitment to the historic creeds, the teachings of the Reformers, and the evangelical movement of more recent years.

Adjusting Programs

While the statement of faith is one of the constants in the life of the campus, nearly all other pronouncements and organizational structures such as the college calendar are subject to redesigning. In the fall of 1981, Wheaton returned to the semester system which it had abandoned in 1970 in order to divide the academic year into quarters. Many months of intense campus debate, by students and faculty, preceded the trustee decision to reestablish a semester program. One administrator noted that one-half of the colleges and universities followed a semester plan while the institutions committed to a program of quarters had declined to 23 percent. Some thought the semester program, with half courses added, known as quads, would offer a wider course selection and would result in a significant annual saving with two registrations rather than three. Others lamented the stress experienced by students, faculty, and staff under the quarter arrangement.[15] Oddly enough, those contentions, and others, were similar to the persuasions used in 1970 that led to dropping the semester arrangement. The trustee action carried the directive that the new program should be continued for a minimum of ten years.

The debate over the calendar was but one of several instances in which some of the faculty found themselves at a measure of variance with the College administration. Points of sensitivity emerged in the 1970s also over campus governance, that is, who shall exercise authority over what matters and to what extent. Concerned faculty noted the steady proliferation of administrative officers and support staff while the number of professors remained constant. The Office of Institutional Research took on a high degree of visibility in the various processes of evaluation, accountability, and "summative reviews." Summative reviews were departmental evaluations, prepared by a panel of outsiders—authorities in their fields—intended to discover areas of strength and weakness, and to recommend procedures for improvement, even the dismissal of teachers judged ineffective.

To many faculty these reviews were a source of uneasiness, even intimidation, although everyone recognized the need for some criteria by which to judge their performance. Some thought that excessive weight was given to student evaluations of their course offerings when they were under consideration for promotion and tenure. At the same time, students felt strongly that they were entitled to an opportunity to express their opinions regarding teachers' classroom performance.

Another instance in which the administration and a faculty body found themselves at variance occurred when the faculty senate in the spring of 1974 recommended opening the campus tennis courts on Sunday, but only from one to five P.M. The resolution was prompted in part by the fact that Wheaton students were using the community courts on Sunday and in so doing were denying local citizens the use of their own facilities. Further, the senate did not regard tennis as an inappropriate activity. But President Armerding, who always referred to Sunday as the Lord's day, and had strong feelings about its appropriate use, vetoed the action. In the spring of 1981, however, the president, in response to a changing cultural climate, joined the four vice-presidents and the Board of Trustees in authorizing the opening of the campus courts on Sunday when worship services were not being held.

In the last year of his administration President Armerding issued a directive reminding faculty, staff, and trustees that they were to abide by the college standards of conduct the year round. The directive was made necessary, the president felt, because there was some uncertainty about the standards and their applicability to nonstudent personnel and trustees. Some faculty thought they were obligated, like the students, to adhere to the standard only while engaged in college business. After the presidential declaration, a one-vote majority of the faculty asked the trustees to consider making the rules uniformly applicable, only when personnel were engaged in college business. The faculty vote had no weight of authority; it was only recommendatory. The president allowed the concerned faculty to meet with the trustees to voice their reasons for the proposed change, and he put the faculty request before the trustees. But in good conscience, he declared, he could not support the faculty request. Subsequently, the trustees sustained the directive unanimously.

Distressed by the rising number of divorces among Christians nationally, a concern widely shared within the Christian community, President Armerding felt that there ought to be a campus policy on divorce and remarriage for college personnel. To that end he appointed a committee in April 1979, headed by Dr. Peter Veltman, to draw up a statement. The committee recognized the complexity of the issue, even when it was basing its criteria on the teaching of Scripture. It resolved not to be guided by a "simplistic, literalistic, legalism," nor by "relative judgments based on pragmatic, emotional, sentimental, or cultural grounds."[16]

The committee's statement of proposed policy was approved by the Faculty Council in October 1979, revised by the faculty at large, and approved by them in November 1980. The final statement was clear, prudent, scripturally sound, sympathetic of the wounds often suffered by innocent victims of divorce. But the policy statement, intended to guide the president and his associates, has not yet become operative.

Students, too, were worried about the escalating rate of divorce among Christians and the consequent effect on the home. Some of them were victims of broken homes. As far as possible they wanted to avoid that unhappy route in their own marriages. Eager for counseling that might give them a good prospect of a happy marriage, they responded well to an invitation to attend the first of a series of marriage preparation seminars in the winter of 1978-79. Authorization for the seminars grew out of a student government report to the Board of Trustees.[17]

The 1983 seminars, held in January and February, were arranged by Deans Sam Shellhamer and Ruth Bamford, and Dr. Zondra Lindblade, professor of sociology. The series, titled "Growing Into Love," offered guidance through such topics as "The Pain and Pleasure of Romance," "Readiness for Responsible Relationship," and "The Language of Love." An attractively designed program carried an arresting quotation introductory to the series of four evenings: "The best time to crystallize your thinking about committed love, engagement, and marriage is now, when love has been awakened, or better still, before you even think about going out with a person of the opposite sex."

Campus Governance: Gains for Faculty and Students

In the matter of governance both the faculty and the student body made marked progress in the 1970s. During the decade a new disposition to share authority—to allow power to filter down from the top to lower levels—was common to the academic environment throughout the country. The Wheaton College Board of Trustees, always a cautious group, was slower than public institutions, and many private ones, to share its governing rights with faculty and students. With a unique heritage to preserve and distinctive values to guard, the caution was understandable. In response to faculty urging, however, the Board invited a faculty member to sit with each of its standing committees: academic, finance, student affairs, development, and Graham Center. Such committees are always free, of course, to declare an executive session without the faculty member present, a right not often invoked.

In 1979 the trustees agreed to allow one faculty member and one student to present a one-page report, together with an oral report at each of its three annual meetings. The representatives were to be present only for their reports. Invited to be present at the same time were the administrative vice presidents for student affairs and academic affairs. The plan was developed after consultation with other Christian colleges and a study of literature supplied by the Association of Governing Boards of Universities and Colleges.[18] Now the vice president of the faculty sits at executive committee meetings and meetings of the full board.

Progress in campus governance was also achieved through bi-monthly meetings of the faculty council and the senior administrative cabinet. The first includes the vice chairman of the faculty committees and the latter the president and his four vice presidents. In alternate months the faculty council, without an agenda, meets with the president in an informal way to share common concerns. All of these faculty gains were in accord with national trends in the management of American colleges.

In the late seventies the faculty felt at liberty—as it would not have a decade or more earlier—through its faculty council, to address the trustees directly about its concerns. In one 1979 memorandum the council said: "Some of us have misgivings about what impact the Graham Center will have upon the College's progress and finances." They also wondered "whether the Lifetime Fitness Center (not yet built) should have the priority it has in our College program." They lamented certain budget cuts and the elimination of the archaeology and anthropology majors without taking "into account faculty opinion." Decisions about administrative appointments without faculty consultation were also a disappointment. Such issues briefly depressed faculty morale from time to time and professors occasionally said so in the *Record.*[19]

Other benefits accrued to the faculty, including the institution of a much delayed sabbatical program, which became operative in 1982-83. Most colleges, and many smaller evangelical colleges, had long-established sabbatical programs. Dr. Buswell had envisioned such academic grants, but they were not financially possible then. Dr. Edman preferred to assign whatever money might have been available for sabbatical leaves to much needed salary increases for the entire faculty. Dr. Armerding found the alumni research and writing grants, generously given for many years, an adequate substitute, especially in an era of high inflation when budget obligations were difficult to meet. But at the end of his tenure in office he gave strong support, together with the vice presidents and the deans, to the program worked out by the faculty and finally announced by Dean Ward Kriegbaum.

Faculty members are now eligible for sabbatical grants after six years of full-time service. Awards approved for study, research, and writing pay half salary for a full year or full salary for a half year. The first sabbatical grants were made to Professors Ann Crawford, biology; Walter Elwell, theological studies; Reginald Gerig, music; Morris Inch, Bible; Joe McClatchey, literature; Sara Miles, biology; James Rogers, psychology; and Helmut Ziefle, German.

Faculty salary levels rose substantially through the seventies, though the

average salary at Wheaton in each rank was still somewhat below the recommendations of the American Association of University Professors, a respected standard. Annual cost of living grants, gratefully received by the
faculty, did not always keep pace with inflation. Salaries were, of course,
dependent on the College's total annual resources. From 1970 to 1983 annual expenditures advanced from $5,900,000 to $24,000,000. These annual,
accelerating costs were in part the consequence of a decade of extraordinary
inflation, exceeding 10 percent at its most severe during the second half of
the decade. Costs were also spurred by an increasingly sophisticated educational program—new student services and the personnel to provide them,
more costly classroom equipment and computers, admissions recruitment,
minority programs, far greater maintenance and energy costs. In 1977-78,
for example, the cost of gas and electricity was $640,000; in 1982-83 it was
$1,200,000.

Approximately 72 percent of Wheaton's $17,800,000 operating funds in
1980 came from tuition, 13 percent from the $35 million endowment fund, 9
percent from gifts and grants, and 6 percent from other sources.[20] Of
Wheaton's annual expenditures, about 63 percent is allocated for faculty
and staff salaries. For all Wheaton personnel benefits improved markedly
through the seventies and early eighties, either by trustee initiative or faculty suggestion. A valuable service to the faculty came in 1982 when retirement preparation seminars were introduced and coordinated by Barbara
Hendrickson, '65, of the personnel office.

New Social Awareness

A new and broader sense of political and social responsibility emerged
among major segments of the faculty and student body in the seventies.
Both off and on campus one heard pronouncements from reform-minded
evangelicals urging commitment to long-delayed social action. New maturity and vitality were emerging on the campus, a bit of it picked up from the
hippies and Jesus people of the sixties, which some observers viewed as part
of an evangelical renaissance. Timothy Smith, a respected historian and several times a speaker at Wheaton, urged evangelicals to surrender their "fortress mentality" and emphasis on social taboos for a new awareness of the
need for social action.[21]

A strong assertion of these concerns came with the publication of the *Chicago Declaration* in 1973, a document produced by the Conference of Evangelicals for Social Concern. The principal convener was John Alexander,
editor of *The Other Side* magazine and a former instructor in philosophy at
Wheaton. Literary finish and organization were given to the *Chicago Declaration* by Dr. Frank E. Gaebelein. Among its signers were a broad spectrum
of evangelical opinion makers: Dr. Robert Webber, Wheaton College professor of Bible; Dr. Paul Henry, '63, then professor of history at Calvin College, subsequently a Michigan State legislator; Dr. Vernon Grounds; Dr.

Ronald J. Sider; Dr. David Moberg; and Jim Wallis, publisher of *The Post American*, later known as *Sojourners* magazine. Sider called the *Declaration*, "An historic moment for biblical social concerns." Among many judgments the document declared that "although the Lord calls us to defend the social and economic rights of the poor and the oppressed, we have mostly remained silent."[22] Professor Webber believes that the *Chicago Declaration* helped to create on the Wheaton campus a climate conducive to a concern for world hunger, a sensitivity to the urban poor, and a feeling of Christian compassion for the needy and oppressed that led students to such spring and summer missionary journeys as the trips to the Dominican Republic, Haiti, and Honduras. These eager youth went out to give themselves to what many people believed to be a spent and drifting world. Such efforts were growing evidence of confidence in the contributions evangelicals could make to the larger society. The new evangelicalism was intensely conscious of its mission to the world community.

The organization of the Jonathan Blanchard Society in 1973 was another example of an increasing sensitivity among Wheaton students about world needs. "What does it mean," the Society asked, "to be the salt and light of the world, to act as a reconciling, redemptive force in society, to stand for the ethics of God's Kingdom?" Members felt that such a group as the Blanchard Society was needed "to raise the political and social consciousness on the campus." In their first year they had as speakers Richard Taylor, '64, (then writing a dissertation on Jonathan Blanchard,) Jim Wallis, and Wes Pippert, UPI correspondent, who was asked to speak on the moral implications of Watergate and a Christian response.

Many of the students who participated in the Christian outreach activities were gaining a new perspective on missions. They were again sharing the Blanchards' vision of Christian love as love that acts, that is responsive to social appeals. No longer were they bound by a fear that social action involved a compromise with faith. The new evangelical outlook emerged during and after World War II. Closely associated with this emphasis were Wheatonites Carl F. H. Henry, Billy Graham, Edward J. Carnell, and Harold Lindsell. Henry's book, *The Uneasy Conscience of Modern Fundamentalism* (1947) led many evangelicals to a new sense of obligation for society's needs. These trends also found encouragement through the founding of the National Association of Evangelicals (1942), the organization of Fuller Seminary (1947), with Wheaton graduates among its first faculty, and the beginning of *Christianity Today* (1956), with Carl F. H. Henry as its founding editor.

Carol Elsen, '82, passes the baton to a teammate at McCully Field.

An appreciation luncheon preceded the opening of the Chrouser Fitness Center pool on August 19, 1981.

CHAPTER 20

The Armerding
Years End

T HE LAST OF THE SEVEN BUILDINGS TO BE ERECTED DURING
President Armerding's administration was the Chrouser Fitness Center,
completed in the summer of 1981. Conceived principally to benefit the student body, it was intended also as a recreational facility for college personnel and for the community.

The idea for the Center had its origins some eight or ten years prior to
trustee approval to construct the facility. Informal suggestions were made to
the campus planning committee, principally by Harvey Chrouser, chairman
of the men's physical education department, that Wheaton should have a
swimming pool. Most people agreed that such an addition to campus life
was long overdue.[1]

Fitness Center: A New Concept

Chrouser felt that a pool should be but one part of a total exercise fitness
program which ought also to include new developments in exercise physiology. The hope was that the campus community could be encouraged,
through a comprehensive program, to develop and maintain a lifelong commitment to personal fitness. "It takes twenty to thirty years of diet neglect to
incubate a heart attack," said Chrouser. "The program will focus on measuring fitness level and improving fitness."

Dr. Paul Parker, college physician from 1973 to 1982, was enthusiastic about the program and urged SAGA, the college food service, to monitor more closely the nutritional quality of its menus. The dining hall director agreed to reduce levels of concentrated sugar, salt, and fried foods, and substitute margarine for butter.[2] An increase in the use of whole grains, fiber, and fresh fruits and vegetables was also agreed to. Dr. Parker further suggested elimination of much of the "junk food" from campus vending machines, a proposal that won both approval and some disapproval.

In 1975 an anonymous donor gave Wheaton $100,000 for the construction of a swimming pool. A year later, when the donor learned of the developing plans for a lifetime fitness center, a second gift of $100,000 was made. In October 1977 the trustees authorized the construction of a $3.5 million health fitness center.[3] The customary practice of starting no campus building until 80 percent of the cost was in hand or pledged was waived and the figure set at 60 percent in 1979 in order to avoid some of the constant inflation of construction costs.

As originally planned the Lifetime Fitness Center was to include—besides the pool and exercise physiology center—racquetball courts, a wrestling room, classrooms, and a rooftop jogging track to be called the Gil Dodds Memorial Jogging Track. But when the cost projection reached $4.3 million in 1979, with the additional need of a maintenance endowment, some retrenchment was necessary. The trustees, therefore, endorsed a Phase I Construction Program which called for beginning the construction of a facility to include a 3.5 meter, eight-lane swimming pool, an exercise and stress physiology laboratory, wrestling room, offices, and locker rooms.[4] J. Emil Anderson and Son were again to be the builders. Phase II, to include the jogging track and handball courts, would be authorized at some later time.

The Fitness Center was now conceived to be a place where, as one of its services, individualized fitness programs for student and faculty could be developed under the direction of a resident exercise physiologist. Dr. Glenn Town was appointed the first such resident. The Center was seen, too, as a significant part of a wholistic concept of education, emphasizing nutrition, exercise, weight control, and stress management (NEWS).[5] General planning for the Center was done by several committees, whose work was coordinated by Dr. Henry Nelson, vice president for student affairs. Fund raising was the responsibility of Dr. Norman Edwards, vice president for development, and Harvey Chrouser. Faculty members Dr. Alan Johnson and Dr. Joseph Spradley were chairmen of committees for program planning and building planning. A few students and faculty members protested that a fine arts center and better classroom facilities should have priority, but the complaints subsided as the plans advanced. Ground was broken for the 30,000-square-foot Center on May 17, 1980, during commencement weekend.

After construction of the Center was well underway, Harvey Chrouser's retirement was made known in September 1980. At a dinner in his honor

President Armerding announced the action of the Board of Trustees, naming the new center at its completion, the Chrouser Fitness Center. For a man who had been associated with Wheaton College for over forty years, it was an epic hour. Chrouser's football teams, during seventeen seasons, had compiled an extraordinary 103-28-7 record and earned him the title, "Winningest coach in Illinois." For twenty-five years he served as athletic director and for thirty years directed Honey Rock Camp, which he conceived and developed.

At dedication ceremonies on October 3, 1981, Homecoming weekend, President Armerding thanked those whose prayers, contributions, and energies had been foundational to the completion of the building. He noted that many friends had contributed, citing Ogle and Lillian Mourer for providing a "substantial gift." The aquatic director's office honors Philip, '32, and Nell Wichern; exercise physiology equipment was provided by the John Benn Snow Memorial Trust, and the room was given by Louis Rathje, '61, and his mother, Mrs. Bert Rathje, '33, in honor of Bert Rathje, '22. Attention was also called to a large mural on the south wall of the swimming pool, suggesting a theme from Philippians 3:14, painted by Marge Gieser, '59, and given by the class of 1981. Dr. Henry Nelson presided at the unveiling of a brass plaque honoring Chrouser.

Adjacent to the Chrouser Fitness Center, at the point where the Center and Centennial Gymnasium are joined, is the Paul M. Avila Memorial Room, where pictures, together with an appropriate plaque, of members of the Wheaton College Hall of Honor are hung. Paul M. Avila was a superb soccer player from 1966 to 1969, All-Conference for three years and All-Midwest in 1979. While engaged in graduate studies, he died at home at the age of twenty-four. Forty-two athletes have been named to the Hall of Honor from football, baseball, basketball, track, soccer, wrestling, and tennis.

The Hall of Honor, funded by the Crusader Club, was largely the inspiration of Harvey Chrouser and Ray Smith, '54. Members of the Hall of Honor are chosen by a selection committee appointed by the Crusader Club. Organized with its own officers and constitution, the Crusader Club came into being in 1970 with the intention of encouraging athletics at Wheaton through contributions for equipment and the scouting program. It was a successor to the Century Club, developed during the Edman era to raise money for scholarship assistance to athletes, a practice that athletic regulatory agencies in time would no longer condone.

Athletics

Athletic teams during the Armerding administration did not quite equal the accomplishments of the "golden years" teams of the Edman period, though there were selected sports in which the record was outstandingly good; and there were selected years for most sports in which team members could take pride. The difference was in part the result of the changing times. The athletic fervor that captivated the college campus, particularly the small campuses throughout the country, in the forties and fifties had moderated to a considerable degree at Wheaton, along with Homecoming bonfires at Lawson and McCully fields the night before the big game, and snake dances through campus streets.

To some extent the decline in interest during this period could be attributable to the lack of marked success in the major spectator sports, basketball and football. Intensification of academic interests, concern for public issues, deeper understanding of international crises, eagerness to respond to service opportunities—all contributed to the decline of athletic fervor. And while Wheaton was the best known evangelical Christian college, fielding a full array of successful athletic teams in the post World War II era, and was named by sports writers "the Notre Dame of the Christian colleges," that edge of superiority began to disappear in the 60s as other Christian colleges from coast to coast grew in size and resources and claimed their share of promising Christian athletes. In addition, the conference in which Wheaton competes—now regarded as the strongest Division III conference in the country—became much more rugged and evenly balanced than it had been in the days of the Crusaders' dominance.

Then, too, Wheaton is sometimes at a disadvantage in enrolling a number of the top athletes by maintaining higher admissions standards than many of the schools with which the College competes. Wheaton's Christian testimony and the required standards for personal living tend further to limit the number of outstanding athletes eager to become members of Crusader teams.

The value of athletics, however, both to the participants and the campus community, cannot be assessed wholly in terms of victories in interschool competition. Many advocates of athletics point to the recreational values, the unifying effect successful teams have on the student body at large, and the public relations value of a quality athletic program. In a Christian college, many athletic directors and coaches contend, good teams, whether in victory or defeat, are a positive witness.

Whatever position one may take on such matters, it is clear that the cost of intercollegiate athletics, both at Wheaton and at comparable institutions, is high. The allotment of funds for athletics at Wheaton far exceeds that made to any other division of the College. However, there are many more people involved, more students, more supervisors and assistants, more equipment, more facilities to be cared for. The college budget for 1983-84 assigned $537,000 for men's and women's athletics, approximately 2.7 percent of the education general budget. That figure has advanced sharply in recent years owing to inflation and the addition of several new sports, but the percentage of the total budget has remained about the same for some years.

Championships that eluded the football and basketball teams in recent years have come in other competition—soccer, wrestling, swimming for men and women, tennis, women's basketball, field hockey, women's tennis, women's track and field. Football was unquestionably hampered by frequent coaching changes—seven head coaches between 1965 and 1982. Coach Jack Swartz, however, had winning seasons in 1966, '67, '68, before deciding to give up coaching to become chairman of the department of physical education.

In 1982 a promising program of rebuilding began under J. R. Bishop, a successful coach at Naperville High School. His 1983 team compiled a 6-3 record, the best since 1978. Quarterback Keith Bishop established several conference and school passing records. His principal pass receiver, Steve Thonn, also established a number of school records. At the end of the season both received Little All-American honors from several organizations, including the Associated Press. Soccer teams were outstanding under the direction of coach Joe Bean. In all, the teams have won, between 1969 and 1982, six conference championships and five NCAA Division III championships.

Coaching by George Olsen and Pete Willson, Wheaton wrestling teams had good success through the Armerding years. They compiled a record during the history of the CCIW of forty-seven individual championships, a number exceeded only by Augustana College.

Lacking their own pool until 1981, swimming teams at Wheaton have been exceptionally successful. Between 1968 and 1980 Crusader teams won the CCIW championship five times. A number of CCIW records are held by both men and women swimmers from Wheaton, and some have been designated NCAA All-American swimmers. Coach Jon Lederhouse called the 1983 season, in which the Wheaton team finished ninth among all Division III teams at Canton, Ohio, the best in the team's seventeen-year history. It was the thirteenth consecutive year in which the Crusaders led all Illinois colleges at the Division II or III meet.

In 1983 Linda Chambers, a freshman from Bethpage, New York, became Wheaton's first women's NCAA division III national swim champion, while Linda Pace also achieved notable success in swimming, qualifying fifteen times for All-American status in various swim lengths and styles during her four years.

Many women athletes have contributed their talents to Crusader teams. In 1981 a superb women's volleyball team compiled a 23-2 record, and in the same season the field hockey team record was 11-1 and the tennis team 11-5. In both 1980 and 1981 the track and field team won the state championship.

Athletic seasons come and go. The shouting and the tumult rises and wanes. Those are times, as one student writer put it, of "excitement, vicarious agony, and exhilaration," times when "participants were exhorted, cajoled, cheered and sometimes mildly denounced by their friends." With

Steve Long, '79, Wheaton's all-time high scorer and two-time All-American, moves the ball toward the goal at East McCully Field.

Linda Petrie, '83, Wheaton's all-time high-scorer in field hockey, moves in on the ball.

victory came joy, with defeat opportunities for graciousness and resolution to try again.

The Armerding Era Closes

At the January 3, 1981, meeting of the Board of Trustees President Armerding announced his intention to retire at the end of the 1982-83 academic year. At the same time he expressed his willingness to terminate his service to Wheaton earlier if a suitable successor were found before the suggested date. While accepting that decision with regret, the trustees without delay established criteria for selecting a new leader and named its selection committee from within the Board. They asked for earnest prayer for the discovery of the right candidate, one fully committed to Wheaton's convictions, sensitive to its heritage, aware of its current needs, and perceptive of future trends in higher education.

Selection committee members were Kenneth Wessner, chairman, Delburt Nelson, George Newitt, Gunther Knoedler, and Kenneth Gieser. To receive recommendations for the presidency the trustees authorized the formation of a committee to represent the interests of the faculty, administration, alumni, student body, and staff. Dr. Joseph Spradley, chairman of the faculty council, represented the faculty and John Knechtle, student government president, was the student committeeman. The Board urged that recommendations be sent to this committee for review prior to their being delivered to the trustee committee.[6] Professor Gerald Hawthorne was designated as liaison person between the Board and the faculty.

The faculty drew up its own list of criteria and eventually recommended several persons. Among the qualities they wished to see in the new president were a deep sense of Christian commitment, demonstrated scholarship, leadership and administrative capability, the capacity to work well with others. They did not feel it essential that he be a graduate of Wheaton, or that he be a minister, though the first five presidents had been ordained. By the end of the screening period, the representative committee submitted to the committee of the trustees for consideration a list of ten names from among the seventy-one suggested.

During the fall there was much speculation on campus by both faculty and students about which candidate might be getting the most serious consideration. In none of those conversations was the name of Dr. J. Richard Chase, president of Biola University, La Mirada, California, advanced. Little wonder, then, that there were expressions of surprise when he was announced, early in January 1982, as the sixth president of Wheaton College. As a California resident he was little known in the Wheaton area, but good things soon began to be heard. Dr. Chase was to begin his duties on August 1, 1982, allowing Dr. Armerding to retire a year early.

The days of President Armerding's last year of service to his alma mater passed swiftly. One high moment of official responsibility he would surely miss—that of preaching the baccalaureate sermon, which he delivered without text from the side of the platform, where he could face the seniors, his young friends, and give them his final counsel and benediction. At this service the graduation class annually offers its best expression of dedication, singing unaccompanied a verse of "May the Mind of Christ My Savior":

> May I run the race before me,
> Strong and brave to face the foe,
> Looking only unto Jesus
> As I onward go.

He would certainly miss, too, other responsibilities, such as the annual Faculty-Staff-Trustee Dinner, over which he presided. On these gracious occasions he commended faculty and staff workers for their service to Wheaton—five, ten, fifteen, twenty years, or more. For many years the award given by the College was simply a lapel pin. More recently small serviceable items for use in the office or home have been given. On one occasion, however, quite exceptional presentations—grandfather clocks—were made to Professors Clyde Kilby and Harvey Chrouser for more than forty years of service. During one of these evenings, held at the DuPage County Complex, rather than in Centennial Gymnasium, the faculty and staff, knowing the president's fondness for horseback riding, turned the tables and presented him with a fine saddle and horse blanket. At the conclusion of the evening Dr. Armerding was escorted to the rear of the building, where he discovered a waiting horse, which he was persuaded to saddle with his new acquisition. He did so faultlessly, and to the admiring cheers of his colleagues, in the dark of night, swung into the saddle.

At his last student press conference the president briefed his hearers on some of the pressing campus needs, like structural repairs to the west wing of Blanchard Hall, renovation of Evans and McManis residence halls, an addition to the dining hall, all creating the need for additional funds, the source of which at the time was uncertain. These were the unglamorous sides of keeping a college efficiently operative.[7] Modesty kept the president from expressing pleasure over the action of an independent group of Christian laypeople in Fort Davis, Texas, together with other friends of the Armerdings, in establishing a scholarship at Wheaton in their honor.

In his final interview with *Record* Editor Mark Dawson, President Armerding spoke of his gratification with an improved faculty and for an educational program based on a solidly Christian philosophy. He spoke of the loss of a number of faculty "star performers" during his tenure, difficult to replace, citing particularly Dr. Merrill C. Tenney and Dr. Clyde S. Kilby. "A strong faculty attracts quality students," he noted. He expressed openness of mind on possible future change in the doctrinal statement and student statement of responsibilities if such changes made the College "even more firmly and explicitly biblical and evangelical."[8]

Armerding Science Hall, named for Wheaton's fifth president.

Wheaton College Board of Trustees, 1983. First row, l. to r.: *William F. (Billy) Graham, Gunther H. Knoedler, George B. Newitt, Kenneth T. Wessner, President J. Richard Chase, Hudson T. Armerding, President Emeritus, Richard H. Seume, P. Kenneth Gieser.* Second row: *C. William Pollard, Delburt H. Nelson, David M. Howard, David L. Burnham, Jeanne B. Blumhagen, Clayton F. Brown, Alan C. Emery, Jr., James M. Lane, V. Gilbert Beers, Irwin W. Killian, Walter C. Kaiser, Jr., Harold Lindsell.*

Tributes for a Retiring President

On Saturday evening, May 15, during commencement weekend, the Board of Trustees hosted an appreciation dinner honoring President and Mrs. Armerding. More than 1,000 trustees, faculty, staff, alumni, students, and parents gathered in Centennial Gymnasium to pay honor to the president for his seventeen years of leadership. Present also were the Armerdings' five children: Carreen, '68, Taylor, '70, Paul, '75, Jonathan, '79, and Mimi— and ninety-four-year-old Dr. Carl Armerding, professor of Bible emeritus and father of President Armerding. After the invocation by Chaplain LeRoy Patterson, Trustee Gunther Knoedler presided as master of ceremonies.

Among the many splendid moments of the evening was a superb wide-screen multimedia survey of the Armerding years, noting the additions to the campus, the academic developments, the growth in ministries, and the esteem in which the retiring president was held by his colleagues and friends. Kenneth Wessner, vice chairman of the Board of Trustees, spoke for that group. He wanted his hearers to know of the many "concrete and measurable achievements" that had come about between 1965 and 1983, the years of the president's service. Degrees were received by 9,700 men and women. The Graduate School enrollment had risen from 97 to 410 at its highest point. The endowment had increased from $8 million to $30 million; the equity in assets had increased from $21 million to $80 million; operating costs had risen from about $4 million to $22 million. Seven new buildings were constructed: Buswell Library, Science Building, Chrouser Fitness Center, Billy Graham Center, Harold Chase Service Center, Fischer Dormitory, and Traber Dormitory. "We thank God for your leadership in strengthing the academic standing of the college" said Trustee Wessner, "and maintaining its spiritual climate. Your integrity, vision, wisdom, judgment, fairness and humility are qualities that will long be remembered."

Tributes were given also by Vice President Henry Nelson for the administration; Dr. Arthur Johnston, alumni president; Delbert Stoner, Parents Council; Lynn Alberti, student government; and Dr. Gerald Hawthorne, vice chairman of the faculty. "Behind his customary reserve," said Professor Hawthorne, "there is a truly warm and friendly person, tender even, with a good sense of humor—a person intelligent and compassionate, dedicated to Christ as Lord and committed to keeping Wheaton College consistent with its motto." To all of those expressions of appreciation President Armerding responded briefly with words of thanksgiving for the providence of God, for the encouragement of his family in times of need, for the support of administrative and staff associates. The evening hymn, long a favorite with the college community, was "Great Is Thy Faithfulness." An announcement at the end of the evening from Dr. Delburt Nelson, chairman of the Board of Trustees, stated that the science building, nameless since its completion in 1971, would be thereafter known as Armerding Hall, and that a plaque indicating the new name would be unveiled following the baccalaureate service.

Words of benediction were offered by Dr. Carl Armerding. The bronze plaque in the lobby of Armerding Hall commends the honoree as an "Administrator, Scholar, Teacher, and Committed Servant of Christ as a Leader in Christian Higher Education."

These were fitting expressions of appreciation for the services of a man who had faced, in the restless sixties, perhaps the severest testings of all of Wheaton's presidents. Yet he remained steady, evidencing Christian love toward those who challenged his positions. He was the man for his times with patience and a warm heart. A man of strong convictions, he realized nonetheless that there are times when discretion calls for adjustment within the range of one's moral values. As an administrator he was steady, orderly, ready to commend achievement by faculty and students. Though there were occasional differences between him and the faculty, they worked well together. The lighter side of his nature, well known to his friends, sometimes was revealed to students—when he donned a ten-gallon hat, or slipped into overalls given him by students, or accepted with grace scrawny caricatures of his angular countenance drawn for student publications in the unsteady 60s. Usually a witty observation or two relaxed his hearers when he began a public address.

Dr. Armerding was the author of two books, *A Word to the Wise*, a series of baccalaureate addresses commemorating his fifteenth anniversary as president, and *Leadership*. He was editor of *Christianity and the World of Thought*.

He was especially pleased with the innovations of his era: faith and learning seminars, Vanguards stress and wilderness education, HNGR, overseas study opportunities, the physical fitness program, personal interviews for all candidates for admission, the sabbatical leaves for faculty, and new graduate programs. He was also pleased with the new international programs that took students to Israel, Europe, South America, and Asia. In the spring of 1983 the Board of Trustees invited him to continue his relationship with Wheaton as a special representative.

PRESIDENT J. RICHARD CHASE, 1982-

CHAPTER 21

J. Richard Chase, Sixth President

T HE SEARCH FOR A NEW PRESIDENT CAME TO AN END ON January 9, 1982, when the Board of Trustees voted unanimously to select Dr. J. Richard Chase, president of Biola University. Public announcement was made at the first chapel service of the new semester in January by Dr. Delburt Nelson, chairman of the Board of Trustees.

"Wheaton has a great history," Dr. Chase told the press on the West Coast when it became known he had been chosen to become Wheaton's sixth president. "Currently it possesses quality faculty, the ability to draw highly capable students, and has growing resources of facilities, funds, and equipment. Drawing these human and physical resources together can usher in its most productive years. The presidency is one of the most exciting and demanding jobs in Christian higher education today."[1]

Dr. Chase had been graduated from Biola College and began to teach there in 1953 while completing his work for a master's degree at Pepperdine University in southern California. From 1957 to 1959 he was in residence for graduate study at Cornell University, Ithaca, New York, from which he earned the Ph.D. degree in rhetoric and public address in 1961. Returning to Biola, he became chairman of the division of humanities and speech and was appointed academic vice president in 1965. His election to the presidency of Biola came in 1970; under his leadership the college enrollment increased from 1,800 to 3,100. Through his direction Talbot Theological Seminary and Rosemead School of Pyschology, Biola affiliates, became graduate schools, allowing Biola to award master's and doctoral degrees. In addition, over a dozen Christian missionary, educational, and community organizations had profited from his participation.

The *Chicago Tribune* headlined its account of Dr. Chase's appointment: "Wheaton College Picks Low Profile President." In a telephone interview, David Hubbard, president of Fuller Theological Seminary, told the *Tribune's* religion writer: "Chase has a blue-chip reputation out here. He is known as a very solid, no-nonsense manager who is cautious, prudent, and laid-back. I suspect he's more interested in the Christian worldview and Christian ethic than in the niceties of theological division. He's more of a centrist than rightist."[2]

Within a month of his election President-elect Chase was on campus to sense the tone of the institution whose future he had agreed to help guide. February greeted the Californian with frigid temperatures, but during his graduate days at Cornell—where he arrived in mid-winter in 1957—he had learned how to endure with fortitude the piercing winter winds of the North. He told a press conference that he wished to consult with the entire campus community in working out a priority list of Wheaton's needs. He expressed the conviction that the Board of Trustees should not only listen to the opinions of the faculty, students, and staff; they should actively seek them out.

On campus again in April, he spoke at his first faculty meeting, pledging that in the decision-making process he would want to consult with them. He liked to "run a fairly open office"; students, faculty, and others would be welcome. That he would support the "statement of responsibility" was clear, though he did not wish it to be seen as a standard of spirituality. He saw it as a cultural necessity, but not central to the spiritual life of Wheaton College.[3]

Wearing a sweater and an open collar he chatted informally with groups of students, his warmth and forthrightness quickly emerging. He wanted them to know that students would be regular guests at the Chase home. Appearing very much at ease, he told them he had grown up on a dairy farm in southern California, where there were 800 dairy cows, a creamery, and delivery trucks. "My first job was feeding calves at 4:30 in the morning, a job I did not like, but it was hard to find help during the war years." He put himself through college by rebuilding cars. At Biola he played on the basketball team and loved the game. Though he was eager to see a strong athletic program developed at Wheaton, he would not sacrifice academic quality to achieve it. While he pledged to maintain the academic vigor of Wheaton College, he did not wish to see the institution become "so strong that people forget we're Christian."[4] In those two visits the new president appeared to be a person who would be relaxed, flexible, easy to approach, cosmopolitan in lifestyle, happy in his job. To the *Chicago Sun-Times* religion editor he said: "It's not necessary to protect religious distinctives by isolationism. I know what my beliefs are, and I'm not interested in isolationism but in involvement as a citizen and a Christian. We don't have to be isolationists to protect our values. Our values are not that fragile."⁵ Speaking for himself and his wife Mary, he expressed the conviction that their spiritual and intellectual journey to the Midwest was divinely guided.

Richard and Mary Chase were married in Los Angeles on December 16, 1950. Mrs. Chase is the daughter of Dr. Samuel H. Sutherland, a dean at Biola at the time of the marriage and later president of that institution. In the same year Richard Chase was ordained to the ministry in Camarillo, California, and served briefly as a youth pastor and pastor. The Chases' children are Ken and Jennifer.

President Chase's Inauguration

The inauguration ceremony for President Chase was held on September 17, 1982. As the carillon sounded across the campus, the academic procession moved into Edman Chapel: Wheaton faculty, trustees, and administration, together with 125 representatives of colleges, universities, and learned societies. The vigorous inaugural organ processional was composed for the occasion by Professor Stephen Cushman. With Dr. Delbert H. Nelson, chairman of the Board of Trustees presiding, Dr. Armerding began the impressive ceremony with the invocation.

Greetings were offered from the academic community by Dr. Patricia O. Thrash, associate director, North Central Association. She noted that "Wheaton graduates have gone on to serve their faith and to provide distinguished leadership to institutions around the world. Through them, Wheaton has become a center and a symbol for Christian service and scholarship." Kenneth Wessner, chairman of the selection committee, reminded his hearers that Dr. Chase succeeded "five other outstanding men who have been used of God to bring our college to where it is today." Professor Hawthorne, who had known President Chase at Biola years before, told an old and admired friend that in the good will of the faculty there were "huge resources already deposited to your account, wholly at your disposal to draw upon, to make full use of, to invest and profit from, so that together we might significantly enrich our generation." Dr. Arthur Johnston, for the alumni family worldwide said: "We embrace you as one of us and pledge the support of our abilities, our gifts, and our prayers." Dale Smith, for the student body, expressed the wish that the new president might "experience the enthusiasm, the fellowship, and above all else, the lives of students, faculty and fellow administrators in a way that draws each of us closer to the Kindgom."

The installation ceremony was conducted by Dr. Nelson; a prayer of commitment by Dr. Billy Graham was read for him in his absence owing to illness. In his charge to his successor President Armerding reminded President Chase of both the joys and heavy responsibilities of the office he was then accepting. "I trust that you will realize in your calling," he said, "that you are responsible to a great host of people who have come here, have studied here, have sent their sons and daughters here, and part of your calling is to safeguard that precious heritage, and I know that you take that very seriously."

In his inaugural address, "Freedom for Excellence," President Chase acknowledged his indebtedness to his predecessors, particularly Dr. Armerding. Although he was not interested in being merely a "caretaker of the past," he pledged himself to be "sensitive to what is ageless and ever contemporary." As he stood there he was conscious of the search on college campuses for a satisfactory system of governance agreeable to faculty and administration. He called for fidelity to the freedom that makes scholarship and constructive inquiry possible. The highest freedom is that which "is ours in Christ." The eloquent address was a strong pledge to preserve a campus climate of free inquiry in which liberal learning, grounded in Christian truth, could flourish. "I pledge to work diligently in making this college a campus where trust and respect are commonplace and where each task is so endowed with nobility that we all willingly pull together. . . . I cannot make a difference: together we can. So help us God."

In the evening of inaugural day the college choirs—Men's Glee Club, Women's Chorale, Concert Choir—offered a concert of celebration in Edman Chapel. A reading of Psalm 23 by Professor Paul Wiens, Concert Choir director, served as a synthesizing theme for an improvization by Professor Stephen Cushman on the Schantz organ and Miss Kathleen Kastner on percussion. The musical notes for the piece came from spelling "Chase" in European note equivalency. The combined choirs sang "Let the People Praise Thee, O God," by William Mathias, a work first performed at the royal wedding of Prince Charles and Lady Diana Spencer. One innovative touch for such an occasion was the dancing of Orchesis, a student women's group who performed to a theme from the Mass of Leonard Bernstein. Director of the group was Susan Fay.

During the evening prior to the inauguration, in the Heritage Room of Edman Chapel, the Wheaton College Women's Club served as hostesses at a reception for Dr. and Mrs. Chase. The campus community and friends of the College were invited to this gathering for which Melissa Lemke provided harp music.

Throughout inaugural week, at the regular chapel services, an academic symposium examined the "Mission of the Christian Liberal Arts College." Faculty members representing the several divisions were speakers, beginning with English professor Beatrice Batson whose concern was the "Intellectual Mission." The "Artistic Mission" was addressed by Dr. James Young, professor of speech; the "Socio-Moral Mission" by Dr. Arthur Holmes, professor of philosophy; and the "Religious Mission" by Dr. Walter Elwell, professor of Bible. An academic convocation on Friday morning presented Dr. Nicholas Wolterstorff, professor of philosophy at Calvin College, speaking on "The Christian Liberal Arts College in World Perspective." The papers were eloquent, imaginative, forward-looking, intellectually probing.

The Chases bought a home with spacious grounds on St. Charles Road, some two miles from campus. Through the year students and faculty, the Board of Trustees, and individuals came to know the Chases' hospitality. At the end of the first year the president invited the entire summer school to the Chase home for a picnic. Of these, seventy-five students came for a barbecue on the lawn, over which Mary Chase presided.

Dr. Chase's first year was given to acquainting himself with Wheaton, planning for major campus repairs, determining space allocations to relieve several departments, preserving and expanding academic resources, confronting the need for additional computer services and terminals, meeting with student and faculty groups, and assessing the needs of the Graduate School and Graham Center. In addressing those concerns, he was proving himself to be a man of insight, resolution, and eloquence. He knew when to be serious, when to be relaxed.

His initial year completed, Dr. Chase set about establishing on-going goals for the College, long-range and current. Since Wheaton exists primarily for its students, it is appropriate that the first of the on-going goals should refer to them—"to develop students who know Christ as Savior, understand the Bible, and seek to live by biblical precepts." Closely associated with that effort will be the continuing endeavor to "attract, retain, and educate gifted students who both desire and can profit from the rigorous academic objectives of Wheaton College."

To teach these promising young students it is necessary "to attract, and retain regular faculty who are supportive of the goals of Wheaton College and who are capable of influencing the lives" of those they teach. The graduate programs must be compatible with the purpose of Wheaton College and its resources, and render "distinctive services not generally found in other institutions." The Graham Center, too, must be effective in its announced intention "to advance biblical evangelism and to contribute to world evangelization." To achieve these and many other associated goals there must be efficient "administrative structures and procedures" as well as "sound fiscal policy." All planning and goal-setting is intended to support Wheaton in its dedication "to serve 'Christ and His Kingdom' in all that it does."

Asked by a student reporter at the end of the first year about his hopes for the second year, President Chase declared that he wanted to develop a little less hectic schedule, allowing for "more time for interpersonal relations in a casual way, with faculty, staff, and students." He expressed a deep interest in service to students, "everything from evaluation to curriculum to teaching techniques." He felt deeply the need to minimize student costs and to be "uncommonly effective with the financial resources we have." Pressed to comment on the students, he replied: "Bright, involved, concerned, creative, at times over-extended. I'm amazed at their involvement."[6]

Two important decisions were made in the fall of 1983, during President Chase's second year: the elimination of the required one summer term for all students and the announcement of a large fund-raising effort. The required summer quarter—begun with the institution of the quarter system in 1970— was never popular with parents or students since it eliminated the prospect of income from summer employment. But the summer requirement made it possible to develop several international study programs, and many students chose one of them rather than remaining on campus.

To help meet growing financial needs the Board of Trustees authorized a fund-raising drive, known as The Campaign for Wheaton, under the general direction of Vice President for Advancement Norman Edwards, to raise $32 million by the end of 1986. Among the major projects to be funded through The Campaign for Wheaton will be the gathering of Wheaton's scattered communications program, including FM Station WETN, into a single facility in the west end of the Graham Center.

Scheduled also for support from the new fund are the construction and renovations of the dining hall and the Student Center, the renovation of Blanchard Hall, and the renovation of the newly acquired Clifford elementary school across from Traber Hall. The elementary school building was named Jenks Hall in 1984 in memory of James L. Jenks, Jr., a Massachusetts insurance executive, since funds for the purchase of the $550,000 building came from a trust established by Jenks. The trust specified that the money was to be used for endowment or for a much needed campus facility. A portion of the building was assigned to the speech communications department for the work in drama.

From the campaign for Wheaton resources $4.5 million will be allocated for the establishment of six endowed faculty chairs. To update and expand campus computer facilities $1 million will be directed.

Assistance for Students

Conscious of the steadily rising cost of an education at Wheaton, the administration and the Board of Trustees have encouraged student participation in whatever programs may be available, in addition to the regular financial assistance grants, to help them meet their needs. One of these, initiated on the Wheaton campus in 1983, is college work study, a government program providing part-time jobs on campus, for which the government pays 80 percent of the students' earnings and the college pays the remainder. CWS opens job opportunities in academic departments, the conservatory, library, WETN radio, news service, and other campus activities. Approximately 100 jobs became available. Most students, however, who are in need of assistance through campus jobs continue to look to the college's own work program. In 1983 this student work force numbered approximately 600.

Of a different order is the President's Award program—once known as

Students at work with library computers: Dan Westergren, Mitch Kinsinger, Rick Young.

An informal chat on the portico of Memorial Student Center: Scott Branks, Tricia Sulita, Jackie Sherrod.

the Merit Award program—revised in 1983. This program intends, in part, to attract students who might cancel their acceptances at Wheaton before the time of enrollment, some of them drawn away by attractive offers from other institutions. Like other schools, Wheaton has experienced an increase in the percentage of cancellations in recent years, principally for financial reasons. For the President's Award program the College set aside $100,000. Ten awards of $1,000 each were given to students, named by Admissions Director Stuart Michael, with outstanding academic records. For the other awards, department heads have an opportunity to recommend promising students who have exceptional records academically and in extracurricular activities. Michael observed that these are the first academic scholarships at Wheaton funded wholly by the College. This kind of "no-need" scholarship is expected to be of value in Wheaton's newly intensified recruiting program.

The largest measure of assistance, however, comes from the Wheaton financial aid program, supported by allotments from student tuition payments. In the fall of 1983 approximately 33 percent of the students were recipients of grants based on need. A minimum of $100 to a maximum of $4,000, received by a few students, was given toward their comprehensive cost of $8,400 a year. In 1983 the total financial aid fund was $1,692,000. A few students qualify for Pell Grants, government funded awards of $1,800 made directly to the student.

All of these programs and remunerative efforts represent trends common to colleges and universities: higher salaries for faculty; higher scholarship and incentive awards; more work opportunities for students to help them meet ever rising room, board, and tuition costs; and the increased use of sophisticated advertising and marketing techniques to attract promising students.

The College is interested not only in providing financial resources but in conserving human resources as well. Students sometimes encounter academic, social, or spiritual difficulties which lead to deeper problems adversely affecting their lives and their future. To minimize or eliminate such casualities the Student Development Office supervises counseling services such as the Academic Assistance Program initiated by students in 1983. One of those who contributed his insights to this program was Dr. Charles Lewis, director of counseling, who came to Wheaton in 1980 from Bradley University.

In an article he wrote for *InForm* in April 1982, Dr. Lewis described the kinds of service his office could render. He observed that there was a time when Christians were distrustful of professional counseling, believing that those who trusted the Lord fully should have no need of psychological help from human sources. Wheaton had experienced that kind of hesitancy in the middle years of the Edman era when students suffering emotional or psychological trauma were referred to off-campus clinics, and there was some reluctance to acknowledge that such matters were the proper concern of the

College. Subsequently, however, the urgency of the need was recognized, and Wheaton responded by providing more student services, including a full-time resident counselor.

Another campus service is the Career Development Center, established in 1976 by Barbara Daly, G'75. Intended to assist students who need guidance in career choices, the Center provides a more complete service than the college employment office had been able to offer. The Center invites freshmen and sophomores to use its facilities and counsel in planning their career goals. In their junior and senior years students are given assistance in preparing a resumé and are invited to participate in interviewing seminars as well as become informed about trends in the job market. The Center maintains a placement service, posts lists of employment opportunities, and serves as host when job recruiters are on campus.

A student employment service had been established in the thirties at the suggestion of professor of education C. B. Eavey, with Rana McDonald, '41, as its director, followed by Jean Rumbaugh, '49. It, too, provided placement service, opportunities for local employment, and information about career opportunities. These campus services have helped give students confidence and direction as they face their future.

For President Chase 1983 was an eventful year as he moved more fully into the life of the campus, witnessing, participating in, or receiving reports of a sequence of activities far too numerous to report. It was a good year for the debate team, winning or placing well in many intercollegiate events, including first place in the Great Western Debate Tournament at the University of Nevada in April. Senior Kevin Rynbrandt was named the tournament's outstanding debater, prompting Debate Coach Edwin Hollatz to say, "Kevin is one of the finest debaters I have worked with in 29 years of coaching."[7] Dr. Hollatz cited Dwight "Butch" Maltby, '78, as an exceptional performer in individual events such as extempore, impromptu, and oration. Traveling as much as 2,000 miles from Virginia to California in a season, students engaged in competitive speech activities have brought back to campus during Dr. Hollatz's career over 200 team trophies. Debate and speech have been consistently one of the campus's most successful activities.

Parents Weekend in October, led by committee chairman John Wright, drew a record attendance of more than 1,500 parents from all parts of the country. Homecoming was a special event in 1983, marking the sixtieth anniversary of that activity initiated in 1923 by Ed Coray, '23, and Clarence Mason, '24. At the Homecoming Chapel the annual Alumni Award for Distinguished Service to Alma Mater was made—this year a joint award—to Robert Noles '40 and Henri Eckhardt '40, both men long engaged in field service for the College. Reunion classes experienced a special time of celebration, exchanging reminiscences at dinner, reminding themselves of the swiftly passing years, expressing thankfulness for God's goodness in returning them to the scenes where so much had transpired to fashion their values, give them direction, and guide them in career choices.

Another outstanding event of the year was the Lutherfest in September honoring the 500th anniversary of the birth of Martin Luther. The academic portion of the celebration, held in Barrows Auditorium, was under the direction of Professor Thomas Kay, chairman of the history department. Scholars from a number of colleges and universities participated in lectures and discussions on Luther's life and influence. A series of three lectures was given by Heiko Obermann, world-renowned Luther scholar and professor of history and theology at the University of Tubingen, West Germany. The second in the series was designated as the annual Cairns History Lecture. Listening to Obermann's energetic presentation of the Luther of the Middle Ages, one could understand why the great reformer emerges as one of the largest figures in the history of the West.

As these final pages are being written, in the waning days of 1983, the first snow of the season has drifted across the campus. Darkness comes early. Amber lights set aglow Blanchard Tower, Edman spire, the Graham Center, the quadrangle, and the dorms. Early evidences of the Christmas season have begun to appear—the lighted wreath on Blanchard tower, the illuminated star on the north side of the building, the glowing sign, JOY, on the roof of Traber Hall.

Standing on the steps of Williston Hall at night and allowing one's vision to sweep the campus slowly, the walkways now empty, one can easily fall into revery. What astonishing developments the years have brought since President Blanchard presided over a tiny prairie college of fewer than fifty students in a single building. One might be tempted to say, "How do you like what you see, Jonathan?"

But history moves forward. When the first reader examines these published pages, nearly a full year will have passed. It is a gentle reminder that the written story of a living institution comes to an end with its history still in progress.

The celebration of the 125th anniversary in 1984-85 of the founding of Wheaton College will encourage the college family to look both forward and backward. With bright hopes for the future, Wheaton enters a new era with a renewed resolve to train young men and women for Christian service, for the enrichment of their lives, for the fullest development of their talents. Wheaton will sustain its commitment to liberal arts education, convinced that it is the best preparation for enlightened citizenship as well as for professional and vocational competence. A liberal arts education must be nurtured with patience; it matures slowly. But its fulfillments endure for a lifetime.

Wheaton has generally received sincere encouragement from its constituency. It will continue to be aware of their expectations and the evaluative assessment of its trustees, administration, faculty, alumni, and friends. As in the past, Wheaton will adjust to altered cultural patterns in the future. It will redefine its educational philosophy from time to time, reassess student life and activities. In the midst of today's flood of information the College will seek to separate the ephemeral from the enduring. It will be vigilant in its resolution to hold fast its unchanging convictions. It will continue to bear witness to those external truths revealed in Scripture and woven into the texture of its history. In the days ahead Wheaton will move forward with confidence, training young men and women "For Christ and His Kingdom."

APPENDIX I

Alumni of the Year
For Distinguished Service to Society

1953   Dr. John R. Brobeck '36, *Physician, Professor, Administrator*
1954   Mr. Howell G. Evans '22, *Business Executive*
1955   Dr. J. Laurence Kulp '42, *Scientist*
1956   Dr. Stephen W. Paine '30, *College President*
1957   Dr. Billy Graham '43, *Evangelist*
1958   Dr. Ruth Kraft Strohschein '27, *Pediatrician*
1959   Dr. Paul E. Adolph '23, *Physician, Missionary, Author*
1960   Dr. Everett D. Sugarbaker '31, *Physician, Author*
1961   Dr. Carl F. H. Henry '38, *Theologian, Christian Journalist, Author*
1962   Dr. & Mrs. Howard F. Moffett '39, *Medical Missionaries, Evangelists*
1963   Mrs. Elisabeth Howard Elliot '48, *Missionary, Author*
1964   Dr. Lawrence H. Andreson '35, *Leader in Church, Youth, and Medical Work*
1965   Dr. Samuel H. Moffett '38, *Leader in the Field of Christian Missions*
        Dr. Elizabeth Jaderquist Paddon '26, *Leader in the Field of Christian Missions*
1966   Dr. Titus M. Johnson '28, *Medical Missionary*
1967   Dr. David H. Paynter '44, *Education Administrator*
1968   Mr. and Mrs. Lyndon B. Hess '31, *Missionaries*
1969   Mr. Norris A. Aldeen '38, *Corporation President*
1970   Mr. Harold G. Mordh '48, *Superintendent of Union Gospel*
1971   Dr. Paul B. Stam '44, *Industrial Research Executive*
1972   Dr. Donald E. McDowell '46, *Surgeon, Missionary*
        Dr. Elois R. Field '45, *Nurse, Teacher, Administrator*
1973   Dr. Eleanor Soltau '38, *Missionary, Physician, Administrator*
        Dr. Paul W. Gast '52, *Scientist*
1974   Mrs. Dorothy Horton Galde '34, *College Professor*
        Dr. & Mrs. John Elsen '42, *Physician, Counselor*
1975   Mr. Charles Hess '25, *Missionary, Bible Translator*
1976   Miss Ruth Hege '30, *Missionary, Author, Speaker*
        Dr. O. Grant Whipple '34, *Christian Camping, Youth Work*

1977   Rev. David M. Howard '49, M.A. '52, *Missionary, Missions Director*

        Dr. Kenneth N. Taylor '38, L.L.D. '65, *Author, Publisher*

1978   Dr. Violet E. Bergquist '39, *College Professor*

1979   Dr. Willard M. Aldrich '31, *Bible College Founder and President*

1980   Miss Gertrude E. Kellogg '44, *Missionary, Translator*

        Dr. Roy W. Lowrie '52, *Christian School Administrator, Executive*

1981   Dr. Richard C. Halverson '39, L.L.D. '58, *Pastor, Author, Counselor, Senate Chaplain*

        Dr. John F. Walvoord '31, D.D. '60, *Seminary President, Author*

        Dr. Larry E. Ward '49, *Relief Organization Founder, President*

1982   Mr. Julius B. Poppinga '50, *Lawyer, Christian Conciliator*

1983   Mr. Robert C. Blaschke '49, *Missionary*

        Dr. & Mrs. William H. Leslie '54, M. Div. '61/'56, *Inner city Pastor/Artist/Teacher*

APPENDIX II

Alumni of the Year
For Distinguished Service to Alma Mater

1953   Dr. Enock C. Dyrness '23, *Registrar, Vice President of Faculty*

1953   Mrs. Mignon Bollman Mackenzie '33, *Professor of Music, Director of Women's Glee Club*

1954   Mr. Herman A. Fischer, Jr. '03, *Attorney, Chairman of the Board of Trustees*

1955   Dr. Edward R. Schell '22, *Dean of the Wheaton College Academy, Emeritus*

1956   Dr. Stanley W. Olson '34, *Medical School Dean, Wheaton College Trustee*

1957   Mrs. Corrinne R. Smith '37, *Dean of Women*

1958   Dr. Russell L. Mixter '28, *Chairman Biology Department*

1959   Mr. Edward A. Coray '23, *Executive Director, Alumni Association*

1960   Dr. Paul M. Wright '26, *Chairman, Chemistry Department*

1961   Dr. P. Kenneth Gieser '30, *Ophthalmologist, Wheaton College Trustee*

1962   Dr. Arthur H. Volle '38, *Professor of Education*

1963   Mr. Charles B. Weaver '24, *Banker, Wheaton College Trustee*

1964   Dr. Clarence B. Hale '28, *Chairman, Foreign Language Department*

1965   Dr. Clarence B. Wyngarden '32, *Wheaton College Physician*

1966   Dr. Angeline Jane Brandt '27, *Professor of Mathematics, Counselor*

1967   Dr. Donald C. Boardman '38, *Chairman, Geology Department*

1968   Mr. Harvey C. Chrouser '34, *Director, Physical Education and Athletics*

1969   Mrs. Ruth Berg Leedy '32, *Professor of Physical Education*

1970   Dr. Bernard A. Nelson '31, *Chairman, Chemistry Department*

1971   Dr. Evan D. Welsh '27, *Wheaton College Chaplain*

1972   Mr. Edward A. Cording '33, *Director, Public Relations; Music Conservatory Director*

1973   Dr. Robert C. Baptista '48, *Vice President, Academic Affairs*
1973   Mrs. Martha Cole Baptista '45, *Assistant Dean of Students*
1974   Dr. Cyril E. Luckman '37, *Professor of Biology*
1975   Mr. David L. Roberts '41, *Director of Development*
1976   Dr. Hudson T. Armerding '41, *President of Wheaton College*
1977   Mr. LeRoy H. Pfund '49, *Coach, Professor of Physical Education; Executive Director, Alumni Association*
1977   Mr. Carter H. Cody '40, *Assistant in Development*
1978   Dr. Arthur F. Holmes '50, M.A. '52, *Professor of Philosophy*
1979   Dr. Harold A. Fiess '39, *Professor of Chemistry*
1980   Mr. Howard W. White '41, *College Controller*
1981   Mrs. Helen Siml deVette '45, *Professor of English*
1981   Dr. Robert O. deVette '41, M.A. '49, *Professor of Spanish; Director of Admissions*
1982   Chaplain H. LeRoy Patterson '40, *Pastor, College Chaplain, Author*
1983   Mr. Henri E. Eckhardt '40, *College Field Representative*
1983   Mr. Robert D. Noles '40, *College Field Representative*

APPENDIX III

Wheaton College Faculty
Twenty-Five Year Alumni Service Awards

The following faculty members were awarded watches by the Alumni Association in recognition of twenty-five years of service to Wheaton College. The date indicates the year in which the award was made.

1956   Fannie Boyce, *Mathematics*
1956   Edward A. Coray, *Physical Education*
1956   Enock Dyrness, *Education and Registrar*
1956   Clarence B. Hale, *Foreign Language*
1956   Agnes Horness, *English*
1956   Mignon B. Mackenzie, *Music*
1957   Stefania Evans, *English*
1960   Joseph P. Free, *Archaeology*
1960   Clyde S. Kilby, *English*
1960   Clarence L. Nystrom, *Speech*
1960   Lamberta M. Voget, *Sociology*
1961   Angeline Brandt, *Mathematics*
1961   V. Raymond Edman, *History and Administration*
1961   Fred B. Gerstung, *Foreign Language*

1961	Ruth B. Leedy, *Physical Education*
1962	John L. Leedy, *Biology*
1963	Edward A. Cording, *Music*
1965	Donald C. Boardman, *Geology*
1965	Harvey C. Chrouser, *Physical Education*
1965	S. Richey Kamm, *Political Science*
1968	Earle E. Cairns, *History*
1968	Clinton O. Mack, *Zoology*
1968	Bernard A. Nelson, *Chemistry*
1968	Ivy T. Olson, *Library*
1968	Merrill C. Tenney, *Bible*
1969	Harold A. Fiess, *Chemistry*
1970	Helen S. deVette, *English*
1970	Frank O. Green, *Chemistry*
1970	George A. Olson, *Physical Education*
1970	June A. Weitting, *Library*
1971	Paul M. Bechtel, *English*
1971	John H. Fadenrecht, *Education*
1971	Karl W. Steele, *Art*
1971	Arthur H. Volle, *Education*
1972	Lois E. LeBar, *Christian Education*
1972	Mary E. LeBar, *Christian Education*
1972	Cyril E. Luckman, *Biology*
1973	Arne T. Howard, *Business and Economics*
1973	Jean R. Kline, *Education*
1973	Peter Veltman, *Education*
1974	Steven Barabas, *Bible*
1974	LeRoy H. Pfund, *Physical Education*
1974	Samuel J. Schultz, Bible
1975	Alton M. Cronk, *Music*
1975	Robert O. deVette, *Foreign Language*
1975	Russell H. Platz, *Music*
1975	Erwin P. Rudolph, *English*
1976	Arthur F. Holmes, *Philosophy*
1976	Ellen R. Thompson, *Music*
1977	Reginald R. Gerig, Music
1977	Eleanor P. Paulson, *Speech*
1978	Gerald P. Hawthorne, *Foreign Language*
1979	LaVern R. Bjorklund, *Physical Education*
1980	Gladys Christensen, *Music*
1980	Edwin Hollatz, *Speech*
1982	E. Beatrice Batson, *English*
1983	Donald L. Church, *Physical Education*
1983	Melvin E. Lorentzen, *Communications*

APPENDIX IV

Present Faculty Members Who Have Served Wheaton College
Twenty-Five or More Years (to the end of the academic year 1983-84)

E. Beatrice Batson, *Professor of English*
Raymond H. Brand, *Professor of Biology*
Gladys Christensen, *Professor of Music*
Donald Church, *Associate Professor of Physical Education*
Reginald Gerig, *Professor of Music*
Gerald Haddock, *Professor of Geology*
Clayton E. Halvorsen, *Professor of Music*
Gerald F. Hawthorne, *Professor of Greek*
Edwin A. Hollatz, *Professor of Speech*
Arthur F. Holmes *Professor of Philosophy*
Thomas O. Kay, *Associate Professor of History*
Melvin E. Lorentzen, *Professor of Communications*
Eleanor Paulson, *Professor of Speech*
LeRoy Pfund, *Professor of Physical Education*
Joseph L. Spradley, *Professor of Physics*
Ellen Thompson, *Professor of Music*
Peter Veltman, *Professor of Education*

APPENDIX V

Teachers of the Year

	Senior Teacher	*Junior Teacher*
1960	Angeline Brandt	
1961	Kenneth Kantzer	Walter Kaiser
1962	Earle Cairns	Robert Baptista
1963	Beatrice Batson	Gerald Hawthorne
1964	Clyde Kilby	James Kraakevik
1965	Howard Claassen	Phillip Hook
1966	Arthur Holmes	William Dixon
1967	S. Richey Kamm	Robert Warburton
1968	Merrill C. Tenney	Marvin Mayers
1969	Russell Mixter	Melvin Lorentzen
1970	John Leedy	Robert Brabenec
1971	Morris Inch	Robert Webber
1972	Cyril Luckman	Leland Ryken

1973	Gordon Fee	Larry Funck
1974	Joseph Spradley	Alan Johnson
1975	Bernard Nelson	LaVern Bjorklund
1976	Ellen Thompson	Joe McClatchey
1977	Russell Platz	Terence Perciante
1978	Zondra Lindblade	Emory Griffin
1979	Albert Smith	Clifford Schimmels
1980	Gerald Hawthorne	Mark Coppenger
1981	Gilbert Bilezikian	Sharon Coolidge Ewert
1982	Derek Chignell	Dorothy Chappell
1983	Leland Ryken	David Benner
1984	Arthur Holmes	Roger Lundin

APPENDIX VI

Wheaton College Faculty Emeriti

Carl Amerding. B.A., D.D., 1948-62, *Professor of Bible and Theology*

Hudson T. Armerding, Ph.D., 1961-82, *President Emeritus, Professor of History*

Paul M. Bechtel, Ph.D., 1946-77, *Professor of English*

LaVern Ruby Bjorklund, M.A., 1954-83, *Professor of Physical Education*

Donald Chapin Boardman, Ph.D., 1940-79, *Professor of Geology*

Fannie Boyce, Ph.D., 1930-62, *Professor of Mathematics*

Earle E. Cairns, Ph.D., 1943-77, *Professor of History*

Howard H. Claassen, Ph.D., 1952-66, 1971-80, *Professor of Physics*

Harvey C. Chrouser, M.A., 1940-77, *Professor of Physical Education*

Edward Atherton Coray, B.A., M.Ed., 1926-51, *Professor of Physical Education*

Edward A. Cording, B.S., 1948-70, *Professor of Educational Administration*

Helen Siml deVette, M.A., 1948-82, *Professor of English*

Robert O. deVette, Ph.D., 1947-82, *Professor of Spanish*

Enock C. Dyrness, M.A., L.L.D., 1924-69, *Registrar and Professor of Education*

John H. Fadenrecht, Ed.D., 1946-73, *Professor of Education*

Harold Alvin Fiess, Ph.D., 1944-83, *Professor of Chemistry*

Frank O. Green, Ph.D., 1945-75, *Professor of Chemistry*

Clarence Hale, Ph.D., 1929-74, *Professor of Foreign Language*

Arne Torkel Howard, M.B.A., 1948-81, *Professor of Economics and Business*

Willard Carrol Jackman, Ph.D., 1958-70, *Professor of Education*

Clyde S. Kilby, Ph.D., 1935-77, *Professor of English; Curator, Marion Wade Collection*

Jean R. Kline, M.A., 1948-80, *Professor of Psychology*

John L. Leedy, Ph.D., 1937-76, *Professor of Botany*

Ruth B. Leedy, M.A., 1935-76, *Professor of Physical Education*

Lois E. LeBar, Ph.D., 1945-75, *Professor of Christian Education*

Cyril E. Luckman, Ph.D., 1947-79, *Professor of Zoology*

Clinton O. Mack, Ph.D., 1943-74, *Professor of Biology*

Mignon Bollman Mackenzie Murray, Mus. M., 1928-67, *Professor of Music*

Russell Mixter, Ph.D., 1928-79, *Professor of Zoology*

Albert S. Nichols, Ph.D., 1944-60, *Professor of Education*

H. Wilbert Norton, Th.D., 1965-80, *Professor of Missions and Evangelism*

Clarence LeRoy Nystrom, Ph.D., 1935-67, *Professor of Speech*

George A. Olson, M.A., 1945-74, *Associate Professor of Physical Education*

Ivy T. Olson, B.S., 1947-82, *Associate Professor of Library Science*

Russell H. Platz, M.A., 1950-83, *Professor of Music*

Erwin P. Rudolph, Ph.D., 1950-81, *Professor of English*

Onas Cudley Scandrette, Ed.D., 1956-67, 1969-79, *Professor of Psychology*

Samuel J. Schultz, Th.D., 1949-80, *Samuel Robinson Professor of Biblical Studies and Theology*

Merrill C. Tenney, Ph.D., 1943-77, *Professor of Bible and Theology*

Arthur H. Volle, Ph.D., 1946-80, *Professor of Educational Administration, Vocational Counselor*

Arlene E. Whiteman, M.S., 1967-80, *Associate Professor of Education*

Johnathan G. Williams, M.A., 1947-62, *Associate Professor of French*

Paul McCoy Wright, Ph.D., 1929-70, *Professor of Chemistry*

END NOTES

Primary sources for a history of Wheaton College are the Minutes of the Board of Trustees, the Minutes of the Executive Committee of the Board of Trustees, and the Minutes of the Faculty of Wheaton College. All of these materials are located in the archives of the College. Housed also in the archives are additional primary sources: papers of the presidents and deans, papers of distinguished members of the faculty and alumni, minutes and reports of special committees, various historical documents, and college catalogs.

Primary sources for information about student life are the student publications: *The Wheaton Record,* the weekly newspaper; *Tower,* the college yearbook; and *Kodon,* the campus literary magazine.

Principal secondary sources are a previous history of Wheaton to 1950 by W. Wyeth Willard, *Fire on the Prairie;* a biography of Jonathan Blanchard by Clyde S. Kilby, *Minority of One;* and Earle E. Cairns's *V. Raymond Edman: In the Presence of the King,* a biography of Wheaton's fourth president. Additional secondary sources are the writings of the presidents and members of the faculty. All other material referred to in the text, and not cited in a bibliographic note, is in the Wheaton College archives.

NOTES

CHAPTER 1

1. Clyde S. Kilby, *Minority of One* (Grand Rapids: Eerdmans, 1959), p. 26.
2. Charles Albert Blanchard, *President Blanchard's Autobiography* (Boone, Iowa: Western Alliance, 1915), p. 27.
3. Jonathan Blanchard, *Sermons and Addresses* (Chicago: National Christian Association, 1892), p. 9.
4. Ibid., p. 9.
5. Kilby, p. 48.
6. Letter, April 26, 1837.
7. Thomas Askew, *The Liberal Arts College Encounters Change* (Evanston: Northwestern University, 1969), p. 12.
8. Kilby, p. 78.
9. *Philanthropist,* January 8 and April 30, 1839.
10. *Notebooks and Diary,* p. 91.
11. Ibid., p. 77.
12. Ibid., p. 79.
13. Knox College Trustees Records, Part A, p. 84.
14. Notebooks and Diary, p. 89.
15. Ibid., p. 90.
16. Kilby, p. 100.
17. *Christian Cynosure,* May 17, 1877.
18. Ernest Elmo Calkins, *They Broke the Prairie* (New York: Scribners, 1937), p. 39.
19. Blanchard to Samuel Williston, April 29, 1849. Williston Letters, Knox College Library.
20. February 14, 25 and June 23, 1846.

21. Jonathan Blanchard, p. 11.
22. Ibid., p. 12.
23. Ibid., pp. 116, 117.
24. Kilby, p. 114.
25. Letter dated June 20, 1849.
26. "Students Farewell," quoted by Kilby, p. 129.
27. Jonathan Blanchard, p. 12.
28. Letter, November 10, 1848.
29. Askew, p. 38.
30. Minutes of the Board of Trustees, Illinois Institute, November 23, 1859.
31. Jonathan Blanchard, p. 13.
32. Subscription list in Wheaton College Archives.
33. Minutes of the Board of Trustees, July 14, 1859.
34. Ibid., December 29, 1859.
35. Ibid.
36. Letter Jonathan Blanchard to Warren L. Wheaton, December 5, 1859.
37. Kilby, p. 151.
38. Charles A. Blanchard, p. 42.
39. Catalog of Wheaton College 1860-61.
40. Ibid., p. 14.
41. Ibid.
42. Herbert Moule, *Unpublished History of Wheaton College.*
43. Charles A. Blanchard, p. 47.
44. Wheaton College Charter.
45. *Republican Register,* September 30, 1925.
46. *Traditions,* ed. by W. Boyd Hunt, p. 7.
47. *Voice of Our Young Folks,* October 1868, p. 4.
48. Catalog of Wheaton College, 1868-69, p. 21.

49. *Voice of Our Young Folks*, October 1868, p. 4.
50. George P. Gardiner, *History of the Beltionian Literary Society*, p. 13.
51. Vol. I, No. 4, April, 1868, p. 3.
52. Ibid., p. 4.
53. Catalog of Wheaton College, 1864-65, p. 17.
54. Ibid., 1865-66, p. 23.
55. Ibid., p. 24.

CHAPTER 2

1. Wheaton, *Illinoisian*, December 23, 1868.
2. Minutes of the Board of Trustees, June 1866.
3. Minutes of the Board of Trustees, June 28, 1864.
4. Herbert Moule, Chapter 8, p. 5.
5. *Voice of Our Young Folks*, September, 1868.
6. Charles A. Blanchard, *Autobiography*, p. 49.
7. Marcus Holt, student diary, October 9, 1871.
8. *CC*, October 10, 1872.
9. Ibid.
10. Kilby, p. 178.
11. Jonathan Blanchard, *Sermons and Addresses*, p. 74.
12. Ibid., p. 156.
13. Ibid., p. 165.
14. Charles A. Blanchard, p. 51.
15. *CC*, July 25, 1868.
16. Ibid., August 12, 1886.
17. Ibid., August 20, 1881.
18. Ibid., September 6, 1888.
19. Kilby, p. 173.
20. Letter, November 12, 1868, Oberlin College Library.
21. *CC*, March 24, 1871.
22. *Wheaton Record*, March 10, 1910, p. 145.
23. Charles A. Blanchard, p. 46.
24. Carl Diehl, *Americans and German Scholarship, 1870-1880* (New Haven: Yale University, 1978).
25. Ibid., Chapter 3.
26. W. Wyeth Willard, *Fire on the Prairie* (Wheaton: Van Kampen, 1950), p. 64.
27. Wheaton College Catalog, 1877-78, p. 20.
28. Merle Curti, *The Growth of American Thought* (New York: Harper & Row, 1943), p. 535.
29. *CC*, September 28, 1871.
30. Askew, p. 83.

31. *CC*, July 11, 1872.
32. Willard, p. 157.
33. Minutes of the Board of Trustees, June 20, 1881.
34. *CC*, April 5, 1877.
35. Ibid., March 8, 1875.
36. Ibid., November 20, 1873.
37. Kilby, p. 188.
38. Ibid., p. 186.
39. Julia Blanchard Fischer, *Blessed Memories* (Wheaton College, N.D.), p. 74.
40. Ibid., p. 76.
41. *CC*, January 29, 1880.
42. Edwin A. Hollatz, *The Development of Literary Societies in Selected Illinois Colleges in the Nineteenth Century, and Their Role in Speech Training* (Evanston: Northwestern University, 1965), p. 90.
43. Comment of Mrs. W. H. Fischer cited in Gordon P. Gardiner, *History of the Beltionian Literary Society*, p. 27.
44. Willard, p. 52.
45. Ibid.
46. Minutes of the Board of Trustees, June 1882.

CHAPTER 3

1. Charles A. Blanchard, *Autobiography*, p. 15.
2. Ibid., p. 23.
3. Frances Carothers Blanchard, *The Life of Charles Albert Blanchard* (New York: Fleming H. Revell, 1932), p. 18.
4. Charles A. Blanchard, pp. 32, 33.
5. Ernest Elmo Calkins, *They Broke the Prairie* (New York: Scribners, 1937), p. 205.
6. Charles A. Blanchard, p. 194.
7. Ibid., p. 36.
8. Ibid., p. 40.
9. Charles A. Blanchard, *Autobiography*, p. 43.
10. Ibid., p. 52.
11. Ibid., p. 61.
12. Ibid., p. 65.
13. Ibid., p. 191.
14. Frances Carothers Blanchard, p. 77.
15. Charles A. Blanchard, Diary.
16. George P. Schmidt, *The Old Time College President* (New York: Columbia University Press, 1930), p. 108.
17. Ibid.
18. Julia Blanchard, Recollections of Julia

E. Blanchard, November 27, 1946, unpublished.
19. Frances Carothers Blanchard, p. 68.
20. Charles A. Blanchard, p. 165.
21. C. F. Thwing, *The College President* (New York: Macmillan 1926), p. 234.
22. Charles A. Blanchard, p. 167.
23. Ibid., p. 166.
24. George P. Schmidt, *The Liberal Arts College* (New Brunswick: Rutgers University Press, 1957), p. 61.
25. Charles A. Blanchard, *The American College: An Address on the Day of Prayer for Colleges*, p. 17. (N.D.)
26. Charles A. Blanchard, "The Christian College" (unpublished address to the Chicago Congregational Association, October 8, 1889).
27. Charles A. Blanchard, *Educational Papers: The People and the Colleges* (New York: Fleming H. Revell, 1890), p. 59.
28. Wheaton College Catalog, 1887-88, p. 32.
29. *Bulletin of Wheaton College*, 1886-87.
30. *CC*, October 18, 1883.
31. Kilby, p. 198.
32. *CC*, June 18, 1885.
33. William Culp Darrah, *Powell of the Colorado* (Princeton: Princeton University Press, 1951), p. 39.
34. Julia Blanchard Fischer, p. 154.
35. Ibid., p. 157
36. *The Advance*, May 19, 1892, quoted by Kilby.
37. *Inter-Ocean*, May 16, 1892, quoted by Kilby.

CHAPTER 4

1. *Wheaton College Record*, March 15, 1890.
2. Ibid., March 22, 1890.
3. Ibid., November 7, 1891.
4. James M. Gray, "An Appreciation," foreword to Frances Carothers Blanchard, p. 7.
5. Charles A. Blanchard, *Educational Papers* (New York: Fleming H. Revell, 1890), p. 80.
6. Ibid., Preface.
7. Ibid., p. 80.
8. *Wheaton College Record*, October 4, 1890.
9. Herbert Moule.
10. W. Wyeth Willard, p. 91.
11. *Wheaton College Record*, April 7, 1972.
12. Ibid., November 5, 1892.

13. Willard, p. 88.
14. *Wheaton College Record*, March 11.
15. Willard, p. 90.
16. W. Boyd Hunt, *Traditions* (Wheaton: Wheaton College, 1938), p. 37.
17. *Wheaton College Record*, May 1899.
18. Ibid., June 1896.
19. *College Echoes '93*, p. 66.
20. *College Echoes '95*, p. 91.
21. Ibid., p. 70.
22. *Wheaton College Record*, June 1898.
23. Ibid., June 1898.
24. Ibid.
25. Ibid., July 1898.
26. Charles A. Blanchard, Miscellaneous papers and notebooks.
27. Ibid.
28. *Bulletin of Wheaton College*, 1919, p. 15.
29. Edward A. Coray, *The Wheaton I Remember* (Chicago: Books for Living, 1974), p.10.
30. *Wheaton College Record*, June 18, 1892.
31. Ibid., September 10, 1892.
32. Ibid., February 18, 1893.
33. *Wheaton College Echo*, 1898, p. 86.
34. Coray, p. 25.
35. *Wheaton College Record*, November 1, 1900.
36. Ibid., March 15, 1901.
37. Ibid., November 15, 1900.
38. Coray, p. 205.

CHAPTER 5

1. *Wheaton College Record*, April 10, 1900.
2. Letter from Bruce Hunt, May 10, 1979.
3. *Wheaton College Record*, March 15, 1910.
4. *Bulletin of Wheaton College*, 1910, p. 12.
5. Ibid., 1915.
6. Charles A. Blanchard, *Autobiography*, p. 67.
7. *Wheaton College Record*, November 15, 1914.
8. Ibid., January 15, 1915.
9. Ibid., March 15, 1916.
10. Ibid., November 15, 1917.
11. Ibid., September 15, 1918.
12. Ibid.
13. Ibid., May 15, 1918.
14. Ibid.
15. Ibid., November 15, 1918.
16. Ibid., January 15, 1919.
17. Conversation with Enock Dyrness, July 19, 1978.

18. *Wheaton College Record*, October 15, 1900.
19. Ibid., p. 5.
20. Ibid., June 1, 1904.
21. Ibid., March 15, 1910.
22. Ibid., July 1910.
23. Ibid.
24. Ibid., June 15, 1910.
25. Ibid., November 3, 1920.
26. Ibid., June 1, 1923.
27. Ibid., March 23, 1921.
28. Ibid., October 24, 1923.

CHAPTER 6

1. Charles A. Blanchard, *Educational Papers*, p. 77.
2. Jonathan Blanchard, *Sermons and Addresses*, p. 57.
3. Ibid., p. 74.
4. March 3, 1878; December 11, 1879; December 9, 1886.
5. Charles A. Blanchard, *An Infallible Guide: Intimate Talks About Divine Guidance*, pp. 9-10.
6. Frances Carothers Blanchard, p. 53.
7. Charles A. Blanchard, "Christian Citizenship" (unpublished and undated sermon notes).
8. Charles A. Blanchard, *Light on the Last Days: Being Familiar Talks on the Book of Revelation* (Chicago: Bible Institute Colportage, 1913), p. 2.
9. Cy Hulsey, *The Shaping of a Fundamentalist: A Case Study of Charles Blanchard* (Unpublished Thesis: Trinity Evangelical Divinity School, 1977), p. 20.
10. Emma Dryer, *Emma Dryer and the Founding of Moody Bible Institute* (n.p.).
11. Charles A. Blanchard, *Light on the Last Days*, p. 119.
12. Ernest R. Sandeen, *The Roots of Fundamentalism* (Philadelphia: Fortress Press, 1968), p. xiii.
13. "Fundamentalism," *Encyclopedia of Social Sciences*, Vol. 5, 1944 edition.
14. *Wheaton College Record*, April 26, 1922.
15. Sandeen, p. 195.
16. Minutes of the Executive Committee, April, 1923, WCA.
17. Sandeen, p. 244
18. Frances Carothers Blanchard, p. 187.
19. Letter from Charles A. Blanchard to Wheaton College Trustees and Faculty, April 25, 1923.

20. Thomas A. Askew, *The Liberal Arts College Encounters Change* (Evanston: Northwestern University, 1969), p. 234.
21. Minutes of the Executive Committee, July 14, 1924.
22. Minutes of the Board of Trustees, March 3, 1926.
23. Steven Barabas,"The Wheaton College Statement of Faith," *Faculty Bulletin of Wheaton College*, November, 1961, p. 55.
24. Conversation with Earl Winsor, May 15, 1979.
25. Julia A. Blanchard, *Faculty Bulletin of Wheaton College*, Vol. 13-14, p. 212.
26. *Wheaton Record*, October 1, 1924, p. 1.
27. Ibid., January 18, 1924.
28. Ibid., December 17, 1924.
29. Ibid., February 4, 1925.
30. Ibid., December 10, 1924.
31. Ibid., March 11, 1925.
32. Ibid., October 16, 1921.
33. Edward A. Coray, p. 158.
34. Letter from Bruce Hunt, May 12, 1979.
35. Edward A. Coray, p. 83.
36. Ibid.
37. *Wheaton College Record*, February 6, 1925.
38. *Bulletin of Wheaton College*, 1925-1926, p. 24.
39. Charles Blanchard, "Psychology," unpublished manuscript, n.d.
40. Wheaton College Faculty Minutes, February 16, 1926.
41. *Bulletin of Wheaton College*, April 1925, p. 42.
42. Charles A. Blanchard file.
43. Frances Carothers Blanchard, p. 209.
44. Charles A. Blanchard file.
45. Acts 11:24.
46. Minutes of the Executive Committee, December 22, 1925.

CHAPTER 7

1. Conversation with Enock Dyrness, June 27, 1979.
2. W. Wyeth Willard, p. 107.
3. *Wheaton Record*, January 6, 1925.
4. Ibid., February 3, 1926.
5. Ibid., February 10, 1926.
6. Minutes of the Executive Committee, February 16, 1926.
7. Ibid., February 19, 1926.
8. Ibid.
9. Ibid.
10. Edward A. Steele, "Buswell the Man,"

Presbyterian, Spring-Fall, 1976, p. 4.
Much of the information about
Buswell's early life used here is from
the article by Edward Steele, who
secured most of his information
through conversations with Dr.
Buswell, "Uncle Buz," as he
affectionately called him in
conversations with the author.

11. *Bulletin of Wheaton College*, May
    1926, p. 3.
12. Ibid., p. 5.
13. Edward A. Steele, p. 6.
14. James Oliver Buswell, Jr., *Bibliotheca
    Sacra*, LXXXII, October 1925,
    p. 405.
15. *Wheaton Record*, March 14, 1934, p.
    1.
16. *Bulletin of Wheaton College*, New
    Series Monthly, May 1926.
17. Miscellaneous Buswell Papers.
18. *Bulletin of Wheaton College*, "A
    Christian College," November, 1926.
19. *Wheaton Record*, August 11, 1926.
20. *Bulletin of Wheaton College*, June
    1927.
21. Letter from Enoch Dyrness, July 28,
    1979.
22. James B. Mack, *Faculty Bulletin*,
    March, 1944, p. 2.
23. Letter from James Oliver Buswell, Jr. to
    George V. Kirk, September 10, 1928.
24. Enoch Dyrness, "A Survey of Wheaton
    College," *Bulletin of the American
    Association of Collegiate Registrars*,
    Vol. 10: No. 1, October, 1934, p. 35.
25. A detailed report of the Russell
    Committee may be found in *Report
    of the Faculty Planning Committee*,
    1944-46.
26. Miscellaneous papers of Julia
    Blanchard.
27. John Laurence Frost, an earnest young
    Christian, died in Italy during his
    senior year as a Stanford University
    student. His parents were Mr. and
    Mrs. Howard Frost of Los Angeles.

CHAPTER 8

1. Minutes of the Wheaton College
   Faculty.
2. Minutes of the Board of Trustees.
3. Wheaton College Catalog, 1931.
4. *Wheaton Record*, March 6, 1935.
5. Conversation with Clyde S. Kilby,
   November 13, 1979.
6. Wheaton College Archives.
7. Conversation with Clyde S. Kilby,
   November 13, 1979.

8. Among his many duties, Dr. Higley
   was authorized by the Executive
   Committee "to sign the monthly
   reports on alcohol consumption
   required by the Federal government."
   Minutes of the Executive Committee,
   June 29, 1937.
9. Minutes of the Executive Committee,
   November 27, 1935.
10. Ibid., May 21, 1937.
11. Ibid., September 14, 1937.
12. Ibid., May 19, 1936.
13. Ibid., May 27, 1936.
14. Ibid., January 15, 1936.
15. Ibid.
16. Minutes of the Wheaton College
    Faculty, February 14, 1935.
17. Ibid., April 19, 1938.
18. Ibid., January 10, 1938.
19. *Wheaton Record*, September 18, 1935.
20. Ibid., December 16, 1936.
21. Ibid., March 16, 1937.
22. *Tower*, 1938, pp. 108-109.
23. W. Boyd Hunt, ed., *Traditions*
    (Wheaton: Wheaton College, 1938),
    p. 13.
24. Ibid.
25. *Wheaton Record*, February 12, 1936.
26. Ibid.
27. *Traditions*, p. 45.
28. Conversation with H. Wilbert Norton,
    February 22, 1980.
29. Conversation with Maurice Dobbins,
    October 15, 1979.
30. *Traditions*, p. 4.
31. Minutes of the Naitermanian Literary
    Society, October 2, 1936.
32. Wheaton College Scholastic Honor
    Society Booklet, Wheaton College
    Archives.
33. Edward A. Coray, *Through Clouds and
    Sunshine*, Vol. I, p. 184.
34. Ibid., p. 189.
35. *Wheaton Record*, May 14, 1938.
36. Ibid., p. 130.
37. Ibid., p. 254.
38. Ibid., p. 261.
39. *Wheaton Record*, January 9, 1940.

CHAPTER 9

1. *Wheaton Record*, April 22, 1936.
2. Ibid.
3. *Bulletin of Wheaton College*, Summer
   1936.
4. *The New York Times*, June 5, 1935.
5. *Wheaton Record*, September 18, 1935.
6. *The New York Times*, July 9, 1935.
7. Ibid., February 27, 1936.
8. Ibid.

9. Minutes of the Executive Committee.
10. Minutes of the Board of Trustees, January 10, 1939.
11. Miscellaneous Buswell papers.
12. Minutes of the Board of Trustees, June 14, 1941.
13. Conversation with Edward A. Coray and LeRoy Patterson, January 24, 1980.
14. Minutes of the Executive Committee, January 19, 1939.
15. Ibid., January 13, 1939. Graham had conduted evangelistic services at Wheaton and had been granted an honorary degree.
16. *Wheaton Daily Journal*, January 25, 1940.
17. Minutes of the Board of Trustees, January 20, 1940. The Alumni statement is attached to the minutes of the Executive Committee meeting January 11, 1940.
18. Earle E. Cairns, *V. Raymond Edman: In the Presence of the King* (Grand Rapids: Moody, 1972), p. 97.
19. Miscellaneous Buswell papers.
20. Cairns, p. 97.
21. Minutes of the Faculty, January 23, 1940.
22. *Bulletin of Wheaton College*, February, 1940.
23. Letter from A. Culver Gordon, February 12, 1940.
24. Letter from Herman A. Fischer to A. Culver Gordon, February 16, 1940.
25. Letter to the Board of Trustees, February 13, 1940.

CHAPTER 10

1. Cairns, pp. 20, 21.
2. Willard, p. 23.
3. Ibid., p. 128.
4. Cairns, p. 30.
5. V. Raymond Edman, *Out of My Life* (Grand Rapids: Zondervan, 1961), p. 42.
6. Willard, p. 133.
7. Cairns, p. 68.
8. Ibid., p. 80.
9. Edman, pp. 57, 59.
10. Minutes of the Board of Trustees, January 11, 1941.
11. Miscellaneous Edman papers.
12. Ibid.
13. *Bulletin of Wheaton College*, June 1941, inaugural number.
14. *Wheaton Record*, May 9, 1941.
15. Conversation with Harvey Chrouser, March 22, 1980.

16. *Wheaton Record*, October 16, 1941.
17. *Bulletin of Wheaton College*, July 1942.
18. Edward A. Coray, *The Wheaton I Remember*, p. 91.
19. Alumni Association Report, 1962.
20. Conversation with Lee Pfund, April 22, 1980.
21. *Wheaton Record*, March 27, 1942.
22. Ibid., August 1, 1939.
23. *The New York Times*, December 9, 1941.
24. Edward A. Coray, *The Wheaton I Remember*, p. 74.
25. *Wheaton Record*, December 9, 1941.
26. Ibid.
27. Ibid., December 12, 1941.
28. Ibid., February 20, 1942.
29. *Wheaton Alumni News*, January-February 1942.
30. Ibid.
31. Ibid.
32. *Faculty Bulletin*, May, 1943.
33. Ibid., August 19, 1942.
34. *Chicago Tribune*, August 1, 1943.
35. Cairns, p. 109.
36. *Wheaton Record*, February 26, 1943.
37. Ibid., August 10, 1943.
38. Ibid., October 21, 1943.
39. Ibid., February 23, 1943.
40. Ibid., May 1, 1942.
41. Ibid., March 22, 1945.
42. *Wheaton Alumni News*, January-February, 1943.
43. Ibid.
44. *Protestant Voice*, March 2, 1945.
45. Conversation with David Roberts, April 29, 1980.
46. *Wheaton Daily Journal*, October 29, 1943.
47. *Armed Forces Tower*, 1945.

CHAPTER 11

1. Faculty Minutes, September 28, 1943.
2. *Wheaton Alumni News*, March-April 1944.
3. Report of the Faculty Planning Committee, 1944-46, chapter 10, p. 2.
4. Ibid., chapter 3, p. 33.
5. Ibid., Appendix II, p. 4.
6. Ibid., chapter 7, p. 70.
7. Ibid., chapter 6, p. 3.
8. Cairns, p. 112.
9. Minutes of the Board of Trustees, October 9, 1943.
10. *Wheaton Record*, November 3, 1949.
11. Conversation with Karl Steele, May 6, 1980.

12. Minutes of the Faculty, February 19, 1946.
13. "Here We Stand," a brief public relations document.
14. *Wheaton Record*, December 14, 1950.
15. Minutes of the Board of Trustees, October 21, 1949.
16. *Wheaton Record*, October 6, 1949.
17. Ibid.
18. Ibid., January 8, 1953.
19. Ibid., September 19, 1957.
20. Earle E. Cairns, *A Blueprint for Christian Higher Education* (Wheaton: Wheaton College, 1953), p. 11.
21. Ibid., p. 37.
22. *Bulletin of Wheaton College*, January 1946.
23. *Wheaton Record*, September 19, 1946.
24. Ibid., August 15, 1946.
25. Ibid., October 30, 1947.
26. Minutes of the Board of Trustees, February 23, 1946.
27. *Bulletin of Wheaton College*, February 1949.
28. Conversation with Russell Mixter, June 18, 1980.
29. *Wheaton Record*, August 15, 1946.
30. Ibid., November 14, 1946.
31. Ibid., August 14, 1947.
32. Ibid., February 18, 1947.
33. Minutes of the Board of Trustees, February 22, 1947.
34. *Faculty Bulletin*, November 1947.
35. Ibid.
36. Ibid.
37. *Wheaton Record*, September 18, 1947.
38. Letter from Roger Voskuyl to Herman A. Fischer, May 24, 1949.
39. Ibid., October 30, 1947.
40. Letter from Voskuyl to Fischer.
41. Conversation with C. Gregg Singer, June 23, 1980.
42. Ibid.
43. Letter from V. Raymond Edman to Norman Burns, Secretary of North Central Association, October 14, 1948.
44. Letter from C. Gregg Singer to V. Raymond Edman, August 3, 1949.
45. Conversation with David Howard, August 25, 1980.
46. *Bulletin of Wheaton College*, March 1950.
47. William H. Leslie, "The Story of the Wheaton Awakening of 1950."
48. Earle E. Cairns, *V. Raymond Edman: In the Presence of the King*, p. 135.
49. Leslie.
50. *Wheaton Record*, September 14, 1950.
51. *Kodon*.

CHAPTER 12

1. Minutes of the Board of Trustees, October 20-21, 1950.
2. Hannah Arendt, *The Human Condition* (Chicago: University of Chicago Press, 1958), p. 1.
3. Minutes of the Board of Trustees, October 20-21, 1950.
4. *Wheaton Record*, September 18, 1952.
5. Names of commissioned officers appear on commencement programs.
6. *Wheaton Alumni*, July 1952.
7. Minutes of the Board of Trustees, June 13, 1952.
8. Ibid., June 9, 1951.
9. Report from the office of the Dean of the College, September 1980.
10. Minutes of the Board of Trustees, June 9, 1980.
11. *Bulletin of Wheaton College*, November 1957.
12. Coversation with Ruby A. Free, September 11, 1980.
13. *Tower*, 1952, p. 140.
14. *Wheaton Record*, October 2, 1951.
15. Letter from Herman A. Fischer to V. Raymond Edman, July 5, 1948.
16. Conversation with Evan Welsh, September 15, 1980.
17. *Bulletin of Wheaton College*, March 1970.
18. Ronald C. Paul, *Billy Graham—Prophet of Hope* (New York: Random House, 1978), p. 77.
19. George M. Wilson, ed., *Twenty Years Under God* (Minneapolis: Worldwide Publications, 1970), p. 6.
20. *Wheaton Record*, February 28, 1952.
21. Ibid., November 15, 1956.
22. Interview with Arthur F. Holmes, May 10, 1978.
23. *Wheaton Record*, January 14, 1960.
24. Title page of *Creation and Evolution* by Russell L. Mixter, published by the American Scientific Affiliation, 1950.
25. Ibid., February 12, 1961.
26. Letter from Katherine B. Tiffany to June Weitting.
27. *Wheaton Record*, April 2, 1953.
28. *Chicago Tribune*, December 1, 1957.
29. *Wheaton Record*, August 9, 1962.
30. Ibid., November 15, 1956.
31. Ibid., February 28, 1963.

32. Thomas Howard, *Christ the Tiger* (Philadelphia: J. B. Lippincott, 1967), pp. 46-47.

CHAPTER 13

1. Chapel address, September 22, 1967.
2. V. Raymond Edman, *Swords and Plowshares* (Chicago: Van Kampen, 1967), p. 1.
3. Ibid., p. 31.
4. Conversation with Robert Walker, October 17, 1980.
5. Earle E. Cairns, *V. Raymond Edman: In the Presence of the King*, p. 201.
6. *Wheaton Leader*, September 28, 1967.
7. Minutes of the Executive Committee, February 28, 1956.
8. Centennial files.
9. *Bulletin of Wheaton College*, May 1959.
10. Minutes of the Executive Committee, March 14, 1959.
11. *Wheaton Alumni*, June 1959.
12. Minutes of the Executive Committee, April 9, 1959.
13. *Wheaton Alumni*, November 1959.
14. Cairns, p. 155.
15. *Wheaton Record*, October 22, 1959.
16. Ibid., October 16, 1959.
17. *Bulletin of Wheaton College*, February 1960.
18. *Wheaton Alumni*, March 1960.
19. Ibid, October 1960.
20. Ibid., July 1960.
21. *Wheaton Record*, September 24, 1959.
22. *Registrar's Annual Reports*, 1960-67.
23. Minutes of the Board of Trustees, January 22, 1955.
24. *Faculty Bulletin*, September 1959.
25. Ibid.
26. *Faculty Bulletin*, Spring 1963.
27. *Wheaton Alumni*, January 1961.
28. Conversation with Arthur F. Holmes, November 12, 1980.
29. Conversation with Arthur Rupprecht, November 14, 1980.
30. *Faculty Bulletin*, November 1960.
31. *Bulletin of Wheaton College*, 1961-62.
32. Charles W. Schoenherr, "Just Who Is Admitted to Wheaton?" *Alumni Magazine*, September 1960, p. 3.
33. Ibid., July-August 1964, p. 6.
34. A Profile of the Class of 1968, Office of Admissions, November 1964.
35. Release from the Office of Admissions, October 19, 1965.
36. *Bulletin of Wheaton College*, 1864-65.
37. Ibid.
38. *Bulletin of Wheaton College*, 1950-51.
39. Ibid., 1939-40.
40. Ibid., 1944-45.
41. Ibid., 1961-62.
42. Ibid., 1952-53.
43. Ibid., 1975-76.
44. Ibid.
45. *Wheaton Record*, October 29, 1959.
46. Ibid., April 5, 1962.
47. Conversation with W. Wyeth Willard, November 24, 1978.
48. Minutes of the Executive Committee, February 1, 1962.
49. *Wheaton Record*, August 2, 1963.
50. Conversation with Alton Cronk, December 5, 1980.
51. Letter from Robert L. Schofield to Mignon Bollman Mackenzie, March 6, 1944.
52. Notes prepared by Edward A. Cording.
53. The Philosophy of Intercollegiate Athletics at Wheaton College.
54. Athletic records compiled by Ray Smith.
55. *Wheaton Alumni*, April 1959.
56. Record book of Moriya's achievements.
57. *Tower*, 1967, p. 142.
58. *Wheaton Record*, May 17, 1962.

CHAPTER 14

1. Report to the North Central Association, March 1964.
2. Minutes of the Board of Trustees, January 11, 1964.
3. Ibid., October 13, 1961.
4. Ibid.
5. Ibid., June 8, 1962.
6. Ibid.
7. Ibid., January 11, 1964.
8. Minutes of the Faculty, October 25, 1960.
9. Wheaton College North Central Report, March 1964.
10. Conversation with John Leedy, April 28, 1981.
11. *Bulletin of Wheaton College*, May 1966.
12. Ibid., October 1959.
13. North Central Report, March 1964.
14. Conversation with Coach Harvey Chrouser, December 2, 1980.
15. *Wheaton Record*, September 27, 1962.
16. Ibid., April 9, 1964.
17. Ibid., September 27, 1962.
18. *Kodon*, Fall 1962, p. 3.
19. Conversation with Melvin Lorentzen, April 15, 1981.

20. *Tower*, 1964, p. 98.
21. *Wheaton Alumni*, June 1962.
22. Minutes of the Board of Trustees, December 8, 1962.
23. Minutes of the Executive Committee, July 9, 1964.
24. Letter of Herman Fischer to members of the Board of Trustees.
25. Earle E. Cairns, *V. Raymond Edman: In the Presence of the King*, p. 184.
26. Memorial publication of the Billy Graham Association.

CHAPTER 15

1. Hudson T. Armerding, "Autobiographical Sketch," unpublished.
2. Ibid.
3. Ibid.
4. Minutes of the Board of Trustees, February 24, 1966.
5. Interview with President Armerding, August 22, 1980.
6. Ibid.
7. Minutes of the Board of Trustees, June 1966.
8. *Bulletin of Wheaton College*, May 1965.
9. *Wheaton Record*, March 25, 1965.
10. Ibid., March 18, 1965.
11. Hudson T. Armerding, Report to the Board of Trustees, May 30, 1969.
12. Ibid., October 7, 1966.
13. Arthur F. Holmes, "The Faculty Viewpoint," May 1967.
14. Ibid.
15. Report of the President's Retreat, May 1969.
16. Ibid., May 1970.
17. Morris Keeton and Conrad Hilberry, *Struggle and Promise: A Future for Colleges* (New York: McGraw-Hill, 1969), pp. vii, viii.
18. Ibid., p. viii.
19. Ibid., p. 25.
20. Ibid., p. 21.
21. Ibid., p. 23.
22. Ibid., p. 39.
23. Ibid., p. 24.
24. Ibid., p. 45.

CHAPTER 16

1. *Wheaton Record*, October 3, 1969.
2. Ibid., October 17, 1969.
3. Ibid., April 29, 1965.
4. Ibid., March 10, 1966.

5. *Tower*, 1967, p. 10.
6. *Wheaton Record*, February 17, 1967.
7. Ibid., , September 25, 1970.
8. *Bulletin of Wheaton College*, June 1969.
9. Ibid., November 1971.
10. James O. Buswell III, "Response for the Family."

CHAPTER 17

1. *Tower*, 1971, p. 10.
2. *Bulletin of Wheaton College*, October 1970.
3. Ibid., November 1971.
4. *Wheaton Alumni*, January 1972.
5. Ibid., June 1972.
6. *Report on the Commission on Institutions of Higher Education of the North Central Association of Colleges and Secondary Schools.* Visit April 1-3, 1974.
7. Ibid.
8. Ibid.
9. Interview with Henry Nelson, November 12, 1981.
10. *Wheaton Alumni*, February 1976.
11. Interview with Henry Nelson, June 8, 1982.
12. *Wheaton Alumni*, February 1976.
13. *Wheaton Record*, September 23, 1977.
14. Interview with David Johnston.
15. Interview with Richard Kriegbaum, December 13, 1982.
16. *Wheaton Record*, October 13, 1972.
17. Interview with Hudson T. Armerding, January 16, 1982.
18. *Wheaton Record*, February 22, 1974.
19. *Wheaton Alumni*, May 1976.
20. *Chicago Tribune*, March 13, 1976.
21. *InForm* (successor to the *Bulletin of Wheaton College*), July 1979.
22. *Wheaton Alumni*, March 1982.
23. Ibid.

CHAPTER 18

1. *Bulletin of Wheaton College*, March 1936.
2. Ibid., December 1937.
3. Ibid.
4. Merrill C. Tenney, "The Graduate School of Wheaton College," *Sunday-School Times*, April 29, 1950.
5. *Bulletin of Wheaton College*, June 1969.
6. Conversation with President

Armerding, November 5, 1981.

7. *Bulletin of Wheaton College,*
November 1977.

8. *Catalog of Wheaton College Graduate
School,* 1982-83, p. 7.

9. Minutes of the Board of Trustees,
January 24, 1969.

10. Ibid., October 10, 1969.

11. Billy Graham Center papers.

12. Dr. Donald Mitchell's report to
President Armerding, Billy Graham
Center papers.

13. Letter from President Armerding to
Allan C. Emery, Billy Graham
Center papers.

14. *Wheaton Record,* September 23, 1977.

15. Billy Graham Center papers.

16. *InForm,* October 19, 1980.

17. *Wheaton Record,* September 19, 1980.

CHAPTER 19

1. Annual Report of the Registrar,
September 1976.

2. Ibid., September 1975.

3. Ibid., September 1978.

4. Data compiled by the Office of
Institutional Research, Franklin and
Marshall College, Lancaster,
Pennsylvania, 1980. Information
supplied by the Board of Human
Resources, National Research
Council.

5. Cyril E. Luckman, "Medical School
Admissions," *Wheaton Alumni,*
October 1974.

6. Office of Christian Outreach, October
21, 1982.

7. *InForm,* July 1982.

8. Program for Missions in Focus 1982.

9. *InForm,* July 1980.

10. *Wheaton Alumni,* December 1982,
p. 5.

11. *Wheaton Daily Journal,* February 2,
1982.

12. Minutes of the Executive Committee of
the Board of Trustees, April 20,
1977.

13. Visitation Report National Association
of Schools of Music, March 28-29,
1978.

14. Arthur F. Holmes, *The Idea of a
Christian College* (Grand Rapids:
Eerdmans, 1975), p. 44.

15. *Wheaton Record,* January 16, 1981.

16. Report of the Committee on Divorce
and Remarriage.

17. *Wheaton Record,* May 11, 1979.

18. Minutes of the Board of Trustees,
November 14, 1979.

19. Faculty letter to the Board of Trustees,
December 4, 1979.

20. President's Annual Report, 1981.

21. Timothy L. Smith, "A Fortress
Mentality: Shackling the Spiritual
Power," *Christianity Today,*
November 19, 1976.

22. Ronald J. Sider, *The Chicago
Declaration* (Carol Stream, Il.:
Creation House, 1974), pp. 11-42.

CHAPTER 20

1. Conversation with Harvey C.
Chrouser, February 21, 1983.

2. *InForm,* January 1979.

3. Minute of the Board of Trustees.

4. Ibid.

5. *InForm,* April 1980.

6. Minutes of the Board of Trustees.

7. *Wheaton Record,* April 16, 1982.

8. Ibid., May 7, 1982.

CHAPTER 21

1. *Whittier News,* Whittier, California,
January 4, 1982.

2. *Chicago Tribune.*

3. *Wheaton Record,* April 12, 1982.

4. Ibid.

5. *Chicago Sun Times,* September 11,
1982.

6. *Wheaton Record,* May 6, 1983.

7. Conversation with Edwin Hollatz,
December 13, 1983.

INDEX OF PERSONS